Market Design

A Linear Programming Approach to Auctions and Matching

The digital economy has led to many new services where supply is matched with demand for various types of goods and services. More and more people and organizations are now in a position to design market rules that are being implemented in software.

The design of markets is challenging as it is necessary to consider the strategic behavior of market participants, psychological factors, and computational problems in order to implement the objectives of a designer. Market models in economics have not lost their importance, but recent years have led to many new insights and principles for the design of markets which are beyond traditional economic theory. This book introduces the fundamentals of market design, an engineering field concerned with the design of real-world markets.

Martin Bichler is Professor of Informatics at the Technical University of Munich (TUM), and a faculty member at the TUM School of Management. He is known for his academic work on market design, and he has acted as a consultant for private and public organizations including regulators, telecoms, and procurement organizations. Projects in which he is involved include the design of auctions for industrial procurement, logistics, advertising, fishery access rights, and spectrum sales. His research addresses algorithmic, game-theoretical, and behavioral questions and has appeared in leading journals in computer science, economics, operations research, and management science. He is currently Editor of *Business and Information Systems Engineering* and serves on the editorial boards of several academic journals.

Market Design

A Linear Programming Approach to Auctions and Matching

MARTIN BICHLER

Technical University of Munich

CAMBRIDGE
UNIVERSITY PRESS

Shaftesbury Road, Cambridge CB2 8EA, United Kingdom

One Liberty Plaza, 20th Floor, New York, NY 10006, USA

477 Williamstown Road, Port Melbourne, VIC 3207, Australia

314–321, 3rd Floor, Plot 3, Splendor Forum, Jasola District Centre, New Delhi – 110025, India

103 Penang Road, #05–06/07, Visioncrest Commercial, Singapore 238467

Cambridge University Press is part of Cambridge University Press & Assessment, a department of the University of Cambridge.

We share the University's mission to contribute to society through the pursuit of education, learning and research at the highest international levels of excellence.

www.cambridge.org
Information on this title: www.cambridge.org/9781107173187

DOI: 10.1017/9781316779873

First published 2018

A catalogue record for this publication is available from the British Library

ISBN   978-1-107-17318-7   Hardback

To my wife Claudia and my daughters Mona and Sonja

Contents

1 Introduction

Market design is a kind of economic engineering, utilizing laboratory research, game theory, algorithms, simulations, and more. Its challenges inspire us to rethink longstanding fundamentals of economic theory.

Paul Milgrom, 2008

The digital economy has led to many new services where supply is matched with demand for various types of goods and services. While only a few years ago academics were mainly concerned with models describing markets, more and more people and organizations are now in a position to design market rules that are being implemented in software. The design of markets is challenging as it is necessary to consider the strategic behavior of market participants, psychological and cognitive factors, and computational problems in order to implement the objectives of a designer. Market models in economics have not lost their importance, but recent years have led to many new insights and principles for the design of markets which are beyond traditional economic theory. In this book, we study *market design*, an engineering field at the intersection of computer science, economics, information systems, and operations research concerned with the design of real-world markets.

Consider a transportation market with multiple lanes on a transportation network, one shipper and multiple carriers. The shipper has a set of truckloads to be shipped from different origins to various destinations. The carriers are available to meet the transportation demand, and they are invited by the shipper to submit sealed bids. Carriers typically have preferences for bundles of lanes on a route such that there are no empty lanes without a shipment, and they also submit respective bids on packages of lanes. This simple logistics procurement example leads to challenges for the shipper.

First, the shipper needs to determine an optimal allocation of bundle bids such that his costs are minimized. Cost minimization is a computationally hard optimization problem in this setting. Second, carriers want to maximize their payoff and it is not necessarily in their interest to reveal their costs truthfully. They might charge a high markup on some lanes where they expect no competition or they might not bid on other lanes where they expect high competition. However, strategic manipulation of this sort can lead to suboptimal allocations of lanes to carriers, high procurement costs for the shipper, and high bid preparation costs for the carriers, who would benefit from information about their competitors. Ideally, a shipper would have an economic mechanism where carriers have incentives to reveal their costs truthfully, and he or she can then determine the cost-minimal allocation optimally. In sales auctions the objectives are typically the maximization of auctioneer revenue or overall welfare. The latter is also referred to as (allocative) efficiency.

Overall, there are fundamental strategic and computational challenges in the design of such multi-object auctions, which are at the core of market design. The 2012 Nobel Memorial Prize in Economic Sciences for Alvin Roth and Lloyd Shapley honored research in this field. Market design uses economic theory, mathematical optimization, systems design, experiments, and empirical analysis to design market rules and institutions. Fundamentally, it asks how the design of the rules and regulations of a market affects the functioning and outcomes of that market. The study includes auction markets but also markets without money such as matching markets, which are used in the assignment of students to courses, in school choice programs, and in kidney exchanges.

This textbook focuses on the design and analysis of efficient multi-object market mechanisms.

1.1   Market Design and Mechanism Design

Market design has theoretical foundations in *mechanism design theory*, an analytical framework for thinking about what a given economic institution can achieve when the information necessary to make decisions is dispersed and privately held. The 2007 Nobel Memorial Prize in Economic Sciences to Leonid Hurwicz, Eric S. Maskin, and Roger B. Myerson was awarded in this field of economic theory. Mechanism design uses an axiomatic method, deriving results from a number of basic assumptions about utility functions or overall design goals of a mechanism. For example, mechanism design has been used to characterize the utility functions of market participants and mechanisms for which the truthful revelation of preferences is an equilibrium, i.e., a situation from which no participant wants to deviate (aka incentive-compatible mechanisms). The mechanism design literature shows that environments which allow for welfare maximization such that participants cannot make a loss and have strong incentives to bid truthfully are limited and require strong assumptions. The celebrated Vickrey–Clarke–Groves mechanism provides dominant strategies for agents to reveal valuations truthfully if they have independent and private values and they can maximize their payoff. If these assumptions are relaxed, so that bidders can have private budget constraints or valuations that are not independent, such positive results no longer exist (unless preferences can be characterized by a single parameter only). Overall, environments where truthful bidding satisfies a strong equilibrium solution concept are quite restricted. Often neither the bidders' preferences in real markets satisfy the assumptions necessary for truthful mechanisms nor is it possible to implement the required mechanisms for practical reasons. Actually, the Vickrey–Clarke–Groves mechanism is rarely used in the field. Still, it is important to understand the assumptions and mechanisms which would make truthful bidding an equilibrium bidding strategy.

Market design starts from the requirements in the field, eliciting the preferences and financial constraints of participants (which might be different from pure payoff maximization), information about competitors available to participants, objectives, and constraints on the allocation problem and on the award process. In many cases these requirements differ from those assumed in mechanism design theory, demanding the development of new models that capture the specifics of a certain type of market. Examples are models of markets for procurement and logistics, for spectrum sales, or for display advertising. Often the specifics of these markets might not allow for mechanisms which are incentive-compatible according to the established equilibrium solution concepts. So, market design takes the market environment as given and derives designs that satisfy some design goals (such as stability or budget balance of the outcome), while relaxing others. In other words, it analyzes tradeoffs and aims for "satisficing" solutions (Simon, 1996) to real types of market design problems rather than finding sets of assumptions that allow for "optimal" designs according to some design desiderata.

Market design complements mechanism design in the level of detail that is specified and analyzed. For example, in mechanism design valuations are typically described as an abstract function of the objects to be allocated, while the parametric forms of the valuation or cost functions, of the utility functions, and of the corresponding bid languages play a significant role in market design. Moreover, market designs almost always need to consider allocation constraints such as restrictions on the number of winners or the quantity awarded to individual bidders or groups of bidders. Therefore market design typically starts out as a mathematical programming task concerned with the design of an appropriate objective function, of appropriate constraints for the overall allocation, and of activity rules and with the definition of a bid language that lets bidders express their preferences in a succinct way. Milgrom (2017) provides an excellent and up-to-date view on market design and how it relates to economic theory.

1.2 Market Design and Mathematical Optimization

One thesis of this book is that *mathematical optimization*, in particular linear and integer linear programming, plays a central role in the design and analysis of multi-object markets and also provides a central foundation for theoretical models of multi-object markets. Many techniques and models introduced in this book use the theory of linear and integer linear programming in one way or another. Compared with algorithms designed for specific problems, there is an amazing versatility in linear and integer linear programming, which makes these techniques very important for market design. Algorithms for the solution of integer linear programs have seen substantial progress in the past two decades, allowing for totally new types of markets in different domains. Before that, in 1975 Leonid Kantorovich and Tjalling Koopmans had already received the Nobel Memorial Prize in Economic Sciences for their work on linear programming and optimal resource allocation. However, the advances in recent years have been staggering and have made many new markets possible that were not considered tractable just a few years ago. The subtitle of this book is reminiscent of the seminal book *Mechanism Design: A Linear Programming Approach* by Vohra (2011), who emphasized the role of linear programming in mechanism design theory.

However, market design is more than mathematical programming, as it takes into consideration bidding strategies and human behavior. Ignoring bidding strategies and different types of manipulation in market-based resource allocation is like optimizing a problem with the wrong parameters. As indicated earlier, strong game-theoretical solution concepts such as dominant-strategy or ex post incentive compatibility are desirable but they might not always be attainable, as a number of impossibility results in mechanism design show. These properties rest on assumptions about bidders' utility functions, which are often not given in the field. Still, in many markets it is possible to devise market rules for which manipulation becomes hard, given the uncertainties about other bidders and their valuations.

Overall, market design aims at design principles and rules for market institutions which are *robust against strategic manipulation and allow bidders to express their preferences*, so that the designer can aim for good or even optimal allocations. This is similar to network security, where designers aim for secure network protocols that are hard to tamper with, knowing that there is no absolute security. Note that "optimality" often refers to social welfare maximization, but the market designer might have different objectives or policy goals. In this sense, market design extends mathematical programming to situations with multiple decision makers. It is a *design science* in the sense of Herb Simon who received both the Nobel Memorial Prize in Economic Sciences (1978) and the Turing Award in Computer Science (1975). Simon's book *The Sciences of the Artificial* (Simon, 1996) motivated the development of systematic and formalized design methodologies relevant to many design disciplines, for example architecture, engineering, urban planning, medicine, computer science, and management science. Market design is therefore a very suitable name for the study of principles and methods in designing markets in the spirit of design science.

1.3   Outline of the Book

This textbook is intended to provide a one-semester course on market design. I am primarily targeting students with a background in computer science, information systems, mathematics, and management science. Hence, I will first introduce in Part I necessary concepts from game theory and mechanism design, as these students typically have not had the respective introductory courses. Parts II and III cover material which is more recent and is often not covered in microeconomics.

One prerequisite for this book is a familiarity with *linear and integer linear programming* and an introductory course in calculus and probability theory. There are many introductory textbooks on these subjects which would provide an excellent start for the topics discussed throughout this book. The appendices summarize important results from mathematical optimization and should serve as a convenient reference for the reader and a brief introduction for those who have not studied the respective courses.

As outlined earlier, this book focuses on the allocation of multiple objects with distributed decision makers. While single-object auctions are fairly well understood, multi-object auctions provide many more design options and they are more challenging to design and analyze. The goal of this book is to introduce important models and principles from game theory, mechanism design, and single-object auction theory for which there are several excellent textbooks. After basic concepts have been introduced, the book focuses on multi-object markets and their properties.

This leads to the three parts of the book: *Part I (Microeconomic Fundamentals)* discusses basic concepts from game theory, mechanism design, and single-object auction theory. The goal of this part is not to discuss each of these topics in breadth but to introduce the terminology and theory required for Parts II and III. The above topics are typically not taught in computer science and management science, and this makes it hard for students from these fields to understand the literature in market design. *Part II (Multi-Object Auction Design)* introduces the more recent theory and specific designs for multi-object markets. *Part III (Approximation and Matching Markets)* analyzes approximation mechanisms which have been designed for markets where the designer cannot hope to solve the allocation problem optimally. Then the design of matching markets where monetary transfers are not possible is discussed. Approximation and randomization play an important role in the recent matching literature. *Part IV (Appendices: Mathematical Optimization)* summarizes the main results from linear and integer linear optimization, on which I draw in Parts II and III.

There is always a tradeoff between the breadth and the depth of a textbook, and it is a matter of choice how much space is devoted to each single topic. If all the various literature streams in computer science, economics, and operations research were covered then a book on market design could easily cover thousands of pages, and it would clearly be beyond a one-semester course. This book provides a fair amount of detail in Part II and also in Part III, but Parts I and IV are limited to a necessary minimum for readers who have not taken the respective introductory courses. Selected references to the original literature are included in the text for those interested in learning more about a specific topic and in reading the original literature.

1.3.1 Part I Microeconomic Fundamentals

Chapter 2 introduces basic game-theoretical notions and solution concepts relevant for market design problems. Solution concepts for normal-form, extensive-form, and Bayesian games are introduced. There are many excellent textbooks on game theory. For example, Shoham and Leyton-Brown (2011) provides a comprehensive introduction for computer scientists, while I cover only a subset of the topics relevant for later chapters.

In Chapter 3 I discuss mechanism design theory, also known as inverse game theory. While the rules of a game are given in game theory, mechanism design tries to design rules such that certain goals and solution concepts are achieved. Market design problems can be considered as games where participants should have incentives to reveal their preferences for objects truthfully. If participants were truthful then the market designer would only need to solve an optimal allocation problem. The first section shows that aggregating general and unrestricted preferences is hard and that simple truthful mechanisms for general preferences are impossible. Then preferences are restricted to independent and private valuations and quasi-linear utility functions, where agents maximize payoff and monetary transfers are allowed. This restriction of preferences allows for a truthful mechanism with a dominant-strategy equilibrium. This means that bidders do not need information about competitors to bid optimally. The Vickrey–Clarke–Groves (VCG) mechanism is a celebrated result which is pivotal for much of the later discussion on auction design.

Chapter 4 introduces the traditional literature on single-object auctions. This literature provides a consistent framework for thinking about phenomena in auction markets, and it formalizes various assumptions. Equilibrium bidding strategies are discussed in a number of standard auction formats, before the outcomes of these auctions in equilibrium are compared. Krishna (2009) provides an excellent textbook which covers auction theory with a focus on Bayesian equilibrium analysis. This chapter is limited to key concepts providing a framework for the analysis of multi-object auctions later on.

1.3.2   Part II Multi-Object Auction Design

Chapter 5 introduces a taxonomy of multi-object auctions. *Multi-unit* auctions (for homogeneous objects) and *multi-item* auctions (for heterogeneous objects) are distinguished. For both types of auction, *sealed-bid* and *open* auction formats have been designed. Open auctions include those that are continuous or organized iteratively in rounds. They can be ascending or descending but always reveal some information about competitors throughout the process. Multi-item auctions are ubiquitous in industrial procurement, in logistics, and also in the public sector (Sandholm, 2012). Much of the remaining discussion is focused on multi-item auctions.

Chapter 6 is devoted to a simple and widespread multi-item auction format, the simultaneous multi-round auction (SMRA). It is a practical auction design and provides an excellent way to introduce some problems that arise in multi-item auctions. The strategic problems in SMRAs led to the development of combinatorial auctions. Combinatorial auctions allow bidders to express all types of preferences including complements and substitutes and can therefore be considered as the most general class of multi-object auction designs.

Chapter 7 introduces sealed-bid combinatorial auctions. The winner determination problem and the respective bid languages are discussed, before the various different payment rules are introduced. The VCG mechanism also leads to dominant-strategy equilibria in combinatorial auctions with payoff-maximizing bidders. However, in contrast with single-object auctions, this mechanism does not necessarily yield a competitive equilibrium, i.e., a stable solution where nobody wants to deviate. Also, the number of possible packages grows exponentially, so that a VCG mechanism might not be practical. The chapter introduces alternative payment rules and illustrates domain-specific bid languages addressing these issues. Combinatorial double auctions are also discussed, but the literature in this field is scarce.

Chapter 8 focuses on open and iterative combinatorial auctions, where bidders are able to outbid each other much as in an English auction. Assignment markets are a restricted type of market, where each bidder wants to win at most one out of several items. This restricted environment allows for ascending auctions with dominant strategies, and, what is more, they provide an excellent environment to illustrate algorithmic models of auctions. These types of model have received much recent attention and complement the literature on sealed-bid auctions. Also, in open multi-item auctions it is even more important to understand the interactions of bidders than it is in the single-item counterparts of these auctions. Note that most high-stakes multi-item auctions are open in format. Unfortunately, open combinatorial auctions cannot always have dominant strategies if modeled as a Bayesian game, where bidders have only distributional information about their competitors.

In Chapter 9 I discuss the single-stage and two-stage combinatorial clock auction formats. These auction formats have been used for the sale of spectrum licenses by governments around the world and provide an excellent example of practical market designs addressing the complexities of multi-object auctions. I also consider some pitfalls and problems that can arise in these auction formats.

1.3.3 Part III Approximation and Matching Markets

Chapter 10 analyzes market design problems in situations where the allocation problem is not tractable. Actually, the allocation problem of many real-world market design problems can be described as a combinatorial optimization problem and so computationally hard to solve. Unfortunately, the VCG mechanism provides dominant strategies only if the allocation problem can be solved exactly. Approximation mechanisms solve the allocation problem in polynomial time to give the objective function value of the underlying allocation problem only within a certain approximation ratio, but the mechanism provides incentives for the truthful revelation of valuations.

Finally, Chapter 11 provides an introduction to matching markets, which do not allow for monetary transfers. The assignment of students to courses at universities serves as a widespread example. There are environments where both sides of the market have preferences (e.g., students and course organizers) and others where only one side has preferences (e.g., the students). Interestingly, there are mechanisms, for both types of matching markets, where the truthful revelation of preferences is a dominant strategy for one side of the market. For example, the well-known deferred acceptance algorithm by Gale and Shapley provides dominant strategies for one side (e.g., the students) in a two-sided matching market, and the outcomes are stable, i.e., in our course allocation example there is no pair of students and course organizers who would want to switch. There are many connections to the theory of multi-object auction markets discussed in Chapter 8 and to approximation mechanisms as they are described in Chapter 10.

Chapter 12 provides an outlook on current trends and frontiers in market design.

1.3.4 Part IV Appendices: Mathematical Optimization

The appendices are intended as a reference to key results in *linear and integer linear programming* that are relevant to multi-object market design in Parts II and III of the book. Linear and integer linear programming is a vast field. I have assumed that readers have had an introduction to linear programming, and the appendices should serve only as a reference or refresher. A textbook introduction to linear programming can be found in Chvatal (1983) and to integer linear programming in Nemhauser and Wolsey (1988).

In the book I will often take a perspective including the reader and therefore will use "we" instead of "I" throughout.

1.4   Acknowledgements

Some sections of the book overlap with parts of papers that have been co-authored with students and colleagues, but I have combined them using a uniform notation with examples geared towards a textbook-style introduction to the field. These papers include Bichler (2010), Bichler *et al.* (2011a, 2013a, 2017b), Diebold *et al.* (2014), Kroemer *et al.* (2014). In preparing this text, I have benefitted from support and advice from many sources. I would like to express my gratitude to my current and former students Franz Diebold, Salman Fadaei, Andor Goetzendorff, Zhen Hao, Dennis Kraft, Richard Littmann, Stefan Mayer, Sören Merting, Per Paulsen, Ioannis Petrakis, Alexander Pikovsky, Stefan Schneider, Thomas Setzer, Pasha Shabalin, Florian Stallmann, Stefan Waldherr, Bernhard Waltl, Jürgen Wolf, and Georg Ziegler. I am thankful to co-authors and colleagues such as Gedas Adomavicius, Larry Ausubel, Haris Aziz, Oleg Baranov, Felix Brandt, Peter Cramton, Vitali Gretschko, Kemal Guler, Alok Gupta, Karla Hoffman, Maarten Janssen, Jayant Kalagnanam, Wolf Ketter, Ramayya Krishnan, Axel Ockenfels, Tuomas Sandholm, Achim Wambach, Christof Weinhardt, and Richard Steinberg for joint work and inspiring discussions. Lauren Cowles, Esther Miguéliz, and the team from Cambridge University Press provided outstanding support for the publication of the book.

I am particularly grateful to Paul Milgrom for all his kindness, advice, and guidance during my sabbatical at the Stanford Department of Economics. Special thanks also go to Dirk Bergemann, Bob Day, and Jacob Goeree for joint work, visits, and the many insights they offered. Last, and certainly not least, I thank my family for supporting me through this time-consuming project. I dedicate this book to them.

Part I

Microeconomic Fundamentals

2 Game-Theoretical Basics

Part I (Microeconomic Fundamentals) of this book provides a succinct introduction to methods and models from microeconomics. In this chapter we introduce and define basic concepts and terminology from game theory will be used throughout the rest of the book. Game theory is the mathematical study of interactions among independent self-interested *agents* or *players* in a game. We limit ourselves to *non-cooperative game theory* and refer the interested reader to more extensive treatments such as Osborne (2004) or Shoham and Leyton-Brown (2009), whose notation we share. *Non-cooperative game theory* focuses on situations where self-interested agents have conflicting goals. This chapter will introduce different types of games and central solution concepts, i.e., methods to predict the outcomes of a game played by rational agents. In some parts of the book we will also draw on *cooperative game theory*, which focuses on predicting which coalitions will form among a group of players, the joint actions that groups take, and the resulting collective payoffs. A cooperative game is a game with competition between groups of players or coalitions. However, we introduce the respective concepts later where needed, in order to keep the chapter concise.

2.1 Normal-Form Games

Let us start with a basic type of game description. In normal-form games, players' actions are simultaneous. In other types of games, called extensive-form games, actions take place sequentially.

Definition 2.1.1 (Normal-form games) A finite normal-form game with n players can be described as a tuple $(\mathcal{I}, A, u)$.

- $\mathcal{I}$ is a finite set of n players indexed by i.
- $A = A_1 \times \cdots \times A_n$, where A_i is a finite set of actions available to player i. A vector $a = (a_1, \ldots, a_n) \in A$ is referred to as an action profile.
- $u = (u_1, \cdots, u_n)$, where $u_i : A \mapsto \mathbb{R}$ is a payoff or utility function for player i.

In definition 2.1.1, *finite* means that there is a finite set of players and each has a finite set of strategies. Typically, a utility function maps the set of outcomes of a game to a real-valued utility or payoff. Here, the actions possible for an agent also describe the outcomes, which is why we use A in the description of a normal-form game. The

Table 2.1 Payoff matrix for the
Prisoner's Dilemma game

	C	D
C	4, 4	1, 5
D	5, 1	2, 2

Prisoner's Dilemma is a well-known example of a normal-form game and is useful to illustrate basic concepts in game theory. There are multiple versions of the game; one version is as follows.

Example 2.1.1 (The Prisoner's Dilemma)   The players of the game are two prisoners suspected of a crime. Each prisoner can either confess (C) or deny (D) the crime. If they both deny, they serve a two-year prison term. If one of them confesses, his prison term will be one year and for the other player five years. If they both confess, they will be in prison for four years each (see table 2.1). The first entry in each cell denotes the row player's time in prison and the second entry denotes the column player's time in prison.

   Regarding the row player, he is always better off by confessing, independently of what the column player does, and vice versa. So, any rational prisoner will adopt the strategy of confessing the crime regardless of the other player's decision. However, if they both denied, they would both be better off.

   One type of strategy available to a player i in a normal-form game is to select a single action a_i and play it. Such a strategy is called a *pure strategy*. In the Prisoner's Dilemma both players might choose the action "confess". But a player is also able to randomize over the set of available actions according to some probability distribution. Such a strategy is called a *mixed strategy*.

Definition 2.1.2 (Mixed strategy) In a normal-form game $(\mathcal{I}, A, u)$ the set of mixed strategies for player i is $S_i = \Delta(A_i)$, where $\Delta(A_i)$ is the set of all probability distributions (aka lotteries) over A_i.

   The probability that an action a_i is played in strategy s_i is denoted by $s_i(a_i)$. When players choose to play a mixed-strategy profile $(s_1, \ldots, s_n)$, the expected utility of player i can be described as $u_i(s) = \sum_{a \in A} u_i(a)(\prod_{j=1}^{n} s_j(a_j))$. Notice that the term in parentheses, $\prod_{j=1}^{n} s_j(a_j)$, is the probability that action profile $a = (a_1, \ldots, a_n)$ will be played. A mixed-strategy profile is the Cartesian product of the individual mixed-strategy sets, $S_1 \times \cdots \times S_n$.

   We analyze games using *solution concepts* or more specifically equilibrium concepts. Solution concepts can be seen as a way to predict the outcome assuming some behavior of rational agents. An economic equilibrium is a state where economic forces such as supply and demand are balanced and the values of economic variables will not change. Solution concepts are principles according to which we identify interesting subsets of the outcomes of a game. The two most fundamental solution concepts are *Pareto optimality* and *Nash equilibrium*.

2.1.1 Dominant-Strategy Equilibrium

In the Prisoner's Dilemma game in table 2.1 a dominant-strategy equilibrium results if both players confess. This means that each rational player would confess, independently of what the other player does. Let us define this more formally. We say that *the strategy s_i strongly dominates* the strategy s_i' if player i always does better with s_i than s_i', i.e.,

$$\forall s_1, \ldots, s_{i-1}, s_{i+1}, \ldots, s_n,$$

$$u_i(s_1, \ldots, s_{i-1}, s_i, s_{i+1}, \ldots, s_n) > u_i(s_1, \ldots, s_{i-1}, s_i', s_{i+1}, \ldots, s_n)$$

The strategy s_i *weakly dominates* s_i' if player i never does worse with s_i than with s_i', and there is at least one case where player i does better with s_i than s_i':

$$\forall s_1, \ldots, s_{i-1}, s_{i+1}, \ldots, s_n, \quad u_i(\ldots, s_i, \ldots) \geq u_i(\ldots, s_i', \ldots)$$

and

$$\exists s_1, \ldots, s_{i-1}, s_{i+1}, \ldots, s_n, \quad u_i(\ldots, s_i, \ldots) > u_i(\ldots, s_i', \ldots)$$

The strategy s_i is a strongly (weakly) dominant strategy if it strongly (weakly) dominates every $s_i' \in S_i$.

Definition 2.1.3 (Dominated strategy) A strategy s_i is strongly (weakly) dominated for an agent i if some other strategy s_i' strongly (weakly) dominates s_i.

In a dominant-strategy equilibrium a player i will do better using s_i rather than a different strategy s_i', regardless of what strategies the other players use.

Definition 2.1.4 (Dominant-strategy equilibrium) A dominant-strategy equilibrium is a set $(s_1, \ldots, s_n)$ such that s_i is dominant for each player i.

Dominant strategies are very useful, as they are simple for players, but they do not always exist. Interestingly, in the standard game-theoretical models of auctions, there is an auction format where the bidders have a simple dominant strategy, as we will see in chapter 4.

2.1.2 Pareto Optimality

Pareto optimality also plays an important role in the Prisoner's Dilemma. A strategy profile is Pareto optimal if there does not exist another strategy profile that Pareto-dominates it. A strategy profile is Pareto-dominated if some player can be made better off without any other player being made worse off.

Definition 2.1.5 (Pareto optimality) Any strategy profile that is not Pareto-dominated is Pareto optimal. A strategy profile s Pareto-dominates strategy profile s' if, for all $i \in \mathcal{I}$, $u_i(s) \geq u_i(s')$ and there exists a $j \in \mathcal{I}$ for which $u_j(s) > u_j(s')$.

Thus, Pareto optimality is a solution concept from the point of view of an outside observer of the game. It gives a partial ordering over strategy profiles, but we cannot generally identify an optimal strategy. Weak Pareto dominance means that at least one

Table 2.2 Payoff matrix for the Matching Pennies game

	Heads	Tails
Heads	1, −1	−1, 1
Tails	−1, 1	1, −1

agent is better off, and no one is made worse off. Strong Pareto dominance means that all agents gain. The Pareto-optimal solution in the Prisoner's Dilemma is for both players to deny but the dominant-strategy equilibrium is for both to confess. This is where the dilemma comes from.

2.1.3   Nash Equilibrium

The Nash equilibrium is arguably the most significant solution concept in game theory. In a Nash equilibrium we look at games from an agent's point of view, as we did in the case of dominant-strategy equilibria.

Definition 2.1.6 (Nash equilibrium) A strategy profile $s = (s_1, \ldots, s_n)$ is a Nash equilibrium if s_i is a best response to s_{-i} for all players i. Here s_{-i} is the profile obtained after removing s_i from the profile s. The *best response* to s_{-i} is a strategy chosen by player i which maximizes his utility given that players other than i play s_{-i}.

Players do not want to deviate unilaterally from a Nash equilibrium. If a predicted outcome was not a Nash equilibrium, it would mean that at least one individual would have an incentive to deviate from the predicted outcome and increase his utility.

Example 2.1.2 (The Matching Pennies game) The Matching Pennies game describes a zero-sum game where both players simultaneously put a penny on the table. If one player wins, the other player loses and the payoff matrix for a row and a column player are described in table 2.2. The game has a mixed-strategy Nash equilibrium, but no pure-strategy Nash equilibrium. In a Nash equilibrium nobody would want to change her strategy if she knew what strategies the other agents were following, and therefore it describes a form of stability. If the column player plays heads with probability p and tails with probability $1 - p$ then the row player must be indifferent between the two actions available to him and so will play a mixed strategy. If she is not indifferent between the two actions, she would play purely the action which gives a better utility by setting a zero probability for the other action. Thus, the only Nash equilibrium is randomization with equal probability over both actions. This is easy to check. For the row player, these probabilities can be derived as follows:

$$E(u_{heads}) = E(u_{tails}) \implies 1p + (-1)(1 - p) = -1p + 1(1 - p) \implies p = 1/2$$

Although computing a mixed Nash equilibrium for small games as above is easy, the problem of finding the Nash equilibrium for a game in general is a computationally hard problem. It was shown to be PPAD-complete (Daskalakis *et al.*, 2009), which means in

Table 2.3 Payoff matrix for the
Battle of Sexes game

	F	B
F	2, 1	0, 0
B	0, 0	1, 2

the worst case that computing an equilibrium is exponential in the number of actions of each player, assuming P $\neq$ PPAD i.e., that the classes P and PPAD describe different sets of problems. Let's take a look at another well-known example of a normal-form game.

Example 2.1.3 (The Battle of Sexes game) The Battle of Sexes game has the bi-matrix representation shown in table 2.3. This game has two players who want to go either to a football game (F) or to a ballet (B). The states (F, F) and (B, B) constitute pure Nash equilibria with rewards (2, 1) and (1, 2), respectively.

We can compute the probabilities for a mixed Nash equilibrium with which the column player needs to play F and B. These probabilities p and $1 - p$ for the column player need to be set such that the expected utility for the row player is the same for both actions:

$$2p + 0(1 - p) = 0p + 1 - p \Longrightarrow p = 1/3$$

The probabilities q and $1 - q$ for the row player are obtained analogously:

$$q + 0(1 - q) = 0q + 2(1 - q) \Longrightarrow q = 2/3$$

Consequently, the expected payoff for each bidder is 2/3 as a result.

Note that we considered only the expected payoffs in the pure equilibria in the Battle of Sexes game, i.e., the expected payoff in (F, F) or (B, B). The *price-of-anarchy* (PoA) has been defined as the ratio between the "worst equilibrium" and the optimal "centralized" solution. It can be defined with respect to pure Nash equilibria or mixed Nash equilibria, for example. In the Battle of Sexes game, the optimal solution would be (F, F) or (B, B) with a total utility of 3 and PoA $3/(4/3) = 9/4$. The price-of-anarchy measures the decrease in the efficiency of a system due to selfish behavior of the players. The concept has received significant attention as it also allows us to analyze the robustness of simple auction formats in the presence of complex utility functions. The PoA can be seen as an analogue of the "approximation ratio" in an approximation algorithm or the "competitive ratio" in an online algorithm.

A *strict Nash equilibrium* is one where every agent's strategy constitutes a unique best response to the other agents' strategies. If, instead, for some player multiple strategies have the same payoff then this constitutes a *weak* Nash equilibrium. The example in table 2.4, with actions U, M, B, L, N, has a unique and pure best response (B, N), because it has the highest utility for both players.

John Nash showed that every game with a finite number of players and action profiles has at least one Nash equilibrium. However, typically there are more than one, which often makes the Nash equilibrium a poor prediction device; if there are multiple Nash

Table 2.4 Normal-form game with a strict
pure-strategy Nash equilibrium in (B, R)

	L	M	N
U	0, 4	4, 0	5, 3
M	4, 0	0, 4	6, 3
B	3, 5	3, 6	7, 7

equilibria in a game, the players face an *equilibrium selection* problem. If some players believe that the equilibrium ultimately played out is s while others believe that it is s' then the profile of strategies actually selected will be a mixture of s and s', a disequilibrium. In our Battle of Sexes example, without coordination bidders might easily end up in a disequilibrium with zero payoff.

Unfortunately, there can be many Nash equilibria. McKelvey and McLennan (1997) showed that, fixing the number of pure strategies for each player, the maximal number of totally mixed Nash equilibria is exponential in the minimum number of pure strategies for any player. A Nash equilibrium is totally mixed if every pure strategy is assigned a positive probability.

There have been several suggestions about how players deal with the equilibrium selection problem. *Payoff dominance* and *risk dominance* are two well-known refinements of the Nash equilibrium solution concept defined by John Harsanyi and Reinhard Selten. A Nash equilibrium is considered payoff dominant if it is Pareto superior to all other Nash equilibria in the game. Risk dominance is best illustrated in the *Stag Hunt game* in table 2.5. A joint action (hunting) in this game yields a higher payoff if all players combine their skills. However, if it is unknown whether the other agent will help in hunting, gathering is the better strategy for each agent because it does not depend on coordinating with the other agent. The strategy pair (Hunt, Hunt) in the Stag Hunt game is payoff dominant since the payoffs are higher for both players compared with the other pure Nash equilibrium (Gather, Gather).

On the other hand, (Gather, Gather) risk-dominates (Hunt, Hunt) since if an uncertainty exists about the other player's action then gathering will provide a higher expected payoff. In this symmetric game it is easy to see this. If each agent assigns a probability 0.5 to Hunt and to Gather then (Gather, Gather) risk-dominates (Hunt, Hunt): $0.5 \times 4 + 0.5 \times 2 \geq 0.5 \times 5 + 0.5 \times 0$. Alternatively, one can look at the product of the deviation losses. If the column player deviates from (Gather, Gather) to Hunt then the deviation loss is 2. The same is true for the column player if the row player deviates. So, the product of the deviation losses is $2 \times 2 = 4$; this is more than the product of the deviation losses from deviations of the (Hunt, Hunt) equilibrium, which is 1. This means that, in this Stag Hunt game, payoff and risk dominance lead to different results.

Table 2.5 Payoff matrix for the Stag
Hunt game

	Hunt	Gather
Hunt	5, 5	0, 4
Gather	4, 0	2, 2

Table 2.6 Payoff matrix for the Chicken game

	C	D
C	6, 6	2, 7
D	7, 2	0, 0

2.1.4 Correlated Equilibrium

The correlated equilibrium is an interesting extension as it generalizes the Nash equilibrium (Aumann, 1987). Let's reconsider the Battle of Sexes game in table 2.3. Now, consider a situation where a "trusted" authority flips a fair coin and, depending on the outcome of the coin toss, tells the players what they should do. For example, if the coin shows heads, the column player is told to choose ballet and the row player is told that as well. No individual player has an incentive to deviate from what they are told to do. In this case, when the row player is told to choose B he knows that the column player is told to choose B as well. So, the row player has no incentive to deviate and switch to F as the payoff would be lower (0 compared with 1). The advantage of following such a procedure is that the expected rewards are now higher (3/2, 3/2) compared with the rewards (2/3, 2/3) from the mixed Nash equilibrium. A more interesting example of correlated equilibria is the game of Chicken in table 2.6.

Example 2.1.4 (The Chicken game) Two drivers drive towards each other on a collision course: one must swerve or both may die in the crash, but if one driver swerves and the other does not then the one who swerved will be called a *chicken*, meaning a coward (C). The worst outcome occurs when both players dare (D). The deterministic or pure Nash equilibria are (D, C) and (C, D) with a payoff of (7, 2) or (2, 7), respectively. A mixed Nash equilibrium has an expected payoff of 14/3 for each player.

  In a correlated equilibrium a trusted third party tells each player what to do, on the basis of the outcome of an experiment with the following probability distribution: (C, D), (D, C), and (C, C) all have a probability of 1/3. If the trusted party tells the column player to dare, then she has no incentive to deviate. She knows that the outcome must have been (C, D) and the row player will obey the instruction to chicken. If the column player is told to chicken then she knows that the outcome must have been either (D, C) or (C, C), each happening with equal probability. The column player's expected payoff on playing C, conditioned on the fact that she is told to chicken, is $0.5 \times 6 + 0.5 \times 2 = 4$. If the column player decides to deviate and play D when told to play C then the expected payoff is $0.5 \times 7 + 0.5 \times 0 = 3.5 < 4$. So, the expected payoff on deviating is lower than the payoff on obeying the instruction of the trusted party. The game is symmetric and the row player has the same incentives. Note that, in the case of the correlated equilibrium, the expected reward for each player is $1/3 \times 7 + 2/3 \times 4 = 5$. This is higher than the expected payoff of 14/3 in the mixed Nash equilibrium.

Definition 2.1.7 (Correlated equilibrium) A *correlated equilibrium* is a probability distribution $\{p_s\}$ on the space of strategy profiles that obeys the following conditions. For each player i, and every two different strategies b, b' of i, conditioned on the event that a strategy profile with b as a strategy was drawn from the distribution, the expected utility of playing b is no smaller than that of playing b':

$$\sum_{s \in \mathcal{S}_{-i}} (u^i_{sb} - u^i_{sb'})p_{sb} \geq 0$$

By $\mathcal{S}_{-i}$ we denote the set of strategy profiles of all other players except for i. If $s \in \mathcal{S}_{-i}$, sb denotes the strategy profile in which player i plays b and the others play s. The inequalities show that if a strategy profile is drawn from the distribution $\{p_s\}$ and each player is told, privately, his or her own component of the outcome, and if furthermore all players assume that the others will follow the recommendation then the expected profit of player i cannot be increased by switching to a different strategy b', so that the recommendation is self-enforcing.

The inequalities in the definition of a correlated equilibrium for the Chicken game can now be formulated as follows:

$$(6-7)p_{C,C} + (2-0)p_{C,D} \geq 0$$
$$(7-6)p_{D,C} + (0-2)p_{D,D} \geq 0$$
$$(6-7)p_{C,C} + (2-0)p_{C,D} \geq 0$$
$$(7-6)p_{D,C} + (0-2)p_{D,D} \geq 0$$
$$\sum_{i,j \in \{C,D\}} p_{i,j} = 1$$
$$0 \leq p_{i,j} \leq 1$$

The first two equations state the optimality of the distribution for the row player by comparing the payoffs for these cases when the column player chooses strategy C or strategy D. In the first equation the recommendation for the row player is C but this player deviates to D when the opponent either plays C (first term) or D (second term). The second equation deals with a row player who is recommended D, but might deviate to C for the two cases where the column player plays C or D. The third and fourth equations are for the column player, whose behavior is symmetric.

For every Nash equilibrium there exists a corresponding correlated equilibrium. Actually, there is an infinite number of correlated equilibria: an intuitive subset is the convex hull of the pure Nash equilibria (D, C) and (C, D) in our example above. There are also correlated equilibria which are not Nash equilibria. For example, if $p_{D,C}$ and $p_{C,D}$ are selected with a probability of 0.5, then this is not a Nash equilibrium but a correlated equilibrium. This means that Nash equilibria are a subset of all correlated equilibria.

The *mediation value* is the ratio of the maximal welfare of a game obtained in a correlated equilibrium and the maximal welfare obtained in a mixed-strategy Nash equilibrium (Ashlagi *et al.*, 2008). In the above example of the Chicken game with two players the mediation value 10/9 can be computed as the maximum welfare of a correlated equilibrium (30/3) divided by the maximum welfare of a Nash equilibrium, which is 9. The price-of-anarchy for the example is $12/9 = 4/3$.

Table 2.7 Normal-form game leading
to (C, E) with iterated dominance

	D	E	F
A	0, 2	2, 1	1, 3
B	1, 4	2, 1	4, 1
C	2, 1	4, 4	3, 2

2.1.5 Further Solution Concepts

For the static solution concepts that we have considered so far, we can define a relationship among the solution concepts, such that dominant-strategy equilibria $\subset$ pure Nash equilibria $\subset$ mixed Nash equilibria $\subset$ correlated equilibria. There are, however, many other solution concepts for normal-form games. In the following, we provide a short description of two widely used concepts and discuss their relationship to the Nash equilibrium.

2.1.5.1 Iterated Elimination of Dominated Strategies

The iterated elimination (or deletion) of dominated strategies is one common technique for solving games that involves iteratively removing dominated strategies. If all players have a dominant strategy then it is natural for them to choose the dominant strategies and so we reach a dominant-strategy equilibrium. Of course, if a player has a dominant strategy then all other strategies are dominated. But there may be cases where a player does not have a dominant strategy and yet has dominated strategies (see section 2.1.1 for a discussion of domination). The iterated elimination of dominated strategies is a common technique for solving games that involves iteratively removing dominated strategies. This process is valid if it is assumed that rationality among players is common knowledge, that is, each player knows that the rest of the players are rational, and each player knows that the rest of the players know that he knows that the rest of the players are rational.

There are two versions of this process. One version involves eliminating only strongly dominated strategies. If, after this procedure, there is only one strategy for each player remaining, that strategy profile is the unique Nash equilibrium. Another version involves eliminating both strongly and weakly dominated strategies. Every equilibrium in dominant strategies is also a Nash equilibrium. However, the Nash equilibrium found by eliminating weakly dominated strategies may not be the only Nash equilibrium.

The order of elimination doesn't matter when we remove strictly dominated strategies. However, the order of elimination does matter when we remove weakly dominated strategies; we might actually discard one or more Nash equilibria of the game. If by iterated elimination of dominated strategies there is only one strategy left for each player, the game is called a *dominance-solvable* game.

Example 2.1.5 Table 2.7 shows an example, where we can first eliminate row A of the row player, because it is strongly dominated by row C. For the remaining rows, we can eliminate column F because it is dominated by the mixed strategy 0.5D + 0.5E. Now we have a payoff matrix with two columns and two rows. Row B is dominated by row

C in this reduced matrix. Finally, in the remaining row, column D is strongly dominated by E. The strategy profile with the column player playing E and the row player playing C is a Nash equilibrium. It is also the unique Nash equilibrium of the game.

2.1.5.2 ε-Nash Equilibrium

In a Nash equilibrium, no player has an incentive to change his behavior. In an approximate or ε-Nash equilibrium, this requirement is weakened to allow the possibility that a player may have a small incentive to do something different. The idea is that players are indifferent to sufficiently small gains, which seems plausible in many situations.

Definition 2.1.8 (ε-Nash equilibrium) A strategy profile $s = (s_1, \ldots, s_n)$ is called an ε-Nash equilibrium if $u_i(s_i, s_{-i}) \geq u_i(s_i', s_{-i}) - \varepsilon$ for all players i and for all strategies $s_i' \neq s_i$.

The concept has a computational advantage compared with Nash equilibrium, as polynomial-time algorithms are known for it (Daskalakis *et al.*, 2009). Every Nash equilibrium is surrounded by ε-Nash equilibria with $\varepsilon > 0$. Unfortunately, a player's payoff in ε-Nash can be arbitrarily less than in a Nash equilibrium of the game. This means that an ε-Nash cannot be used to approximate agents' payoffs in a Nash equilibrium.

2.2   Extensive-Form Games

The normal-form game does not incorporate any notion of sequence. In game theory, a *sequential or dynamic game* is a game where one player chooses his or her action before the others choose theirs. The extensive-form representation makes temporal structure in the game explicit. We only mention extensive-form games briefly, for the sake of completeness, because we will rarely draw on such models in subsequent sections. This might appear surprising, because many auction formats are organized in sequential rounds. In the next chapter, on mechanism design, we will discuss the revelation principle, given in Theorem 3.3.1, which provides theoretical reasons why auctions are typically modeled as games in which bids are submitted simultaneously. We do use extensive-form games, however, to illustrate strategic problems as they arise in the simultaneous multi-round auction in Chapter 6.

A perfect-information extensive-form game can be modeled as a tree, where each node describes the choice of an agent between possible actions represented by edges. The leaves represent the outcomes for which each player has a utility. In each stage of the game, the players know the node they are in. Every perfect-information game can be converted to an equivalent normal-form game. However, the transformation to a normal-form game comes at the expense of exponentially many outcomes in the resulting game. The reverse transformation, of normal-form games to perfect-information extensive-form games, is not always possible. Every perfect-information game in extensive form has a pure-strategy Nash equilibrium in normal-form representation. Yet there might exist some unsatisfying Nash equilibria which are based on "non-credible threats".

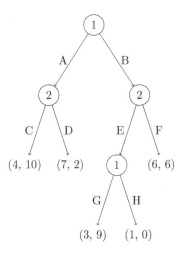

Figure 2.1 Example of a perfect-information game in extensive form.

Hence, we use a stronger concept called subgame-perfect equilibrium. A subgame is a smaller game that forms part of the larger game.

Definition 2.2.1 (Subgame-perfect equilibrium) A strategy profile s of a game is a subgame-perfect equilibrium if it represents a Nash equilibrium of every subgame of the original game.

Every perfect-information extensive-form game has at least one subgame-perfect equilibrium, which is also a Nash equilibrium. Backward induction eliminates branches which would involve any agent making a move from that node that is not credible (i.e., not optimal) for the agent.

Example 2.2.1 Figure 2.1 provides a simple example of an extensive-form game with actions A and C as subgame-perfect equilibria; this is easy to derive through backward induction from the leaves to the root node. For example, agent 1 can choose between actions G and H. Action G provides a higher payoff, of 3, so that agent 1 selects G. Now, agent 2 can anticipate this and, needing to make a choice between E and F, selects E, and so on.

There might be Nash equilibrium strategies which rely on a (non-credible) threat that will harm the agent making the threat. For instance, in the Chicken game in example 2.1.4, if one agent has the chance to remove the steering wheel from his car he should always take it because it leads to a subgame in which his rational opponent would swerve away, because it would otherwise kill both of them. The agent who rips out the wheel will always win the game, and the opponent's threat not to swerve is not credible.

An extensive-form game has *perfect information* if each agent, when making a decision, is perfectly informed of all the events that have previously occurred. Tic-tac-toe (noughts and crosses) is an example of a game with perfect information, as each agent can see all the pieces on the board at all times. Combinatorial game theory studies

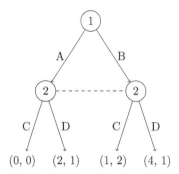

Figure 2.2 Example of an imperfect-information game in extensive form.

sequential games with perfect information such as chess or Go. An important notion in combinatorial game theory is that of a *solved game*, meaning for example that, as one can prove, the game of tic-tac-toe results in a draw if both players play optimally.

Complete information is different from perfect information, which implies that each player is perfectly informed of all the events that have previously occurred. A complete-information game may or may not be a perfect-information game. Card games where each player's cards are hidden from the other players are examples of games with *imperfect information*. Imperfect-information games are extensive-form games in which each player's choice nodes are partitioned into information sets. If two or more choice nodes are in the same information set then they have the same actions and the player to whom that set belongs does not know which node in the set has been reached. However, the actions in different choice nodes of the information set lead to different outcomes. In the imperfect-information extensive-form game in figure 2.2, the information set is indicated by a dotted line connecting the nodes in that set. Player 2 doesn't know whether player 1 played action A or B. Player 1 would like to make player 2 think that she has played A when she has actually played B so that player 2 will play D and player 1 will receive 4. The equilibria depend on the beliefs of player 2.

So far, we have assumed complete-information games. However, a player might only have probabilistic information about the payoffs of the game for other players. This means that bidders are of different types, and there is a prior probability for a player to be a particular type. For example, a bidder might have a high or a low valuation in an auction. This is a game with *incomplete information*, as will be discussed in the next section. There are solution concepts for normal-form games but also for extensive-form games with incomplete information. Incomplete-information games are also referred to as *Bayesian games*.

2.3   Bayesian Games

In complete-information normal-form games, we assume that all players know all relevant information about the game, in particular, the number of players, the action available to each bidder, and the payoff associated with each action. This is often unrealistic and so in our game-theoretical discussion of auctions we model them as games with incomplete information. Now the expected payoff and the strategies of player i depend on her beliefs about others' payoffs. A player's optimal action can depend on her beliefs about other player's beliefs about his beliefs, etc. Harsanyi (1967) introduces the *type* of a player, a random variable $\theta_i \in \Theta_i$ which contains the information about player i's payoffs. The probability distribution of this random variable is assumed to be common among the players (aka a common prior), and the players use Bayes' rule to update their beliefs and reason about probabilities. We denote $\theta = (\theta_1, \ldots, \theta_n)$ and $\theta_{-i} = (\theta_1, \ldots, \theta_{i-1}, \theta_{i+1}, \ldots, \theta_n)$.

Definition 2.3.1 (Bayesian games) A finite Bayesian game is a tuple $(\mathcal{I}, A, \Theta, u, F)$ in which:

- $\mathcal{I}$ is a set of players;
- A_i is the set of actions available to player i, with $a_i \in A_i$ as a specific action and $A = A_1 \times \cdots \times A_n$;
- $\Theta = \Theta_1 \times \cdots \times \Theta_n$ is the set of all possible types, where Θ_i is the type space of player i and a type θ_i in this space could be the value that player i has for an object;
- $u_i : A \times \Theta \mapsto \mathbb{R}$ or $u_i(a_1, \ldots, a_n; \theta_1, \ldots, \theta_n)$ is the payoff or utility function for player i with $u = (u_1, \ldots, u_n)$;
- F is the probability distribution (aka a common prior) of the players' types. If the Θ_i are finite then F is a discrete probability distribution on Θ and we denote the probability of realization θ by $p(\theta_1, \ldots, \theta_n)$.

Note that, in this chapter, we assume that the actions A are equivalent to the outcomes O of a game. In Bayesian games, only the type θ_i is private to player i; everything else, including the probability distribution, is common knowledge. First, for each player i, θ_i is chosen randomly from Θ_i according to F, and player i observes his or her realized type θ_i. Then the players update their beliefs about other players' types based on F. The distribution conditional on θ_i can be described as $F_i(\theta_{-i}|\theta_i)$. The players then choose their actions simultaneously.

It's now possible to define strategies $s_i : \Theta_i \mapsto A_i$ by combining types and actions. A strategy s_i may assign different actions to different types, and $s_i(\theta_i) \in A_i$. The utility of a bidder is calculated by taking expectation over types using the bidder's conditional beliefs about opponents' types:

$$Eu_i(s_i|s_{-i}, \theta_i) = \sum_{\theta_{-i} \in \Theta_{-i}} u_i(s_i(\theta_i), s_{-i}(\theta_{-i}), \theta_i, \theta_{-i}|\theta_i)p_i(\theta_{-i}|\theta_i)$$

In the above formula, player i uses the pure strategy s_i, and other players use strategy s_{-i}. A Bayesian Nash equilibrium may seem conceptually more complicated. However, we can construct a normal-form representation that corresponds to a given Bayesian game. The induced normal form for Bayesian games has an action for every pure strategy. Each agent's payoff given a pure strategy profile s is her ex ante (original) expected utility under s. The Bayesian Nash equilibria of a Bayesian game are then the Nash

Table 2.8 Payoff matrix of a Bayesian game

		Type 1			Type 2	
		L	R		L	R
Type 1	U	4, 4	6, 6	U	4, 2	6, 2
	B	2, 4	4, 6	B	2, 4	4, 2
		L	R		L	R
Type 2	U	2, 4	4, 6	U	2, 2	4, 4
	B	4, 4	2, 6	B	4, 4	2, 2

equilibria of its induced normal form. Example 2.3.1 shows how the payoff matrix of a Bayesian game is transformed to this induced normal form.

Example 2.3.1 (Payoff matrix of a Bayesian game) Table 2.8 provides an example of a Bayesian game. It consists of four 2×2 games. Each agent has two types which are publicly known to each occur with probability 0.5. The actions are U, B, L, R (up, bottom, left, right).

We can define a 4×4 normal-form game in which the actions are the four strategies of the two agents and the payoffs are the expected payoffs in the individual games, given the agents' common prior beliefs. The complete payoff matrix can be constructed as shown in table 2.9.

2.3.1   Bayesian Nash Equilibrium

A Bayesian Nash equilibrium is basically the same concept as a Nash equilibrium with the addition that players need to take expectations over opponents' types.

Definition 2.3.2 (Bayesian Nash equilibrium) A Bayesian Nash equilibrium (BNE) is the Nash equilibrium of a Bayesian game, i.e.,

$$E(u_i(s_i|s_{-i}, \theta_i)) \geq E(u_i(s_i'|s_{-i}, \theta_i))$$

for all $s_i'(\theta_i)$ and for all types θ_i occurring with positive probability.

Every finite Bayesian game has a Bayesian Nash equilibrium. Bayesian Nash equilibria play a significant role in the analysis of first-price auctions. Chapter 4, on single-object auctions, will describe in more detail how such equilibria are derived. The

Table 2.9 Induced normal form of the game from table 2.8

	LL	LR	RL	RR
UU	3, 3	4, 3.5	4, 4	5, 4.5
UB	4, 3.5	4, 3	4, 4.5	4, 4
BU	2, 3.5	3, 3.5	3, 4.5	4, 4.5
BB	3, 4	3, 3	3, 5	3, 4

assumption of a prior distribution $F(\cdot)$ in Bayesian games that is known to all players might be considered strong. However, in some applications such as display advertisement auctions or keyword auctions, where participants have access to large volumes of historical bid data, it is reasonable to assume that these bidders can estimate the prior distribution of the valuations from the bids.

For extensive-form games with imperfect information, the *perfect Bayesian equilibrium* provides an alternative, and it can be seen as an extension of the subgame perfect equilibrium discussed in section 2.2. Extensive-form games with incomplete information are often modeled via a root node representing nature, which randomizes over the types of a player. Depending on the type of player there are different subgames. This can lead to different types of perfect Bayesian equilibria. In *separating* perfect Bayesian equilibria, different types of player choose different actions. If different types of player choose the same action, this is referred to as a *pooling* strategy. Chapter 6 provides examples of extensive-form games with incomplete information in the context of ascending auctions. In such a signaling game there is uncertainty about the type or budget a bidder has, and this bidder bids aggressively in the initial phases independent of her type, thus playing a pooling strategy. We postpone a more detailed discussion to chapter 6.

2.3.2   Ex Post Equilibrium

An ex post equilibrium is a refinement of the Bayesian Nash equilibrium in which each player's equilibrium strategy remains an equilibrium even after the player learns the other players' private information. An ex post equilibrium is robust to the distribution of private information, i.e., such a strategy remains a best response regardless of the distribution of private information. We denote $s_i \in S_i$ as the set of all player i's mixed strategies, and write $s_j(a_j|\theta_j)$ to denote the probability under mixed strategy s_j that agent j plays action a_j, given that j's type is θ_j. The ex post expected utility of a Bayesian game can be described as

$$E(u_i(s, \theta)) = \sum_{a \in A} \left(\prod_{j \in I} s_j(a_j|\theta_j) \right) u_i(a, \theta)$$

Note that the ex post expected utility is computed on the basis of the actual types θ of the players. This allows us to introduce an ex post equilibrium.

Definition 2.3.3 (Ex post (Nash) equilibrium) A mixed-strategy profile s is an ex post (Nash) equilibrium if $s_i \in \arg \max_{s_i' \in S_i} E(u_i(s_i', s_{-i}, \theta)) \, \forall \theta, \forall i$.

In other words, no agent would ever want to deviate from her mixed strategy even if she knew the complete type vector θ. Players only need assumptions about the strategies s_{-i} of the other players. This means that the equilibrium is robust under perturbations in the type distribution. Unfortunately, an ex post equilibrium is not guaranteed to always

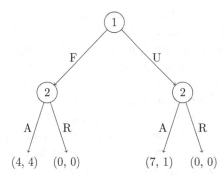

Figure 2.3 Example of an Ultimatum game.

exist. For auction markets, an ex post equilibrium is very desirable because then bidders do not need information about the prior distribution of valuations, i.e., the type distribution.

2.4   Games and Human Behavior

We have discussed a number of well-known games such as the Battle of Sexes, the Prisoner's Dilemma, and the Chicken game, which describe abstract strategic problems. Such games have been studied in game theory, assuming some solution concept, and also in the laboratory. Not surprisingly, the behavior of subjects in laboratory experiments cannot always be explained with game-theoretical solution concepts and corresponding notions of rationality. The Ultimatum game and the Public Goods game are two examples where laboratory subjects often do not behave as game theory predicts.

In the *Ultimatum game* two players need to decide how to divide a sum of money that is given to them. Both players know the amount. The first player proposes how to divide the sum between the two players, and the second player can either accept or reject this proposal. If the second player rejects it, neither player receives anything. If the second player accepts it, the money is split according to the proposal. The game is played only once so that reciprocation is not an issue. Figure 2.3 provides an example where player 1 can make a fair (F) or unfair (U) proposal. Player 2 then has the possibility of accepting it (A) or rejecting it (R).

If player 2 acts rationally, he should accept any division in which player 1 offers him anything at all, since doing so leaves him with more money than he would have had otherwise. If player 1 knows that player 2 will act rationally, and if she acts rationally herself, then she should offer player 2 only one dollar and take seven dollars. However, divisions which player 2 regards as unfair are often rejected. In industrialized cultures people typically offer "fair" (i.e., 50 : 50) splits, and offers of less than 20% are often rejected in experiments. Apparently, fairness considerations play a role in human decision making.

In the *Public Goods* game subjects secretly choose how many of their private tokens to put into a public pot. The tokens in this pot are multiplied by a factor (greater than one and less than the number of players) and this "public good" payoff is evenly divided among players. Each subject also keeps the tokens they do not contribute. The group's total payoff is maximized when everyone contributes all their tokens to the public pool. The Public Goods game can be seen as a Prisoner's Dilemma with more players. Unfortunately, the Nash equilibrium in this game is simply to have zero contributions by all; if the experiment were a purely analytical exercise in game theory it would resolve to zero contributions because any rational agent does best contributing zero, regardless of whatever anyone else does. However, the Nash equilibrium is rarely seen in experiments.

Both the Ultimatum game and the Public Goods game are examples challenging the type of rational choice by human decision makers that is assumed in game theory. Behavioral economics develops alternative models to explain human behavior in such games (Kahneman, 2003). This literature tries to reflect issues such as fairness, inequity aversion, and reciprocity, to arrive at models which might be more predictive in some areas. Still, in many market design problems the rationality assumptions implied by traditional game-theoretical solution concepts which focus on selfish maximization of expected utility or payoff can be a useful baseline to predict and understand market outcomes. Gilboa *et al.* (2014) provides an excellent discussion about the role of game-theoretical models in economics and how they complement empirical data and experimental results. It is also the combination of theory, experiment, and field data that allows for a thorough understanding of market designs.

2.5   Summary

This chapter provides a brief introduction to solution concepts designed to predict the equilibrium outcomes of a game. These concepts will be refined and applied in subsequent chapters. Equilibrium concepts are very important as a prediction device for markets, because market models should make predictions about humans who understand the models. A purely descriptive analysis of markets, or non-equilibrium predictions, would not deliver good predictions in the long run, because the players would respond and adapt their behavior. This is what makes the game-theoretical analysis of markets different from the types of prediction found in other fields of computer science and operations research, which typically do not need to consider interactions among decision makers.

In particular, Bayesian games will be important in subsequent chapters on mechanism design; furthermore, auctions are typically modeled as Bayesian games. For example, Bayesian Nash equilibrium strategies have been derived for first-price sealed-bid auctions of a single object. Deriving such equilibria for sealed-bid multi-object auctions turns out to be much harder. Stronger solution concepts such as ex post equilibria are desirable for multi-object auctions, but they are limited to a restricted set of mechanisms and specific assumptions about the utility functions. Auctions which exhibit such solution concepts are desirable, because they do not require prior information about the valuation distributions of other bidders.

There are many recent developments in game theory which might become important for market design in the future. For example, behavioral game theory analyzes interactive strategic decisions and behavior using the methods of game theory, experimental economics, and experimental psychology. It covers phenomena such as regret and loss aversion, which certainly play a role for human behavior in markets. We will point to the respective literature in later chapters where appropriate.

2.6   Comprehension Questions

1. Describe the dilemma in the Prisoner's Dilemma.
2. Why is there no pure-strategy Nash equilibrium in the Matching Pennies game?
3. Is every Nash equilibrium also a correlated equilibrium?
4. Why must all actions in the support of a mixed strategy that is part of a Nash equilibrium have the same expected utility?
5. What is the difference between an ex post equilibrium, a Bayesian Nash equilibrium, and a Nash equilibrium?
6. How do you distinguish between a game with incomplete information and a game with imperfect information?

2.7   Problems

Subgame Perfect Equilibrium

Consider a market that is serviced by a monopolist which we call the *incumbent* and a new *entrant*. If the entrant decides not to enter the market the incumbent obtains a high profit of 10. If the entrant enters the market then, depending on the high or low price chosen by the two businesses, the payoffs in table 2.10 can be achieved. The entrant is the row player and the incumbent is the column player.

1. Find the pure Nash equilibria of the game.
2. Find a subgame perfect equilibrium of the game.

Table 2.10 Payoff matrix

	H	L
H	4, 6	−1, 2
L	−3, 3	−2, 1

Bayesian Nash Equilibrium

Consider the following Bayesian game:

1. Player 1 (row) has two types and player 2 (column) has only one type. Player 1 knows her type but player 2 doesn't know player 1's type.

Table 2.11 Payoff matrix I

	F	N
F	$1, -2$	$2, -1$
N	$-1, 2$	$0, 0$

Table 2.12 Payoff matrix II

	F	N
F	$-2, 1$	$2, -1$
N	$-1, 2$	$0, 0$

2. The payoffs for the two cases can be found in payoff matrices I and II (see tables 2.11 and 2.12) with probability p, and $1 - p$, respectively.

3. The two players choose F or N as their action. (Choices are made simultaneously.)

Find pure Bayesian Nash equilibria, if any, for the two cases $p > 2/3$ and $p < 2/3$. Also find mixed-strategy Bayesian Nash equilibria for $p = 2/3$.

3 Mechanism Design

Mechanism design studies the construction of economic mechanisms in the presence of rational agents with private information. It is sometimes called reverse game theory, as mechanism designers search for mechanisms which satisfy game-theoretical solution concepts and achieve good outcomes. For example, an auctioneer might want to design an auction mechanism which maximizes social welfare of the participants and exhibits dominant strategies for bidders to reveal their true valuations. We mostly discuss market mechanisms in this book, but mechanism design is not restricted to markets and the basic principles can be applied to various types of interactive decision making.

Mechanism design has relations to *social choice theory*, which is a field in economics focusing on the aggregation of individual preferences to reach a collective decision or social welfare. Social choice theory depends upon the ability to aggregate individual preferences into a combined *social welfare function*. Therefore, individual preferences are modeled in terms of a utility function. The ability to sum the utility functions of different individuals, as is done in auction theory in chapter 4, depends on the utility functions being comparable with each other; informally, individuals' preferences must be measured with the same yardstick. The mechanism design literature on auctions typically assumes cardinal utility functions and interpersonal utility comparisons, as in the early social choice literature such as Bergson (1938) and Samuelson (1948). Note that Arrow (1950) and much of the subsequent literature assumes only ordinal preferences and rejects the idea of interpersonal utility comparisons. This means that utility cannot be measured and compared across individuals. The auction design literature as discussed in this book is an exception and assumes *quasi-linear utility functions*, where bidders have cardinal values for an allocation and maximize their payoff on the basis of prices in the market. Also, utility is comparable across agents. Cardinal preferences allow agents to express intensities, which is not possible with ordinal preferences only. For example, an agent might much prefer a diamond to a rock, but this information about intensity will be ignored if only ordinal preferences (diamond $\succ$ rock) are expressed.

Mechanism design is not limited to cardinal or even quasi-linear utility functions, but quasi-linear utility allows for mechanisms where social welfare functions can be implemented and the truthful revelation of preferences by agents is a dominant strategy. Such results are rare outside quasi-linear mechanism design (section 3.4), which is why this set of assumptions has received significant attention. There is a long-standing discussion between the proponents of cardinal and ordinal theory (Alt, 1936; Koebberling, 2006) regarding the situations where either one or the other model is justified. For example, in environments where the valuation of an item or a set of items is based on the net present value of future revenue streams, cardinal measures of valuation can be defended and interpersonal or inter-company comparisons of such valuations are appropriate. Such situations are different from measuring the personal utility of an individual for a consumer good which is not intended for resale.

Depending on the type of utility function assumed, various difficulties arise when a mechanism designer wants to implement a social choice function in the presence of self-interested agents. In this chapter, we discuss first some fundamental problems in the aggregation of ordinal preferences in the context of social choice theory. In section 3.1 incentives of agents to misrepresent their preferences are ignored, but even with truthful agents the aggregation of ordinal preferences is challenging. In section 3.2 ordinal preferences are translated into a real-valued utility function. Then mechanism design theory for general preferences is introduced (section 3.3), after which section 3.4 focuses on quasi-linear mechanism design. The notation used in the chapter largely follows Shoham and Leyton-Brown (2011), which provides a more comprehensive discussion of the material. An advanced textbook on mechanism design covering very recent trends is Borgers *et al.* (2015).

3.1   Social Choice

Results in social choice have uncovered the logical incompatibility of various desiderata. We first introduce some simple voting rules and then discuss what is arguably the central result in social choice, Arrow's impossibility theorem. We restrict ourselves to a very short introduction, mainly to help readers understand some of the difficulties in aggregating ordinal preferences; we refer the interested reader to Arrow *et al.* (2010) or Brandt *et al.* (2012). If we assume cardinal utility then aggregating preferences in a cardinal social welfare function becomes easier, but the strategic manipulation of agents is still an issue.

3.1.1   Voting Rules

Voting can be found everywhere. One can vote over political representatives, award nominees, where to go for dinner, joint plans, allocations of resources, etc. A voting rule takes as input a vector of votes (submitted by the voters) and as output produces either the winning alternative or an aggregated ranking of all alternatives. Each voter ranks all the alternatives or outcomes. For example, if the set of alternatives is $O = \{a, b, c, d\}$, then one possible ranking or vote is $b \succ a \succ d \succ c$. Such a submitted ranking is called a vote. We assume that voters make rational choices, i.e., consistent choices among alternatives. If in our example the voter prefers $d \succ a$ once he is left with only two choices $O = \{a, d\}$, then this would be inconsistent given his earlier vote.

Table 3.1 Example votes
without a Condorcet winner

Martin	$a \succ b \succ c$
Marianne	$b \succ c \succ a$
Oliver	$c \succ a \succ b$

More formally, let $\mathcal{I} = \{1, 2, \ldots, n\}$ denote the set of voters, and $o_j \in O$ the set of m alternatives. Voter i weakly prefers alternative o_1 to o_2 ($o_1 \succeq o_2$), or he has a strict preference $o_1 \succ o_2$. We capture indifference as $o_1 \sim o_2$, assume preferences to be transitive, and assume a total ordering of all alternatives for each voter. Transitivity means that if $o_1 \succeq o_2$ and $o_2 \succeq o_3$ then $o_1 \succeq o_3$. We can now define $\succeq_i \in L$ as a preference ordering or ranking of alternatives $o \in O$ by agent $i \in \mathcal{I}$, where L is the set of all possible preference orderings. Sometimes we omit the subscript for brevity. A preference profile $[\succeq] \in L^n$ can now be described as a tuple with a preference ordering for each agent. From now on, we distinguish between a social choice and a social welfare function.

- A *social choice function* is a function $C : L^n \mapsto O$ that takes the votes as input and selects one alternative as output.
- A *social welfare function* is a function $W : L^n \mapsto L$ that takes the votes as input and ranks alternatives as less desirable, more desirable, or indifferent for every possible pair of alternatives.

Many social choice functions have been suggested in the past. For example, *plurality voting* (aka majority rule with two alternatives) is a simple rule where each voter casts a single vote and the alternative with most votes is selected. In *approval voting* each voter can cast a single vote for as many alternatives as she wishes, and again the alternative with the most votes is selected. *Borda voting* is such that each voter submits a full ordering on the alternatives. This ordering contributes points to each alternative. If there are m alternatives, it contributes $m - 1$ points to the most preferred alternative, $m - 2$ points to the second most preferred alternative, etc. The winners are those whose total sum of points from all the voters is maximal.

One can now define different criteria with which to compare these voting rules. For example, a social choice function satisfies the *Condorcet condition* if it always picks a Condorcet winner when one exists.

Definition 3.1.1 (Condorcet winner)   A Condorcet winner is an outcome $o \in O$ such that $\zeta(o \succ o') \geq \zeta(o' \succ o) \ \forall o' \in O$.

Here, $\zeta(o \succ o')$ denotes the number of agents who prefer outcome o to o'. In other words, an alternative is a Condorcet winner if it wins all its pairwise elections. A Condorcet winner does not always exist. Consider a widespread example with three alternatives and three voters, Martin, Marianne, and Oliver (see table 3.1), to illustrate the point. This is also referred to as the Condorcet paradox, because we get an intransitive relationship among the alternatives when the Condorcet criterion is used.

Table 3.2 Example votes and plurality voting

Martin	$b \succ a \succ c \succ d$
Marianne	$c \succ a \succ b \succ d$
Oliver	$d \succ a \succ b \succ c$

Even if a Condorcet winner exists, the Condorcet criterion is not satisfied by all voting rules. In the example in table 3.2, alternative a would be a Condorcet winner, but it does not win under the plurality voting rule, where b, c, or d could win.

One could also look at the *majority criterion*; i.e., if an alternative is ranked first by most votes, that alternative should win. Unfortunately, again this intuitive criterion is not satisfied by all voting rules. For example, in the example in table 3.3, alternative a is the majority winner but does not win under the Borda rule, where alternative b would be the winner.

3.1.2 Arrow's Impossibility

The examples in the previous subsection illustrate that some popular voting rules can violate desirable properties. May's theorem shows that with *two alternatives* only, a voting rule is anonymous, neutral, and monotonic if and only if (iff) it is the plurality rule (May, 1952). Actually, any reasonable rule coincides with plurality for two alternatives. Anonymity just means that the names of voters are irrelevant, and neutrality that the names of the alternatives are irrelevant. Monotonicity is satisfied if, when a particular alternative wins and a voter improves her vote in favour of this alternative, then it still wins. With two alternatives, voters even have dominant strategies to reveal their preferences truthfully with a plurality rule. Unfortunately, Arrow's celebrated impossibility theorem shows that with *three or more alternatives* no voting protocol can satisfy a small set of intuitive criteria. We first define these simple criteria (Pareto efficiency, the independence of irrelevant alternatives, non-dictatorship), which are often seen as notions of fairness.

For now, we assume that all voters' preferences are strict total orderings on the alternatives. The preference ordering selected by the social welfare function W given the preference profile $[\succeq] \in L^n$ is described as $\succeq_W$.

Definition 3.1.2 (Pareto efficiency, or unanimity) A social welfare function W is Pareto efficient (satisfies unanimity) if, whenever all voters agree that $o_1 \succ_i o_2$, this implies that $o_1 \succ_W o_2$ for any $o_1, o_2 \in O$ and $\forall i$.

Table 3.3 Example votes and Borda voting

Martin	$a \succ b \succ c \succ d \succ e$
Marianne	$a \succ b \succ c \succ d \succ e$
Oliver	$c \succ b \succ d \succ e \succ a$

In other words, Pareto efficiency means that, when all agents agree on the ordering of two outcomes, the social welfare function must select that ordering. The independence of irrelevant alternatives demands that the selected preference ordering between two alternatives should depend only on the relative orderings given by the voters and should be independent of other alternatives.

Definition 3.1.3 (Independence of irrelevant alternatives, IIA) A social welfare function W is independent of irrelevant alternatives, if for any $o_1, o_2 \in O$ and any two preference profiles $[\succeq'], [\succeq''] \in L^n$ that leave the preference between o_1 and o_2 unchanged for all voters but might change other preferences, the social preference order between o_1 and o_2 remains unchanged, i.e., ($o_1 \succ_{W([\succ'])} o_2$ iff $o_1 \succ_{W([\succ''])} o_2$).

Overall, we aim for consistency, which means that if an alternative o_j is chosen from a set of alternatives then it is also chosen from all its subsets. For example, if a political candidate is chosen out of four competitors, the same candidate should also be selected on the basis of the votes submitted, if two of the other candidates withdrew their candidacy. Non-dictatorship means that there does not exist a single voter whose preferences always determine the social ordering.

Definition 3.1.4 (Non-dictatorship) The social welfare function W does not have a dictator if there does not exist a voter i such that for all o_1, o_2 the preference of the dictator determines the social preference, i.e., $o_1 \succ_i o_2 \implies o_1 \succ_W o_2$.

Interestingly, Arrow (1950) showed that no social welfare function W satisfies these properties for all possible inputs and three or more alternatives.

Theorem 3.1.1 (Arrow, 1950) *If $|O| \geq 3$, any social welfare function W that is Pareto efficient and independent of irrelevant alternatives is dictatorial.*

Proof sketch: Consider a choice over the set of alternatives A, B, C. Let us say that at the beginning every agent ranks B last and therefore prefers A and C over B. If now agents start ranking B first, we eventually reach an agent k such that the social welfare function ranks B first as well, after agent k changes her preference regarding B. This is true since it follows from Pareto efficiency once every agent has changed her preference order. On the contrary, suppose that the welfare function moves B to an intermediate point instead of the top. Without loss of generality, assume that $A \succ_W B \succ_W C$ holds, where $\succ_W$ is the order given by the social welfare function. If now every agent moves C above A we get $C \succ_W A$ by Pareto efficiency. By definition 3.1.3 (IIA) we know that $B \succ_W C$ still holds. Therefore, we get $C \succ_W A \succ_W B \succ_W C$; a contradiction.

We now show that agent k is a dictator over $\{A, C\}$. Let profile 1 be any profile where k prefers A over C. We then construct additional profiles by changing the position of B. Let profile 2 be a profile where the first $k - 1$ agents rank B first while k and the succeeding agents rank B last. Let profile 3 be a profile where the first k agents rank B first while every agent $i > k$ ranks B last. Finally, in profile 4 the first $k - 1$ agents rank B first, k ranks $A \succ_k B \succ_k C$ and every agent $i > k$ ranks B last. We observe that profiles 2 and 4 have the same order ($A \succ_W B$) on $\{A, B\}$. Also, profile 4 has the same order ($B \succ_W C$) on $\{B, C\}$ as profile 3. Since the relative ordering on $\{A, C\}$ does not change through profiles 1 to 4 we conclude that $A \succ_W C$ for profile 1. Therefore, k is a dictator over $\{A, C\}$ because we only fixed her order on $\{A, C\}$ for profile 1. Finally, it is only necessary to show that the pivotal voter is a dicator over all pairs of outcomes, and that there must only be one dictator.   □

Unfortunately, the result extends to social choice functions C where only a single top-ranked outcome must be selected, as was shown by Muller and Satterthwaite (1977). Note that so far we have not discussed strategic manipulation. The Gibbard–Satterthwaite theorem (see theorem 3.3.2) is based on Arrow's theorem and shows that for general preferences we cannot hope for a deterministic mechanism that is non-manipulable.

There is a huge literature in social choice characterizing the properties of different voting systems, which is beyond this textbook. Several scholars have tried to relax the independence of the irrelevant alternatives assumption or Pareto optimality, with little success. One fruitful line of research relaxed the consistency requirements of a social choice function. The top cycle, the uncovered set, the Banks set, and the tournament equilibrium set are examples of social choice functions satisfying such weaker notions of consistency (Brandt *et al.*, 2015).

Another line of research is *randomization*, although it might not always be acceptable. In random dictatorship one voter is picked uniformly at random and his most preferred alternative is selected. This mechanism is even strategy-proof for voters, i.e., voters have no incentive to lie about their preferences (Gibbard, 1977). We will discuss these topics in more detail in chapter 11 on matching theory.

The above results hold for general ordinal preferences. A possibility for circumventing Arrow's theorem is to restrict the types of preference. For example, we typically assume specific cardinal preferences, where bidders maximize payoff in the context of auctions. Before we get there, we will discuss the general concept of a utility function, which describes the preferences of agents formally.

3.2   Utility Functions

In large parts of this book we assume the existence of a utility function, which represents the preferences of an agent and transforms preferences into real numbers. This does not yet mean that these numbers are comparable across agents, but we will make this assumption later, in Section 3.4. First, however, we want to understand if there are any assumptions at all under which ordinal preferences can be represented by a utility function. The answer was provided by Von Neumann and Morgenstern (1947) and covers decisions under certainty and also uncertainty. Uncertainty is typically modeled via lotteries.

Definition 3.2.1 (Lottery)   Let $O = (o_1, o_2, \ldots, o_m)$ be a set of outcomes and $p = (p_1, \ldots, p_m)$ a lottery on the set of outcomes, where $p \in \Delta(O)$ is the probability of outcome $o_j \in O$ occurring; $p_j \geq 0$ for all $o_j \in O$ and $\sum_{i=1}^{m} p_j = 1$. Here, $\Delta(O)$ is the set of lotteries on O.

Example 3.2.1   Suppose a coin is tossed and we win \$100 if heads comes up and nothing if tails comes up. The set of outcomes in this case is $O = (100, 0)$. A fair coin represents the simple lottery $p = (0.5, 0.5)$ over O. A manipulated coin could for instance give us the simple lottery $q = (0.3, 0.7)$ over O.

The St. Petersburg paradox, originally proposed in a letter by Nicolas Bernoulli in 1713, shows that the *expected value* of a gamble can lead to unrealistic decisions when bidders take into account only the expected value. In this paradox one person offers to flip a coin until it comes up heads. The person offers \$1 if heads appears on the first trial; otherwise the payoff doubles each time tails appears, with this compounding stopping, and payment being given, at the first heads. The St. Petersburg gamble has an infinite expected value; however, most people share the intuition that they should not offer more than a few dollars to play. Explaining why people offer such small sums to play a gamble with infinite expected value is a question that has attracted significant attention. The earliest discussions of the St. Petersburg paradox led to the idea of utility functions, now a central concept in economics.

If agents have preferences over the simple lotteries (p, q) on O, we write $p \succeq q$ to denote that the agent weakly prefers p to q, and $p \succ q$ to denote that the agent strictly prefers p to q. In 1738, Daniel Bernoulli proposed that rational behavior should be described as that maximizing the expectation of a function U, thus accounting for risk aversion. This is referred to as the *expected utility hypothesis*. Utility functions $U : \mathbb{R}_{\geq 0} \mapsto \mathbb{R}_{\geq 0}$ map expected value to expected utility as a way to describe diminishing marginal utility. Let's assume U is twice continuously differentiable. If $U'(o) > 0$ and $U''(o) < 0 \quad \forall o \in O$ then U is concave and the subscript i describes a *risk-averse* agent, as we now illustrate in example 3.2.2.

Example 3.2.2 (Expected utility)   Suppose that an agent has the utility function $U(o) = \ln(o)$ and has to choose between the following two lotteries: win \$100 or \$1, each with a probability of 50%, $p = ([0.5, 100], [0.5, 1])$, or win \$50 with certainty, $q = ([1, 50])$. From the utility function we can construct $u(p) = E_p[U(o_i)] = 0.5 \ln(100) + 0.5 \ln(1) = 2.3$ and $u(q) = E_q[U(o_i)] = \ln(50) = 3.9$, so that q will be preferred.

The *expected utility theorem* of Von Neumann and Morgenstern (1947) provides axioms describing when the expected utility hypothesis holds:

1. $\succeq$ is *complete*, i.e., either $p \succ q$ or $q \succ p$ or $q \sim p$ for all $p, q \in \Delta(O)$;
2. $\succeq$ is *transitive*, i.e., if $p \succeq q$ and $q \succeq r$ then $p \succeq r$ for all $p, q, r \in \Delta(O)$;
3. $\succeq$ is *continuous*, so that if $p \succeq q \succeq r$ with $p, q, r \in \Delta(O)$ then there exists a probability $\alpha \in [0, 1]$ with $\alpha p + (1 - \alpha)r \sim q$;

4. *independence if $p \succ q$ and $p, q, r \in \Delta(O)$ $\forall \alpha \in (0, 1]$ then $\alpha p + (1 - \alpha)r \succ \alpha q + (1 - \alpha)r$.*

Von Neumann and Morgenstern (1947) showed in the expected utility theorem that any agent whose preferences satisfy these four axioms has a utility function. Such an agent's preferences can be represented on an interval scale and the agent will always prefer actions that maximize the expected utility.

Theorem 3.2.1 (Von Neumann and Morgenstern, 1947) *Suppose that the rational preference relation $\succeq_i$ on lotteries $\Delta(O)$ satisfies the continuity, completeness, transitivity, and independence axioms. Then there exists a function $u : \Delta(O) \mapsto \mathbb{R}_{\geq 0}$. That is, we can assign a number u_j to each outcome o_j with $j = 1, \ldots, m$ such that, for any two lotteries $q, p \in \Delta(O)$, we have*

- $p \succeq q$ *iff* $\sum_{j=1}^{m} p_j U(o_j) \geq \sum_{j=1}^{m} q_j U(o_j)$

In other words, if and only if the axioms of von Neumann and Morgenstern hold, there is a utility function $U(o_i)$ such that, for all $p, q \in \Delta(O)$, $p \succeq q \equiv u(p) = E_p(U(o_j)) = \sum_{j=1}^{m} p_j U(o_j) \geq \sum_{i=j}^{m} q_j U(o_j) = E_q(U(o_j)) = u(q)$. Note that the von Neumann–Morgenstern utility function is not unique. If the expected utility hypothesis does not characterize rationality, then one of the axioms of von Neumann and Morgenstern must be rejected.

Let's now discuss specific forms of utility functions as found in the literature to model the risk attitudes of decision makers. A (strictly) risk-averse agent is one whose von Neumann–Morgenstern utility function is (strictly) concave. Similarly, a (strictly) risk-loving individual is one whose utility function is (strictly) convex. When comparing the risk aversion of two agents, the derivative $U'(x)$ alone is of little help, as U and U' can be multiplied by any positive constant and still represent the same preferences. The Arrow–Pratt coefficients are widely used to compare the risk aversion of agents.

Definition 3.2.2 (Absolute risk aversion) The *Arrow–Pratt coefficient of absolute risk aversion is $\mathscr{A}_A(x) = -U''(x)/U'(x)$.*

That the utility function U exhibits *increasing (constant, decreasing) absolute risk aversion*, IARA (CARA, DARA) $\Longleftrightarrow$ $\mathscr{A}'_A(x) > (=, <) 0 \ \forall x$. This ratio is the same for U and $aU + b$.

Definition 3.2.3 (Relative risk aversion) The *Arrow–Pratt coefficient of relative risk aversion is $\mathscr{A}_R(x) = x\mathscr{A}_A(x)$.*

That the utility function U exhibits *increasing (constant, decreasing) relative risk aversion*, IRRA (CRRA, DRRA) $\Longleftrightarrow$ $\mathscr{A}'_R(x) > (=, <) 0 \ \forall x$. CARA or IARA imply IRRA, and CRRA or DRRA imply DARA. Let's look at some examples of utility functions and their risk measures. A quadratic utility (with IARA, IRRA) can be described as follows:

$$U(x) = x - \frac{b}{2}x^2, \qquad b > 0$$

$$U'(x) = 1 - bx$$

$$U''(x) = -b < 0$$

$$\mathscr{A}_A(x) = \frac{b}{1 - bx}$$

$$\frac{d\mathscr{A}_A(x)}{dx} = \frac{b^2}{(1 - bx)^2} > 0$$

$$\mathscr{A}_R(x) = \frac{bx}{1 - bx}$$

$$\frac{d\mathscr{A}_R(x)}{dx} = \frac{b}{(1 - bx)^2} > 0$$

With a quadratic utility function the marginal utility is positive and the utility is increasing. In contrast, a negative-exponential utility has constant absolute risk aversion (CARA, IRRA) and can be described as follows:

$$U(x) = -e^{-bx}, \qquad b > 0$$

$$U'(x) = be^{-bx} > 0$$

$$U''(x) = -b^2 e^{-bx} < 0$$

$$\mathscr{A}_A(x) = b$$

$$\frac{d\mathscr{A}_A(x)}{dx} = 0$$

$$\mathscr{A}_R(x) = bx$$

$$\frac{d\mathscr{A}_R(x)}{dx} = b$$

The equilibria of auctions are often analyzed assuming risk-averse bidders and we will revisit risk aversion in the context of single-object auctions.

Although the axioms of expected utility theory appear plausible, there are situations where human decision makers violate them. Allais' paradox (Allais, 1953) is an example of a simple experiment where people show an inconsistency of actual observed choices with the predictions of expected utility theory. The typical outcome of this experiment cannot be explained by risk aversion. In particular, the independence assumption has been criticized and there have been numerous experiments in recent years showing that humans often do not maximize expected utility in various situations (Ariely, 2008). Difficulties such as this have given rise to alternative forms of utility function, including those used in prospect theory (Kahneman and Tversky, 1979). These models should allow a wider range of behavior than can be found in the laboratory. Nevertheless, the axioms of von Neumann and Morgenstern can provide a useful baseline for models of human subjects on a market. Moreover, more and more market transactions are automated by artificial agents where rational decision making according to these axioms is a reasonable assumption.

3.3   Mechanism Design Theory

So far, we have not discussed the possibilities of strategic manipulation by agents. Mechanism design assumes that agents want to maximize their individual preferences and therefore can have an incentive to misrepresent preferences. A key question in mechanism design is whether an economic mechanisms can implement a social choice function under some game-theoretical solution concept if agents are self-interested, their preferences are private information, and they want to maximize their payoff.

Typically, mechanism design problems are modeled as Bayesian games (see definition 2.3.1); this is known as Bayesian mechanism design. Note that in chapter 2 on game theory we assumed that actions A are equivalent to outcomes O. We will relax this assumption now and define a Bayesian game $(\mathcal{I}, O, \Theta, F, u)$ on the outcomes. Preferences in a Bayesian game are assumed to be information private to the agents. Hence, they are known neither to the other agents nor to the mechanism and only distributional information (the common prior distribution F) is available to agents.

Definition 3.3.1 (Mechanism)   A mechanism $(A, \mathcal{M})$ in a Bayesian game $(\mathcal{I}, O, \Theta, F, u)$ consists of the following:

- $A = A_1 \times \cdots \times A_n$, where A_i is the set of actions of agent $i \in \mathcal{I}$;
- a function $\mathcal{M} : A \mapsto \Delta(O)$ from actions to a distribution over outcomes.

Definition 3.3.1 includes deterministic and randomized mechanisms. If a mechanism determines one specific outcome o on a set of actions with certainty, we talk about a *deterministic* mechanism, otherwise a *randomized* mechanism. Now, given a Bayesian game, we define what it means to implement a social choice function C in dominant strategies.

Definition 3.3.2 (Implementation in dominant strategies)   A mechanism $(A, \mathcal{M})$ is an implementation of a social choice function C in dominant strategies if, for any vector of utility functions u, the Bayesian game $(\mathcal{I}, O, \Theta, F, u)$ has an equilibrium in dominant strategies. In such an equilibrium $\mathcal{M}(a) = C(u)$.

We also refer to mechanisms with dominant strategies for participants as *strategy-proof* mechanisms or as *dominant-strategy incentive-compatible* (DSIC). Incentive-compatibility refers to incentives to reveal preferences truthfully.

We talk about a truthful implementation in the case of dominant strategies but, as indicated above, truthful reporting can also be implemented in weaker solution concepts such as Bayesian Nash equilibria. Next, we discuss *Bayesian Nash incentive compatibility* or *ex post incentive compatibility*, where truthful reporting of the preferences is a Bayesian Nash equilibrium or an ex post equilibrium, respectively. We also use the term *truthfulness* instead of incentive compatibility.

Definition 3.3.3 (Implementation in a Bayesian Nash equilibrium)   A mechanism $(A, \mathcal{M})$ is an implementation of a social choice function C in a Bayesian Nash equilibrium if there exists a Bayesian Nash equilibrium of the Bayesian game $(\mathcal{I}, O, \Theta, F, u)$

such that $\mathcal{M}(a) = C(u(\cdot, \theta))$ for all $\theta \in \Theta$ and every action profile $a \in A$ that can arise given the type profile θ in this equilibrium.

Note that in the following we implicitly assume that *utility is comparable between agents* and we can compute a social choice function C, such as the utilitarian social choice function, maximizing the sum of the utilities of all individuals in the economy. We discussed differences between cardinal and ordinal utility in the introduction to this chapter. While cardinal utilities might be a strong assumption for some markets they can be reasonable for others, for example, markets involving business decision makers.

There is a huge number of mechanisms one can imagine, including multi-round mechanisms or aggregate mechanisms combining multiple mechanisms. Gibbard (1973) made a useful observation which allows us to concentrate on *direct revelation* (or just *direct*) *mechanisms*, i.e., mechanisms in which the only action available to agents is to announce their private information.

Theorem 3.3.1 (Revelation principle; Gibbard, 1973) *Every social-choice function C that can be implemented in dominant strategies can also be implemented by a strategy-proof direct mechanism.*

Proof. We consider an arbitrary mechanism that implements a social choice function C in dominant strategies. Then we show how to construct a new mechanism which *truthfully* implements C. Let $s_1, \ldots, s_n$ denote the dominant strategies. Consider a mechanism that implements the social choice function C in these dominant strategies for n bidders.

The new mechanism will ask the agents for their types, use them to determine $s_1, \ldots, s_n$, the agents' dominant strategies under the original mechanism, and then choose the outcome that would have been chosen by the original mechanism for agents following the strategies $s_1, \ldots, s_n$. In other words, any solution to a mechanism design problem can be converted into one in which agents always reveal their true preferences, if the new mechanism "lies for the agents" in just the way they would have chosen to lie to the original mechanism.

It is easy to see that no bidder will lie to such a mechanism. Assume that some agent i would be better off declaring a different type θ_i' to the new mechanism rather than her true type θ_i. This implies that i would have preferred to follow some different strategy s_i' in the original mechanism rather than s_i, which contradicts the assumption that s_i is a dominant strategy for i.   □

The revelation mechanism was extended to Bayesian Nash incentive-compatible mechanisms (Dasgupta *et al.*, 1979). In other words, for any Bayesian Nash equilibrium of any arbitrary mechanism, there exists a very simple incentive-compatible direct revelation mechanism that is equivalent. Therefore, by analyzing incentive-compatible direct mechanisms, what can be accomplished in all possible equilibria of all possible mechanisms can be characterized. This is an important result as it allows a designer to focus on direct mechansims rather than having to explore all possible mechanisms.

Unfortunately, for general preferences there is no strategy-proof mechanism. Gibbard (1973) proved that any non-dictatorial voting scheme with at least three possible outcomes cannot have dominant strategies for all bidders. Satterthwaite (1975) showed that if a committee is choosing among at least three alternatives, then every strategy-proof voting procedure is dictatorial.

Theorem 3.3.2 (Gibbard, 1973; Satterthwaite, 1975) *If there are at least three outcomes, $|O| \geq 3$, there is a preference profile $[\succeq]$ such that $C([\succeq]) = o$ for every $o \in O$, and C is dominant-strategy truthful then a social choice function C is dictatorial.*

The Gibbard–Satterthwaite theorem can be proved using Arrow's impossibility theorem. Given a social choice function C one can build a ranking of alternatives. The outcomes o_1 and o_2 are moved to the top of all agents' preferences and then C is used to determine whether $o_1 \succeq o_2$. One can then show that if C is an incentive-compatible and non-dictatorial social choice rule then the ranking which is based on C is unanimous and independent of irrelevant alternatives. However, this is impossible according to Arrow's theorem. It is worth mentioning that this result is specific to dominant-strategy implementations, not to Bayesian Nash implementations, of a social choice function.

One possibility is to give up strategy-proofness and focus on fairness and other design desiderata. Another possibility is to restrict the types of preferences allowed. Indeed, there are also a few remarkable results describing environments where we can aggregate preferences such that participants have dominant strategies to reveal their preferences truthfully. For example, *quasi-linear preferences* are an escape route from the impossibilities found above. They require monetary transfers and participants who maximize payoff. The well-known result by Green and Laffont (1979) shows that the Vickrey–Clarke–Groves mechanism is the unique quasi-linear mechanism which allows for strategy-proofness and efficiency. We discuss quasi-linear mechanism design in the next section. However, there are also mechanisms which do not require monetary transfers. One famous example is provided by *matching mechanisms*, which will be discussed in chapter 11. Matching is used for course assignment, for example, where students are assigned to course organizers but they each have their own course preferences. In the "men-proposing" Gale–Shapley deferred-acceptance algorithm, men have dominant strategies to report their ordinal preferences truthfully (see section 11.2.2).

Yet another environment which allows for dominant strategies is that of *single-peaked preferences*. Assume that the alternatives voters can choose from are numbered as $O = \{o_1, \ldots, o_m\}$ and that the valid preferences of the voter are single-peaked in the sense that the preference order is completely determined by the voters' choices of peak alternatives, o_p. In other words, a group of voters or agents have single-peaked preferences over a group of outcomes if they each have an ideal choice in the set and outcomes that are further from their ideal choice are preferred less. An example would be that of different persons in a room who want to agree on the optimal loudness of the radio. Formally, $o_i \succeq o_j$ if and only if $|j - p| \geq |i - p|$. The median social choice function $\mathcal{M}(p_1, \ldots, p_n) = \text{median}(p_1, \ldots, p_n)$ chooses the median alternative of all peak alternatives. In his 1948 paper Black provided a formal analysis of majority voting that included the *median voter theorem* (see Black (1948) and Moulin (1991)).

Theorem 3.3.3 *Suppose that the domain of preferences is single-peaked. Then the median social choice function is implementable in dominant strategies.*

Proof sketch: Consider a mechanism where each voter reports a peak alternative and the mechanism outputs the median of all peaks. Suppose that the other voters reported p_{-i}, and that the true peak of voter i is p_i. Let p_m be the median of all reported peaks. If $p_i = p_m$ then voter i cannot gain by declaring a different peak. Now, suppose that $p_i < p_m$ and let us examine a false report p'_i of voter i. If $p'_i \leq p_i$ then p_m remains the median, and the voter did not gain. If $p'_i > p_m$ then the new median is $p'_m \geq p_m$ and, since $p_i < p_m$, this is less preferred by i. Thus, voter i cannot gain by declaring a false peak alternative if the true peak alternative is smaller or equal to the median alternative. A similar argument holds for the case $p_i > p_m$. $\qquad\square$

In a voting situation with two alternatives, the median rule becomes the same as the *majority rule* and the domain is single-peaked. This observation coincides with the fact that with only two alternatives the majority rule exhibits a dominant strategy equilibrium. In the majority rule, each voter reports his preferred alternative and the alternative that is preferred by the majority of the voters is chosen. It is straightforward to see that, in this two-alternative setting, it does not make sense for voters to report preferences other than their preferred alternative. When we have three or more alternatives, it is obvious that the majority rule is different from the median rule and it loses its dominant strategy (see theorem 3.3.2).

As indicated earlier, there are other escape routes from this impossibility which have drawn considerable attention in recent years. Randomization and approximation can provide truthful mechanisms for some environments (see chapter 10). In particular, the theory of matching with preferences has led to remarkable algorithms which are strategy-proof at least for one side of the market and which have found widespread application (see chapter 11). We will discuss these topics in Part III of the book. For now, we focus on the most widespread assumption in mechanism design, that of a quasi-linear utility function.

3.4   Quasi-Linear Mechanism Design

In this and the subsequent section on auction theory, we assume that preferences can be described with quasi-linear utility functions. Quasi-linearity can be seen as the standard assumption in auction theory, and it allows for a non-dictatorial mechanism which is dominant-strategy incentive-compatible. We introduce the celebrated Vickrey–Clarke–Groves mechanism, which is the unique strategy-proof mechanism in quasi-linear mechanism design and a landmark result in this field.

3.4.1   Quasi-Linear Utility Functions

Quasi-linear utility functions are linear in one argument, generally the money involved. Therefore, we will adapt our notation. An outcome $o = (x, p)$ is an element of O, where

$x \in X$ is an allocation and $p \in \mathbb{R}^n$ a price or payment. From now on, we describe an agent's valuation for an allocation $x \in X$ as $v_i(x, \theta)$, where θ is again the type of an agent in a Bayesian game. Sometimes we will write $v_i(x)$ or v_i for brevity. The set V_i of all possible valuations of agent i is a random variable with a publicly known distribution function $F_i(\cdot)$ which has a strictly positive and continuously differentiable density function $f_i(\cdot)$ on its support $[\underline{v}_i, \overline{v}_i]$. This is the common prior valuation distribution of the Bayesian game.

Definition 3.4.1 (Quasi-linear utility function) A quasi-linear utility function of an agent i is given by $u_i(o, \theta) = v_i(x, \theta) - p_i$, where $o = (x, p)$ is an element of the outcomes O, θ is the joint type, and $v_i : X \times \Theta \mapsto \mathbb{R}$.

In definition 3.4.1 we model risk-neutral agents and have chosen a simple quasi-linear form that will be convenient for our analysis of auctions in the following. Risk-aversion can be modeled based on such a quasi-linear utility function with $u_i(o, \theta) = U(v_i(x, \theta) - p_i)$, where $U : \mathbb{R}_{\geq 0} \mapsto \mathbb{R}_{\geq 0}$ is a strictly monotonically increasing utility function as discussed in section 3.2. This function would no longer be quasi-linear, however; it needs to be linear in one argument.

First, we aim for strategy-proof mechanisms. If a mechanism is strategy-proof then the risk attitude of bidders is irrelevant and truthfulness is always a dominant strategy independently of the risk attitude. This is different for Bayesian Nash equilibria, where risk aversion matters. Let us first define a deterministic mechanism in a quasi-linear setting.

Definition 3.4.2 (Deterministic quasi-linear mechanism) A deterministic mechanism $\mathcal{M} = (A, f, p)$ is defined by a set of actions A available to agents, a deterministic choice function $f : A \mapsto X$, and a payment rule $p_i : A \mapsto \mathbb{R}$ for each agent i.

Note that mechanisms do not need to be deterministic and could be randomized, which is what we discuss in chapter 10. A (deterministic) direct mechanism $\mathcal{M} = (f, p)$ in the quasi-linear setting is one in which each agent i is asked to state her type $A_i = \Theta_i$, so that we do not explicitly mention the available actions A when we describe the mechanism. In market design problems it is convenient to substitute the type of a bidder by her valuation for an allocation, which describes her maximal willingness to pay for an allocation. In such problems, f is the function determining the allocation or resources to agents. In a single-object auction, this would just be a function computing the maximum of all bids submitted. In multi-object auctions, obtaining f often involves solving hard computational optimization problems.

Given an agent's reported valuations $w_i \in V_i$, the mechanism $\mathcal{M} = (f, p)$ computes an outcome $f(w)$ and charges each agent i a price $p_i(w)$. However, since agents are taken to be self-interested, any reported valuation w_i does not necessarily reflect the true valuation v_i. Instead, agents try to optimize their personal utility $v_i(f(w)) - p_i(w)$. However, a strategy-proof quasi-linear mechanism can offer a monetary incentive to reveal their actual valuations.

Definition 3.4.3 (Strategy-proofness of quasi-linear direct mechanisms) A mechanism $\mathcal{M} = (f, p)$ is *strategy-proof* if for all agents $i \in \mathcal{I}$ and all valuations $w \in V$ it holds that

$$v_i(f(v_i, w_{-i})) - p_i(v_i, w_{-i}) \geq v_i(f(w)) - p_i(w)$$

3.4.2   The Vickrey–Clarke–Groves Mechanism

For now, we focus on the objective of computing an outcome $x \in X$ which maximizes the agents' aggregated preferences or social welfare, $\sum_{i \in \mathcal{I}} v_i(x)$. Later, we will also discuss alternative design goals such as the maximization of the auctioneers' revenue. Note that in quasi-linear settings we assume that interpersonal utility comparisons are possible, which is a prerequisite for social welfare maximization.

Interestingly, the Vickrey–Clarke–Groves (VCG) principle (Clarke, 1971; Groves, 1973; Vickrey, 1961) provides a general solution to designing truthful mechanisms in a quasi-linear setting.

Definition 3.4.4 (Vickrey–Clarke–Groves mechanism) A mechanism $\mathcal{M} = (f, p)$ is a VCG mechanism if the social choice function f maximizes the social welfare with respect to the reported valuations $w \in V$,

$$f(w) \in \arg\max_{x \in X} \sum_{i \in \mathcal{I}} w_i(x)$$

and if for each agent $i \in \mathcal{I}$ there exists a function $h_i : V_{-i} \mapsto \mathbb{R}$ such that the pricing scheme p_i is computed as

$$p_i(w) = h_i(w_{-i}) - \sum_{j \in \mathcal{I} \setminus \{i\}} w_j(f(w))$$

The VCG payment scheme aligns an agent's utility with the objective of optimizing the social welfare. To achieve this, the second term of the VCG pricing scheme pays each agent i the sum over all valuations reported by the other agents. Together with the agent's personal valuation, this sum equals the social welfare. Furthermore, since no agent has a direct influence on the first term of her pricing scheme h_i, her utility is indeed optimized if she reveals her valuation truthfully. Formally, the truthfulness of the VCG principle can be proven as follows.

Theorem 3.4.1 (Vickrey, 1961) *The VCG mechanism $\mathcal{M} = (f, p)$ is strategy-proof.*

Proof. For any agent $i \in \mathcal{I}$ and valuation $w \in V$, let $a = f(v_i, w_{-i})$ denote the outcome for the agent's true valuation while $b = f(w)$ denotes the outcome with respect to the reported valuation. Since the social choice function maximizes over the reported valuations, it holds that $v_i(a) + \sum_{j \in \mathcal{I} \setminus \{i\}} w_j(a) \geq v_i(b) + \sum_{j \in \mathcal{I} \setminus \{i\}} w_j(b)$. Thus, agent i cannot gain utility by misrepresenting his true valuation:

$$v_i(f(v_i, w_{-i})) - p_i(v_i, w_{-i}) = v_i(a) - \left(h_i(w_{-i}) - \sum_{j \in \mathcal{I} \setminus \{i\}} w_j(a) \right)$$

$$\geq v_i(b) - \left(h_i(w_{-i}) - \sum_{j \in \mathcal{I} \setminus \{i\}} w_j(b) \right)$$

$$= v_i(f(w)) - p_i(w) \qquad \square$$

A payment scheme p_i should not only be truthful but should also avoid negative payments. In addition, the mechanism should not charge prices which exceed the reported valuations.

Definition 3.4.5 (Individual rationality)   A mechanism $\mathcal{M} = (f, p)$ is individually rational if, for all agents $i \in \mathcal{I}$ and valuation tuples $w \in V$, the reported value of outcome $f(w)$ to agent i is greater than or equal to the payment $p_i(w)$:

$$w_i(f(w)) \geq p_i(w)$$

Individual rationality is an important requirement that ensures that no agent has negative utility if she reveals his true valuation. Clarke's pivot rule specifies a VCG payment scheme which is individually rational and avoids charging negative prices.

Definition 3.4.6 (Clarke's pivot rule)   A pricing scheme for a VCG mechanism implements Clarke's pivot rule if for all agents $i \in \mathcal{I}$ and valuation tuples $w_{-i} \in V_{-i}$ it holds that

$$h_i(w_{-i}) = \max_{a \in A} \sum_{j \in \mathcal{I} \setminus \{i\}} w_j(a)$$

The resulting pricing scheme $p_i = (\max_{a \in A} \sum_{j \in \mathcal{I} \setminus \{i\}} w_j(a)) - \sum_{j \in \mathcal{I} \setminus \{i\}} w_j(f(w))$ charges each agent the difference between the optimal social welfare with and without her participation. In other words, her payments reflect the externalities she causes the other agents, which are neither negative nor exceed $w_i(f(w))$.

Theorem 3.4.2   *A VCG mechanism $\mathcal{M} = (f, p)$ which implements Clarke's pivot rule has non-negative payments and is individually rational.*

Proof.   For any agent $i \in \mathcal{I}$ and valuation tuple $w \in V$, let $a = f(w)$ be the optimal outcome with respect to the reported valuations while $b = \arg\max_{c \in A} \sum_{j \in \mathcal{I} \setminus \{i\}} w_j(c)$ maximizes Clarke's pivot rule. By the definition of b it holds that $\sum_{j \in \mathcal{I} \setminus \{i\}} w_j(a) \leq \sum_{j \in \mathcal{I} \setminus \{i\}} w_j(b)$ and therefore no negative payments are made:

$$p_i(w) = \left(\sum_{j \in \mathcal{I} \setminus \{i\}} w_j(b) \right) - \left(\sum_{j \in \mathcal{I} \setminus \{i\}} w_j(a) \right) \geq 0$$

Furthermore, no valuation function maps to a negative value. In particular the value of $w_i(b)$ must be greater than or equal to 0. Together with the fact that outcome a is optimal with respect to the reported valuations, this implies that

$$w_i(a) + \left(\sum_{j \in \mathcal{I} \setminus \{i\}} w_j(a) \right) \geq w_i(b) + \left(\sum_{j \in \mathcal{I} \setminus \{i\}} w_j(b) \right) \geq \left(\sum_{j \in \mathcal{I} \setminus \{i\}} w_j(b) \right)$$

which in turn proves individual rationality:

$$w_i(f(w)) = w_i(a) \geq \left(\sum_{j \in \mathcal{I} \setminus \{i\}} w_j(b) \right) - \left(\sum_{j \in \mathcal{I} \setminus \{i\}} w_j(a) \right) = p_i(w) \qquad \square$$

The VCG principle is very general and applies to all types of quasi-linear mechanism design problems including auctions on one or multiple objects and public goods problems. We will discuss the VCG mechanism in more detail in the context of auction theory. It has been shown that the VCG mechanism is the unique strategy-proof auction mechanism when modeled as a Bayesian game with independent and private values (Green and Laffont, 1979; Holmstrom, 1979).

However, there are also a number of fundamental limitations of the VCG mechanism. First, the VCG mechanism implements a utilitarian social choice function, i.e., a function that maximizes a weighted sum of values. Sometimes mechanism designers might want to implement different social choice functions. However, a theorem by Roberts (1979) states that only weighted utilitarian functions can be implemented with incentive-compatible mechanisms if the agents' valuation functions are unrestricted and there are at least three different possible outcomes. Second, the VCG mechanism does not always give a competitive equilibrium. Such an equilibrium should satisfy buyer maximization, seller maximization, and market clearing. This can lead to collusion and a lack of revenue monotonicity. We discuss this issue in more detail in the design of combinatorial auctions (see section 7.3.2).

Third, the VCG mechanism is not necessarily *budget balanced*, a problem which arises in two-sided markets. For example, in an exchange which allows multiple buyers and sellers to submit bids and asks, the auctioneer might incur a substantial loss when using a VCG mechanism. Even for single-sided auctions, though, we require an additional assumption for the VCG mechanism to be budget balanced: that there is still a feasible allocation even if one bidder is removed from the market. This is sometimes called the no-single-agent effect.

Apart from these problems, the VCG requires agents to reveal all their valuations, which is a problem in combinatorial auctions where bidders can have an exponentially large set of valuations. Also, they need a trusted auctioneer, which might not always be available. These might be reasons why the VCG mechanism can rarely be found in the field. Unfortunately, even in quasi-linear mechanism design no mechanism can satisfy budget balance, incentive compatibility, individual rationality, and efficiency. This was shown by Myerson and Satterthwaite (1983) in a simple bilateral trade model.

3.4.3   The Myerson–Satterthwaite Theorem

The simplest model of a two-sided market is the bilateral trade model with one seller and one buyer, who are privately informed about their values for a single indivisible good. This model is sufficient to show what is arguably one of the central results in mechanism design, the theorem of Myerson and Satterthwaite.

Theorem 3.4.3 (Myerson and Satterthwaite, 1983) *In the bilateral trade problem there is no mechanism that is efficient, Bayesian Nash incentive-compatible, individually rational, and at the same time budget balanced.*

In the following short proof, we use the VCG mechanism in a similar way to Krishna (2009) rather than using the original line of argument of Myerson and Satterthwaite

(1983). The proof leverages the revenue equivalence theorem, which we discuss in the next chapter (see theorem 4.4.1), which says that, for risk-neutral bidders, any symmetric and increasing equilibrium of any auction where the expected payment of a bidder with the lowest type is zero yields the same expected revenue to the seller.

Proof. Suppose that there is a buyer with a privately known value v_b drawn from a strictly positive and continuously differentiable density function $f_b(\cdot)$ on its support $[\underline{v_b}, \overline{v_b}]$. Similarly, a seller has a privately known value or cost for the object, v_s, drawn from a strictly positive and continuously differentiable density function $f_s(\cdot)$ on its support $[\underline{v_s}, \overline{v_s}]$. These distributions are independent and commonly known and have full support on the respective intervals. We also assume that $\underline{v_b} < \overline{v_s}$ and $\overline{v_b} \geq \underline{v_s}$, so that the supports overlap.

In a VCG mechanism the buyer announces a valuation w_b and the seller announces w_s. If $w_b \leq w_s$, the object is not exchanged and no payments are made. If $w_b > w_s$ then the object is exchanged and the buyer pays $\max\{w_s, \underline{v_b}\}$ and the seller receives $\min\{w_b, \overline{v_s}\}$. It is straightforward to see that it is a weakly dominant strategy for the buyer and the seller to be truthful. The mechanism is also efficient, because the object is transferred if $v_b > v_s$. Buyer and seller cannot make a loss in equilibrium and the VCG mechanism is individually rational. A seller with value $\overline{v_s}$ and a buyer with value $\underline{v_b}$ have an expected payoff of zero. All other agents have a positive expected payoff. However, the VCG mechanism yields a deficit $w_b - w_s$ for every $w_b > w_s$, which equals the gains from trade.

Suppose that there is some other mechanism that is individually rational, incentive-compatible, and efficient. By the revenue equivalence theorem (see theorem 4.4.1), the expected payment for any buyer with value v_b under this mechanism can differ from the expected payment under the VCG mechanism by a constant K. Also, the expected payment of any seller with value v_s under this mechanism can differ from her expected payment or receipts under the VCG mechanism by a constant L. In the VCG mechanism a buyer with value $\underline{v_b}$ gets an expected payoff of zero, so that $K \leq 0$. Similarly, since a seller with value $\overline{v_s}$ gets an expected payoff of 0, we must have $L \geq 0$. The expected deficit under the alternative mechanism is the expected deficit under the VCG mechanism plus $L - K \geq 0$. However, since the VCG mechanism yields a deficit, the other mechanism also leads to a deficit. Therefore, there does not exist an efficient mechanism that is incentive-compatible, individually rational, and budget balanced. □

In a simplified example with uniformly distributed valuations, Myerson and Satterthwaite (1983) analyzed a simple mechanism splitting the gains from the bilateral trade based equally on the reported values. Both participants shade their bids in equilibrium, so that some welfare is lost. In a similar way, some authors fix budget balance, individual rationality, and incentive compatibility but relax the goal of welfare maximization. For example, McAfee (2008) provides a simple price-setting mechanism which yields one half of the optimal social welfare.

Double auctions can be seen as a generalization of the bilateral trade problem, with more buyers and sellers. For double auctions with single-unit demand and supply, McAfee (1992) gave a dominant-strategy mechanism which is weakly budget balanced (i.e., the auctioneer might make money) at the expense of a welfare loss. Although the results of Myerson and Satterthwaite (1983) for bilateral trade with two agents suggest that there will be a significant welfare loss, the possibilities for strategic manipulation are typically much reduced in large markets with many bidders and many objects. Still, it is interesting to see that, even in a simple model of bilateral trade, some fundamental design desiderata are incompatible.

d'Aspremont and Gérard-Varet (1979) showed that if we relax strategy-proofness to Bayesian Nash incentive compatibility then one can achieve budget balance. Their *expected externality mechanism* is budget balanced and Bayesian Nash incentive-compatible, but it is not individually rational because it may give negative expected gains from trade to some agents. In other words, an agent who already knows her true preferences may expect to do worse in the expected externality mechanism than if no trade took place. This might not be acceptable in many applications.

3.5   Summary

Quasi-linear mechanism design as discussed in this chapter considers a Bayesian game with a given number of bidders and a publicly known common prior distribution. It is the standard approach used to model auction markets. The realities of markets in the field can be quite different from the assumptions made in quasi-linear mechanism design. However, game-theoretical predictions are sensitive to the model assumptions. Therefore, it is important to understand what happens if some assumptions are relaxed.

There is often also no common prior distribution, and bidders might have widely differing beliefs about their competitors. This has been the focus of *robust mechanism design*. Also, we have analyzed only single-shot games where demand and supply are present at the same time, but in many situations the interaction between buyers and sellers occurs dynamically over time; this has been the focus of *dynamic mechanism design*. *Algorithmic mechanism design* has emphasized in particular the role of approximation and randomization, which has led to new insights and extended the scope of mechanism design theory. Finally, we will shed light on the question of truthful mechanism design for environments where utility functions are not quasi-linear. In the following, we provide an brief overview of these fields. Mechanism design is still a very active field of research, so this can only be a selection of more recent topics.

3.5.1   Robust Mechanism Design

Assumptions about common prior distributions in game-theoretical models have long been criticized as they are typically not given in the field. Hurwicz (1972) postulated the use of "non-parametric" mechanisms which are independent of the distributional assumptions regarding the willingness-to-pay of the agents. Later, Wilson (1987) wrote: "I foresee the progress of game theory as depending on successive reductions in the base of common knowledge required to conduct useful analyses of practical problems. Only by repeated weakening of common knowledge assumptions will the theory approximate reality." He states that trading rules should be made "belief-free" by requiring that they "should not rely on features of the agents' common knowledge, such as their probability assessments".

Fang and Morris (2006) analyzed a symmetric two-bidder private value auction in which each bidder observes her own private valuation as well as noisy signals about her opponent's private valuation. This model of private information is different from the standard Bayesian Nash analysis of auctions with private values, which we will discuss in the next chapter; in this case each agent's belief about her competitor is simply assumed to coincide with the common prior. With such a multi-dimensional private signal, the revenue equivalence between the first and the second price auction (see section 4.4) fails to hold. Moreover, the agents' types might not be independent but *interdependent*. This means that an agent's preferences depend not only on her private information but also on the private information of other agents. For example, private information about the market conditions of a bidder in a spectrum auction can affect other bidders' valuations for licenses, not only their own. Bergemann and Morris (2005) used a model where agents have payoff types and belief types, and they characterize a direct mechanism as robust if in the interim it is incentive-compatible for agents to report their payoff types truthfully to the mechanism for all possible belief types. They characterized robust incentive-compatible mechanisms as more specifically ex post incentive-compatible mechanisms. Jehiel *et al.* (2006) showed that, in environments with interdependencies, only constant rules, according to which the same alternative is chosen for every type realization, are incentive-compatible. The result is very general and highlights that an environment with independent and private values and quasi-linear utility functions is remarkable in that it allows for strategy-proof and truthful mechanisms that maximize social welfare.

3.5.2   Algorithmic Mechanism Design

Since a common prior distribution in Bayesian mechanism design is a strong assumption, a large body of work in computer science has focused on strong game-theoretical solution concepts which do not require distributional assumptions such as dominant-strategy or ex post implementations. While such equilibria can be considered as more robust predictions, they restrict the design space for mechanisms substantially. Algorithmic mechanism design (Nisan and Ronen, 2001) allows for approximation of the social choice function rather than an exact solution. First, this is important because the underlying social choice function is computationally hard. Second, relaxing social welfare maximization as a goal can also allow for new ways to achieve truthfulness in a mechanism. We will discuss algorithmic mechanism design in more detail in chapter 10.

3.5.3   Dynamic Mechanism Design

Mechanism design has typically focused on static, one-time, decisions such as those which occur in isolated markets when buyers and sellers are present at the same time.

Dynamic mechanism design focuses on a sequence of interdependent decisions where the parameters (e.g., the number of agents or their types) vary over time. Examples are advance ticket sales of airlines where buyers receive information over time or sequential auctions for search advertising. Advance ticket sales require an airline to decide how to price seats on a flight over a certain time frame in response to changing inventory and customer demand. Similarly, display advertising exchanges conduct a large number of sequential auctions (billions per day) for user impressions, and advertisers compete for these impressions in separate auctions one after the other. Market participants arrive and depart over time, and both the maximization of efficiency and the maximization of seller revenue in such environments are important considerations. We largely focus on static markets in this book, but we will discuss recent literature on dynamic auctions in section 5.4. Nevertheless, for many environments such as online advertising markets there are no widely accepted market models.

3.5.4   Non-Quasi-Linear Mechanism Design

Although quasi-linearity is a reasonable abstraction of many real-world environments, it does not always hold. The theorems of Gibbard and Satterthwaite (see section 3.3) already tell us that no strategy-proof mechanism exists for general preferences. However, it is also the case that, for various restricted utility functions, positive results don't seem to exist. There have been a number of articles on assignment problems without money (see section 11.3), which gave impossibility results and some form of dictatorship (Ehlers and Klaus, 2003; Hatfield, 2009). Two-sided matching, as is discussed in chapter 11, provides an exception because some mechanisms achieve strategy-proofness for one side of the market with ordinal preferences. Also, randomization and approximation are being used to achieve truthful mechanisms for specific market environments.

Often utility functions are cardinal and money can be transferred, but still the utility functions are not quasi-linear. Baisa (2016) analyzed general non-quasi-linear utility functions, which only increase in wealth. He showed that no dominant-strategy, individually rational, weakly budget-balanced, and efficient mechanisms exist for multi-dimensional types. Also, restricted utility functions can be analyzed for specific domains. In advertising markets, agents might not maximize payoff but rather the value of items (e.g., user impressions on a web site) subject to a budget constraint for a marketing campaign. In the presence of private budget constraints, bidders could manipulate reports about the valuations and about the budgets and it is not obvious whether truthful mechanisms with reasonable guarantees on welfare exist. Fadaei and Bichler (2017) analyzed markets where bidders maximize value subject to a budget constraint and used approximation to achieve truthfulness. Unfortunately, the approximation ratios achieved can be quite low. Maximizing value subject to a budget constraint might be a reasonable model in the case where budgets are provided by a principal and the money spent is not taken into account by an agent bidding in the auction (Bichler and Paulsen, 2017).

Behavioral economists have analyzed human decision behavior in the laboratory and have found that human subjects are often loss averse or overweight small probabilities and underweight large probabilities (Kahneman, 2003). This is also different from the expected utility maximizers which have been discussed so far. In market design it is important to have realistic models of bidders' utility functions for a specific domain, even though such models might not admit dominant-strategy incentive-compatible mechanisms.

3.6   Comprehension Questions

- You are confronted with a new voting rule. If the votes of persons A and B are the same then the social welfare function will coincide with their preference. Otherwise the social welfare function will return the vote of person C. Which of Arrow's axioms is violated by this rule?
- Suppose we are trying to show that no truthful mechanism exists for a given setting. There are multiple options for a possible such mechanism including sealed-bid, iterative-bid, or a combination thereof. Explain why we do not need to reason about all these possibilities and it is enough to limit ourselves to direct revelation mechanisms.
- Why is a quasi-linear utility function important in mechanism design?
- What is specific about Clark's pivot rule in a VCG mechanism?
- Which mechanism design desiderata are incompatible in the bilateral trade model?
- Explain the revelation principle and its significance for mechanism design.

3.7   Problems

Voting
Suppose that for a given set of votes there is a Condorcet winner. Consider the following. If we then apply the Borda voting rule to these votes, the candidate which has the highest Borda score will always be the Condorcet winner. Is the latter statement true?

Auction Design with Verification
A set of items $\mathcal{K}$ is being assigned to a group of bidders $i \in \mathcal{I}$. Each bidder has different valuations for different packages of items. The mechanism designer can only verify the valuation of a bidder for the package assigned to that bidder. In other words, if bidder i gets package $S \subseteq \mathcal{K}$ the mechanism can decide whether the reported $v_i(S)$ is true. In the case where a lie is detected the liar will get fired, an unacceptable outcome for him or her. Valuations are strict, i.e., $v_i(S) \neq v_i(T)$ for $S \neq T$. Can you design a truthful and Pareto-optimal mechanism for this environment?

Decide on a Printer
A company needs to decide whether to buy a 3D printer for a cost C. The company has just two employees with values v_1 and v_2 and the mechanism should have the following properties.

1. If $v_1 + v_2 > C$ then the printer is purchased and if $v_1 + v_2 < C$ then it is not.
2. If the printer is purchased then the employees are charged at least C in total (i.e., there is no subsidy by the company) and player i is never charged more than v_i.

Can you show that there is no incentive-compatible direct revelation mechanism for this problem?

4 Single-Object Auctions

An auction can be defined as "a market institution with an explicit set of rules determining resource allocation and prices on the basis of bids from the market participants" (McAfee and McMillan, 1987). The competitive process serves to aggregate the scattered information about bidders' valuations and to set a price dynamically. The *auction format* describes an economic mechanism which determines the rules governing when and how a deal is closed. The mechanism includes the social choice function or allocation rule and the payment rule, as we described it for deterministic quasi-linear mechanisms (see definition 3.4.2).

The social choice function of an auction is either *(allocative) efficiency* or *revenue maximization* for the auctioneer. Allocative efficiency measures whether the objects end up with those bidders who value them most, while revenue maximization focuses on the expected selling price. An auction which maximizes the social welfare $f(v)$ of all agents, so that $f(v) \in \arg\max_{x \in X} \sum_{i \in \mathcal{I}} v_i(x)$, is called an efficient auction. For single-object auctions this means that the object is allocated to the bidder with the highest value. Revenue-maximizing auctions are also referred to as *optimal auctions*.

4.1 Single-Object Auction Formats

Single-sided single-object auctions are auctions where one seller sells a single item or object to one out of many bidders. *Open auctions* reveal price quotes and require public and adjustable bids. After a certain elapsed time the auction clears, meaning that it matches buyers and sellers and determines the price if no further bids are received within this time frame. In the case of an ascending *English auction* the auctioneer begins at the seller's reservation price and solicits progressively higher oral bids from the audience until only one bidder is left, thus making the reservation prices of all unsuccessful bidders known. The winner claims the item at the price of the last bid. In a *clock auction* the price rises continuously while bidders gradually quit the auction. In contrast with the English auction there is no possibility for jump bids, i.e., bids which are higher than the minimum bid increment or auctioneer's ask price. Both auction formats are purely *ascending* formats.

A *descending* auction works in the opposite way: the auctioneer starts at a very high price, and then lowers the price continuously. In a *Dutch auction* the auctioneer begins with a price too high for anyone in the audience to pay and lowers the price until one bidder calls out that she will accept the current price. The winner claims the item and pays the price she bid. This auction format is often used for perishable goods such as flowers, where it is important to determine the winners fast.

Sealed-bid auctions do not reveal price quotes, and require private, committed bids which are opened simultaneously. After the sealed bids are received by the auctioneer, she arranges them in decreasing order. The highest bidder acquires the object and pays the seller his own bid price in a *first-price sealed-bid auction*. In contrast, the highest bidder pays only the second highest bid price in a *second-price sealed-bid auction*. A little reflection shows that the second-price sealed-bid auction (aka a Vickrey auction) is an instance of a VCG mechanism (see section 3.4.2), and it exhibits a weakly dominant strategy for bidders. Neither bidding lower nor bidding higher than her true valuation would increase the payoff of a bidder, as we discuss further below. Of course, these single-sided auctions can also be reversed and used in the context of procurement. We talk about *reverse auctions* in this case.

Double auctions admit multiple buyers and multiple sellers at once. The *continuous double auction* (CDA) matches bids in the order received. When a new buy bid is processed, the auction checks whether the offered price matches the lowest (i.e., best) existing sell bid, and vice versa. On detection of a match, the auction clears at the price of the existing bid, and generates a new price quote. A transaction is completed when an outstanding bid or ask is accepted by another trader. The CDA is a common mechanism for organized exchanges such as stock and commodity markets. A periodic version of the double auction, termed a *call market or clearing house*, collects bids over a specified interval of time and then clears the market at expiration of the bidding interval at a price that maximizes the turnover, for example. In this chapter we focus on the standard auction formats for single-object auctions in single-sided markets, which we introduced above:

- ascending (clock) auctions
- first-price sealed-bid auctions
- second-price sealed-bid auctions
- descending (Dutch) auctions.

Before we introduce game-theoretical models of the individual auction formats, we discuss frequently used model assumptions.

4.2   Model Assumptions

One way to classify auctions is based on differences in the values bidders put on what is being auctioned. Quasi-linear mechanism design provides a standard framework to analyze and design auctions. In an auction with *independent private values*, a bidder can learn nothing about his value from knowing the values of the other bidders. An example is the sale of an artwork to someone who will not resell it. If there were the possibility of resale then a bidder's value would depend on the price at which she could resell, which would depend on the other bidders' values. Knowing all the other values might well change her bidding strategy.

Definition 4.2.1 (Independent private-value model, IPV) The value v_i of bidder $i \in \mathcal{I}$, is independently and identically distributed (i.i.d.) according to a continuous cumulative probability function $F(v) : [\underline{v}, \bar{v}] \mapsto [0, 1]$. The distribution function $F(v)$ has full support with $f(v) > 0$ for all $v \in [\underline{v}, \bar{v}]$.

As in our discussion of quasi-linear mechanism design, the traditional auction literature models such auctions as a Bayesian game (see definition 2.3.1), where the distribution function $F(v)$ is common knowledge while it is assumed that bidders have independent and private values and quasi-linear utility functions (see definition 3.4.1).

We distinguish between the *independent private-value* (IPV) *model*, in which a bidder's knowledge of her own value tells her nothing about other bidders' values, and more general models which allow for *interdependent values* where each bidder has private information about the object and a net value that depends on her own signal and that of others. For example, $\theta_i = \theta + v_i$ has a common-value component (θ) and a private-value (v_i) component. The two components can be correlated so that one bidder's private valuation can influence another bidder's valuation.

A *pure common-value model* refers to an extreme case where the bidders have ex post identical values but each bidder forms her own estimate on the basis of her own ex ante private information. An example is bidding for oil drilling rights. A bidder's estimate might change if she could have a look at the other bidders' estimates, because they are all trying to estimate the same underlying value of the object. A common phenomenon in such auctions is the *winner's curse*, i.e., winners tend to overpay. Since the auctioned object is worth the same to all bidders, they differ only in their estimates of the value. The winner is the bidder with the highest estimate. If we assume that the average bid is accurate then the highest bidder overestimates the item's value. In the following we focus on markets with independent and private values. Krishna (2009) provides an extensive treatment of the material.

4.3 Equilibrium Bidding Strategies in the IPV Model

A simple way to analyze auctions is to assume complete information. This makes optimal bidding simple. In a private-value auction for a single object, the highest-valuing bidder can bid just above the second-highest value. In a common-value auction, the bidders will take into account each others' information and their value estimates will converge to a single joint estimate. However, with complete information the seller should not be using an auction. She would just charge a price that she knows will be accepted by one of the bidders. Therefore, auctions are typically modeled as a Bayesian game where all bidders have a common prior distribution of their valuations. In what follows, we discuss the main single-sided auction formats in the independent private-value model and derive equilibrium bidding strategies in a Bayesian game setting. We start with ascending auctions and second-price sealed-bid auctions as they have a simple weakly dominant strategy.

4.3.1   Ascending Auctions

Let's start with *ascending* single-object auctions. In our analysis we assume a simple clock auction, which works as follows. Before the auction starts, bidders decide whether they will participate. This decision is made public. A single clock visible to all bidders is used to indicate the price $p \in \mathbb{R}$ of the object. The reserve price set by the seller is $r \in \mathbb{R}$. The clock starts at an initial price $p = r$ and increases continuously. Bidder messages can take only two values and a bidder can indicate whether she is "in" or "out" (equivalently, she wants to "continue" or "stop") by pressing or releasing a button. A bidder releasing the button at a price p indicates her decision to stop bidding, that is, that her demand is zero at that price. The price clock stops when only a single bidder remains pressing the button, who is then determined the winner. The winner's payoff is her value v_i minus the current standing price at the time of winning p. The losers' payoffs are zero.

A bidder's dominant strategy in such a private-value ascending auction is to stay in the bidding until bidding higher would require her to exceed her value, and then to stop. This is optimal because she always wants to buy the object if the price is less than its value to her, but she wants to pay the lowest price possible. All bidding ends when the price reaches the second-highest value of any bidder present at the auction.

A dominant strategy is independent of risk neutrality if bidders know their own values with certainty in the independent private-value model. Note that only the clock auction has a dominant strategy; this is not true for the English auction, where bidders can submit jump bids (Isaac *et al.*, 2007). The transparency of ascending auctions together with dominant strategies make them popular auction formats in the field. In Part II we analyze whether these compelling properties can be maintained when multiple objects are being sold.

4.3.2   Second-Price Sealed-Bid Auctions

In a second-price sealed-bid auction each bidder submits one bid but does not learn about other bidders' bids. The bids are opened and the highest bidder pays the amount of the second-highest bid and wins the object. The winning bidder's payoff is her value minus the second-highest bid. The seller's payoff is the second-highest bid. Second-price auctions are considered outcome-equivalent to ascending auctions. Bidding one's value is a weakly dominant strategy: a bidder who bids less is no more likely to win the auction but she pays the same price, the second-highest bidder's bid, if she does win. Bidding more than the value of an object could lead to a negative payoff. Bidder 1 might bid an amount that is strictly more than her value. Bidder 2 might bid less than bidder 1, but more than bidder 1's value. Consequently, bidder 1 would win at a loss. The auction format belongs to the class of VCG mechanisms and is strategy-proof.

In practice, in the past Vickrey auctions have rarely been used. With the advent of Internet advertising auctions, this has changed (Varian and Harris, 2014). In *display ad auctions*, users navigate to various web pages. Publishers of these web pages contact an ad exchange with information about the user and a reserve price for an ad on this page. Ad exchanges then contact advertisers to bid on the ad. Such display ad exchanges typically use Vickrey auctions to determine the winner and the prices, and then the ad of the winner is displayed on the user's page. There are millions of such auctions and they need to be run in milliseconds.

Sponsored search auctions (aka keyword auctions) are similar but they assign multiple slots on a web page. Google and other companies use a *generalized second-price auction* (GSP) for this purpose. Facebook's ad system is based on the VCG mechanism (see section 3.4.2). Strictly speaking, sponsored search auctions are already a form of a multi-item auction as discussed in chapter 5. We discuss the GSP auction here, however, because it shows nicely that a second-price auction does not have to be incentive-compatible.

In GSP each bidder places a bid for a search keyword on a search engine. The highest bidder gets the first slot, the second-highest the second slot, and so on. Then the highest bidder pays the price bid by the second-highest bidder, the second-highest pays the price bid by the third-highest, and so on. While this auction is also a second-price auction, it is not strategy-proof unless there is only one slot.

Example 4.3.1 Suppose that there are two slots and three bidders. The first slot gets 100 clicks per hour and the second slot gets 70 clicks per hour. Bidders 1, 2, and 3 have values per click of $10, $7, and $4, respectively. Under the GSP auction, the payments for slots one and two are $7 and $4 per click. The total payments of the winning bidders 1 and 2 are $700 and $4 \times 70 = $280, respectively. Now, if all bidders bid truthfully, the payoff of bidder 1 is ($10 − $7) \times 100 = $300. However, if she bid $6 and wins the second slot, her payoff would be ($10 − $4) \times 70 = $420, which is more than her payoff when bidding truthfully.

In contrast, the payment of the first bidder in a VCG auction would be less. Essentially, she is charged the externality that she imposes on bidders 2 and 3. The externality she imposes on bidder 3 is $4 \times 70 = $280, by forcing him out of position 2). In addition, she moves bidder 2 from position 1 to position 2 and thus causes him to lose 30 clicks per hour. This leads to an additional $30 \times 7 = $210. In total, the VCG payment of the first bidder would be $280 + $210 = $490, which is less than the $700 that she has to pay in the GSP auction. Now her payoff in the VCG auction is $1000 − $490 = $540. The payment of bidder 2 would remain the same under the VCG mechanism.

Edelman *et al.* (2007) showed in an elegant model that the unique perfect Bayesian equilibrium in this auction is for bidders to shade their bid by some fraction. They also showed that the resulting positions and payoffs for bidders are the same as in the Vickrey auction, and that this is an ex post equilibrium, i.e., it is independent of other bidders' values.

4.3.3 First-Price Sealed-Bid Auctions

In a first-price sealed-bid auction each bidder again submits one bid but does not learn about other bidders' bids. The highest bidder pays her bid and wins the object. A bidder's strategy is her bid as a function of her value. In the first-price auction a bidder should submit a sealed bid just large enough to outbid the second-highest bid. Unfortunately, no dominant strategies exist in these auctions. If all the bidders' values are common knowledge and a bidder can predict the second-highest bid perfectly, this is a simple problem. If the values are private information and only a common prior distribution of the values is available, a Bayesian Nash equilibrium strategy is more complex to derive.

A bidder's tradeoff is between bidding high, thus winning more often, and bidding low, thus benefitting more if the bid wins. A Bayesian Nash equilibrium bidding strategy also depends on the bidder's degree of risk aversion and the prior distribution $F(\cdot)$. Therefore, the resulting Bayesian Nash equilibrium is less robust to mistakes in the assumptions of the model than the equilibria of ascending and second-price sealed-bid auctions. For now, we assume that bidders are risk neutral and that the ex ante distribution of values is the same for all bidders, i.e., bidders are *symmetric*.

We now discuss the equilibrium strategy more formally. Suppose that n risk-neutral bidders i have values $v_i \in V$, a random variable which is distributed according to a continuous density function $f(v) \geq 0$ with cumulative probability $F(v)$ on the support $[0, \bar{v}]$. This is the common prior distribution of the Bayesian game. We refer to a bidder's symmetric, increasing, and differentiable equilibrium bid function as $\beta(v_i)$.

We focus on a specific bidder, bidder 1, and determine the optimal price p she should bid conditionally on the common prior distribution $F(\cdot)$. We now denote the highest value among the $n - 1$ remaining bidders by a random variable Y_1. This is equivalent to the highest-order statistic of $V_2, V_3, \ldots, V_n$, which describe the random variables of subsequent draws. The kth-order statistic of a statistical sample is equal to its kth-smallest value in several draws from the same distribution. We use G to denote the distribution function of Y_1, where $G(y) = F(y)^{n-1}$.

Bidder 1 wins the auction whenever $\max_{i \neq 1} \beta(V_i) < p$. Now, $\max_{i \neq 1} \beta(V_i) = \beta(\max_{i \neq 1} V_i) = \beta(Y_1)$ and so bidder 1 wins whenever $\beta(Y_1) < p$ or $Y_1 < \beta^{-1}(p)$. This allows us to formulate the expected payoff of bidder 1 as

$$G(\beta^{-1}(p))(v - p)$$

We can now maximize with respect to p and derive the first-order conditions (with $g = G'$)

$$\frac{g(\beta^{-1}(p))}{\beta'(\beta^{-1}(p))}(v - p) - G(\beta^{-1}(p)) = 0$$

In a symmetric equilibrium we have $p = \beta(v)$, so we can formulate the following differential equation:

$$\frac{vg(v)}{\beta'(v)} - \frac{g(v)\beta(v)}{\beta'(v)} - G(v) = 0$$

Thus

$$G(v)\beta'(v) + g(v)\beta(v) = vg(v) \equiv \frac{d}{dv}(G(v)\beta(v)) = vg(v)$$

We know that $\beta(0) = 0$, so we get

$$\beta(v) = \frac{1}{G(v)} \int_0^v yg(y)dy = E[Y_1|Y_1 < v]$$

Theorem 4.3.1 *The symmetric Bayesian Nash equilibrium strategy in a first-price sealed-bid auction is given by $\beta(v) = E[Y_1|Y_1 < v]$, where Y_1 is the highest of the $n - 1$ independent values of competing bidders.*

In order to establish that this is a symmetric Bayesian Nash equilibrium strategy, one needs to prove that if the other $n - 1$ bidders follow β, it is optimal for bidder 1 to follow β, i.e., it is a best response and neither bidding higher nor bidding lower could increase the expected payoff of bidder 1.

The conditional expectation of Y_1 given that $Y_1 < v$ is $E[Y_1|Y_1 < v]$, which can be rewritten as

$$\beta(v) = v - \int_0^v \frac{G(y)}{G(v)} dy$$

as a result of integration by parts. Remember that

$$\frac{G(y)}{G(v)} = \left[\frac{F(y)}{F(v)}\right]^{n-1}$$

so that

$$\beta(v) = v - \int_0^v \left[\frac{F(y)}{F(v)}\right]^{n-1} dy.$$

This shows that the number of bidders n determines by how much a bidder in a first-price sealed-bid auction shades his bid below the valuation. Note that we are assuming symmetric bidders. The analysis with asymmetric bidders is more involved. Now, suppose we have symmetric bidders and the common prior distribution is the uniform distribution $F(v) = v/\bar{v}$; then the last equation becomes

$$\beta(v) = v - \frac{\int_0^v (x/\bar{v})^{n-1} dx}{(v/\bar{v})^{n-1}}$$

$$= v - \frac{\left.(1/\bar{v})^{n-1}(1/n)x^n\right|_{x=0}^v}{(v/\bar{v})^{n-1}}$$

$$= v - \frac{(1/\bar{v})^{n-1}(1/n)v^n - 0}{(v/\bar{v})^{n-1}}$$

$$= v - \frac{v}{n} = \left(\frac{n-1}{n}\right)v$$

If there are two bidders and values are uniform on $[0, 1]$, a bidder should bid $\beta = v/2$. With $n = 100$ bidders, the equilibrium bid would be $99v/100$. Then the expected payoff would be $v^{100}/100$.

We can also compute the ex ante expected seller revenue of a first-price sealed-bid auction with a uniformly distributed prior. The expected value of V can be determined via order statistics for the uniform distribution. The kth-highest order statistic resulting from n draws from a uniform distribution is

$$E[v_k(n)] = \frac{n-k+1}{n+1}\bar{v}$$

So, the highest order statistic is $n\bar{v}/(n+1)$. In equilibrium every bidder shades his bid to $\beta(v) = (n-1)v/n$, so that the expected revenue is

$$E[\beta(v)] = \frac{n-1}{n+1}\bar{v}$$

Interestingly, this is equivalent to the second-highest order statistic of the distribution, which is the outcome of a second-price sealed-bid auction. We discuss this observation in more detail in section 4.4.

4.3.4   Descending Auctions

The seller in a descending auction (aka Dutch auction) announces a bid, which he continuously lowers until some bidder stops him and takes the object at that price. A bidder's strategy involves deciding when to stop the bidding as a function of her value. The descending auction is considered *strategically equivalent* to the first-price sealed-bid auction, which means there is a one-to-one mapping between the strategy sets and the equilibria of the two games. The reason for this strategic equivalence is that no relevant information is disclosed in the course of the auction, only at the end when it is too late to change anybody's behavior. In the first-price auction a bidder's bid is irrelevant unless it is the highest, and in the descending auction a bidder's stopping price is irrelevant unless it is the highest. Therefore, the equilibrium bid function is calculated the same way for both auctions.

Note that strategic equivalence is different from *outcome equivalence*. The latter means that two auction formats achieve the same price and the same allocation. The English auction is outcome equivalent to the Vickrey auction, but not strategically equivalent. The English auction offers information about when other bidders drop out, and bidders can respond to competitors' bids. Therefore, the two auction games are not considered strategically equivalent. However, in both cases bidders have a weakly dominant strategy to bid an amount or set a limit equal to their own true value. Therefore, the equilibrium outcomes are the same as long as bidders' valuations are not affected by observing others' bidding behavior, which always holds true in the private-value environment.

4.4   Comparing Equilibrium Outcomes

We can now compare the revenue of these auctions in equilibrium. We have seen that the first-price and descending auctions are strategically equivalent, so the payoffs to the bidders and seller will be the same under each rule regardless of whether values are private or common and whether the players are risk neutral or risk averse. Also, the second-price and ascending auctions are the same in the sense that the bidder who values the object most highly wins and pays the second highest value of all the bidders present (outcome equivalence), even though the strategies can be different in the two auctions. However, how can we compare the revenue of the first-price and the second-price sealed-bid auction? Arguably, the central result in single-object auction theory is the *revenue equivalence theorem* (Vickrey, 1961), which shows that, in the symmetric independent private-value model with risk-neutral bidders, the expected revenue of all auctions introduced in the previous section is the same. There are several versions of the revenue equivalence theorem.

Theorem 4.4.1 (Revenue equivalence theorem) *Let all agents be risk neutral with private values drawn independently from the same strictly increasing distribution function $F(v)$ with support $[\underline{v}, \bar{v}]$. If two auction formats satisfy the following criteria,*

1. *the winner of the object is the agent with the highest value, and*
2. *the lowest bidder type, $v = \underline{v}$, has an expected payment of zero,*

then the symmetric equilibria of the two auction rules have the same expected payoffs for each type of bidder and for the seller.

Proof. Using the revelation principle (theorem 3.3.1) we focus on direct mechanisms. Let us analyze the truthful equilibrium of a direct mechanism in which one bidder deviates from truth telling, pretending type z instead of her actual type v, and then bids $\beta(z)$. By criterion 1 of the theorem, the probability that an agent wins the object, given that she pretends type z, equals $F(z)^{n-1}$, which is the probability that all $n - 1$ other agents have types $v < z$. Let us denote this winning probability by $G(z)$, with a continuous density function $g(z)$.

It is useful to abstract from the details of the auction format A and consider only the expected payoff of the agents, $\Pi^A(v, z)$. The expected payoff of any agent of type v is the same, since we are restricting ourselves to symmetric equilibria. It equals

$$\Pi^A(v, z) = G(z)v - m^A(z)$$

The expected payment $m^A(z)$ depends on the other agents' strategy β and on z but is independent of the true type value, v. The first-order condition with respect to the agent's choice of type message z is

$$\frac{d\Pi(v, z)}{dz} = g(z)v - \frac{dm^A(z)}{dz} = 0$$

so

$$\frac{dm^A(z)}{dz} = g(z)v$$

We are looking at a truthful equilibrium, so we can replace z with v:

$$\frac{dm^A(v)}{dv} = g(v)v$$

Next, we integrate this last equation over all values from $\underline{v}$ to v, adding $m^A(\underline{v})$ as the constant of integration:

$$m^A(v) = m^A(\underline{v}) + \int_{\underline{v}}^{v} xg(x)dx$$

We can use the previous equation to substitute for $m^A(z)$ in the payoff equation for $\Pi^A(v, z)$ and, after replacing z with v and setting $m^A(\underline{v}) = 0$ (because of assumption 2), this becomes

$$\Pi(v, v) = G(v)v - \int_{\underline{v}}^{v} xg(x)dx$$

The expected payoff $\Pi(v, v)$ of a bidder with type v depends only on the distribution $G(v)$, which depends only on the distribution $F(v)$ and not on $\beta(z)$ or other details of the auction format. However, if the bidders' payoffs do not depend on the auction rule, the seller's revenue is independent of the auction rule.   □

Although the different auctions have the same expected payoff for the seller, they do not have the same realized payoff. In the first-price sealed-bid auction, for example, the winning bidder's payment depends entirely on his own value. In the second-price auction the winning bidder's payment depends entirely on the second-highest value, which is sometimes close to his own value and sometimes less.

4.5   Robustness of the Revenue Equivalence Theorem

The revenue equivalence theorem holds for the symmetric independent private-value model with risk-neutral bidders. If two auction formats in this environment implement the same allocation then the revenue of the auctioneer is the same. Of course, the model assumptions are not always satisfied in the field. Next, we discuss common deviations from these assumptions and their impact on revenue.

4.5.1   Risk-Averse Bidders

Risk neutrality implies that the expected utility of a bidder is just equal to the difference between the expected gain and the expected payment. Now, we examine the consequences of the adoption of a utility function $U : \mathbb{R}_{\geq 0} \mapsto \mathbb{R}_{\geq 0}$ describing risk aversion, i.e., with $U' > 0$ and $U'' < 0$. If bidders are risk averse, the extent of their aversion to risk will influence their bidding behavior in Bayesian Nash equilibria. Therefore, with risk aversion the first-price and Dutch auctions generate higher expected revenues, while the ascending clock auction or the second-price auction for a single object are not affected because they have dominant strategies. Let's examine the situation of a risk-averse agent in a first-price sealed-bid auction. If she loses she gets nothing, while if she wins she obtains a positive profit. By marginally increasing her bid, she lowers her profit if she wins but increases the probability of winning. The increment in wealth associated with winning the auction at a reduced bid counts less than the possible loss of not winning owing to such a bid. This risk aversion works to the seller's advantage, because risk-averse bidders bid higher in the first-price and in the descending auction.

Theorem 4.5.1 *If bidders have symmetric independent private values and the same risk-averse utility function then the expected revenue in a first-price sealed-bid auction is greater than in a second-price sealed-bid auction.*

Proof. Note that if bidders are risk averse, this does not affect a dominant-strategy equilibrium under the second-price sealed-bid auction. Let us next analyze the first-price sealed-bid auction. To solve for the equilibrium of a first-price sealed-bid auction with risk-averse bidders, let us look at a bidder's incentive to report her true type v as z in an auction. Let U describe a utility function which might either be concave (i.e., risk averse) or linear (risk neutral). The bidder maximizes her utility by her choice of z:

$$\Pi(v, z) = G(z)U[v - \gamma(z)]$$
$$= F(z)^{n-1}U[v - \gamma(z)]$$

where γ is an increasing and differentiable equilibrium bid function and where $\Pi(v, 0, \gamma(0)) = 0$ because $F(0) = 0$. The first-order condition is

$$\frac{\partial \Pi(v, z)}{\partial z} = (n-1)F(z)^{n-2}f(z)U[v - \gamma(z)] + F(z)^{n-1}U'[v - \gamma(z)][-\gamma'(z)] = 0$$

In a symmetric equilibrium, it must be optimal to choose $z = v$. Using that fact, for all $v > \underline{v}$ (since $F(\underline{v}) = 0$) we can solve the previous equation for $\gamma'(z)$ to get

$$\gamma'(v) = \left(\frac{(n-1)f(v)}{F(v)}\right)\left(\frac{U[v - \gamma(v)]}{U'[v - \gamma(v)]}\right)$$

Now let's look at the effect of risk aversion on $\gamma(v)$. If U is linear with $U(x) = x$ then the second term on the right-hand side of the last equation becomes

$$\frac{U[v - \gamma(v)]}{U'[v - \gamma(v)]} = v - \gamma(v)$$

but if the bidder is risk averse, so that U is strictly concave, with $U' > 0$ and $U'' < 0$, then

$$\frac{U[v - \gamma(v)]}{U'[v - \gamma(v)]} > v - \gamma(v)$$

The above inequality holds because the average gradient $U(x)/x$ of U at any point x is strictly greater than the gradient $U'(x)$ for any strictly concave function. Thus, for a given v, the bid function in the last inequality makes the bid higher if the bidder is risk averse than if she is not. The bid for every value of v except $v = \underline{v}$ increases. Note that $\gamma(\underline{v}) = \underline{v}$, regardless of risk aversion. By increasing her bid from the level optimal for a risk-neutral bidder, the risk-averse bidder insures herself. If she wins then her surplus is slightly less because of the higher price, but she is more likely to win and so avoid a surplus of zero. □

The result can be developed for the CARA or CRRA utility functions introduced in section 3.2. In summary, a risk-neutral seller faced by risk-averse bidders prefers the first-price or Dutch auction over the Vickrey or English auction, because they lead to a higher expected revenue. A more extensive discussion can be found in McAfee and McMillan (1987).

4.5.2   Interdependent Values

Another crucial assumption of the IPV model is the independence of bidders' valuations. In section 3.5 we gave a brief discussion of interdependent values, i.e., the case when one agent's private information affects other agents' preferences. For more general environments, where agents have multi-dimensional signals, the efficient social choice rule is not Bayesian implementable, i.e., there are no mechanisms such that truth-telling is a Bayesian Nash equilibrium.

Let us now discuss the strategic problem in pure common-value auctions, where we assume bidders have only an estimate of the true value of an object and each bidder can extract useful information about the object's value to herself from the bids of the other bidders. The obvious strategy, especially following our discussion of private-value auctions, is for a risk-neutral bidder to bid up to her unbiased estimate of the value. But this strategy can make the winner's payoff negative, because the winner is the bidder who has made the largest positive error in her estimate. The bidders who underestimated the value lose the auction but their payoff equals zero, which they would receive even if the true value were common knowledge. Only the winner suffers from her estimation error: the *winner's curse*.

Once bidders recognize the possibility of the winner's curse and adjust their bidding strategies, the winner will no longer have to regret her victory. Having adjusted their bids by scaling down to be lower than their unbiased estimates, the winner may still be the bidder with the biggest overestimation error but the winning bid would now be less than the true value. Thus, the problem is to decide how much less than one's value-estimate to bid. The strategic problem is similar to deciding how much to bid in a first-price sealed-bid auction in the IPV model. There, a bidder wants to bid less than her value, but she also wants to win if she can do so as cheaply as possible. She therefore tries to estimate the value of the second-highest bid conditionally upon she herself having the highest value.

There are also other forms of interdependency between bidders' valuations. Milgrom and Weber (1982) introduced the concept of affiliation in bidders' valuations: "Bidders' valuations of an object are affiliated if they are not negatively correlated." In practice, affiliation means that, given that one bidder believes an object is worth a large amount, the other bidders will not think the object is worth less. Again, when bidders with affiliated values participate in English auctions, the information disclosed during the bidding can cause the remaining bidders to privately revise their valuations and possibly raise them. This could be one reason why English auctions tend to yield higher average selling prices (McAfee and McMillan, 1987). Therefore, in the case of affiliated values, sellers should use the English auction because it yields the highest expected revenue, followed by the Vickrey auction. The first-price auction should yield lower revenues as bidders learn less information during the auction.

This insight has also become known as the *linkage principle*, which implies that open auctions generally lead to higher expected prices than sealed-bid auctions (Milgrom and Weber, 1982). The intuition provided by the linkage principle for the potential benefits of ascending over sealed-bid auction formats, and the benefits of information revelation generally, has been quite influential in practical auction design.

4.5.3 Asymmetry of Bidders

If the symmetry assumption from the IPV model is removed then bidders fall into recognizably different classes, i.e., the private values are not drawn from a single common distribution but multiple distributions. This again has no effect on the English auction. However, the revenue equivalence breaks down in the case of a first-price sealed-bid or Dutch auction. The first-price sealed-bid or Dutch auction can even lead to inefficient outcomes (McAfee and McMillan, 1987). Suppose that, for example, there are two bidders, A and B, characterized by their random valuations in the ranges [0, 5] and [3, 7]. Consider a Dutch auction. Obviously, B could always win and have a gain by bidding the amount 5 and could do even better by shading his bid further. But then the low-valuation bidder A could win with positive probability, violating Pareto efficiency. This is an important observation for auctions where efficiency is crucial.

4.5.4 Uncertainty about the Number of Bidders

Of course, the number of bidders also has an effect on the outcome of an auction. The more bidders there are, the higher the valuation of the second-highest bidder is, on average. Thus, on average the number of bidders increases the revenue of the seller. In many auctions, bidders are uncertain about the number of participants. McAfee and McMillan (1987) showed that if bidders were risk averse and had constant or decreasing absolute risk aversion then numbers uncertainty leads to more aggressive bidding in a first-price sealed-bid auction. However, numbers uncertainty has no effect on bidding strategies under the three other auction rules.

In summary, the common single-object auction formats are all simple and robust. Ascending auctions possess a number of characteristics that help explain their popularity. They lead to efficient outcomes in a wide range of environments and economize on information gathering and bid preparation costs.

4.6 Bidder Collusion

A crucial concern about auctions in practice is the ability of bidders to collude (in bidder or auction rings), but the theoretical work on this issue is rather limited. To rank different auctions from the point of view of collusion, suppose that all potential bidders have come to a collusive agreement. They have selected their designated winner, who is assumed to be the one with the highest valuation, advising her to follow a particular strategy and committing others to abstain from bidding.

Robinson (1985) makes the point that a collusive agreement may be easier to sustain in a second-price auction than in a first-price auction. In a Dutch or first-price sealed-bid auction the designated winner will be advised to place a bid slightly higher than the seller's reserve price, whereas all other ring members are asked to abstain from bidding. However, each bidder can gain by in fact placing a slightly higher bid, in violation of the ring agreement. This is not so under the English or Vickrey auction. Here, in a bidder ring, the designated bidder is advised to bid up to her own valuation and everybody else is advised to abstain from bidding. No one can gain by breaking the agreement because no one will ever exceed the designated bidder's limit. Thus, the English auction is particularly susceptible to auction rings and the designer should opt for a Dutch instead of an English auction if she is dealing with an auction ring.

Even if auction rings can write enforceable agreements, the ring faces the problem of how to select the designated winner and avoid strategic behavior by ring members. This can be done by running a pre-auction. In a pre-auction, every ring member is asked to place a bid and the highest bidder is chosen as the ring's sole bidder at the subsequent auction. However, if the bid at the pre-auction affects only the chance of becoming designated winner at no cost, each ring member has a reason to exaggerate her valuation. This problem can only be solved if the designated winner shares her alleged gain from trade.

4.7   Optimal Auction Design

An important branch of traditional auction design theory is concerned with the design of optimal auctions. This theory uses mechanism design techniques to characterize, in general terms, the auction that maximizes the seller's expected revenues. Myerson (1981) proposed a general approach towards optimal auction design based on the revelation principle. That is to say, in the context of auctions a designer may restrict attention, without loss of generality, to incentive-compatible direct auctions (see section 3.3). Therefore, the auction that is optimal among incentive-compatible direct auctions is also optimal for all types of auction. Myerson (1981) essentially reduces the optimal auction problem for a single-object auction to the optimal choice of reserve price.

A *reserve price r* is a bid put in by the seller, secretly or openly, before the auction begins, which commits her not to sell the object if nobody bids more than r. That is, an optimal auction requires the seller to set a reserve price r below which she will not sell the item. She can still use a Vickrey auction and this auction would not lose its dominant-strategy incentive compatibility by introducing a reserve price, which can be seen as another bidder. The reserve price is set to mimic the expected bid of the second-highest bidder and is greater than the seller's reserve valuation. The optimal level of the reserve price is determined by a tradeoff. The disadvantage of setting a reserve price is that it is possible for the remaining bidders to have a valuation that lies between the seller's valuation and the reserve price. In this case, the seller loses the sale even though the bidder would have been willing to pay the seller more than the product is worth. On the other hand, if the reserve price is above the second-highest bidder's valuation, the bidder pays more than she would have paid in the absence of a reserve price. In summary, the seller imposes the reserve price in order to capture some informational profits that would otherwise have gone to the winner.

There is a relationship between optimal auction design for risk-neutral bidders with private values and the theory of price differentiation in monopolies (Bulow and Roberts, 1989). In an optimal auction the objects are allocated to the bidders with the highest marginal revenues, just as a price-discriminating monopolist sells to buyers with the highest marginal revenues. Moreover, just as a monopolist should not sell a unit of a commodity below the price where marginal revenue equals marginal cost, an auctioneer should not sell below a reserve price equal to the value of the bidder whose marginal revenue equals the value of the auctioneer's retention of the unit.

So, how would the auctioneer set r? If there is just one bidder, the seller will do badly under any of the auction rules we have discussed so far. A single bidder would bid $p(v) = 0$ and win, and any standard auction yields zero revenue. So, posting a price offer to the bidder makes more sense; if the auction has a reserve price, it can be equivalent to posting a price.

Let the bidder have a value distribution $F(v)$ on $[\underline{v}, \bar{v}]$ which is differentiable and strictly increasing, so that the density $f(v)$ is always positive. Let the seller value the object at $v_s \geq \underline{v}$. The seller's payoff is

$$\Pi(r) = \Pr(r < v)(r - v_s) + \Pr(r > v)(0)$$
$$= [1 - F(r)](r - v_s)$$

This has the first-order condition

$$\frac{d\Pi(r)}{dr} = [1 - F(r)] - f(r)(r - v_s) = 0$$

On solving the last equation for r we get

$$r = v_s + \frac{1 - F(r)}{f(r)}$$

as a necessary condition. For example, if F is uniformly distributed on $[0, 10]$ then $r = 5 + v_s/2$. If there was only a single bidder and $v_s = 0$ then the expected revenue would be $\Pi(5) = 0.5 \times 5 + 0.5 \times 0 = 2.5$. Remarkably, the optimal reserve price r is independent of the number of bidders n and is also above the seller's value, v_s. The reason is that the optimal reserve price occurs when the marginal revenue equals the seller's cost, and a bidder's marginal revenue is independent of other bidders' marginal revenues when the values are independent.

Remember that by setting a positive reserve price r the auctioneer runs the risk that, if the highest value Y_1 among the bidders is smaller than r, the object will remain unsold. However, this potential loss is offset by the possibility that the highest value Y_1 exceeds r and the second-highest value Y_2 is smaller than r. Then the object will be sold at r rather than the second highest bid price. The probability of the first case is $F(r)^2$ and the loss is at most r, i.e., the expected loss is $rF(r)^2$. The probability of the second case is $2F(r)(1 - F(r))$ and the gain is of order r, so that the expected gain is of order

$2rF(r)(1 - F(r))$. The expected gain from setting a reserve price exceeds the expected loss.

In summary, optimal single-object auction theory suggests that a revenue-maximizing auctioneer should use an efficient (e.g., second-price sealed-bid) auction with an appropriately set reserve price r. This is an interesting result, as no restrictions are placed on the types of policy that the seller could use. For instance, the seller could have several rounds of bidding, or charge entry fees, or allow only a limited time for the submission of bids. None of these procedures would increase the expected price for the seller. Our discussion assumes an environment where bidders are symmetric. Myerson (1981) proved optimal auctions for very general settings by looking at the *virtual valuation* of a bidder, which is her true valuation shaded down by a function of the common prior distribution. This concept allows for a remarkably general result that also includes asymmetric bidders. These results have even been extended to settings with correlated and common bidders (Cremer and McLean, 1988) or risk-averse bidders (Maskin and Riley, 1984).

Interestingly, encouraging the entry of additional bidders can outweigh the benefits of an optimal reserve price. Bulow and Klemperer (1996) showed in a symmetric independent private-values model that an additional bidder is worth more to the seller in an ascending auction than the ability to set a reserve price. In contrast, optimal auction theory has been used more recently to set reserve prices for online advertisements, where auctioneers can estimate valuations on the basis of large volumes of historical data. Ostrovsky and Schwarz (2011) showed in a large field experiment that, following the introduction of new reserve prices, revenues in these auctions increased substantially, in particular for categories with a high theoretical reserve price, a high search volume, or only a few bidders.

While optimal single-object auctions are relatively well understood, the design of optimal multi-object auctions is technically very challenging and the subject of much recent research. For the remainder of this book we will focus on the design of efficient auctions rather than optimal auctions, which is why we have skipped the detailed proofs for optimal auction design in this subsection.

4.8   Selected Experimental Results

> If a law disagrees with experiment, it's wrong. In that simple statement is the key to science.
>
> Richard Feynman

Many experiments have been conducted in order to test game-theoretical results and, therefore, they deploy similar experimental procedures. An experimental session typically consists of several auction periods in each of which a number of subjects bid for a single unit of a commodity under a given auction design. The item is often referred to as a "fictitious commodity", in order to keep the terminology as neutral as possible. Subjects' valuations are decided randomly prior to each auction and are private information. Typically the valuations are independent and identical draws from a uniform distribution where the lower and the upper boundary are common knowledge. In each period, the highest bidder earns a profit equal to the value of the item minus the price; other bidders earn zero profit for that auction period. Subjects are sometimes provided with examples of valuations and bids along with profit calculations to illustrate how the auction works. Sometimes experimenters perform dry runs, with no money at stake, to familiarize subjects with the auction procedures. Various guidelines for laboratory experiments help to achieve internal and external validity of the results.

Tests of the revenue-equivalence theorem are of two basic types. Some types test the strategic equivalence of first-price and Dutch auctions, and of second-price and English auctions. Other types test the revenue equivalence between first-price or Dutch auctions and second-price or English auctions. Given the strategic equivalence of these different auctions, average prices are predicted to be the same, independent of bidders' attitudes towards risk.

The experimental data show that subjects do not behave in strategically equivalent ways in first-price and Dutch auctions or in outcome-equivalent ways in English and second-price auctions (Cox *et al.*, 1982). Bids in first-price and Dutch auctions are commonly above the *risk-neutral Bayesian Nash equilibrium* (RNBNE) strategy. The discussion about overbidding was played out in a controversy among experimental economists in the December 1992 issue of the *American Economic Review*, a well-known academic journal in economics. It raised the question how to provide sufficient experimental control to establish empirical regularities in the laboratory and how to modify the theory in light of countervailing empirical evidence. Ever since, overbidding has been the subject of substantial research in the experimental auction literature. Risk aversion, regret about the outcome of an auction, and uncertainty about the rationality of others have served as explanations for overbidding.

A number of authors have used risk aversion to explain bids above the RNBNE (Cox *et al.*, 1988). However, measuring the risk aversion of lab subjects turns out to be a challenge. Overall, risk attitudes not only differ across assessment methods but also vary within a given method.

Post-auction regret served as another explanation for the bidding behavior in first-price sealed-bid auctions. Engelbrecht-Wiggans and Katok (2008) found support for the regret model in experiments with information feedback about the highest or second-highest bid after the auction. Deviations from the RNBNE bid function could also be due to wrong expectations of the bidders about the bids of others. Goeree and Holt (2002) demonstrated that misperceived probabilities of winning the auction would explain over-bidding as well as risk aversion.

Interestingly, prices are also above the equilibrium weakly dominant bidding strategy in second-price sealed-bid auctions, although here bidding is independent of risk attitudes. In English auctions, bidding generally converges to the dominant-strategy pre-diction. There are several explanations for the lower bidding in Dutch versus first-price auctions. In one model, Dutch auction bidders update their estimates of their rivals' val-uations, assuming them to be lower than they initially anticipated as a consequence of no one having taken the item as the clock ticks down.

In summary, in private-value auctions the revenue-equivalence theorem fails in most experimental tests with human subjects. In many auction experiments, subjects do not behave in strategically equivalent ways in first-price and Dutch auctions or in English and second-price auctions, even in controlled laboratory environments which mirror the theoretical assumptions. It is even less likely that equilibrium bidding strategies of first-price auctions can be found in the field, where the assumptions of the independent private-value model are often violated. Bidding above the dominant strategy in second-price auctions is relatively widespread whereas, in English auctions, market prices rapidly converge to the dominant-strategy price. The situation is different in display advertisement auctions or sponsored search auctions, where automated bidding agents have access to historical bid data allowing for estimates of the valuations compete. Assumptions of a common prior distribution, which have otherwise often been challenged, appear as a reasonable assumption in these types of application.

4.9   Summary

The analysis of standard auction formats as Bayesian games has taken center stage in economics. Bayesian Nash equilibrium strategies provide a rigorous way to think about rational bidding in the first-price sealed-bid and Dutch auctions. Unfortunately, Bayesian Nash equilibrium strategies are not always predictive in the laboratory, and various behavioral conjectures have been used to explain deviations from the equilibrium strategies in the laboratory. It has also turned out to be difficult to derive Bayesian Nash equilibrium strategies for multi-object auctions, because the informational assumptions of bidders having common prior distributions for various packages are strong.

The revenue equivalence theorem is arguably the central result, and it illustrates the assumptions at work when the expected revenue of the auctioneer is the same for different standard auction formats. The analysis helps one to understand which assumptions (e.g., risk attitudes of bidders, the symmetry of common prior type distributions, the independence of valuations, etc.) are important and have an impact on the outcomes of auctions in the field. Even though Bayesian Nash equilibria do not appear to be good predictors for human bidding behavior, the models show what the assumptions would have to be like for an unregulated market to be Pareto efficient and revenue equivalent.

In traditional auction theory the number of bidders is often assumed to be exogenous (i.e., growing). In practice, auctioneers can often encourage bidders to enter, which can have a significant positive effect on revenue. Klemperer (2002) emphasized that collusion and a low number of bidders are among the most important reasons why in practice some auctions fail.

In this chapter, we focused on ascending, Dutch, first-price, and second-price sealed-bid auctions, which are considered the four standard single-object auction formats. There are also other auctions with interesting properties. An all-pay auction is an auction in which every bidder must pay regardless of whether they win. A type of *all-pay auction* is a Tullock auction in which everyone submits a bid but both the losers and the winners pay their submitted bids. The *dollar auction* (Shubik, 1974) is a two-player Tullock auction in which only the two highest bidders pay their bids. This means that the second-highest bidder is the loser by paying the top amount she bids without getting anything back. Typically, bidders start bidding and the auction continues with the second-highest bidder trying to become the highest bidder. This easily leads to outcomes where the highest and the second-highest bidder make a loss. Another form of an all-pay auction is a *war-of-attrition* game, where all bidders pay their bid except the winner, who pays the second-highest bid. Sometimes, the term all-pay auction also refers to specific auction formats where all bidders including the winner pay their bid. Various auction types have been invented and studied, but an understanding of the four standard auction formats is a useful basis for the discussion of multi-object auctions discussed in Part II of the book.

4.10   Comprehension Questions

1. Discuss differences between the independent private-values and the common values models.
2. Describe the four standard auction formats for a single-object auction.
3. Would you choose a first-price sealed-bid auction or an English auction to maximize the expected revenue in the presence of risk-averse bidders?
4. How does the optimal reserve price of a seller maximizing expected revenue depend on the number of bidders?
5. What's the difference between the efficiency and revenue of an auction?
6. Suppose you are in an auction where the winner is the highest bidder, who then pays the third highest bid. Is truthful bidding a dominant strategy in such third-price auctions?

4.11   Problems

Efficiency and Revenue
Consider a sealed-bid auction with the bids shown in Table 4.1. Describe an efficient outcome, an inefficient outcome, and one with optimal revenue.

Table 4.1 Bidder valuations

	Bidder A	Bidder B	Bidder C	Bidder D
Valuation	12	10	4	16

Equilibrium Strategies
Consider an auction in which a single seller is selling an item to one of two bidders, who both demand only a single unit.

1. Which mechanism ensures that the item goes to the bidder with the higher value for it?
2. Now consider a market where two sellers are selling two items simultaneously to two unit-demand bidders. If a bidder wins both items then her value for both will

equal her value for the item she preferred. Explain why organizing two second-price auctions will not lead to truthful strategies. Assume that there is no coordination between the two sellers.

Auctions with Complete Information

Consider an auction in which three bidders compete for a single item and there is complete information about the values of the bidders. Show that any pure Nash equilibrium of the game is efficient.

Part II

Multi-Object Auction Design

5 An Overview of Multi-Object Auctions

We now focus on markets where multiple related and indivisible objects are sold. These objects might be homogeneous or heterogeneous. In general, a seller can decide to sell the objects in multiple auctions or in a single auction. Let's assume that the seller decides to sell the objects either one at a time in a sequence of single-object auctions or simultaneously; then she needs to decide on the auction format. If the seller decides to sell all objects in a single auction, there are open and sealed-bid auction designs, which we briefly introduce next. Note that we assume independent and private values of bidders and quasi-linear utility functions unless mentioned explicitly.

Since we have multiple objects, we need additional notation. Let $\mathcal{K}$ denote the set of objects to be auctioned ($|\mathcal{K}| = m$) and $k \in \mathcal{K}$ (also $l \in \mathcal{K}$) denote a specific object. Again, let $\mathcal{I}$ denote the set of bidders participating in the auction ($|\mathcal{I}| = n$) and $i \in \mathcal{I}$ (also $j \in \mathcal{I}$) denote a specific bidder. We distinguish between *multi-unit auctions*, where multiple identical objects are sold, and *multi-item auctions*, where heterogeneous objects are sold.

Models of multi-object markets have been developed in economics for a long time, starting with Adam Smith's famous conjecture about the invisible hand of the market. Therefore, we begin with a brief history of multi-object markets and respective models in economics, before we classify multi-unit and multi-item auction formats.

5.1 General Equilibrium Models

The supply and demand model of a single type of good is a partial equilibrium model where the clearance on the market of some specific good is obtained independently from prices and quantities in the markets for other goods. This makes analysis much simpler than in a general equilibrium model which includes multiple goods or objects. In *partial equilibrium analysis* the supply and demand for *one type of good* in markets with multiple buyers and sellers is analyzed in order to understand how prices arise in a competitive equilibrium. We will introduce the term competitive equilibrium more formally in definition 8.1.2. For now, such an equilibrium is a state where supply and demand are balanced and, in the absence of external influences, prices and allocation will not change.

The widespread graphical illustration of a partial equilibrium in figure 5.1 has price on the vertical axis and quantity on the horizontal axis, and it describes how competitive

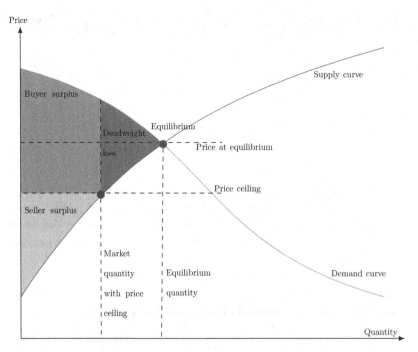

Figure 5.1 Partial equilibrium in a market for homogeneous goods.

equilibrium prices on such markets arise and what the impact of a shift in either demand or supply implies. It provides a good initial intuition of the dynamics that can arise on exchanges. In equilibrium the gains from trade (the lighter shaded area in figure 5.1) are maximized. If some price ceiling is set then a *deadweight loss* arises. This is a loss of economic efficiency, which can occur when equilibrium for a good or service is not achieved or is not achievable.

In contrast with a partial equilibrium for a single type of good, general equilibrium theory attempts to explain supply, demand, and prices in a whole economy with many types of objects to be traded. A baseline model is that of a *perfect market*, where a large number of buyers and sellers are present at the same time and know all the prices of the objects and the utilities each participant would get from owning each object. No participant has the market power to set prices, and there are no transaction costs or scale economies. Also, there are no barriers to enter or exit the market, and no externalities. When the conditions of a perfect competition hold, it has been shown that a market will reach a competitive equilibrium in which the quantity supplied for every product or service, including labor, equals the quantity demanded at the current price. This equilibrium is a Pareto optimum, and no participant can be made better off, by changing the allocation, without making someone else worse off.

Leon Walras, a French economist, proposed a dynamic process by which general equilibrium might be reached, that of the *tâtonnement*. Prices are announced by an auctioneer, and agents state how much of each good they would like to offer or purchase.

Prices are lowered for goods with positive prices and excess supply, and are raised for goods with excess demand. Trades only occur in equilibrium, when the process stops. This raises the question under what conditions such a process will terminate in an equilibrium and when these equilibria are unique. Kenneth Arrow, Gérard Debreu, and Lionel W. McKenzie provided a rigorous mathematical treatment of general equilibrium in the 1950s. They asked the more general question, if equilibria in a market exist, when they are stable and efficient?

This line of research resulted in two famous welfare theorems. The *first fundamental welfare theorem* asserts that competitive equilibria are Pareto efficient. The *second fundamental welfare theorem* states that every efficient allocation can be supported by some set of equilibrium prices. To guarantee that an equilibrium exists, it suffices that consumer preferences and production sets are convex, i.e. there are no economies of scale, and goods are perfectly divisible. These central results are existence theorems about conditions when a market can be in equilibrium, but they reveal little about how these equilibria emerge. Some critics of general equilibrium modeling contend that general equilibrium models have little connection to actual economies, as their assumptions are almost never given in the field (Georgescu-Roegen, 1979). For example, goods are typically not divisible and preferences are not convex. Production processes cannot be scaled up or down without losing efficiency. For example, car manufacturing is far more efficient when done at large scales. Such effects are ignored in traditional general equilibrium models. In very large markets, the non-convexities of bidder preferences might be ignored but more often the number of objects and bidders is such that they matter. In what follows, we focus on multi-object markets where the objects are indivisible and bidders can influence the price with their bids. This means that game-theoretical equilibrium solution concepts matter.

5.2 Multi-Unit Auction Formats

We first discuss the sale of multiple identical objects. As in case of single-object auctions, there are sealed-bid (aka closed) and open auction formats. Typically, bidders are assumed to have *weakly decreasing marginal valuations* for an additional unit in this literature, i.e. $v(k) - v(k-1) \geq v(k+1) - v(k)$. This is a restriction on the set of possible valuations. For example, there are markets where bidders have super-additive valuations for specific numbers of units. Here, a bidder might have a positive valuation for four units but no value for less than four. Such general preferences are discussed in the context of combinatorial auctions in chapter 7.

5.2.1 Sealed-Bid Multi-Unit Auction Formats

Three multi-unit auction formats are well known: the discriminatory, the uniform-price, and the Vickrey auction. In each auction, a bidder is asked to submit bids indicating how much she is willing to pay for one, two, . . . , m units.

In a multi-unit *Vickrey auction* a bidder who wins k^i units pays the k^ith-highest losing bids, not including his own. In a Vickrey auction it is again a weakly dominant strategy to bid truthfully.

In a *uniform-price auction* all m units are sold at a clearing price such that the total amount demanded is equal to the total amount supplied. Any price between the highest losing bid and the lowest winning bid equates demand and supply. Unfortunately, the uniform-price auction is not truthful. *Demand reduction* is often an issue in uniform-price auctions (Ausubel and Baranov, 2014). Consider a simple example with six units of a good and three bidders, each interested in two or three units. If all bidders submit a bid on only two units at most, they all pay zero. Such strategies are not truthful and they can lead to inefficient allocations. Note that if bidders have only single-unit demand then the uniform-price auction is truthful. Some also argue that in large markets, with many bidders and many units, the uniform-price auction is truthful because the influence of single bidders on the price is low.

In a *discriminatory auction*, each bidder pays an amount equal to the sum of her winning bids. This is equivalent to perfect price discrimination relative to the submitted demand functions. Demand reduction is also an issue in this type of auction. Even if we assume symmetric bidders, no closed-form expressions for equilibrium bidding strategies are available for the discriminatory auction.

5.2.2   Open Multi-Unit Auction Formats

For single-object auctions we found that the clock auction implements the outcome of the Vickrey (second-price) auction. An ascending multi-unit auction which is strategy-proof or ex post incentive-compatible is also highly desirable, because neither solution concept requires assumptions about the other bidders' valuations. While the English and Dutch auctions do not satisfy a strong solution concept, the so-called clinching auction does.

In the uniform-price *multi-unit English auction*, the auctioneer begins by calling out a low price and then gradually raises it. Bidders indicate how many units they are willing to buy at the first price. As the price rises, bidders reduce the number of units they are willing to buy. The auction ends when the total number of units demanded is exactly m and all m units are sold at the price where the total demand changes from $m + 1$ to m. Demand reduction can also be an issue in these auctions. Uniform price rules are used in open ascending auctions for Treasury bills by the US government. But one can also view the uniform-price English auction as a simplified model of the simultaneous multi-round auction, to be described in chapter 6.

In the *multi-unit Dutch auction* the auctioneer calls a price high enough that no bidder is willing to buy any units at that price. The price is then gradually lowered until a bidder indicates that she is willing to buy a unit at the current price. The bidder is then sold an object at the price and the auction continues; the price is lowered further until another unit is sold and so on, until all m units have been sold.

Table 5.1 Example valuations for a clinching auction with six bidders

	1 unit	2 units	3 units
Bidder A	123	113	103
Bidder B	75	5	3
Bidder C	125	125	49
Bidder D	85	65	7
Bidder E	45	25	5
Bidder F	49	9	3

The *clinching auction* (Ausubel, 2004) is an ascending-price format that is outcome-equivalent to the Vickrey auction. The auctioneer begins by calling out a low price and then raises it. Each bidder indicates her demand at the current price p, and the quantity demanded is reduced as the price rises. A bidder is credited a unit of a good at the current price when the rest of the bidders lower their demand for this good. A unit of a good is debited from a bidder at the current price when the rest of the bidders increase their demand for this good. The auctioneer calculates the set of goods in excess demand and adjusts the prices accordingly. The auction ends whenever a market-clearing allocation is demanded by bidders at the current price. We now provide a complete-information example which nicely illustrates the mechanism (Ausubel, 2004).

Example 5.2.1 Suppose that there are 5 units of a homogeneous good for sale and six bidders (A–F) each interested in buying up to 3 units. The marginal values of each bidder are given in table 5.1. If bidder A purchased 3 units at a price of $50 then his utility was $123 + 113 + 103 - 3 \times 50 = \$189$.

In a clinching auction, the auctioneer starts the auction at a reserve price r and proceeds to increment a continuously ascending price lock. At each price, bidders indicate how many units they are willing to purchase at the current unit price. The quantity required is to be non-increasing in price. When a unit price p^* is reached such that the aggregate demand no longer exceeds supply, then each bidder i is assigned the quantity that she demanded at the final price. Let us now determine the payments.

Suppose that $r = \$10$. Then the bidders A–F indicate demands of 3, 1, 3, 2, 2, and 1 unit, respectively. Thus the aggregate demand is 12 units while the supply is only 5; the clock is incremented until the price is $25, and again at $45. At the price of $45, bidder E drops out of the auction. At a price of $49 bidder C reduces her demand from 3 to 2 units and bidder F drops out, so that the aggregate demand becomes 8. At a price of $65 bidder D reduces her demand to 1 unit, so that the aggregate demand becomes 7. Now bidder A knows that she will certainly win 1 unit, because if we reduce the supply of 5 by the demand of 4 of the other bidders, 1 unit remains. In other words, bidder A has *clinched* winning a unit. Clinching is an expression from American sports-writing jargon.

At a price of $75 bidder B drops out and the aggregate demand is now 6 units. As a consequence, bidder C has clinched a unit, and bidder A has clinched a second, because the aggregate demand of all other bidders for bidder C is 4 units. For bidder A the aggregate demand of the other bidders at the price of $75 is 3 units, so that she clinches a second unit. Finally, at a price of $85 bidder D drops out. Consequently the auction ends and the supply equals the demand at 5 units.

With a uniform-price rule, the payment for each unit would be $85. According to the payment rule of the clinching auction, each bidder is charged the price at which she clinched a unit. Bidder A would win 1 unit for a price of $65, 1 unit for $75, and 1 unit for $85. Bidder C would win 1 unit for $75 and 1 unit for $85.

It is interesting to note that the payments in a clinching auction differ from the prices used in the auction. In a single-object clock auction or an ascending uniform-price auction for one object the final clock prices are equivalent to the payments. It can be shown that the payments are equivalent to those in the VCG auction. This is a necessary condition for straightforward bidding to be an ex post equilibrium, as we discuss in chapter 8. Note that, as in the VCG auction, the payments of a bidder i in a clinching auction are a function of only the responses of other bidders and therefore are independent of bidder i's bids.

5.2.3   Sequential Sales

In cases where a seller has several units of a homogeneous good, she may also sell them sequentially, one unit after another. This is often done in the auctioning of wine, horses, and used cars. In some of these markets, it has been observed that prices tend to follow a declining pattern. Several explanations have been proposed for this phenomenon. Declining prices follow readily if each bidder's valuations for the different objects are independently drawn from an identical distribution, bidders are not strategic, and each bidder wants to buy only one unit. In this case, the competition and the prices would decrease over time. Some authors recommend that bidders should bid less than their valuation in the first round to account for the option value of participating in subsequent rounds. Even though they are easy to implement and widely used, sequential sales lead to a number of strategic challenges for a bidder, depending on whether the bidder is interested in buying one object or in buying more objects. Basic models analyze bidders with single-unit demand in sequential first-price and second-price auctions. Typically, one is interested in equilibria that are sequentially rational, i.e., for any outcome of the first-period auction the strategies in the second period form an equilibrium. While the VCG mechanism would be truthful if allocation and payments could be determined at the end, after all bids have arrived, it is not truthful if allocation and payments are determined one object after the other, as we now illustrate in example 5.2.2.

Example 5.2.2   Suppose that there are three unit-demand bidders and two homogeneous objects, which are to be sold sequentially. The bidder types are $100 and $70 for the first two bidders and $50 for the third bidder, who only arrives for the second auction. In case of truthful bidding bidder 1 pays $70 in the first auction and bidder 2 pays $50 in the second auction. However, if bidders 2 and 3 do not change their bids, bidder 1 could bid $60 in the first auction, and lose, and then bid truthfully in the second auction, which would get him the object for $50.

If modeled as a Bayesian game, bidders would be truthful in the last auction but would shade their bids for earlier auctions in equilibrium (Krishna, 2009). This is so because, in any period before the last, there is an option value associated with winning not the current auction but a later auction.

5.3   Multi-Item Auction Formats

Multi-unit auctions are designed for restricted environments where objects are homogeneous. This is relevant and many real-world auctions satisfy these restrictions. Now we allow objects to be heterogeneous, a generalization of the multi-unit environment. In the following, we will not require weakly decreasing marginal valuations but bidder valuations that can include complements or substitutes for different packages of objects. Complementary valuations describe synergies among items, where the value of a bundle (aka package) of items is greater than the sum of the individual item values, i.e., it is super-additive. Substitute valuations do not allow for complementarities. Different types of valuation are described in more detail in chapter 7. We assume that the items are not divisible, as is the case in most markets, and this leads to complexities which are at the core of the subsequent chapters.

5.3.1   Simultaneous Auctions

A simple way to sell multiple objects is to auction them simultaneously, so that bidders can submit bids on each item individually. A famous example of such a multi-object auction format is the *simultaneous multi-round auction* (SMRA), which has been used for spectrum sales worldwide. We will discuss this specific auction format in chapter 6, because it has become important in the field. However, SMRA is not necessarily efficient with general valuations. Bidders with complementary valuations face risks that they may end up winning only a subset of items from their desired bundle and that they may end up paying too much for this subset. This is called the *exposure problem* (Rothkopf *et al.*, 1998). The exposure problem leads to significant strategic problems in the SMRA. Similar problems arise in the sequential sales of objects. Eventually, this problem has led to the development of combinatorial auction designs.

5.3.2   Combinatorial Auctions

Combinatorial auctions allow for bundle bids, i.e., a price is defined for a subset of the items for auction (Cramton *et al.*, 2006). The price is valid only for the entire set and the set is indivisible, which solves the exposure problem. For example, in a combinatorial auction a bidder might want to buy 10 units of item x and 20 units of item y for a bundle price of $100, which might be more than the total of the prices for items x and *y* sold individually. We refer to a bidding language as a set of allowable bid types (e.g., bundle bids or bids on price and quantity) in an auction. A bidding language allowing for bundle bids is also useful in procurement markets with economies of scope, where suppliers have cost complementarities owing to reduced production or transportation costs for a set of items. In this case, we talk about either a combinatorial procurement auction or a combinatorial reverse auction.

Various types of valuation can easily be expressed in combinatorial auctions, and therefore such auctions can be considered to be the most general types of market mechanisms.

Combinatorial auctions have found application in a variety of domains such as the auctioning of spectrum licenses (Bichler and Goeree, 2017), truck load transportation (Caplice and Sheffi, 2006), bus routes (Cantillon and Pesendorfer, 2006), or industrial procurement (Bichler *et al.*, 2006). Original designs had already been proposed by Rassenti *et al.* (1982) for the allocation of airport time slots. However, the design of combinatorial auctions is such that several types of complexity can arise.

- The auctioneer faces *computational complexity* when determining an optimal allocation. The winner determination problem in combinatorial auctions (see section 7.2) is an NP-hard problem (Garey and Johnson, 1972). In addition, in iterative auctions the auctioneer needs to derive ask prices, which is typically a hard computational problem as well.
- A bidder needs to determine his valuations for $2^m - 1$ bundles, where m is the number of items. We refer to this as *valuation complexity*. Without restrictions, this would require 1023 valuations to be elicited for an auction with only 10 items of interest. There are spectrum auctions with around 100 licenses to be sold; this can lead to the fact that, with a fully enumerative bid language, bidders can bid only on a small subset of packages. This is also referred to as the "missing bids problem" and can have a significant negative impact on efficiency.
- Even if the bidders knew their valuations perfectly, they would still need to decide how high to bid during the auction. The issues relate to when and how they reveal their preferences. We describe this as *strategic complexity*. Researchers have proposed different auction formats, which exhibit various degrees of strategic complexity for bidders.
- Finally, *communication complexity* describes the number of messages that need to be exchanged between the auctioneer and the bidders in order to determine the optimal allocation. It has been shown that the communication complexity in combinatorial auctions is exponential (Nisan and Segal, 2006).

We discuss different approaches to address these underlying complexities of combinatorial auctions in the following chapters. Combinatorial auctions can be considered as a very general class of auction markets allowing bidders to express general preferences. Unfortunately, we will see that there cannot be a truthful and ascending auction for bidders with general valuations. This result does not hold, however, if we allow for certain restrictions on the bidders' valuations. The remainder of Part II focuses on various types of multi-object auction formats and respective theoretical models.

5.4   Online and Dynamic Auction Design

The discussion of strategies in sequential sales has shown that equilibrium bidding strategies are not truthful in a repeated second-price auction. It is of interest to understand whether there are truthful auctions for sequential sales which are strategy-proof. This question has caused significant attention in recent years, because many important applications such as sponsored-search auctions or display ad auctions are dynamic. In computational complexity theory, dynamic problems are problems stated in terms of the changing input data. The term *dynamic mechanism design* refers to problems, where agents or objects arrive over time (Bergemann and Said, 2011) (see section 3.5.3).

There is a large number of possible model assumptions one can explore. Bidders or objects can arrive dynamically over time. In many articles bidders have unit demand to keep the analysis simpler, but in the field they often have multi-unit demand. If bidders arrive dynamically, consumption might happen immediately after arrival or within a certain time frame after arrival. There could be a fixed and publicly known supply of goods, or the supply is unknown. As always, goods can be homogeneous or heterogeneous. Payments might need to be determined at the time of the allocation or the environment can allow the determination of payments later in time.

In some problems the population of bidders changes over time, but their private types are fixed. This environment is often referred to as online auction design. In other problems the population of bidders is fixed but their private information changes over time. For example, an object loses some value if a bidder has to wait. Interestingly, Bergemann and Välimäki (2010) provided an individually rational and efficient mechanism that is ex post incentive-compatible in these dynamic environments. This can be seen as a generalization of the static VCG mechanism. Bergemann and Välimäki (2010) considered an infinite-horizon dynamic model in which participants observe a sequence of private signals over time and a sequence of decisions must be taken in response to these signals. The signals may depend on previously observed signals or decisions, and they are independent across agents. In the dynamic pivot mechanism each bidder's net utility is equal to her marginal contribution to the social welfare. Athey and Segal (2013) considered a setting similar to Bergemann and Välimäki (2010), but they were also interested in budget balance, i.e., a mechanism that does not require external subsidies. They generalized the expected externality mechanism of d'Aspremont and Gérard-Varet (1979) to a dynamic model. While some authors aim for welfare maximization, others focus on revenue maximization (Pai and Vohra, 2008). The literature in this field is still developing. In the following we will focus on static markets, where supply and demand are present at one point in time.

5.5   Summary

Multi-object auction markets present a broad field of study. General equilibrium theory has focused on competitive equilibria in multi-object markets, but some of the assumptions about the participants' preferences can be considered strong. For example, goods are typically assumed perfectly divisible and bidders are considered as price takers who cannot influence the prices of goods. Part II of this book studies auction markets for multiple indivisible objects, where bidders can influence the resulting prices with their bids. This means, as in our discussion of single-object auctions, we will use game-theoretical equilibrium solution concepts. In this chapter, we introduced a taxonomy of multi-object markets and described some wide-spread auction markets. Multi-unit auctions are designed for the sale of multiple homogeneous objects, while multi-item auctions refer to mechanisms for the sale of heterogeneous objects. Of course, there are also combinations, i.e., multi-unit and multi-item auctions. While multi-unit auctions typically assume weakly decreasing marginal values, combinatorial auctions allow bidders to express various types of preferences including substitutes and complements. They can be considered the most general types of multi-object auction markets and will be the focus of Part II of this book.

5.6   Comprehension Questions

1. Describe the different types of multi-unit auction format.
2. Under what circumstances is the multi-unit uniform-price English auction incentive-compatible?
3. Why does the simultaneous sale of multiple objects in parallel auctions not necessarily lead to efficient outcomes?
4. Which problems arise in the design of combinatorial auctions?

6 The Simultaneous Multi-Round Auction Format

Before we introduce various combinatorial auction formats, we will discuss a simple and widespread auction format for selling multiple objects, the simultaneous multi-round auction (SMRA). It allows bidders to bid on multiple objects simultaneously and win multiple objects. The SMRA was designed for the US Federal Communications Commission in the early 1990s, and it has been the standard auction format for selling spectrum worldwide for many years. It is also easy to implement and therefore a natural candidate for many multi-object markets. However, it can also lead to substantial strategic problems for bidders. We discuss several opportunities for profitable manipulation, which will provide a motivation for the alternative auction designs discussed in the remainder of this book.

6.1 SMRA Rules

The SMRA is an extension of the English auction to more than one item. All the items are sold at the same time, each with a price associated with it, and the bidders can bid on any number of items. The auction proceeds in rounds, which are specific periods of time in which all bidders can submit bids. After a round is closed the auctioneer discloses who is winning and the price of each item, which coincides with the highest bid submitted on the item. There are differences in the level of information revealed about other bidders' bids. Sometimes all bids are revealed after each round; sometimes only prices of the currently winning bids are published.

The bidding continues until no bidder is willing to raise the bid on any item further. In other words, if in one round no new bids are placed, the bidders receive the spectrum for which they hold the highest active bid; then the auction ends, with each bidder winning the blocks on which she has the highest bid, and paying this bid price for any item won.

The SMRA uses simple *activity rules*, which force bidders to be active from the start. Without such rules, bidders might be tempted to hide their demand and wait to see how prices develop before they start bidding. Monotonicity rules, where bidders cannot bid on more items in later rounds, are regularly used. This forces bidders to be active from the start. Activity rules can be considered to be a major innovation of this auction format. Typically, bidders get eligibility points assigned at the start of the auction; these define the maximum number of items or licenses for which they are allowed to bid.

If the number of items they win in a round and the new bids they submit require fewer eligibility points than in the last round then they lose points.

Apart from the activity rules, there are additional rules that matter. Auctioneers typically set *reserve prices* for each item, which describe prices below which an item will not be sold. They need to define *bid increments* and how bid increments might change throughout the auction. A bid increment is the minimum amount by which a bidder needs to increase his bid beyond the ask price in the next round. Sometimes, auctioneers allow for *bid withdrawals* and sometimes bidders get bid waivers, which allow bidders not to bid in a round without losing eligibility points. Auctioneers often set *bidding floors and caps*, which are limits on how much a winner in the auction needs to win as a minimum and how much she can win at most. These rules should avoid unwanted outcomes such as a monopoly after the auction or a winner who wins so little spectrum that it is not sufficient for viable business. In some SMRA versions bidders cannot submit jump bids but just accept clock prices for each item type, and this price rises as long as there is excess demand on an item.

The auction format is popular, because it is easy to implement and the rules are simple. If the valuations of all bidders are additive, the properties of a single-object ascending auction carry over. Unfortunately, this is rarely the case and bidders have often synergies for specific items in a package or their preferences are substitutes. Only if bidders have substitute preferences and bid straightforwardly does the SMRA terminate at a Walrasian equilibrium (Milgrom, 2000), i.e., an equilibrium with linear, i.e., item-level, prices. *Straightforward bidding* means that a bidder bids on bundles of items which together maximize the payoff at the current ask prices in each round. Milgrom (2000) also showed that with at least three bidders and at least one non-substitute valuation (for example a super-additive valuation for a package if items), no Walrasian equilibrium exists. A more in-depth theoretical discussion of environments and conditions where item-level ask prices allow for Walrasian equilibria and even satisfy strong game-theoretical solution concepts will be provided in chapter 8.

For now, let us discuss the types of manipulation that can often be found in the field. Bidders in an SMRA can benefit from prior information about others' valuations. Owing to the fact that SMRA does not satisfy a strong solution concept such as the VCG mechanism, bidders in high-stakes spectrum auctions spend a considerable time (months or even years) in estimating the valuations of other bidders and developing strategies.

6.2   Tactics in the SMRA

Despite the simplicity of its rules there can be considerable strategic complexity in the SMRA when there are synergies between items that cover adjacent geographic regions or between items that are linked in other ways. Bidders who compete aggressively for a certain combination of items risk being exposed when they end up winning an inferior subset at high prices. When bidders rationally anticipate this *exposure problem*, competition will be suppressed with adverse consequences for the auction's performance. A number of laboratory experiments document the negative impact of the exposure problem on the performance of the SMRA (Brunner *et al.*, 2010; Goeree and Lien, 2016; Kagel *et al.*, 2010; Kwasnica *et al.*, 2005).

Other strategic challenges are due to the activity rules. The monotonicity rule does not allow bidders to submit bids on more items than in the previous round. Sometimes, a less preferred alternative can have more blocks, which can lead to inefficiencies in cases where a bidder is outbid on the preferred allocation. These activity rules lead to *eligibility management* and the *parking* of eligibility points in less desirable blocks, which has been observed in the context of spectrum auctions (Porter and Smith, 2006). Sometimes a bidder might also prefer to bid on a bundle with a higher number of eligibility points rather than the preferred bundle of items, in order to have the option to return to it later.

The SMRA also allows for various forms of *signaling and tacit collusion*. Jump bidding is usually seen as a strategy to signal strength and preferences and to post threats. Sometimes even the standing bidder will increase his winning bid for the same purpose. However, there are more reasons for jump bids. In later rounds, jump bids are used to avoid ties (Boergers and Dustmann, 2003). *Retaliatory bids* are bids submitted on items desired by rivals to force them not to bid on the items the bidder desires. For example, if a bidder is interested in block x and another bidder is interested in items x and y, the first bidder can drive up the price of y, signaling that the second bidder should cease bidding on x. Sometimes bidders might also not signal interest in an item, as others could take advantage of this interest to park and maintain their own eligibility at no cost because they know they will be overbid (Salant, 1997).

Also, *budget bluffing* is a well known tactic (Porter and Smith, 2006). Bidders typically track the bid exposure of other bidders. The bid exposure is the sum of a bidder's previous-round provisionally winning bids plus the bidder's new bids in the present round. This can provide an indication of a competitor's potential budget (Bulow *et al.*, 2009). Bidders can bid above their budget, knowing that they will be outbid on some items, in order to fool rivals into believing their budget is larger than it is. Strategies like this lead to a complex decision situation for bidders. Furthermore, *demand reduction* is an issue. Demand reduction can easily occur in the presence of budget constraints and no complementarities, as the following example illustrates.

Example 6.2.1 Suppose that there are two bidders (1 and 2) and two items. We assume complete information, where bidder 1 has a valuation of $v_1 = 10$ for each item and bidder 2 has a valuation of $v_2 = 11$ for each item. Bidder 1 has a binding budget constraint of $w_1 = 10$. When bidder 1 reduces her demand to one item, bidder 2 has an incentive to reduce his demand as well. If he does not reduce his demand, bidder 1 could drive up the price to 10 on the first item until bidder 2 is overbid, and then drive up the price on the second item. This would leave bidder 2 with a payoff of $11 - 10 = 1$ for each of the two items. If bidder 2 reduced his demand to a price of zero and bidder 1 agreed, they would both achieve a payoff of 10 or 11, respectively.

Overall budget constraints are often ignored and are typically considered to be outside quasi-linear mechanism design, but they often matter in the field. Let's assume a spectrum sale with only three items and two bidders. Bidder 1 wants to win all three items. If bidder 2 has a budget limit of w and is willing to spend the whole budget even on a single item, he could drive up the prices of all three items to w, until he gets overbid. In order for bidder 1 to win all three items she would have to invest three times the budget of bidder 2. Note that in a combinatorial auction it would be sufficient for a bidder to submit a bundle bid on all three items, which amounts to $w + \epsilon$, in order to win all three items. Weak bidders can drive up prices on items which are of interest to their rivals in order to bind the rivals' budget and have less competition on items they prefer. This is sometimes referred to as *budget binding*. Brusco and Lopomo (2009) provided a game-theoretical analysis considering complementarities and budget constraints.

In summary, the following tactical considerations typically come into play when bidders prepare for an SMRA:

- tactics to deal with the exposure problem
- eligibility management
- signaling and tacit collusion
- budget bluffing
- demand reduction
- budget binding

Bidders need to have a good understanding of their rivals' preferences and their financial strength so that they can find a best response to opposing strategies. As a consequence, telecom operators typically spend months or even years preparing for high-stakes spectrum auctions using SMRA.

6.3   Strategic Situations in SMRA

Equilibrium strategies in SMRA depend heavily on the information that bidders have about competitors and on whether their valuations include substitutes or complements. In the field, bidders often have specific beliefs about the valuations of other bidders and the type distributions are asymmetric. These information sets can lead to strategies which are quite different from those assuming symmetry of the bidders and a common prior distribution.

We look at two specific spectrum auctions in Germany as examples to illustrate the strategic challenges that bidders can face in such auctions. We do not aim for a precise description of the auctions, and so we simplify the environment at the expense of the accuracy of our description. While we cannot go into every detail and there might be different views about these auctions, the discussion should provide a better understanding about strategic challenges in such auctions in the field. The auction in 2015 can be compared to a war of attrition game, while the auction in 2010 is closer to a traditional English auction. A classic example of a war of attrition is an all-pay auction, where each agent makes a bid on an item and the highest bidder wins but each agent pays his bid. This means also that the losing bidders accumulate more cost the longer the auction takes. In a single-object English auction only the winner pays. The discussion below draws on Cramton and Ockenfels (2016), which provides an excellent summary of a German spectrum auction in 2010 and, in particular, on the model of Bichler *et al.*

(2017a), who focused on an auction in 2015. The analysis of the strategic challenges in these two auctions should motivate the search for alternative auction formats which are efficient and have simple truthful strategies for bidders; this will be the goal of the subsequent discussion of theoretical models in Part II.

6.3.1   War of Attrition

In the German spectrum auction in 2015, the regulator offered spectrum for mobile use in four different bands: 700, 900, 1800, and 1500 MHz. Spectrum in the 700, 900, and 1800 MHz band was offered in 2×5 MHz paired blocks (frequency division duplex (FDD) spectrum), whereas spectrum in the 1500 MHz band was offered in 1×5 MHz (time division duplex (TDD) spectrum) blocks. There were six licenses in the 700 Mhz band, seven licenses in the 900 MHz band, and 10 licenses in the 1800 MHz band. We ignore the 1500 MHz band in the following as it was of much less value; low-frequency and FDD bands can generally be considered more valuable for all bidders in the auction. There were three bidders (Telefónica, Telekom, and Vodafone), who were already present in the market. All three bidders were considered strong international players, but there was uncertainty about how much Telefónica would be willing to invest in the German market and whether they would be willing to go as high as their competitors, for various reasons. Note that the German auction formats reveal information about all bids to the bidders after each round. Typically, implementations of the SMRA in other countries reveal information only about winning bids to the bidders after each round.

Of course, the competitors in such a market can always try to split the licenses in a fair manner and have the auction end after a few rounds. Such strategic demand reduction happened in the German spectrum auction in 1999, where Telekom and Mannesmann competed for 10 spectrum licenses. Mannesmann bid EUR 18.18 million on blocks 1–5 and EUR 20 million on blocks 6–10. This was an acceptable outcome for both bidders, and the auction closed after just two rounds (Grimm *et al.*, 2003). However, often bidders have different views about how a fair split of the spectrum licenses would look, a conflict of interest arises and prices go up. Let's introduce a simple two-stage model of these auctions in which the possibility of demand reduction plays an important role. In the first stage of this two-stage model, bidders send signals about acceptable packages. If these acceptable packages lead to a feasible solution without excess demand then the auction will end. The second stage can be seen as a game where bidders try to resolve the conflict of interest in cases where they cannot agree on an allocation.

6.3.1.1   A Brief Summary of the Auction

In the auction in 2015, the first 30 rounds can be seen as the first stage of our two-stage model. All bidders started out with high demands signaling interest in a significant part of the spectrum licenses but reduced their demand quickly. With specific jump bids and knowledge of the position of the licenses in a band the bidders communicated alternative packages of interest. For example, Telekom reduced demand to 233; we use a 3-tuple as a shorthand describing how many licenses the package included in the 700 MHz, 900 MHz, and 1800 MHz bands, respectively. In round 19, after an initial bid of 234, Telefónica reduced demand from 225 to 224 in round 21. This was followed by Vodafone, who originally signaled 234 but eventually reduced to 225 in round 30. In total, the demand of the three bidders after round 20 was six licenses in the 800 MHz band, seven licenses in the 900 MHz band, and 12 licenses in the 1800 MHz band. This meant that there the excess demand was only two licenses in the 1800 MHz band, and the auction would have ended if two bidders had reduced their demand by one more license. The total revenue of the regulator was less than €2 billion at this point.

However, none of the bidders wanted to give up an additional license in the 1800 band and there was a conflict of interests among the bidders after significant demand reductions in the first 30 rounds. Therefore, the bidders tried to resolve the conflict of interest in the second stage, in which all three bidders signaled strength in order to convince the opponents to give in and reduce another block. These signals were jump bids describing the desired package, sometimes geared towards a specific opponent. For example, Telefónica temporarily increased demand from 224 to 225 in rounds 58 and 59, which could be interpreted as a threat. In round 74, Vodafone went back from 225 to 234, which might have indicated that, if no agreement could be reached, it would go back to its original goal of 234. Telekom also increased demand again to 234 in round 76, which was mirrored by Telefónica in round 77, who also bid on 234. After a few rounds all bidders reduced demand again, but the excess demand of two licenses in the 1800 MHz band could not be resolved. In round 84, Telefónica reduced to 223 so that there was only one license of excess demand in the 1800 MHz band. However, neither of the other two bidders followed, and the auction did not end.

There were several rounds of demand inflation and demand reduction subsequently, which led to strong price increases in the 1800 MHz band, and also in the 900 MHz band. For example, in round 134 Telekom bid on eight blocks in the 1800 MHz band, before Vodafone started bidding aggressively on four blocks in the 700 MHz band in round 155. The prices in the 700 MHz band were at the level of the reserve prices until then, and the fact that Vodafone even jeopardized a low-price outcome in this band was probably seen as an aggressive signal of strength. Eventually, in round 174 Telefónica reduced to 222 and the auction closed soon after in round 181, after some more rounds of bidding in the 1500 MHz band. The rules and results of the individual auction rounds can be found at www.bundesnetzagentur.de.

6.3.1.2 A Model with Costly Signals

Let us now introduce a *signaling game* with costly signals (each new bid incurs a cost increment to the bidder) as a simple model. A signaling game is a sequential Bayesian game (see section 2.2) with two agents, the sender and the receiver. The sender has a certain type, θ, which is given by "nature". The sender observes her own type while the receiver does not know the type of the sender. On the basis of her knowledge of her own type, the sender chooses to send a message signaling her type. The receiver observes the message but not necessarily the true type of the sender; he knows that the sender might not signal her true type. Then the receiver chooses an action, which determines the payoffs. The two agents receive payoffs dependent on the sender's type and the action chosen by the receiver. Such a model can be used to characterize the strategic difficulties in the auction in 2015 and in 2010 and to highlight their differences.

Jump bids were not cost-free in this auction, where every bidder needed spectrum in every band. The more rounds there were, the more expensive the auction became to all bidders, similarly to a war of attrition. Some rounds with jumps even came at a cost of more than EUR 200 million to a bidder. While this is a significant amount of money, the net present values of packages of licenses can be in the billions. Note that licenses are granted for a period of 15 years. The jump bids in the auction could be seen as a signal of strength, with the purpose of convincing opponents to reduce the demand for another license. They showed that a bidder was willing to accept a significant difference in the prices for the licenses (if the auction ended sooner than expected) and indicated that she was willing to raise prices even higher.

In the model, we consider a simpler band plan with only a single band and five homogeneous spectrum licenses. Bidders are interested in acquiring one or two licenses, and we assume they have a strictly higher value or budget for two licenses than for one license. There are three bidders in this market and we index them with $i = 1, 2, 3$. For simplicity, the value of m licenses is taken to be mv_i for bidder i, i.e., there are no complementary valuations. The bidders have common beliefs about the ranking of bidders' valuations, but they do not know the exact valuation of the players. Bidder 3 plays a pivotal role and has two possible types, v_{3s} (strong) and v_{3w} (weak) with $v_{3s} > v_{3w}$, and a probability $0 < p = \Pr\{V_3 = v_{3s}\} < 1$ for the strong type. The values of all three bidders can be rank ordered as $v_1 > v_{3s} > v_2 > v_{3w}$, which is common knowledge. Suppose that bidder 1 is strong enough to win two licenses with certainty, so that we can focus on the strategies of bidders 2 and 3 to win either two licenses (a "win" action, w) or one license only (an "agree" action a). Telefónica was widely considered the weaker player, but there was significant uncertainty about the budget Telefónica would want to invest in the auction. Telefónica can be considered as bidder 3 in our model.

If one bidder, i, wants to win (she chooses action w_i), then either she or the opponent will win one license. We consider the valuations to be budgets and assume that each bidder will bid up to his budget for two licenses if he chooses w_i. Action a_i means that he only bids on one license. The full dynamic Bayesian game is illustrated in figure 6.1; N, "nature", decides whether bidder 3 has a strong type, with probability p, or a weak type with probability $1 - p$. The leaf nodes describe the payoffs of both bidders if they follow a particular strategy. Bidder 2 observes the action of bidder 1 (e.g., she bids for two licenses) and needs to decide whether he agrees to win one license or wants to win two licenses himself.

Let's analyze the strategies of the two bidders and how they depend on their valuations and the probability p. Bidder 3 can select one of the two actions w_3 or a_3. If bidder 3 plays a *separating strategy*, with w_3 if she has a strong type and a_3 if she has a weak type, then prices would not rise in the case of a weak type v_{3w} and bidder 3 could achieve a payoff of v_{3w} by winning one license with certainty (lowest left branch). In this case, bidder 3 is satisfied with one license and leaves two licenses to bidder 2. Thus, there is no competition and zero prices. In cases where both bidders agree, we assume that the

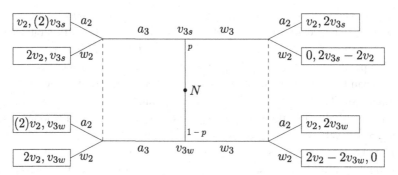

Figure 6.1 Signaling game with five licenses.

one with the higher value gets two licenses (in the figure this is indicated by "(2)") at a price of zero. If bidder 3 has a strong type v_{3s} then she would bid on two licenses and actually win this package (right uppermost branch). Her payoff depends on bidder 2 and whether he agrees or also wants to win two licenses. Again, we assume that bidder 2 bids up to his valuation $2v_2$ for two licenses, i.e., he chooses action w_2. Therefore, the payoff of bidder 2 is 0 if he tries to win and bidder 3 has a strong type. In this model, there does not exist a *separating equilibrium*, because if only the strong bidder shows strength, bidder 2 will want to "agree" and, if that is the case, the weak bidder 3 will also want to choose "win".

Bidder 3 can play a *pooling strategy* of w_3 if she bids for two licenses no matter whether she has a strong or a weak type (the right-hand branches). If bidder 2 believes that there is a high probability, p, that bidder 3 has a strong type (v_{3s}), then bidder 2 would play a_2; if he thinks p is low, and $2v_2 - 2v_3 > v_2$, he would rather play to win (action w_2). Whether bidder 2 agrees or tries to win depends on his valuations but also heavily on p. Actually, there exists a *pooling equilibrium* with both types of bidder 3 playing "win" if the probability that bidder 3 is a strong type is large enough. This can be seen as follows. If both types of bidder 3 choose "win" then bidder 2 will "agree" if and only if

$$p(v_2 - 0) + (1 - p)(v_2 - 2v_2 + 2v_{3w}) \geq 0$$

which reduces to

$$(1 - 2p)v_2 \leq 2(1 - p)v_{3w}$$

If bidder 2 "agrees" in this information set then both types of bidder 3 will want to "win". Thus, a pooling equilibrium exists if p is relatively large or if the value of the weak bidder 3 is close to the value of bidder 2. There are also equilibria with mixed strategies in this game which, like the pooling equilibrium, can explain the results.

In the auction in 2015, Telefónica submitted jump bids until very late in the auction to influence the beliefs that others had about p. Vodafone and Telekom (bidder 2 in the model) responded with signals to show Telefónica that they considered themselves stronger. In the initial rounds of an auction, the cost of jump bids is low compared with the net present values. As the number of rounds increases, however, the total cost and the cost of additional jump bids becomes significant. As a consequence, such signals become more credible. Since companies have already invested significant amounts of money in earlier stages of the auction, there can be a tendency to stay in the game and send costly signals (jump bids) in order to win the most desired package, much as in a war of attrition.

6.3.2   English Auction vs. War of Attrition

In the 2015 auction discussed above, one could assume that each of the three bidders needs spectrum in each band. This was not the case in the German auction in 2010, however. E-Plus was the smallest service provider, and they had competively low prices in the end consumer market but also a lower quality of service compared with other carriers. The company could either win significant spectrum to improve the quality of its network or keep its position as a low-cost carrier with no spectrum in the valuable 800 MHz band and a lower quality of service compared with its competitors. This provided significant strategic leverage in the auction, making it closer to an English auction, where only the winner pays. In the following, we describe this 2010 auction and then highlight the differences from the 2015 auction.

6.3.2.1   A Brief Summary of the 2010 Auction

In the 2010 auction the German regulator sold 41 spectrum licenses in four bands. These included six licenses in the valuable 800 MHz band, five licenses in the 1800 MHz band, six licenses in the 2 GHz band, and 14 licenses in the 2.6 GHz band. The competitive situation in 2010 was different from that in 2015 as there were four bidders, two larger bidders (Telekom and Vodafone) and two smaller competitors, Telefónica and E-Plus, with market shares of approximately 19% and 17%, respectively. (Telefónica and E-Plus merged before the 2015 auction.) It was expected that Telekom and Vodafone would both get two licenses, which was also the maximum they were allowed to win. So the key question was whether Telefónica and E-Plus would both win one of the remaining licenses or whether E-Plus would go away with no license in the 800 MHz band. In this way E-Plus would remain the weakest player in the German market, but its position was viable assuming that it got some spectrum in the 2.6 GHz band.

E-Plus indicated in the early rounds that it wanted to win one license in the 800 MHz band, while Telefónica showed that it wanted two licenses in the 800 MHz band. In rounds 59 and 60 E-Plus submitted substantial jump bids of EUR 335 million. They continued to bid aggressively in the 800 MHz band until the total revenue increased from less than EUR 500 million to almost EUR 3 billion. In round 123 Telefónica reduced demand from two licenses to one license in the 800 MHz band and the bidding was mainly focused on the 1800 MHz and the 2.6 GHz bands. In round 199 Telefónica came back and bid aggressively for two lots in the 800 MHz band again until eventually E-Plus stopped bidding in this band in round 222. However, the fact that it had dropped out of the 800 MHz band completely led to a substantial difference in the payments, so that Telefónica, Telekom, and Vodafone, but not E-Plus, had to bear the high prices in the 800 MHz band.

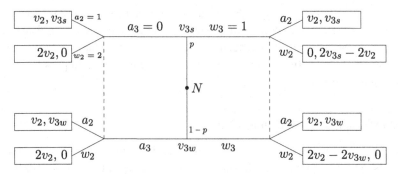

Figure 6.2 Signaling game with four licenses.

6.3.2.2   A Model with (Potentially) Costless Signals

We again use a signaling game similar to that in figure 6.1, to illustrate the strategic situation in the 2010 auction. We will slightly modify the setup to account for the differences. Let's assume the auction has four licenses and that it models the 800 MHz band. Again, assume that bidder 1 has a high enough budget that she will certainly win two licenses. Bidder 1 is a proxy for Telekom and Vodafone in the German auction in 2010 auction, as it was expected ex ante that they would each win what they wanted in the 800 MHz band.

Therefore, we can again focus on the competition of bidders 2 and 3 for the two remaining licenses, i.e., Telefónica and E-Plus in the 2010 auction. The main difference from the signaling game described in section 6.3.1.2 is that bidder 3 does not have to bear the cost of high prices when she is overbid. Therefore, the setting leads to different payoffs, which are summarized in figure 6.2. Now action a_2 means that bidder 2 agrees to win a single license only, while a_3 means that bidder 3 agrees to win no license. Similarly, w_2 means that bidder 2 wants to win both licenses and w_3 means that bidder 3 wants to win one license.

If both bidders agree, we assume that both get one license at a price of zero. If bidder 3 agrees and bidder 2 wants to win then bidder 2 gets both licenses at a price of zero. Note that, for bidder 3, playing w_3 dominates a_3. No matter how bidder 2 responds, bidder 3's payoff when playing w_3 is either equal to or higher than that obtained by playing a_3 (comparing the payoffs of bidder 3 on the left-hand side and the right-hand side of figure 6.2). If bidder 2 assumes that bidder 3 is trying to win one unit (w_3) then he will get a payoff of v_2 if he agrees. If bidder 2 is trying to win two units then either he might drive up the prices until his valuation and therefore have zero profit or he gets a profit of $2v_2 - 2v_{3w}$. Whether he chooses w_2 depends on p and on whether $v_2 > 2v_2 - 2v_{3w}$.

6.4   Summary

The SMRA is a simple auction format. Different versions of this format are found not only in spectrum sales. Electronic procurement auctions often provide the possibility to bid for multiple objects in parallel. Note that the level of transparency varies for different implementations. The auction design used in the German spectrum auctions described in this chapter reveals all information about all bids to the bidders. In other countries, only the standing bid on each item is revealed after each round and sometimes not even the identity of the standing bidder on an item is known. While activity rules are similar in spectrum auctions, there is a wider variety of rules in procurement. Clearly, these differences have an impact on the types of manipulation possible in an auction.

The analysis of the German spectrum auctions with their high level of transparency is an interesting case study of the strategic challenges in such auctions. The resulting prices do not necessarily reflect the valuations of bidders and they are a result of the various strategies and signals sent in the auction. The process resembles a bargaining situation where bidders haggle over the final allocation. Interestingly, in some situations such as the German auction in 2010, the auction rules and the specific preferences and strength of the bidders can induce (almost) dominant bidding strategies for some bidders. The exposure problem is arguably a central strategic challenge for bidders in many multi-object auctions, and it can lead to substantial inefficiencies. While we have discussed the problem only briefly in this chapter, we will focus on combinatorial auctions as a way to eliminate the exposure problem in subsequent chapters.

6.5   Comprehension Questions

1. What are the consequences of the exposure problem in the SMRA for bidding strategies and outcomes?
2. Which activity rules are being used in the SMRA for spectrum sales?
3. Which types of manipulation have been observed in the SMRA?
4. Explain the analogy of the two German spectrum auctions with an English auction and a war of attrition, respectively.

7 Sealed-Bid Multi-Object Auctions

The strategic complexity of bidding in simultaneous auctions such as the SMRA has led to the development of combinatorial auctions. They allow bidders to express super- and subadditive valuations, which is not the case in SMRA. We first focus on sealed-bid combinatorial auction designs, before we discuss iterative auctions in the next chapter. There are two important design parameters for sealed-bid combinatorial auctions: the bid language and the payment rule. First, we discuss generic bid languages as they are widely used in the literature and the resulting allocation or winner determination problem. Then we discuss payment rules such as those used in the Vickrey–Clarke–Groves (VCG) mechanism and those used to compute bidder-optimal core payments. The latter were designed to address some of the problems in the VCG mechanism. Finally, we introduce examples of compact bid languages for specific domains. Such bid languages make additional assumptions on the shape of the value or cost functions, but they allow bidders to express their preferences with a low number of parameters, which is typically important for generic bid languages.

7.1 Generic Bid Languages

A bid in an auction is an expression of the bidder's willingness to pay particular monetary amounts for various outcomes. Bidders formulate bids according to their private preferences and bidding strategies. A *bid language* defines the way (the format of the communicated messages and the interpretation rules) in which bidders are allowed to formulate their bids.

In combinatorial auctions every auction outcome corresponds to a particular allocation. From the point of view of a particular bidder, the auction outcome is defined by the set of items allocated to her and the monetary amount she has to pay for it. Therefore, the most direct way of bid formulation is to let each bidder attach a bid price to each possible bundle. This allows a bidder to express any kind of preference, but in the worst case it requires an exponential number ($2^m - 1$) of bundles to be evaluated and monitored by every bidder and the same amount of messages to be communicated to the auctioneer. Although in many cases not every possible combination of items has a positive value for every bidder, the number of interesting bundles can quickly become overwhelming.

Bid languages for combinatorial auctions are typically built from *atomic bids* and *logical rules* that allow several atomic bids either to win simultaneously or not.

Definition 7.1.1 (Bundle)   A *bundle* (or *package*) S is a subset of the item set $\mathcal{K}$ ($S \subseteq \mathcal{K}$).

The empty set ($|S| = 0$), single-item sets ($|S| = 1$) and all-items set ($S = \mathcal{K}$) are all considered bundles.

Definition 7.1.2 (Atomic bid)   An *atomic bid* $b_i(S)$ is a tuple consisting of a bundle S and a bid price $p_i(S)$ submitted by the given bidder i with $b_i(S) = \{S, p_i(S)\}$.

The two most popular and intuitive bid languages are *exclusive-OR* (XOR) and *additive-OR* (OR).

Definition 7.1.3 (XOR bid language)   The bid language *exclusive-OR* (XOR) allows bidders to submit multiple atomic bids. For each bidder at most one of her atomic bids can win. This means that she either gets *all* items contained in the bundle listed in *exactly one* of her atomic bids or she gets nothing. By submitting her atomic bids, the bidder expresses her willingness to pay at most the amount specified in her winning atomic bid (if any).

Definition 7.1.4 (OR bid language)   The bid language *additive-OR* (OR) allows bidders to submit multiple atomic bids. For each bidder any non-intersecting combination of her atomic bids can win. This means that the bidder either gets *all* items contained in the bundles listed in *some non-intersecting set* of her atomic bids or she gets nothing. By submitting her atomic bids, the bidder expresses her willingness to pay at most the sum of the amounts specified in her winning atomic bids (if any).

The XOR bid language lets each bidder define a bid price for each possible combination that she can win, exactly as described above. From this point of view, it can be considered the most powerful of all possible bid languages for combinatorial auctions (CAs). However, it suffers from the exponential number of bundles that have to be evaluated. For example, in some spectrum auctions there have been 100 licenses for sale; thus, without considering spectrum caps imposed on the bidders, in the worst case 2^{100} packages could be enumerated, which is a number of order 1.267×10^{30}. As a comparison, 3×10^{23} is an estimate of the number of stars in the observable universe. It is clear that bidders interested in many licenses can specify only a small proportion of their bids of interest. Note that the winner determination problem for auctions with a fully expressive XOR bid language treats missing package bids as if a bidder had no value for the package. Laboratory experiments have shown that this "missing bids problem" can itself lead to substantial efficiency losses, even with the much lower number of possible packages compared with SMRA, where bids can be submitted only on individual items (Bichler *et al.*, 2013a).

In a simultaneous multi-round auction the bids are additive (corresponding to the OR bid language) and, for each package, there is an estimate of the valuations for this package which is just the sum of the bids on the individual items. This allows for higher efficiency in larger markets than some combinatorial auction designs, even though bidders cannot express their complementarities without the risk of winning only parts of a bundle of interest and having to pay more than this subset of items is worth to the bidder. Combinatorial auction designs therefore face a natural tradeoff between the efficiency gains of allowing bids on packages and the efficiency losses due to missing bids.

Consequently, auction designers try to use information about the structure of the bidders' valuations to design *compact bid languages*, which still allow bidders to represent their preferences but with a low number of parameters. The OR bid language is sufficient if no subadditive valuations exist. Unfortunately, this is often not the case, e.g., in the presence of budget restrictions (if the bidder cannot afford every combination of bundles for which she bid).

Alternatively, the OR* bid language has been proposed; thus allows bids to be submitted on dummy items. These items will have no intrinsic value to any of the bidders, but they will be used to express constraints. Suppose that there are two items A and B and a dummy item D. A bidder can now submit an OR bid on AD and BD, which prevents her from winning the package AB. In this way bidders need to bid for fewer packages than in an OR bid language and at the same time they avoid situations where they win multiple packages but are only interested in one of them. For more information on generic bid languages the reader is referred to Nisan (2006) and Boutilier and Hoos (2001). Often the number of packages that bidders need to specify is still not practical. For example, in a combinatorial auction with an XOR bid language and only 10 items and six units of each item, a bidder could already specify more than 282 million bids. Domain-specific compact bid languages leverage domain knowledge about utility functions and they can provide a remedy for this combinatorial explosion (see section 7.5).

7.2   The Winner Determination Problem

Let's now focus on the winner determination problem (WDP) in combinatorial auctions (Lehmann *et al.*, 2006; Rothkopf *et al.*, 1998; Sandholm, 2006). It is a good example of the types of optimization problem that one encounters in various multi-object auctions with different bid languages. This and subsequent sections draw on linear and integer programming techniques and we assume a basic familiarity with these topics (see the appendices).

Example 7.2.1   The following example with four bids and three items illustrates a simple procurement application (see table 7.1). The buying organization needs different quantities of grain in different production sites. In this case, the buyer aggregates demand for multiple production sites, as suppliers might be able to provide better prices owing to reduced production and transportation costs. Suppliers bid on subsets of the locations and each subset has a bundle price. We assume that suppliers provide the entire quantity for an item or location as an example of a single-unit combinatorial auction. In the case when bidders can provide subsets of the quantity demanded, e.g., only 500 t of grain for Berlin, this would become a multi-unit combinatorial auction.

Table 7.1 Example with bundle bids

Items	Bids			
	B1	B2	B3	B4
1000 t grain in Berlin	1	0	1	1
800 t grain in Munich	0	1	1	1
800 t grain in Vienna	1	1	1	0
Bid price (in thousands)	$150	$125	$300	$125

A forward or sales auction as the term is used throughout the book will maximize revenue rather than minimize costs. This will transform the winner determination problem from a weighted-set covering problem (in procurement) to a weighted-set packing problem (in sales), which is discussed below. In both cases we talk about the *winner determination problem* (WDP) or alternatively the *combinatorial allocation problem* (CAP).

Let's briefly recap the notation. Remember that we denote a set of items as $\mathcal{K} = \{1, \ldots, m\}$ and index it with k, and we denote a set of bidders as $\mathcal{I} = \{1, \ldots, n\}$ and use the index i for private valuations $v_i(S) \geq 0$ of bundles $S \subseteq \mathcal{K}$ with price $p_i(S)$. This means that each bidder i has a valuation function $v_i : 2^{\mathcal{K}} \rightarrow \mathbb{R}_0^+$ that attaches a value $v_i(S)$ to any bundle $S \subseteq \mathcal{K}$. In addition, we assume the bidder values $v_i(S)$ to be independent and private (i.e., known only to the bidder) and the bidder's utility function to be quasi-linear (i.e., the payoff of a bidder $\pi_i(S) = v_i(S) - p_i(S)$) with free disposal (i.e., if $S \subset T$ then $v_i(S) \leq v_i(T)$).

The WDP in a single-unit combinatorial sales auction can be formulated as a binary program using the decision variables $x_i(S)$ which indicate whether the bid of the bidder i for the bundle S is part of the allocation:

$$\max_{x_i(S)} \sum_{S \subseteq \mathcal{K}} \sum_{i \in \mathcal{I}} x_i(S) v_i(S) \qquad \text{(WDP)}$$

$$\text{s.t.} \quad \sum_{S \subseteq \mathcal{K}} x_i(S) \leq 1 \qquad \forall i \in \mathcal{I}$$

$$\sum_{S:k \in S} \sum_{i \in \mathcal{I}} x_i(S) \leq 1 \qquad \forall k \in \mathcal{K}$$

$$x_i(S) \in \{0, 1\} \qquad \forall i, S$$

In the objective function the total sum of valuations or welfare is maximized. Here, we assume that we have access to the true valuations of bidders $v_i(S)$ rather than only the bids $b_i(S)$. The first set of constraints guarantees that any bidder can win at most one bundle, which is only relevant for the XOR bid language. Without this constraint bidders can win multiple bundles, which is referred to as an OR bid language. This problem is equivalent to the well-known weighted-set packing problem. The second set of constraints ensures that an item is allocated to at most one bidder.

As indicated, the WDP of a *single-unit combinatorial procurement* or *reverse auction* (the WDPR) is a version of the set-covering problem, which is the minimization version of the set-packing problem. The WDP of the *multi-unit combinatorial procurement auction* (the WDPMR), where bidders can specify the quantities $c_{i,k}(S)$ offered of each item $k \in \mathcal{K}$, and d_k is the demand of the buyer on this item, can be modeled as a multi-dimensional knapsack problem:

$$\min_{x_i(S)} \sum_{S \subseteq \mathcal{K}} \sum_{i \in \mathcal{I}} v_i(S) x_i(S) \qquad \text{(WDPMR)}$$

$$\text{s.t.} \quad \sum_{S \subseteq \mathcal{K}} x_i(S) \leq 1 \qquad \forall i \in \mathcal{I}$$

$$\sum_{S:k \in S} \sum_{i \in \mathcal{I}} c_{i,k}(S) x_i(S) \geq d_k \qquad \forall k \in \mathcal{K}$$

$$x_i(S) \in \{0, 1\} \qquad \forall i, S$$

It has actually been shown that the WDP (with an OR bid language) is NP-complete (see Appendix B.1).

Theorem 7.2.1 (Rothkopf *et al.*, 1998) *The decision version of the WDP with an OR bid language is NP-complete even if restricted to instances where every bid has a value equal to* 1 *and every bidder bids only on subsets of size of at most* 3.

The well-known NP-complete set packing problem can be reduced to the WDP with an OR bid language in polynomial time. The same holds for the WDP with an XOR bid language, even when bidders bid only on subsets of size of at most 2. The three-dimensional matching problem has been reduced to the WDP with an XOR bid language. A comprehensive overview of complexity results for different version of the WDP is provided in Lehmann *et al.* (2006).

There are, however, tractable cases of the WDP if we restrict bids or valuations in a way that gives the bids a structure that allows for efficient solution methods. For example, if the *goods are substitute* property (aka *gross substitutes* in definition 8.3.2 below) holds then this leads to integral solutions of the LP-relaxation of the WDP. Note that the substitute condition allows for additive valuations but not for complements or super-additive valuations. This will play a role when we compute ask prices in ascending combinatorial auctions, in chapter 8.

A good overview of other restrictions on the valuations that lead to tractable cases of the WDP was provided by Mueller (2006). Unfortunately, most of these restrictions are so severe that auctioneers cannot rely on them in most applications of combinatorial auctions. Apart from the theoretical complexity analysis, extensive analyses of the empirical hardness of the WDP (Leyton-Brown *et al.*, 2009) illustrate that satisfactory performances can be obtained for the problem sizes and structures occurring in practice. Note that problem sizes with up to a dozen bidders and items only, as often found in procurement practice, can typically be solved in seconds. In transportation auctions with hundreds of lanes, the computational complexity might defy exact optimal solutions. However, exact solutions to the WDP have been computed in spectrum auctions worldwide.

7.3   Payment Rules

Much as in single-item auctions, one can use a pay-as-bid rule in a first-price sealed-bid combinatorial auction but also implement a Vickrey–Clarke–Groves (VCG) mechanism. The latter is sometimes referred to as a *generalized Vickrey auction*. This auction format exhibits a dominant-strategy equilibrium, but it faces a few problems which do not appear in single-item auctions. Most notably, the outcome of a VCG auction might not be in the core (see section 7.3.2.1), and losing bidders could make themselves better off together with the auctioneer. Bidder-optimal core-selecting payment rules have been designed to address this problem. In this section we discuss the computation of pay-as-bid, VCG, and bidder-optimal core-selecting payment rules before we elaborate on equilibrium strategies.

7.3.1   Pay-as-Bid Payment Rules

Arguably, the most widely used combinatorial auction design in applications is the first-price sealed-bid combinatorial auction. Published examples of such auctions in procurement include transportation auctions, industrial procurement, the auctioning of bus routes in London, or auctions for food provisioning in schools. Strategically, pay-as-bid payment rules are difficult because bidders need to decide not only which packages they want to bid for, but also by how much to shade their bids. Unfortunately, the derivation of Bayesian–Nash equilibria similar to those for single-item auctions has proved to be very tedious. So far, no closed-form equilibrium strategy for first-price sealed-bid combinatorial auctions with general valuations exists. We discuss equilibrium strategies further in section 7.4.

7.3.2   Vickrey–Clarke–Groves Payment Rules

The Vickrey–Clarke–Groves principle introduced in section 3.4.2 can easily be applied to combinatorial auctions. The winners are also determined by the WDP. The VCG payments of the winners are then computed as

$$p_i^{VCG} = v_i(x^*) - [w(\mathcal{I}) - w(\mathcal{I}_{-i})]$$

Here p_i^{VCG} is the Vickrey price, while $w(\mathcal{I})$ is the objective value to the WDP of the valuations of all bidders, and $w(\mathcal{I}_{-i})$ is the objective value to the WDP of all bidders except the winning bidder i. We use the valuation $v_i(x^*)$ in the optimal allocation x^* rather than the bid, because we expect the bidder to reveal her valuation truthfully in a direct revelation mechanism. In a combinatorial auction, this means that a bidder needs to submit bids on all possible bundles, the number of such bids being exponential in the number of items. Each winning bidder receives a Vickrey payment, which is the amount that she has contributed to increasing the total value of the auctioneer.

Example 7.3.1   Let's take as an example two items A and B which are to be sold in a combinatorial auction. The bids of bidders 1 and 2 are indicated in table 7.2. The total value is maximized at \$34 (see the items marked with an asterisk), when $\{A\}$ is sold

Table 7.2 Bids submitted in a VCG auction

	{A}	{B}	{A, B}
Bidder 1	20*	11	33
Bidder 2	14	14*	29

to bidder 1 and {B} to bidder 2. Bidder 1 bids $20 for {A} but she receives a Vickrey payment of $34 − $29 = $5, since without her participation the total value would be $29. In other words, the net payment or Vickrey price p_1^{VCG} which bidder 1 has to pay to the auctioneer is $20 (bid price) − $5 (Vickrey payment) = $15. Bidder 2 bids $14 on B but receives a Vickrey payment of $34 − $33 = $1, because without his participation the total valuation of this auction would be only $33. The auctioneer's revenue would then be $15 + $13 = $28.

In this auction bidders have a dominant strategy of reporting their true valuations $b_i(S) = v_i(S)$ on all bundles S to the auctioneer, who then determines the allocation and the respective Vickrey prices. The proof for the dominant-strategy incentive compatibility of the VCG mechanism carries over.

7.3.2.1   Solutions Outside the Core

The central problem of the VCG is best understood if the auction is modeled as a *cooperative* (aka *coalitional*) game (Ausubel and Milgrom, 2006b). In chapter 2 we focused exclusively on non-cooperative game theory, which is the main theory used to model markets. Now it is convenient to extend the scope to cooperative games, where groups of agents (aka coalitions) may enforce cooperative behavior; hence the game is a competition between coalitions of players rather than between individual players. Suppose that (N, w) is the coalitional game derived from the trade between the seller and the bidders. Here, N is the set of all bidders $\mathcal{I}$ plus the auctioneer, with $i \in N$, and $M \subseteq N$ is a coalition of bidders with the auctioneer; $w(M)$ denotes the coalitional value for a subset M, which is equal to the objective value of the WDP with all bidders $i \in M$ involved.

Definition 7.3.1 A *core* payoff vector Π is defined as

$$\text{Core}(N, w) = \left\{ \Pi \geq 0 \middle| \sum_{i \in N} \pi_i = w(N), \sum_{i \in M} \pi_i \geq w(M) \; \forall M \subset N \right\}$$

This implies that there should be no coalition $M \subset N$ which can make a counter-offer that leaves the coalition members and the seller at least as well off as the currently winning coalition. The payoff vector Π is also referred to as a *strong* core. A *weak* core, in contrast, requires that all members in a coalition are better off.

Unfortunately, in the VCG auction there can be outcomes which are not in the core. To see this, assume again a combinatorial sales auction with three bidders and two items A, B (see table 7.3).

Example 7.3.2 Referring to table 7.3, bidder 1 bids $b_1(A) = \$0$, $b_1(B) = \$2$, and $b_1(A, B) = \$2$. Bidder 2 bids $b_2(A) = \$2$, $b_2(B) = \$0$, and $b_2(A, B) = \$2$. Finally,

Table 7.3 Bids submitted in a VCG auction

	$\{A\}$	$\{B\}$	$\{A, B\}$
Bidder 1	0	2*	2
Bidder 2	2*	0	2
Bidder 3	0	0	2

bidder 3 has only a bid $b_3(A, B) = \$2$ but no valuation for the individual items. In this situation the net payments of the winners (bidders 1 and 2) are zero, and bidder 3 could have found a solution with the auctioneer that would have made both better off. We leave the computation of the Vickrey prices as an exercise.

Outcomes which are not in the core lead to a number of problems, such as low seller revenues or non-monotonicity of the seller's revenues in the number of bidders and the amounts bid; to see this, just omit bidder 1 from the auction in the previous example. Also, such auction results are vulnerable to collusion by a coalition of losing bidders. Therefore, it has been argued that the outcomes of combinatorial auctions should be in the core (Day and Raghavan, 2007).

This raises the question under what conditions the VCG payments are in the core. The *bidders-are-substitutes* condition (BSC) is necessary and sufficient to support VCG payments in the core (Bikhchandani and Ostroy, 2002). A bidder's payment in the VCG mechanism is always less than or equal to the payment by the bidder in any other core solution.

Definition 7.3.2 (Bidders-are-substitutes condition, BSC) The BSC condition requires that

$$w(N) - w(N \setminus M) \geq \sum_{i \in M} [w(N) - w(N \setminus i)], \quad \forall M \subseteq N$$

In words, BSC holds whenever the incremental value of a subset of bidders to a grand coalition is at least as great as the sum of the incremental contributions of each of its members. We discuss this in more detail in section 8.3, and show why this condition is necessary.

7.3.2.2 Potential Issues

Apart from efficiency and strategy-proofness, the *law of one price* is often cited as a desirable goal in market design. We also refer to anonymous prices as prices for a package which are independent of the identity of the bidder. This means that the same type of object should have the same price for different bidders. This avoids arbitrage between markets, but it also avoids envy between bidders. Unfortunately, the VCG auction violates this design goal.

Example 7.3.3 Suppose that there are two bidders and two homogeneous units of one item. Bidder 1 and bidder 2 both have preferences for only one unit and they each submit a bid of $5 on one unit. In this case, they both pay zero. Now, assume that bidder 2 also

Table 7.4 Valuations of bidders in a VCG auction with budget constraints of 10

	1 unit	2 units	3 units
Bidder 1	10	20	30
Bidder 2	10	20	30

bids $9 for two units. As a consequence, bidder 2 would still pay zero, while bidder 1 would pay $4 for a unit.

This can also be an issue in combinatorial auctions with core payment rules, as will be discussed in the next subsection. Apart from these problems, many practical issues arise (Rothkopf, 2007). In a combinatorial auction bidders need to submit bids on all possible packages; the number of bids is exponential in the number of items. Not only is this difficult for bidders in larger auctions, it also makes it difficult for the auctioneer to solve the NP-hard allocation problem and obtain the payment computations for all winners, with a large number of bids.

Of course, a trusted auctioneer is also needed. In particular, in situations where the outcome is not in the core the auctioneer has an incentive to manipulate the outcome. Bidders might feel uncomfortable revealing so many package valuations truthfully in one step, and the VCG auction can also lead to problems with budget-constrained bidders where multiple equilibria can arise. Let's take a look at the following example (see table 7.4) to illustrate the possible bidding strategies and outcomes of a VCG auction with budget constraints.

Example 7.3.4 There are two bidders for three units of an object. Initially, all the bidders submit bids at their budget constraint of $10, although they all value an additional unit at $10, i.e., $v_i(S) = 10|S|$.

If bidder 1 bids $\min\{v_i(S), 10\}$ for all packages $S \neq \emptyset$ and bidder 2 bids $v_i(S)/3$, then bidder 1 wins one unit for a price of 10/3 and bidder 2 wins two units for a price of 0. This means, with bidder 1 revealing her budget constraint, bidder 2 could make sure that he wins two units and pays nothing.

The example only scratches the surface, and in fact budget constraints lead to significant strategic challenges for bidders. Dobzinski *et al.* (2012a) showed that, when bidders have private budgets, there is no strategy-proof multi-unit auction that yields an efficient outcome and satisfies weak budget balance. However, they also showed that, for homogeneous goods, additive valuations, and *public budgets*, there are deterministic and randomized mechanisms. The deterministic mechanism for public budgets is a version of Ausubel's clinching auction (see section 5.2.2). There are also positive results for randomized multi-unit auctions with private budget constraints and additive valuations (Bhattacharya *et al.*, 2010). We discuss randomized approximation mechanisms in chapter 10.

Table 7.5 Example bids for a core-selecting auction

	{A}	{B}	{A, B}
Bidder B1	28*		
Bidder B2		20*	
Bidder B3			32
Bidder B4	12		
Bidder B5		11	

7.3.3 Bidder-Optimal Core Payment Rules

Vickrey–Clarke–Groves solutions outside the core, where it is possible that a subset of bidders might have been able to pay more than the winners paid, are often seen as undesirable. Ascending combinatorial auctions, discussed in the next chapter, will be in the core if bidders bid truthfully because every losing coalition of bidders could have outbid the winning coalition if this would have been profitable. While such a payment rule is not strategy-proof, it has been argued that, with the uncertainties in large multi-object markets, bidders have sufficient incentives to bid truthfully. In particular, one can try to find a vector of core prices which is closest to the VCG payments. This means that such payments are minimal for the bidders, i.e., bidder-optimal. The idea is that bidder-optimal core (BOC) payments minimize the incentive to deviate from truthful bidding. A simple example from Day and Cramton (2012) should illustrate the basic idea.

Example 7.3.5 Let's assume two blocks A and B and five bidders 1 to 5. The winning allocation is indicated by asterisks (table 7.5). In this example the VCG payments would be $12 + 11 = 23$, which is outside the core and less than 32, the bid price of bidder 3 for $\{A, B\}$. The minimal core price would be 32, which would lead to payments of 16.5 and 15.5 for bidders 1 and 2 respectively. This payment is called bidder-optimal and core-selecting, and it is determined in such a way that it is nearest to the VCG payment. Figure 7.1 describes the example graphically.

The computation of such core payments is non-trivial. One could add a constraint, for each possible losing coalition, to the optimization problem which minimizes payments. However, the number of constraints grows exponentially with the number of bidders (see definition 7.3.1 of the core). However, such core constraints can be generated dynamically, which leads to an effective computation of such payments; this has also been used in spectrum auctions.

In the computational approach discussed in the literature (Day and Raghavan, 2007) core prices are found by iteratively creating new price vectors p^t and then checking at each iteration t whether there is an alternative outcome which generates strictly more revenue for the seller and which every bidder in this new outcome weakly prefers to the current outcome. If such a coalition $\mathscr{C}$ exists, it is called a *blocking coalition* and a constraint is added to the partial representation of the core in the payment space until no further blocking coalitions can be found. In order to discover the most violated blocking coalition $\mathscr{C}^t$ relative to the current payments at iteration t, the WDP is extended as in

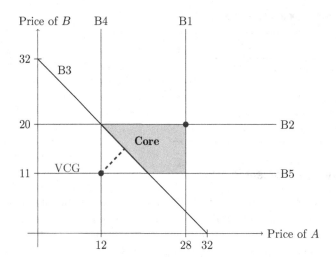

Figure 7.1 Example of a bidder-optimal core payment (see note at end of chapter).

the separation problem SEP^t:

$$z(p^t) = \max \left\{ \sum_{i \in \mathcal{I}} \sum_{S \subseteq \mathcal{K}} b_i(S) x_i(S) - \sum_{i \in \mathcal{W}} [b_i^*(S_i) - p_i^t] \gamma_i \right\} \qquad \text{(SEP}^t\text{)}$$

$$\text{s.t.} \quad \sum_{S:k \in S} \sum_{i \in \mathcal{I}} x_i(S) \leq 1 \qquad \forall k \in \mathcal{K}$$

$$\sum_{S \subseteq \mathcal{K}} x_i(S) \leq 1 \qquad \forall i \in \mathcal{I} \backslash \mathcal{W}$$

$$\sum_{S \subseteq \mathcal{K}} x_i(S) \leq \gamma_i \qquad \forall i \in \mathcal{W}$$

$$x_i(S) \in \{0, 1\} \qquad \forall i \in \mathcal{I}, S \subseteq \mathcal{K}$$
$$\gamma_i \in \{0, 1\} \qquad \forall i \in \mathcal{W}.$$

Here, $\mathcal{W}$ is the set of winners from the solution of the WDP and $b_i^*(S)$ represents bidder i's winning bid. If the sum of the current payments p^t is less than the solution to SEP^t then a violated core constraint has been found, and we must add a constraint to our partial representation of the core. Following Day and Raghavan (2007) this partial representation is given by the following linear program for finding equitable bidder-Pareto-optimal (EBPO) payments, which is then solved to find the next tentative set of payments p^{t+1} until no further constraints can be found:

$$\theta(\epsilon) = \min \sum_{i \in \mathcal{W}} p_i \qquad \text{(EBPO}^t\text{)}$$

$$\text{s.t.} \quad \sum_{i \in \mathcal{W} \backslash \mathscr{C}^\tau} p_i \geq z(p^\tau) - \sum_{i \in \mathcal{W} \cap \mathscr{C}^\tau} p_i^\tau \qquad \forall \tau \leq t \qquad \text{(EBPO}^t.1\text{)}$$

$$p_i \leq b_i^*(S) \qquad \forall i \in \mathcal{W}$$
$$p_i \geq p_i^{vcg} \qquad \forall i \in \mathcal{W}$$

As in SEP^t, $b_i^*(S)$ is the winning bid for i and the parameters $p_i^{vcg} = b_i^*(S) - (\text{WDP} - \text{WDP}_{-i})$ represent VCG payments. We then use the value of each p_i in the solution for the next iteration (i.e., use set $p_i^{t+1} = p_i$).

7.4   Equilibrium Bidding Strategies

As already discussed in section 7.3.2, the VCG mechanism is the unique strategy-proof auction mechanism in the independent private-values setting (Green and Laffont, 1979; Holmstrom, 1979). The general argument also extends to combinatorial auctions. Consequently, bidder-optimal core payments or pay-as-bid payment rules cannot be strategy-proof. Bayesian Nash equilibrium analysis is the standard approach to model such sealed-bid auctions and much recent research has aimed to extend the analysis of single-object to multi-object auctions (Krishna, 2009).

Deriving a risk-neutral Bayesian Nash equilibrium (RNBNE) for multi-object auctions is technically more challenging than that for single-object auctions and, as of yet, there is only a small number of papers deriving RNBNE strategies for specific combinatorial or non-combinatorial multi-object auction formats. We first summarize the results on core-selecting sealed-bid combinatorial auctions, before we discuss bidding strategies in first-price sealed-bid combinatorial auctions. In the absence of RNBNE strategies, we sometimes discuss Nash equilibria in the respective complete-information game.

7.4.1   First-Price Sealed-Bid Auctions

As discussed earlier (see section 7.3.1), so far no closed-form Bayesian Nash equilibrium characterization for first-price sealed-bid combinatorial auctions has been found that is similar to the one that we have seen for single-object auctions in section 4.3. The complete-information game was analyzed early on, while the Bayesian analysis of restricted environments led us to additional insights.

Bernheim and Whinston (1986) characterized the Nash equilibria that can arise in the complete-information game; this work provides a good intuition about the strategic problem in such auctions. They showed that multiple Nash equilibria can emerge, several of them being inefficient. To see this consider a simple example.

Example 7.4.1 Consider the sale of two objects $\{A, B\} \in \mathcal{K}$ and two bidders 1 and 2 in a first-price sealed-bid combinatorial auction, as shown in table 7.6. There are several Nash equilibria which arise from these valuations. For example, both bidders might submit a bid of $7 on the package $\{A, B\}$ only. This is an example of an inefficient equilibrium, because in the efficient solution A would be assigned to bidder 1 and B would be assigned to bidder 2. If one of the bidders bid on only one item, this would not be a best response to the bid of the opponent. However, there is a Nash equilibrium where bidder 1 bids $3 on $\{B\}$ and $6 on the package and bidder 2 bids $3 on $\{A\}$ and $6

Table 7.6 Example of valuations for a first-price sealed-bid combinatorial auction

	{A}	{B}	{A, B}
Bidder 1	6*	5	8
Bidder 2	5	6*	7

on the package; then bidder 1 gets {B} and bidder 2 gets {A}, which is also inefficient. Of course, there are also efficient Nash equilibria.

The incomplete-information environment is harder to model. In addition to single-object first-price sealed-bid auctions there are many more possible environments, with different numbers of bidders and bidder preferences, which makes the analysis challenging. However, for specific environments it is possible to characterize Bayesian Nash equilibria.

The following analysis of split-award auctions suggests that equilibrium selection problems remain also in the incomplete-information analysis of first-price sealed-bid combinatorial auctions. We stick to the procurement version, as it is widely used for combinatorial auctions in business practice. Actually, procurement and logistics are arguably the most frequent applications of combinatorial auctions. Note that the goal of a procurement manager is cost minimization and that lower bids from bidders or suppliers have a higher likelihood of winning.

In *split-award auctions* a procurement manager splits her demand for a larger quantity of a good into two (or more) shares (aka lots), for example 30% and 70% shares or two 50% shares. In an ex post split-award auction, the buyer allows suppliers to submit bids on individual shares as well as on 100% of the order, which differentiates ex post split-award auctions from their ex ante counterparts. In ex ante split-award auctions only bids on individual items are allowed (Bichler *et al.*, 2014b).

Ex post split-award auctions without the possibility of package bids could lead to an *exposure problem* for bidders if they had economies of scale, i.e., the average cost is lower for two shares than for one. In this case they could aim to win the package and bid aggressively on both lots below cost, but then win only one of them. If they did not succeed in winning the package, they would then incur a loss. Many procurement auctions are not business-critical and bidders have strict guidelines not to bid below cost. In such situations, if bidders cannot bid on the package then this will obviously lead to high procurement costs for the buyer.

In what follows, we limit our attention to the case with two bidders and two shares only and *diseconomies of scale*. We also assume that the suppliers know the scale economies in the market but the buyer does not, which is why she is using an ex post split-award auction. This environment allows us to characterize Bayesian Nash equilibria, and it is strategically interesting because suppliers *need to coordinate on a split award for an efficient solution*. Anton and Yao (1992) showed that in such markets suppliers can coordinate on the efficient split award in equilibrium but that there are also inefficient equilibria where both bidders try to win the package. This means, as in the complete-information game in example 7.4.1, that there is an equilibrium selection problem.

Let's introduce the model more formally. A buyer conducts a split-award auction in order to award a business between $n = 2$ ex ante symmetric, risk-neutral, and profit-maximizing suppliers. We focus on a simple setting in which the bidders can win a contract for either 50% or 100% of the business, which makes it technically a combinatorial (reverse) auction, with two identical units and the whole package up for auction. Bidder i's (with $i \in \{1, 2\}$) costs for 100% of the business, k_i^s, are determined by a private cost parameter θ_i. The cost type is independently drawn from an arbitrary distribution function $F(\cdot)$, with support $[\underline{\theta}, \overline{\theta}]$ ($0 < \underline{\theta} < \overline{\theta}$), with the density f positive and continuous. A constant efficiency parameter $0 < C < 1$, which is equivalent for and known to all suppliers, determines the costs for 50% of the business, $k_i^\sigma = C\theta_i$. The costs for no award are zero. Furthermore, the buyer does not know the efficiency parameter C, which can be a realistic assumption in procurement markets where the buyer is less well informed about the economies of scale.

The pair of two price functions for 100% and 50% of the business, $(p^s(\theta_i), p^\sigma(\theta_i))$, characterizes the bidding strategy of supplier i ($i \in \{1, 2\}$); both price functions are strictly increasing and continuous. Bidders are assumed to be individually rational, which means that all submitted bids, $p^s(\cdot)$ and $p^\sigma(\cdot)$, must be at least as high as the supplier's costs for the respective allocation. The auctioneer is ex-ante indifferent between awarding 100% of the business to a single supplier (a sole-source award) and awarding 50% of the business each to two different suppliers (a split award). Hence, the winner determination in a split-award auction must satisfy the auctioneer's indifference condition.

Hereafter, the ith lowest order statistic out of n different cost types is denoted by $\theta_{i:n}$. A split-award auction which implements the auctioneer's indifference condition must ensure that the sole-source award (split award) is the winning award if and only if $\min_{i\in\{1,2\}}\{p^s(\theta_i)\} < (\geq) p^\sigma(\theta_1) + p^\sigma(\theta_2)$.

As indicated, we are focusing on markets with strong diseconomies of scale in which suppliers must coordinate in the efficient solution. Dual source efficiency (DSE) describes a setting in which it is always efficient for the buyer to award 50% of the business to each of two different suppliers. Anton and Yao (1992) showed that, independently of the two draws of the bidders' cost types, the split is always the efficient award if the efficiency parameter C lies below $\underline{\theta}/(\underline{\theta} + \overline{\theta})$. An ex-ante-defined risk premium by the procurement manager extends the scope of DSE.

The same types of equilibria emerge in a setting with a constant risk premium r for the sole-source award and with $C < (\underline{\theta} + r)/(\underline{\theta} + \overline{\theta})$, which also allows values for C of greater than 0.5, e.g., a setting with $C = 0.52$, $\theta \in [100, 140]$, and $r = 25$ in which a Bayesian Nash equilibrium exists, where both bidders coordinate even though suppliers have economies of scale. We refer to such a coordinate equilibrium as a σ-equilibrium.

In the first-price sealed-bid split-award auction, both suppliers $i \in \{1, 2\}$ learn their respective cost parameters θ_i before they simultaneously submit two bids, one for the 50% share, $p^\sigma(\theta_i)$, and one for the 100% share, $p^s(\theta_i)$. There are two possible allocations at the end of the auction, which depend only on the prices submitted for each share.

1. The bidder with the lowest price for 100% of the business wins the sole source award if this allocation yields lower purchasing costs for the auctioneer than the sum of the two prices for 50% of the business, i.e., $\min_{i\in\{1,2\}}\{p^s(\theta_i)\} < p^\sigma(\theta_1) + p^\sigma(\theta_2)$.
2. The split award is allocated to both suppliers if the sum of their split prices is lower than or equal to the lowest sole-source price, i.e., $\min_{i\in\{1,2\}}\{p^s(\theta_i)\} \geq p^\sigma(\theta_1) + p^\sigma(\theta_2)$.

Hence, the indifference condition of the auctioneer is implemented by the auction. Interestingly, in this two-bidder model, coordination on a split award is a σ-*equilibrium*. However, there is also a winner-takes-all (WTA) equilibrium, in which both bidders compete for only the whole package. This WTA equilibrium coincides with the equilibrium bid strategy for a single-object reverse auction. Both suppliers would charge a markup on their costs, which is derived as in the first-price sealed-bid forward auction in section 4.3, and they would not bid on a single object only. This equilibrium is not efficient in DSE.

Interestingly, there is also an efficient σ-equilibrium, which has constant pooling prices for 50% of the business. Various σ-equilibria with different pooling prices $p^\sigma \in [\bar\theta C, (1-C)\underline\theta]$ exist.

Lemma 7.4.1 *Consider the FPSB split-award auction model with $n = 2$ bidders and DSE. Then, if a σ-equilibrium exists, the split price p^σ must be constant and $p^\sigma \in [\bar\theta C, \underline\theta(1-C)] \ \forall \ \theta \in [\underline\theta, \bar\theta]$.*

Proof sketch: Suppose that the equilibrium split prices are not constant; then the bidder with the lower split price always has an incentive to deviate from the equilibrium strategy. Let's now show that $\bar\theta C \leq p^\sigma \leq \underline\theta(1-C)$. The left-hand inequality follows from noting that type $\bar\theta$ must earn a non-negative equilibrium payoff. For the right-hand side consider $\underline\theta$ and the equilibrium payoff $p^\sigma - \underline\theta C$. Suppose that $\underline\theta$ deviates and bids $(2p^\sigma - \varepsilon, p^\sigma)$ where $\varepsilon \searrow 0$. When the other bidder is using $(p^s(\cdot), p^\sigma)$ this bid will result in a sole-source award with probability 1 for $\underline\theta$ and a profit of $2p^\sigma - \underline\theta$. In equilibrium this deviation cannot be profitable, so $2p^\sigma - \underline\theta \leq p^\sigma - \underline\theta C$, which reduces to $p^\sigma \leq \underline\theta(1-C) + \varepsilon$. $\qquad\square$

Lemma 7.4.1 can then be used to prove σ-equilibrium for the case with two bidders. Bidders submit high sole-source prices that support the equilibrium, but they must not be higher than a given boundary $G(p^\sigma, \theta)$ in order to avoid profitable deviations for the sole-source award.

Theorem 7.4.1 *In the FPSB split-award auction model with $n = 2$ bidders and DSE, there are different efficient σ-equilibria with $p^\sigma \in [\bar\theta C, (1-C)\underline\theta]$. Let $p^s(\cdot)$ be a continuous and strictly increasing bid function with $p^s(\underline\theta) = 2p^\sigma$ and $p^s(\theta) \leq G(p^\sigma, \theta)$ for all θ; then $(p^s(\cdot), p^\sigma)$ is a σ-equilibrium.*

A long proof with the derivation of $G(p^\sigma, \theta)$ can be found in Anton and Yao (1992). In summary, the analysis suggests that the equilibrium selection problems in the complete-information game of the first-price sealed-bid package auction remain also in the incomplete-information analysis. Such coordination problems can lead to significant inefficiency in the laboratory and in the field. An analysis of the n-bidder case and experimental results can be found in Kokott *et al.* (2017).

7.4.2   Bidder-Optimal Core-Selecting Auctions

As for first-price sealed-bid combinatorial auctions, bidder-optimal core-selecting auctions can be modeled as complete information games. Day and Milgrom (2008) showed that bidder Pareto optimality implies optimal incentives for truthful revelation over all core-selecting auctions, among other supporting results, including decreased vulnerability to false-name bidding and collusive behavior relative to other auction formats discussed in the literature, in particular the VCG mechanism. Day and Raghavan (2007) noted that *total-payment-minimizing* core payments are further resistant to certain forms of collusion with side payments. Selecting a bidder-optimal point in the core polytope is also supported by the fact that if the truth-revealing VCG price vector is in the core then the algorithm described in section 7.3.3 will produce VCG as its output.

Unfortunately, a core-selecting auction only provides a dominant strategy if the VCG outcome is in the core; otherwise it does not. Goeree and Lien (2016) actually showed that no Bayesian incentive-compatible core-inducing auction exists when the VCG outcome is not in the core. In specific settings where the VCG outcome is outside the core, the equilibrium bidding strategy is to shade bids below one's true valuation, speculating that the reduced bid can lower one's payment and yet acquire the same bundle of goods.

Simple threshold problems where multiple local bidders interested in only one item compete against a global bidder who is interested only in obtaining all the items, provide an illustrative example. If the sum of the local bidders' valuations exceeds the valuation of the global bidder then the VCG payments are not in the core. Local bidders can now try to free-ride on each other; this means that a bidder tries to win at a low price at the expense of a competitor, who then needs to pay a high price. The core prices computed in section 7.3.3 are equivalent to the prices resulting from ascending combinatorial auctions. We will discuss core prices in more detail in the context of ascending auctions in section 8.3.3 and will provide an example of a threshold problem. Even if the threshold environment is simple, the free-rider problem that arises is fundamental and can also be found in spectrum auctions in the field where regional bidders compete against national bidders.

7.5   Domain-Specific Compact Bid Languages

So far we have assumed generic bid languages such as the XOR or OR bid languages in our analysis. However, in many multi-unit multi-item markets the number of possible packages from which a bidder can choose is so large that the auctioneer can expect to elicit only a small number of the package valuations with these bid languages, even if bidders are truthful. We referred to this problem as the "missing bids" problem.

In this section, we discuss compact and domain-specific bid languages as a remedy for efficiency losses due to missing bids. Often, prior knowledge about the shape of the bidders' value or cost functions allows for compact bid languages with a low number of parameters that bidders need to specify in order to describe their preferences adequately. The design of the bid language is a central task in most market design problems, and it is important that such languages allow bidders to express their preferences well (Sandholm, 2007). In what follows, we provide two examples of compact bid languages which nicely illustrate the flexibility of domain-specific and compact bid languages.

In procurement markets with economies of scale, the various discount policies which are regularly used in pricing can be elements of a bid language (Bichler *et al.*, 2013b; Goossens *et al.*, 2007). Such bid languages follow established market practices and bidders do not need to change their established discount policies. In a similar way, we discuss a bid language for TV ad markets which is natural to media agencies, allowing them to express their preferences with a few parameters only by describing substitutes in a succinct way. Such *domain-specific* bid languages require adequate optimization models to compute cost-minimal allocations in procurement or revenue-maximal allocations in forward TV ad auctions.

Other bid languages allow for the specification of qualitative attributes such as weight or color, which matter in the allocation decision. Such auctions are often referred to as *multi-attribute auctions*. In contrast with the requests for quotes or tenders regularly used in procurement, the purchasing manager specifies a scoring function to be used to evaluate multi-attribute bids. This enables competitive bidding with heterogeneous but substitutable offers. Multi-attribute auctions differ in the types of scoring rules or functions used and in the type of feedback that is provided to bidders. Depending on the type of bids submitted, and on the type of scoring function, the auctioneer faces differing optimization problems (Bichler and Kalagnanam, 2005).

7.5.1   Procurement Markets with Economies of Scale and Scope

In procurement practice, suppliers employ various types of discount policies in different settings. Figure 7.2 provides an example of total-quantity discounts, where a procurement manager has a demand for 3000 units of one item only, and suppliers are restricted to deliver at most 2000 units. Supplier 1 charges a unit price of $3.50 for up to 2000 units, while supplier 2 charges $4 for up to 1500 units but only $2.50 per unit for the entire quantity if the purchasing manager buys 1500 to 2000 units. Such types of discounts have been referred to as *total-quantity bids* (Goossens *et al.*, 2007). Alternatively, *incremental volume-discount bids* apply discounts only to additional units in a specific price interval (Davenport and Kalagnanam, 2000). The resulting total cost curves are monotonic whereas the total-quantity bids lead to jagged curves.

The winner-determination problem for such types of bids is also a hard computational problem, as is illustrated by the total-quantity bids in figure 7.2. A "greedy" solution would be to purchase 2000 units from supplier 3 and the remaining 1000 units from supplier 1, which would cost $7500. The optimal solution would be to buy 1500 units from supplier 2 and 1500 units from supplier 3, resulting in a total cost of $1500 \times \$2 + 1500 \times \$2.5 = \$6750$. Typically, there is not just a single commodity but dozens,

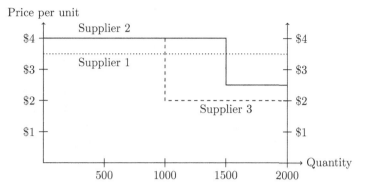

Figure 7.2 Example of volume discounts on a single item.

and the procurement manager needs to consider allocation constraints on the number of winners or on the allocation per winner, which makes this a computationally hard problem.

In addition to volume-discount bids and total-quantity bids one can find lump-sum rebates on total spend, and such discounts can be based on the quantity or spend of one or a few items that are being auctioned. In this section, we introduce a powerful bid language to describe various types of volume discount found in practice and a rather involved mixed-integer program to find the cost-minimal solution. This should serve as an illustration of how mixed-integer programs can be solved to obtain flexible bid languages that allow for a large number of different discount policies (see also Bichler *et al.*, 2010). After the above introductory example, we will now get more specific about bid languages for procurement.

7.5.1.1   Compact Bid Languages

Bid languages should be expressive enough to allow for the description of different shapes that cost functions can assume, including concave and convex shapes. At the same time, a bid language should allow the description of bids in a compact way with only a few parameters. Compact bid languages, which allow bidders to describe their preferences on multiple items and quantities as a function, can alleviate the missing-bids problem.

Definition 7.5.1 (Compact bid language)   A *compact bid language* allows one to define the bid price as a function $p_i : \mathbb{R}^{\mathcal{K}} \to \mathbb{R}$ of quantity for one or more items $k \in \mathcal{K}$.

We use the term *bid function* for p_i. Such a bid function has a particular parametric form. Clearly, the most compact format would reveal the parameters and the specification of the true total-cost function in a direct revelation mechanism to an auctioneer. The parametric shape of such a cost function might be non-linear and different between suppliers and industries, which is one reason why the true specification of the function is typically not revealed in practice. It is rather common to specify volume discounts or markups for economies or diseconomies of scale. Such volume discounts can be formulated as piecewise linear functions. Bids in a compact bid language are an approximation to the underlying cost function.

Bid languages should allow for a close approximation of widespread types of cost functions but at the same time should require a low number of parameters. A bad approximation will make it difficult for the auctioneer to find an efficient allocation, even if suppliers bid truthfully. Multi-unit bundle bids in combinatorial auctions allow for close approximations, as they specify only discrete points but at the expense of the huge number of bids required to describe a bidder's costs. Next, we discuss a bid language for procurement markets with economies of scale and scope ($\mathcal{L}_{ESS}$). This language allows for various types of discount and rebate as found in procurement practice.

7.5.1.2   The $\mathcal{L}_{ESS}$ Bid Language

Offers from suppliers can come in any combination of incremental or total quantity discounts, depending on multiple conditions. To accommodate the richness observed in practice one needs a language R_d that allows for different discount types. In the case of diseconomies of scale, for example, when the volume awarded is beyond the production capacity of a supplier, she might want to charge respective *markups* R_m to cover her increased per-unit costs. While markups are conceptually equivalent to volume discounts, we use a separate notation R_m as they need to be modeled differently in our optimization model.

In addition, there are *lump sum discounts* R_l, which describe refunds of part of the total price. For example, if the volume purchased exceeds a threshold, a supplier might be willing to reduce the overall payment by a fixed amount $R_l = \$10\,000$ on the total price. These lump sum discounts R_l can also be defined on the spend S_l or the quantity Q_l and are often used to describe economies of scope.

In $\mathcal{L}_{ESS}$, bidders should be able to express these different types of discounts. Every supplier $i \in \mathcal{I}$ submits a base price $P_{k,i}$ for every item $k \in \mathcal{K}$ and also the maximum quantity $E_{k,i}$ she is willing to supply. In addition, she specifies volume discounts $d \in \mathcal{D}$, lump sum discounts $l \in \mathcal{L}$, and markups $m \in \mathcal{M}$ to modify the base price when there are certain *spend conditions*. Note that we use the symbol for a set also for its cardinality. The total bid-price function $p_i : \mathbb{R}^{\mathcal{K}} \to \mathbb{R}$ of a set of items $\mathcal{K}$ can be written as

$$p_i(x_1, \ldots, x_\mathcal{K}) = \sum_{k \in \mathcal{K}} P_{k,i} x_{k,i} - \sum_{d \in \mathcal{D}} R_d y_d 1_{\{C_d\}} + \sum_{m \in \mathcal{M}} R_m y_m 1_{\{C_m\}} - \sum_{l \in \mathcal{L}} R_l 1_{\{C_l\}}$$

where R_d describes the *volume discount* per unit that is awarded on a quantity y_d if a *spend condition* C_d is true, e.g., after the quantity exceeds a certain lower bound on the quantity Q_d or the spend S_d. Note that Q_d and S_d can be defined either on a particular item provided by the supplier or on a set of items from this supplier. We use the term *discount interval* and refer to *spend conditions*, which define a unit price for a particular quantity interval. The volume discounts of a specific bidder can be valid for the total quantity purchased (*total-quantity discounts*) or for the amount exceeding a prespecified threshold (*incremental (volume) discounts*). This also holds for markups R_m. Lump sum discounts R_l are defined on overall spend or quantity, not per unit.

The *spend conditions* (C) are an important language feature, which allows for much flexibility. Spend conditions can be defined on a set of items and based on the spend (S) or the volume (Q) purchased. For example, if the spend on the items A and B is more than $\$100\,000$, a supplier offers a lump sum discount of $R_l = \$4000$. An elementary spend condition C is treated as a literal in propositional logic, for example $S_{A,B} > \$100\,000$ or $Q_A > 2000$. Composite spend conditions take the form of a conjunction of m elementary conditions. So, in general, a discount rule takes the form of a Horn clause, with $C_1 \wedge C_2 \wedge \cdots \wedge C_\sigma \implies R$. We have limited the discount rules to Horn clauses, in order to keep the corresponding allocation problem of the auctioneer concise.

Definition 7.5.2 (Discount rule) A discount rule F is a Horn clause of the form $C_1 \wedge C_2 \wedge \cdots \wedge C_\sigma \implies R$, where

- C_σ is a literal defined on the spend levels or quantity levels for a set of items, with $\sigma = \{1, \ldots, \Sigma\}$ the set of respective spend conditions,
- R is a discount, i.e., a lump sum discount, an incremental volume discount, a total quantity discount, or a respective markup.

The supplier is also able to specify disjunctive discount rules, i.e., two or more rules cannot be active at the same time. For example, if the supplier purchases more than $\$10\,000$ of items A and B, there is a discount of $\$1.77$. Alternatively, if the supplier buys more than 5000 units of item A, the discount is $\$1.02$. Only one of these two discounts is eligible, and the auctioneer will choose the discount that minimizes his total cost.

Definition 7.5.3 An $\mathcal{L}_{ESS}$ bid is a tuple $(\mathcal{P}, \mathcal{E}, \mathcal{H}, \Sigma)$, where

- $\mathcal{P}$ is a set of base unit prices for each item $k \in \mathcal{K}$,
- $\mathcal{E}$ is a set of maximum quantities $E_{k,i}$ that a supplier s can provide for each item $k \in \mathcal{K}$,
- $\mathcal{H}$ is a set of discount rules $F \in \mathcal{H}$, and
- Σ is a set of disjunctions specified on the set of rules in $\mathcal{H}$.

Overall, $\mathcal{L}_{ESS}$ is an example of a compact bid language, which provides expressiveness for a low number of parameters specified by the bidder. Let us now describe how such a bid language can be modeled as a mixed-integer program in order to compute cost-minimal allocations subject to the allocation constraints typically present in procurement (Sandholm and Suri, 2006).

7.5.1.3   The Allocation Problem with $\mathcal{L}_{\mathcal{ESS}}$

In the following, we model the buyer's problem. The buyer needs to select quantities from each supplier providing bids in $\mathcal{L}_{\mathcal{ESS}}$ such that her costs are minimized and her demand is satisfied. We refer to this as a WDPSQS problem (a supplier quantity-selection problem) and introduce a respective mixed-integer program (MIP) in the following. We first introduce some necessary notation. We use uppercase letters for parameters, lowercase letters for decision variables, and a calligraphic font for sets. Sets indexed by a member of another set represent the subset of all elements that are relevant to the index. For example, $\mathcal{K}_d$ describes all items that are included in a discount rule $d \in \mathcal{D}$, and x_{k,i_d} describes the quantity purchased from supplier i on item k, which is part of the discount pricing rule $d \in \mathcal{D}$. Such discount rules can be defined on different items or sets of items per supplier. The buyer's problem is then modeled as follows:

$$\min \left\{ \sum_{k \in \mathcal{K}} \sum_{i \in \mathcal{I}} P_{k,i} x_{k,i} - \sum_{d \in \mathcal{D}} R_d y_d + \sum_{m \in \mathcal{M}} R_m y_m - \sum_{l \in \mathcal{L}} R_l c_l \right\} \qquad \text{(WDPSQS)}$$

$$\text{s.t.} \quad \sum_{i \in \mathcal{I}} x_{k,i} \geq W_k \qquad\qquad\qquad \forall k \in \mathcal{K} \qquad (1)$$

$$x_{k,i} \leq E_{k,i} \qquad\qquad\qquad \forall k \in \mathcal{K}, \forall i \in \mathcal{I} \qquad (2)$$

$$\sum_{k \in \mathcal{K}_d} x_{k,i_d} - D_d c_d \geq y_d \qquad\qquad \forall d \in \mathcal{D} \qquad (3d)$$

$$\sum_{k \in \mathcal{K}_m} x_{k,i_m} + B c_m \leq y_m + D_m + B \qquad \forall m \in \mathcal{M} \qquad (3m)$$

$$B c_d \geq y_d \qquad\qquad\qquad \forall d \in \mathcal{D} \qquad (4d)$$

$$\sum_{n \in \mathcal{N}_d} j_n - \sum_{\bar{d} \in \bar{\mathcal{D}}_d} c_{\bar{d}} \geq |\mathcal{N}_d| c_d \qquad \forall d \in \mathcal{D} \qquad (5d)$$

$$\sum_{n \in \mathcal{N}_l} j_n - \sum_{\bar{l} \in \bar{\mathcal{L}}_l} c_{\bar{l}} \geq |\mathcal{N}_l| c_l \qquad \forall l \in \mathcal{L} \qquad (5l)$$

$$|\mathcal{N}_m|^{-1} \left(\sum_{n \in \mathcal{N}_m} j_n + 1 \right) - \sum_{\bar{m} \in \bar{\mathcal{M}}_m} c_{\bar{m}} \leq c_m + 1 \qquad \forall m \in \mathcal{M} \qquad (5m)$$

$$\sum_{k \in \mathcal{K}_n} P_{k,i_n} x_{k,i_n} - \sum_{d \in \mathcal{D}_n} R_d y_d + \sum_{m \in \mathcal{M}_n} R_m y_m \geq S_n j_n \qquad \forall n \in \mathcal{N} \qquad (6l,d)$$

$$\sum_{k \in \mathcal{K}} x_{k,i_n} \geq Q_n j_n \qquad\qquad\qquad \forall n \in \mathcal{N} \qquad (7l,d)$$

$$\sum_{k \in \mathcal{K}} x_{k,i_n} - Q_n < B j_n \qquad\qquad \forall n \in \mathcal{N} \qquad (8m)$$

$$x_{k,i}, y_d, y_m \geq 0 \qquad\qquad\qquad \forall k \in \mathcal{K}, \forall i \in \mathcal{I}, \\ \forall d \in \mathcal{D}, \forall m \in \mathcal{M}$$

$$c_d, c_m, c_l, j_n \in \{0, 1\} \qquad\qquad \forall d \in \mathcal{D}, \forall l \in \mathcal{L}, \\ \forall n \in \mathcal{N}, \forall m \in \mathcal{M}$$

The objective function of WDPSQS minimizes the product of all base prices $P_{k,i}$ and quantities $x_{k,i}$ of item k purchased from supplier i, subtracts the sum of all discounts R_d and lump sum discounts R_l, and adds the markups R_m.

The first set of constraints, (1), ensures that the demand W_k is fulfilled, and the second set of constraints, (2), ensures that the amount purchased of a product k does not exceed the maximum quantity $E_{k,i}$ provided by each supplier of each item. The constraint sets (3d) and (3m) determine the relevant volume, y_d or y_m, for which the discount or markup respectively is defined; B is a sufficiently large number. For example, if $D_d = 0$ then (3d) defines a total quantity discount, where $y_d = x_{k,i}$; otherwise, D_d is set to the threshold above which the volume discount is valid, as such describing an incremental volume

$y_d = x_{k,i} - D_d$. Typically, the discount intervals and markups hold for a single item, but they can also be defined on multiple items $k \in \mathcal{K}_d$.

For each discount rule, we introduce binary variables c_d, c_l, and c_m. Such decision variables are determined on the basis of the spend conditions, which we define in constraint sets (4d), (5d), (5l), and (5m). Constraint (4d) ensures that a discount is provided ($y_{k,i} > 0$) only if the respective binary variable for this discount, c_d, is true. Constraint sets (5d), (5l), and (5m) ensure that if a particular set of spend conditions is given ($j_n = 1$) which form preconditions for a discount, markup, or lump sum discount then the respective binary variable c_d, c_l, or c_m is also true. The factors $|N_d|$, $|N_m|$, and $|N_l|$ describe the numbers of conditions that need to be true for the respective binary variable to become true. These constraints also allow one to specify sets of discount rules $\bar{\mathcal{D}} \subset \mathcal{D}$, $\bar{\mathcal{M}} \subset \mathcal{M}$, and $\bar{\mathcal{L}} \subset \mathcal{L}$, which cannot be active at the same time as the respective rule.

The final sets of constraints (6)–(8) model individual conditions on spend or quantity that need to be fulfilled for a particular discount rule in constraint sets (5). For example, the constraint set (6l), (6d) specifies a minimum spend condition for volume discounts and lump sum discounts. In words, if the total cost including markups and discounts (not considering other lump sum discounts) exceeds S_n then an additional lump sum discount will be granted. Constraint set (7l), (7d) determines a minimum quantity condition used in volume and lump sum discounts. Constraint set (8m) defines a minimum quantity condition for a markup rule. One can show that the decision version of the WDPSQS is strongly NP-complete (Bichler *et al.*, 2010; Goossens *et al.*, 2007). It has been shown that problems with up to 30 suppliers, 30 items, and five quantity schedules can be solved to near optimality in less than 10 minutes on commodity hardware, which makes such problems practically viable.

7.5.2 Distributed Scheduling in TV Ad Markets

Different domains allow for different bid languages. Let us provide a second example, from the field of TV advertisement sales. Revenues from TV ad sales are an important income stream for TV stations. Parts of the advertisement capacity of a typical TV station are sold via large long-term contracts of about a year, and these will not be considered in our study. We focus instead on the sale of the remaining ad slot inventory to specific marketing campaigns that run in the short term. Such buyers are large media agencies, who purchase a set of slots with the intent to procure the best slots for each of their customers' campaigns. Because the amount of air-time filled by long-term customers varies, the length of a slot available in the short-term market can vary between 2 and 5 minutes, while the length of an ad also varies considerably, lasting up to 1 minute. For a particular channel, there are of the order of 150 short-term slots available during programs per week.

Different slots have a different reach for different customer segments or for the population overall. The reach of a particular slot varies over time, but there are estimates based on historical panel data available to clients of the media agencies. Clients use the reach per segment (based on gender, age, or other demographics) or per population to determine their willingness-to-pay for different slots. Clearly, the value of some slots, such as those during the finals of the national soccer league, may be difficult to estimate and their valuation varies considerably depending on the target market of an advertiser. Apart from these high-value slots there is also typically a segment of low-value slots, which are also difficult to price as the demand is hard to predict and are therefore suitable for an auction market.

The allocation of TV ad slots can be modeled as a multi-knapsack problem, in which each time slot k in the set $\mathcal{K} = \{1, 2, \ldots, m\}$ is treated as a knapsack with a maximum capacity or duration of c_k, which cannot be exceeded. As mentioned above, each slot can potentially hold a number of ads, though some slots may have been previously allocated to larger customers, so we assume that c_k reflects only short-term capacity in the current market; this creates a potentially heterogeneous list of c_k values, even for a TV station with slots of the same size when considering all the ads to be aired. We also assume that each slot k has a reservation value or minimum price per unit time, r_k, which reflects the station's ability to offload excess capacity at a low price to existing customers if needed. Station call signs and other brief announcements can also be used to fill any excess unused time.

Each bidding advertiser i in the set $\mathcal{I} = \{1, 2, \ldots, n\}$ has an ad of duration d_i to be shown repeatedly (at most once per time slot) if she wins a bundle of time slots in the auction. To ensure adequate reach, each bidder specifies an abstract "priority vector" or "weight vector" W_i, containing an arbitrary weight value w_{ki} for each time slot. These "weights" conveying "strength of priority" could specifically represent the expected viewership, the expected viewership of a particular demographic, or the viewership weighted by expected sales, etc., reflecting the advertiser's performance metric of choice. She can then bound the total priority value in the auction outcome to be greater than or equal to a minimum amount.

Thus, after specifying the priority vector and ad duration, a bidder places one or more tuples $(w_j^{\min}, b_j)$ containing the desired sum of priority values $w_j^{\min}$ necessary to justify a monetary bid b_j. At most one bid placed by a bidder can win, making the bid language an XOR of "weight threshold levels". For example, if the bidder sets the priority weights w_{ki} at the expected viewership of each slot k, the XOR structure lets her set an exact price for any particular price point of interest. She can set a price for a total of $w_j^{\min} = 1$ million viewers, a price for $w_j^{\min} = 2$ million viewers, etc., regardless of which slots are chosen to reach this total viewership. This price-point structure reflects the ability of the language to represent the fundamental complementarity in this type of market; a small number of ad slots (or a small reach, etc.) may have little or no value, but several of them together are worth more than the sum of the parts.

The set J_i contains all bid indexes j of a bidder i, and a superset J is defined as $J := \bigcup_{i \in \mathcal{I}} J_i$. We assume these bids are submitted in a sealed-bid format, in which bids are submitted once to a proxy. In such markets it is not practical for media agencies to participate in an ascending auction every week or two. After the bids have been submitted, the market is cleared at a particular point in time and the allocation is determined for some period, for a time (e.g., two weeks) in the future.

The formulation WDPTV given below maximizes the value of the accepted bids given that: ad durations do not exceed capacity in any slot, (1a); the bid values are not less than the seller's reservation values, (1b); the priority threshold level $w_j^{\min}$ of a bid j is met if and only if that bid is accepted, (1c), (1d); at most one bid j is accepted for each bidder i, (1e). The decision variables x_{kj} and y_j indicate the time if slot k is assigned to bid j and if bid j itself is accepted, respectively, while M is a sufficiently large positive constant parameter. The formulation is as follows:

$$\max \sum_{j \in J} b_j y_j \qquad \text{(WDPTV)}$$

$$\text{s.t.} \quad \sum_{j \in J} d_j x_{kj} \leq c_k \qquad \forall k \in \mathcal{K} \qquad (1a)$$

$$d_j \sum_{k \in \mathcal{K}} r_k x_{kj} \leq b_j \qquad \forall j \in J \qquad (1b)$$

$$\sum_{k \in \mathcal{K}} w_{ki} x_{kj} \leq M y_j \qquad \forall j \in J \qquad (1c)$$

$$w_j^{min} - \sum_{k \in \mathcal{K}} w_{ki} x_{kj} \leq M(1 - y_j) \qquad \forall j \in J \qquad (1d)$$

$$\sum_{j \in J_i} y_j \leq 1 \qquad \forall i \in \mathcal{I} \qquad (1e)$$

$$x_{kj} \in \{0, 1\} \qquad \forall k \in \mathcal{K}, j \in J \qquad (1f)$$

$$y_j \in \{0, 1\} \qquad \forall j \in J \qquad (1g)$$

The priority vector W_i provides flexibility to the bidders in expressing their preferences over ad slots, and we propose that this novel bid language could be relevant in a number of other areas.

For example, a bidder in the ad slot auction might want her ad to be on the air at least five times within one week between 8 and 10 pm. That is, all ad slots between 8 and 10 pm are substitutes (see definition 8.3.2) but the bidder needs at least five; this is a complementarity valuation for a sufficient volume from a group of substitutes. The priority-vector format would then have weights equal to 1 for the selected set of substitute times and $w_j^{min} = 5$. Let's look at the computational complexity of the problem.

Theorem 7.5.1 *The decision version of the WDPTV problem is strongly* NP-*complete.*

Proof. There is a reduction from the decision version of the strongly NP-hard multiple-knapsack problem, i.e., given a set of n items and a set of m knapsacks $(m \leq n)$, with a profit b_j and a weight d_j for each item j, and a capacity c_k of each knapsack k, can one select m disjoint subsets of the set of n items such that the total profit of the selected items exceeds a given target profit T, with each subset assigned to a knapsack and the total weight of any subset not exceeding the capacity of the assigned knapsack?

To see that this problem is a special instance of the WDP, let the minimum price per unit $r_k = 0$; let each bidder i bid for only a single item j with bid price b_j and priority vector W_i with $w_j^{min} = 1$. This means that she wants her ad, with length (weight) d_j, to be assigned to one out of all the slots (knapsacks) k with duration (capacity) c_k. The multiple-knapsack decision problem can be answered affirmatively if and only if this specific WDPTV instance has an optimal objective value greater than or equal to T. The problem is in NP because it is straightforward to check whether a given solution is correct. □

The decision version of the multiple knapsack problem is strongly NP-complete (Chekuri and Khanna, 2006). While weakly NP-complete problems may admit efficient solutions in practice as long as their inputs are of relatively small magnitude, strongly NP-complete problems do not admit efficient solutions in such cases. Unless P = NP, there is no fully polynomial-time approximation scheme (FPTAS) for strongly NP-complete problems (Garey and Johnson, 1972). Even if we cannot hope for FPTAS, near-optimal solutions with standard mixed-integer programming solvers can be obtained for practically relevant problem sizes (Goetzendorff *et al.*, 2015).

7.6   Combinatorial Double Auctions

So far we have focused on single-sided auctions with one auctioneer and multiple bidders. More and more markets facilitate trade among multiple buyers and sellers. The simplest example of a two-sided market is the *bilateral trade scenario* discussed in section 3.4.3, in which there is a single seller and a single buyer only. The Myerson–Satterthwaite theorem shows that no mechanism can be efficient, Bayesian Nash incentive-compatible, individually rational, and at the same time budget balanced. With more buyers and sellers on each side, we have an exchange institution. A *double auction* for multiple copies of homogeneous goods is an *exchange institution*, where multiple buyers and sellers simultaneously submit their ask prices to an auctioneer and then the auctioneer chooses some price p that clears the market: all the sellers who asked less than p sell, and all buyers who bid more than p buy at this price p.

A *combinatorial double auction* or combinatorial exchange brings together multiple buyers and sellers to trade multiple heterogeneous and indivisible objects. Combinatorial exchanges have been discussed for various application domains including transportation (Wang and Kopfer, 2014), fishery (Innes *et al.*, 2014), supply chain formation (Walsh *et al.*, 2000), and vegetation markets (Nemes *et al.*, 2008). The winner determination problem for a combinatorial exchange (WDPCE) is similar to that of a single-sided combinatorial exchange. Here, $c_{i,k}(S)$ can assume a positive or negative quantity, i.e., a quantity that a bidder wants to buy or, rather, to sell on the market. The value $v_i(S)$ can also be a positive or a negative number. For example, if a market participant wants to sell a package then this ask price would enter as a negative amount. The exchange will then maximize the difference between buy bids and asks, i.e., the gains from trade subject to the allocation constraints which guarantee feasibility. Here is the formulation for a combinatorial exchange:

$$\max_{x_i(S)} \sum_{S \subseteq \mathcal{K}} \sum_{i \in \mathcal{I}} v_i(S) x_i(S) \qquad \text{(WDPCE)}$$

$$\text{s.t.} \quad \sum_{S \subseteq \mathcal{K}} x_i(S) \leq 1 \qquad \forall i \in \mathcal{I}$$

$$\sum_{S:k \in S} \sum_{i \in \mathcal{I}} c_{i,k}(S) x_i(S) \leq 0 \qquad \forall k \in \mathcal{K}$$

$$x_i(S) \in \{0, 1\} \qquad \forall i \in \mathcal{I}, S \subseteq \mathcal{K}$$

The VCG mechanism is general, and it also leads to strategy-proofness in a combinatorial exchange. Unfortunately, this mechanism is not budget balanced in a combinatorial exchange. The amount of loss incurred by the auctioneer in a combinatorial exchange with a VCG payment rule can be substantial. Given the fact that the VCG mechanism is the only strategy-proof mechanism, there has been research on payment rules which are in the core with respect to the bids and which are budget balanced, so that the auctioneer does not make a loss (Day, 2013; Parkes, 2001). These rules cannot be strategy-proof, however.

An application where combinatorial exchanges have been used for some years is *day-ahead energy markets*. In this context, bidders are allowed to submit block orders (i.e., package bids). Electricity production exhibits substantial non-convexities owing to the start-up costs and minimum power output of power plants. Non-convexities also exist on the buyers's side, because bidders are interested in winning a certain quantity of energy for several hours in a row. This is why day-ahead energy markets allow for package bids of multiple subsequent hours.

The main design problem in these exchanges is the requirement to determine anonymous and linear (hourly) prices. This means that Walrasian equilibrium prices are required. Such prices typically do not exist in a market that allows for package bids and indivisible items, as we will discuss in more detail in chapter 8. Owing to the impossibility of linear (item-level) prices in the optimal solution, there are two approaches. In the USA, markets implement the welfare-maximizing solution but deviate from linear prices by using side payments. Due to these non-convexities, there will be some accepted bids which should not have been accepted at those prices. These bids are financially compensated via so called uplifts. Unfortunately, such uplifts might be very high. In Europe, exchanges implement linear prices and accept inefficient allocations in terms of social welfare (Van Vyve *et al.*, 2011). There are a number of proposals about how to compute or approximate linear prices on energy markets (Hogan and Ring, 2003; Martin *et al.*, 2014; O'Neill *et al.*, 2005; Van Vyve *et al.*, 2011). Some of these are based on the dual of linear programming relaxation; others define a separate problem to minimize the uplift. However, there can be bids that should be winning on the basis of the market price and yet they are not. Participants in these markets seem to prefer linear and anonymous prices in spite of these shortcomings.

7.7 Empirical Results

There is relatively little work on bidder behavior in sealed-bid multi-object auctions. With a VCG payment rule bidders are expected to submit their valuations truthfully. In experiments with a low number of items, this is often but not always the case (Scheffel *et al.*, 2011). However, in larger combinatorial auctions with many items, bidders might not be able to bid on all possible packages, owing to the exponential growth of these packages.

As indicated in section 7.4.1, Bayesian models of first-price sealed-bid combinatorial auctions are largely unexplored. However, there are Bayesian Nash equilibrium strategies for sealed-bid ex ante split-award auctions. There are closed-form Bayesian Nash equilibrium strategies for such auctions (Bichler *et al.*, 2014b), and we discuss these experiments to understand to what extent equilibrium strategies are predictive of the behavior of human subjects in the laboratory. One could argue that if Bayesian Nash equilibrium strategies cannot even explain simple ex ante split-award auctions with two lots, there is little hope that they can explain bidder behavior in more complex combinatorial auctions with many items. Bichler *et al.* (2014b) designed laboratory experiments, with different levels of control, where human bidders competed either against other human bidders or against computerized bidders. The latter were designed to mitigate the impact of behavioral influences, such as risk aversion, regret, and inconsistent expectations. Bichler *et al.* observed significant underbidding in split-award procurement auctions for low-cost draws similar to that observed in earlier experiments on single-lot first-price sealed-bid auctions. Although the impact of risk aversion should be reduced with many repeated auctions, residual risk aversion, wrong expectations about other bidders, or regret can all serve as explanations for this underbidding. Interestingly, there was no significant underbidding in computerized experiments, where bidders submitted bids only once but their bids were reused in 100 computerized auctions. This provides evidence that strategic complexity cannot serve as an explanation for underbidding in these two-object auctions. Computerized experiments where the bid function of a bidder is used only once rather than in 100 auctions again exhibited significant underbidding, which indicates that risk aversion has a considerable impact on bidding strategy.

The results provided evidence that bidders in the laboratory behave as expected utility maximizers and that they are able to mimic the complicated equilibrium strategies with surprisingly high precision in the computerized experiments, if regret and risk aversion are controlled. However, in the field, wrong expectations about others, risk aversion, and regret can all influence bidder behavior and Bayesian Nash equilibrium strategies might not be a good predictor for human bidding behavior. Here, we have only discussed a single set of experiments on ex ante split-award auctions, where there is a unique Bayesian Nash equilibrium strategy. The situation in ex post split-award auctions is even more difficult, as there is a substantial equilibrium selection problem and it is difficult for bidders to coordinate on an equilibrium. While Bayesian Nash equilibrium strategies might not be a good prediction tool in procurement applications, where risk aversion matters and bidders often have beliefs about their competitors rather than a common prior distribution, they might well be predictive in advertising markets where bidders are automated and all have access to the same historical bid data. There is a larger number of experiments on open multi-object auctions, which we summarize at the end of the next chapter.

7.8   Summary

In chapter 6 we discussed the SMRA, a simple auction format, which restricts bidders to bidding on individual items. Bidders cannot express complementary valuations or substitute valuations, which can lead to inefficiencies. Combinatorial auctions, however, allow bids on bundles of items and bidders can express all types of valuation. Bundle bids address the exposure problem of larger bidders, but they can make it harder for small bidders to jointly outbid a large bidder with a package bid. This expressiveness of an XOR bid language in combinatorial auctions comes at a cost. Winner determination turns into a computationally hard problem. In addition, bidders need to express a large number of package bids with general bid languages. The number of possible package bids is exponential in the number of items with an XOR bid language. This motivates the design of compact bid languages, which require bidders to specify a much smaller number of parameters to describe their preferences. We provided two longer examples about compact bid languages in procurement and in TV ad scheduling. They illustrate that, with some prior information about the shape of the bidders' value or cost functions, it is possible to elicit bidder preferences even in complex multi-unit multi-object environments.

We discussed different payment rules including pay-as-bid, VCG, and bidder-optimal core payment rules. While the VCG mechanism is strategy-proof, it is not necessarily in the core. On the other hand, a Bayesian Nash equilibrium analysis of pay-as-bid and bidder-optimal core payment rules is challenging and requires strong assumptions about common prior distributions being available to bidders. Experiments can be quite useful to understand such sealed-bid market mechanisms better. The results of existing laboratory experiments indicate that bidder idiosyncrasies with respect to their risk aversion or beliefs matter a lot in multi-object auctions with a pay-as-bid payment rule, and the outcomes are hard to predict.

Even in high-stakes spectrum auctions, sealed-bid auction formats are rarely used, and some argue that, owing to the many possible bids that a bidder can submit and possible value interdependences, multi-object auctions should rather be organized as open auctions. Arguably, the understanding of ascending auction formats plays a much more important role in multi-object auctions than in single-object auctions, and we will discuss open auctions in the next chapter.

Notes

Figure 7.1 was adapted with permission from Robert W. Day and Peter Cramton, Quadratic core-selecting payment rules for combinatorial auctions, *Operations Research* **60**(3) 2012. Copyright (2012), the Institute for Operations Research and Management Sciences, 5521 Research Park Drive, Suite 200, Catonsville, MD 21228, USA.

7.9   Comprehension Questions

1. What is the winner determination problem (WDP) in combinatorial auctions? Can you characterize its computational complexity?
2. What problems arise when the VCG mechanism is applied to combinatorial auctions?
3. What is the value of the bundle $\{a, b, c, d\}$ for the following bid languages?
   - $(\{a, b\}, 10)\text{XOR}(\{c, d\}, 6)$
   - $(\{a, b\}, 10)\text{OR}(\{c, d\}, 6)$
4. Why is it sometimes necessary to develop domain-specific bid languages?

7.10 Problems

Winner Determination

Consider the auction shown in table 7.7 with three items $\{A, B, C\}$ and three bidders $\{1, 2, 3\}$.

Table 7.7 Bidder valuations

	$\{A\}$	$\{B\}$	$\{C\}$	$\{A, B\}$	$\{A, C\}$	$\{B, C\}$
Bidder 1	8	8	–	–	8	–
Bidder 2	–	6	8	–	8	9
Bidder 3	6	–	–	13	12	13

Model this problem as an integer program (IP) where each bidder can get at most one package. The objective is to assign packages of items to the bidders such that the social welfare is maximized.

VCG Payments

Three bidders bid for two items and their bids are provided in table 7.8.

Table 7.8 Bidder valuations

	$\{A\}$	$\{B\}$	$\{A, B\}$
Bidder 1	7	8	13
Bidder 2	9	5	12
Bidder 3	–	–	16

(a) Model the problem as an integer program.
(b) Compute the allocation and VCG payments.
(c) Compute the utilities of the bidders and the seller.

Winner Determination and VCG Payments

Consider three indivisible items A, B, C and two bidders. Each item has an individual size for each bidder. Table 7.9 shows the values and sizes of the two bidders.

Table 7.9 Bidder valuations

	Bidder 1		Bidder 2	
Item	Size	Value	Size	Value
A	0.5	1	1	2
B	0.5	2	0.5	2
C	1	2	0.5	1

The capacity of each bidder is 1. The goal is to assign items to the bidders such that the social welfare is maximized and the size of the allocation respects the bidder's capacities.

- Model this problem as an integer program.
- What is the optimal solution of the integer program and the relaxed program?
- Compute the VCG payments by the bidders.
- Compute the utilities of the bidders and the seller.

8   Open Multi-Object Auctions

The revelation principle (see theorem 3.3.1) suggests that if a social-choice function can be implemented by an arbitrary indirect mechanism (e.g., an open auction) then the same function can be implemented by a truthful direct revelation mechanism. Analyzing direct mechanisms is often more convenient, and the revelation principle allows one to argue that this restriction is without loss of generality. Yet there are cases where one prefers to implement and model the indirect version of a mechanism rather than its direct counterpart.

One argument used in the literature refers to interdependent valuations. The *linkage principle* implies that open auctions generally lead to higher expected revenue than sealed-bid auctions, with interdependent bidder valuations. Milgrom and Weber (1982) wrote: "One explanation of this inequality is that when bidders are uncertain about their valuations, they can acquire useful information by scrutinizing the bidding behavior of their competitors during the course of an (ascending) auction. That extra information weakens the winner's curse and leads to more aggressive bidding in the (ascending) auction, which accounts for the higher expected price."

Another argument for open auctions is that the winners of an ascending auction do not need to reveal their true valuation to the auctioneer, only that it is above the second-highest bid. With respect to multi-object auctions, Levin and Skrzypacz (2017) write that economists think of open auctions as having an advantage because bidders can discover gradually how their demands fit together. Most spectrum auctions are open auctions, largely for these reasons.

As a result, much recent research has focused on ascending multi-object auctions, i.e., generalizations of the single-object English auction where bidders can outbid each other iteratively. The models can be considered as algorithms, and we will try to understand the game-theoretical properties of these algorithms. In particular, we want to understand if there is a generalization of the English auction to ascending combinatorial auctions that also has a dominant strategy or ex post equilibrium. Unfortunately, the answer is negative for general valuations. However, there are positive results for restricted preferences.

A strong restriction of preferences is found in assignment markets, where bidders bid on multiple items but want to win at most one. This restriction allows us to formulate the allocation problem as an assignment problem, and there exists an ascending auction where truthful bidding is an ex post equilibrium. The game-theoretical analysis of ascending assignment markets has led to algorithmic models of ascending auctions, which we discuss first. These models have been influential for modeling open combinatorial auctions, which we discuss thereafter. We introduce restrictions on the valuations in open combinatorial auctions that allow for ex post implementations. Unfortunately, these auction algorithms rely on a number of non-linear and personalized prices, which are exponential in the number of objects. They also lead to many auction rounds. The discussion of theoretical models is useful before we introduce open combinatorial auction formats as they are used in the field, in the next chapter.

8.1 Primal–Dual Auctions for Assignment Markets

In assignment markets each bidder can bid on multiple items but wants to win at most one. As a consequence, the allocation problem reduces to an assignment problem (AP), i.e., the problem of finding the maximum weight matching in a weighted bipartite graph. The variables $p(k)$ and π_i in the following formulation describe the dual variables of the linear program:

$$\max \sum_{i \in \mathcal{I}} \sum_{k \in \mathcal{K}} v_{i,k} x_{i,k} \qquad \text{(AP)}$$

$$\text{s.t.} \sum_{i \in \mathcal{I}} x_{i,k} = 1 \qquad \forall k \in \mathcal{K} \qquad (p(k))$$

$$\sum_{k \in \mathcal{K}} x_{i,k} = 1 \qquad \forall i \in \mathcal{I} \qquad (\pi_i)$$

$$x_{i,k} \in \{0, 1\} \qquad \forall k \in \mathcal{K}, \forall i \in \mathcal{I}$$

The assignment problem (AP) can be modeled as a binary program and is illustrated as a bipartite graph where the edges are the valuations of the bidders (see figure 8.1). The variable $x_{i,k}$ represents the assignment of agent i to item k, taking the value 1 if there is an assignment and 0 if this is not the case. This formulation also allows fractional variable values, but there is always an optimal solution where the variables take integer values, because the constraint matrix is totally unimodular (see appendix A.4). The first constraint requires that every item is assigned to exactly one agent, and the second constraint requires that every agent is assigned to one item. The dual variables are added on the right, with $p(k)$ describing the anonymous item prices and π_i the payoff of each bidder.

Note that in this chapter we typically focus on ex post equilibria (see definition 2.3.2) rather than dominant-strategy equilibria. None of these equilibrium concepts requires assumptions about other bidders' valuations. Ex post equilibria are slightly weaker than dominant-strategy equilibria, because they require the assumption that other bidders will play their best response. Dominant strategies require assumptions neither about others' valuations nor their strategies. Let's look at a simple example to see why dominant-strategy equilibria are difficult to attain in ascending multi-object auctions.

Example 8.1.1 Suppose that there are two bidders with additive valuations competing for two heterogeneous items $\{A, B\}$ in parallel English auctions. Bidder 1 has a value

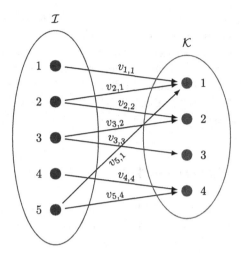

Figure 8.1 The assignment problem as a bipartite graph.

of $4 for item A and $3 for item B. Bidder 2 has a value of $3 for item A and $2 for item B. Bidder 1 will win both items, if both bidders bid straightforwardly. Now, let's assume that bidder 2 will bid up to $100 on both items, if she sees that bidder 1 starts bidding on item A. In this case, straightforward bidding would not be the best response as bidder 1 would make zero payoff. Knowing this strategy of bidder 2, bidder 1 is better off bidding only on item 2.

Obviously, bidder 2 is irrational in this example. However, in iterative multi-object auctions we cannot rule out irrational behavior and so need to make this mild assumption that others play their best response as rational bidders. This assumption requires us to restrict ourselves to ex post equilibria. Actually, with additive valuations, straightforward bidding is an ex post equilibrium in the example above, which is a simultaneous multi-round auction. This is true because with additive valuations each of the two parallel auctions can be analyzed separately.

If straightforward bidding in an ascending auction always yields the VCG allocation and payments then it is also ex post incentive-compatible. This is so because the VCG mechanism is the *unique* strategy-proof and welfare-maximizing mechanism (Green and Laffont, 1979; Holmstrom, 1979) and because, by applying the revelation principle to an ex post incentive-compatible mechanism, we then obtain a direct-revelation strategy-proof mechanism. In the following sections, we therefore analyze whether the resulting allocation of an ascending auction is welfare maximizing and whether the payments are equivalent to the VCG payments.

8.1.1 Dual Prices and VCG Payments

In this section we draw on duality theory from linear programming. We recommend the reader to revisit linear programming and duality theory (see appendix A.3). Every linear program (LP) such as the assignment problem AP, referred to as a primal problem, can be converted into a dual problem. There are two ideas fundamental to duality theory. One is the fact that (for the symmetric dual) the dual of a dual linear program is a linear program which is equivalent to the original, primal, linear program. Additionally, every feasible solution for a linear program gives a bound on the optimal value of the objective function of its dual. The *weak duality theorem* states that the objective function value of the dual for any feasible solution is always greater than or equal to the objective function value of the primal problem for any feasible solution (assuming a primal maximizing the objective function). The *strong duality theorem* states that if the primal has an optimal solution, x^*, then the dual also has an optimal solution. If we interpret the primal LP problem as a classical resource-allocation problem, its dual can be interpreted as a resource valuation or the price of a scarce resource described by a constraint. These prices hold only for convex optimization problems and as long as the allocation or basis of the LP is optimal. Integer programs do not exhibit such dual prices in general unless the optimal solution is a feasible integer allocation.

The AP is modeled as an integer program; more specifically, as a binary program. Binary programming problems are typically NP-hard, but this is not the case if the constraint matrix is totally unimodular as for the AP (see appendix A.4). An auctioneer could solve the allocation problem with a Simplex algorithm or use even more efficient algorithms such as the well-known Hungarian algorithm, which has a runtime of $\mathcal{O}(n^3)$. Total unimodularity does not only make the allocation problem tractable; it also allows for efficient ascending auctions, where straightforward bidding is an ex post Nash equilibrium.

Definition 8.1.1 (Straightforward bidding)   Straightforward bidding (aka sincere bidding or myopic bidding) describes a strategy where, in each stage of an ascending auction, a bidder bids on all packages which maximize his payoff.

In a market with perfectly divisible objects, every Walrasian allocation is in the core (Debreu and Scarf, 1963). Also, any core allocation can be approximately decentralized by price as the number of agents becomes large (Anderson, 1978). With indivisible objects and small numbers of agents, the weak core and Walrasian equilibria are not always equivalent. The assignment market in this section and the housing market (without money) in section 11.3.1 are examples where there is equivalence. Both assume that bidders are interested in a single object only. Let's discuss the assignment market in more detail.

Assignment markets were first analyzed by Shapley and Shubik (1971), who found that the weak core of an assignment game is non-empty and is precisely the set of solutions of the dual of the corresponding linear program. The theorem follows directly from linear programming duality. This means that at core prices there is no coalition $M \subset N$ which can make a counter-offer that leaves the members of M and the seller at least as well off as the currently winning coalition while at least one member of M is better off (see section 7.3.2.1). Again, N is the set of bidders $\mathcal{I}$. Shapley and Shubik (1971) showed that a core of this game exists, and we know effective computational procedures for the core (given that bidders submit sealed bids). Let us now look at the dual of the AP described above:

$$\min\{\sum_{i\in\mathcal{I}}\pi_i + \sum_{k\in\mathcal{K}}p(k)\} \qquad\qquad\text{(DAP)}$$

$$\text{s.t.}\quad \pi_i + p(k) \geq v_{i,k} \qquad\qquad \forall k \in \mathcal{K}, \forall i \in \mathcal{I}$$
$$\pi_i, p(k) \text{ unrestricted} \qquad \forall k \in \mathcal{K}, \forall i \in \mathcal{I}$$

A different formulation minimizes the set of prices $P = (p(1), \ldots, p(k), \ldots, p(m))$ and is bidder-optimal in this respect as it maximizes the payoffs of bidders:

$$\min \sum_{k\in\mathcal{K}}p(k) \qquad\qquad\text{(DAP2)}$$

$$\text{s.t.}\quad \pi_i + p(k) \geq v_{i,k} \qquad\qquad \forall k \in \mathcal{K}, \forall i \in \mathcal{I}$$

$$\sum_{i\in\mathcal{I}}\pi_i + \sum_{k\in\mathcal{K}}p(k) = W^*$$

$$\pi_i, p(k) \geq 0 \qquad\qquad \forall k \in \mathcal{K}, \forall i \in \mathcal{I}$$

The second set of constraints ensures that the sum of prices equals the objective function value W^* of the AP. It can be shown that the resulting prices P are equivalent to the prices with a VCG payment rule and consequently are incentive-compatible as well (Leonard, 1983). There is an equivalence between the core of the coalitional game and the competitive equilibrium for assignment markets and combinatorial auctions (Bikhchandani and Mamer, 1997; Kelso and Crawford, 1982), which we discuss later.

Definition 8.1.2 (Competitive equilibrium, CE)   A price vector P and a feasible allocation x^* are in competitive equilibrium if the allocation x^* maximizes the payoff of every bidder and the auctioneer revenue, given the prices P.

The efficient allocation x^* is said to be *supported* by the price vector P in CE. We talk about CE prices and core prices interchangably in what follows. If we have a CE price vector with item-level (i.e., linear) prices, we talk about a *Walrasian equilibrium* and *Walrasian prices*, in a way reminiscent of the fictional Walrasian auctioneer. As indicated in the introduction of this chapter, the first fundamental welfare theorem asserts that market equilibria are Pareto efficient (see section 5.1). This is true for the assignment market as well.

Theorem 8.1.1 (First welfare theorem for assignment markets)   *A Walrasian equilibrium in the assignment market maximizes social welfare.*

Proof. Let x^* be a welfare-maximizing allocation with welfare W^*. In a Walrasian equilibrium, if a bidder i prefers item $x_{i,k}$ to $x^*_{i,k}$ at prices P then $v_i(x_{i,k}) - p(x_{i,k}) \geq v_i(x^*_{i,k}) - p(x^*_{i,k})$. We can sum this inequality over all bidders:

$$\sum_{i\in\mathcal{I}}v_i(x_{i,k}) - \sum_{i\in\mathcal{I}}p(x_{i,k}) \geq \sum_{i\in\mathcal{I}}v_i(x^*_{i,k}) - \sum_{i\in\mathcal{I}}p(x^*_{i,k})$$

Now, $\sum_{i\in\mathcal{I}}v_i(x_{i,k}) = W$ and $\sum_{i\in\mathcal{I}}v_i(x^*_{i,k}) = W^*$. In a Walrasian equilibrium, an item $k \in \mathcal{K}$ is unsold if prices are null. The sum $\sum_{i\in\mathcal{I}}p(x_{i,k})$ runs over all items with a non-zero price, and $\sum_{i\in\mathcal{I}}p(x^*_{i,k}) \leq \sum_{i\in\mathcal{I}}p(x_{i,k})$. Rearranging terms shows that the welfare of x is at least that of x^*, and therefore x is also welfare-maximizing. $\qquad\square$

8.1.2 An Ascending Auction for the Assignment Problem

We now introduce a simple ascending auction by Demange et al. (1986) for an assignment market which always ends in CE and which is based on a Hungarian algorithm by Kuhn (1955). Primal–dual algorithms employ a widespread algorithm design principle often used to solve linear programs, and the Hungarian algorithm is a primal–dual algorithm. A second algorithm described in Demange et al. (1986) draws on an earlier auction proposed by Crawford and Knoer (1981). Each bidder $i \in \mathcal{I}$ assigns a value $v_i(k)$ to every item $k \in \mathcal{K}$, where $v_i(k) \in \mathbb{N}$. The payoff of i in an ascending assignment market is given as $v_i(k) - p(k)$. An assignment $\mu : \mathcal{I} \mapsto \mathcal{K}$ maps bidders to items, and $\mu(i) = k$ means that item k is assigned to bidder i. The auctioneer announces a start price $r(k)$ for each item $k \in \mathcal{K}$, which can be zero. Each bidder now announces which item or items she wants to buy at the start prices, i.e., her demand set $D_i(P)$.

Definition 8.1.3 (Demand set) The demand set $D_i(P)$ of a bidder i includes all bundles which maximize the bidder's payoff π_i at the given prices P:

$$D_i(P) = \{S \mid \pi_i(S, P) \geq \max_{T \subseteq \mathcal{K}} \pi_i(T, P), \pi_i(S, P) \geq 0, S \subseteq \mathcal{K}\}$$

If it is possible to assign each item k to a bidder i who demands it, the auction is in CE. If no such assignment μ exists, a set of items is overdemanded. This means the number of bidders demanding only items in this set is greater than the number of items in the set. In CE there cannot be an overdemanded set. An ascending auction locates a minimal overdemanded set, that is, an overdemanded set where none of its proper subsets is overdemanded. The ask prices of each item on such a minimally overdemanded set are raised by the auctioneer. Then the bidders are again asked for their demand set $D_i(P)$. After the new bids are announced, the auctioneer again finds either a complete assignment or a new minimal overdemanded set, whose prices she again raises. This procedure cannot continue infinitely with finite valuations but will end at some set of prices P.

Example 8.1.2 We provide an example with three bidders $\mathcal{I} = \{1, 2, 3\}$ and three items $\mathcal{K} = \{A, B, C\}$ to illustrate the ascending algorithm for the assignment market in tables 8.2–8.4. The true valuations of the bidders are given in table 8.1.

In round $t = 0$ there is overdemand on item B, so that the price for this item goes up. A set of items is overdemanded if the number of bidders demanding only items in this set is greater than the number of items in this set. In round $t = 2$ the set of overdemanded items is A and B. In the example, in round $t = 5$ the algorithm finds an efficient solution, marked with primes (see table 8.4, right). The social welfare of this efficient auction is $8 + 2 + 6 = 16$ (marked with asterisks in tables 8.1 and 8.2, left). The VCG payment for bidder 1 would be $2 - (16 - 14) = 0$; for bidder 2 it would be $8 - (16 - 11) = 3$ and for bidder 3 it would be $6 - (16 - 15) = 5$. These are actually equivalent to the CE prices for this auction: bidder 1 pays a price of $0 for item 3, bidder 2 pays a price of $3 for item 1, and bidder 3 pays a price of $5 for item 2. None of the bidders would have an incentive to deviate from straightforward bidding.

Table 8.1 Valuations of bidders $\mathcal{I}$ for items $\mathcal{K}$

	A	B	C
Bidder 1	5	7	2*
Bidder 2	8*	9	3
Bidder 3	2	6*	0

Table 8.2 Example of an ascending auction market. The boxed values indicate those items for which payoff is maximized at the current prices

$t=0$	$\mathcal{K}$			$t=1$	$\mathcal{K}$		
$\mathcal{I}$	A	B	C	$\mathcal{I}$	A	B	C
1	5	[7]	2*	1	5	[6]	2
2	8*	[9]	3	2	[8]	[8]	3
3	2	[6]*	0	3	2	[5]	0
$p^1(k)$	0	1	0	$p^2(k)$	0	2	0

Table 8.3 Example of an ascending auction market (contd.)

$t=2$	$\mathcal{K}$			$t=3$	$\mathcal{K}$		
$\mathcal{I}$	A	B	C	$\mathcal{I}$	A	B	C
1	[5]	[5]	2	1	[4]	[4]	2
2	[8]	7	3	2	[7]	6	3
3	2	[4]	0	3	1	[3]	0
$p^3(k)$	1	3	0	$p^4(k)$	2	4	0

Table 8.4 Example of an ascending auction market (contd.)

$t=4$	$\mathcal{K}$			$t=5$	$\mathcal{K}$		
$\mathcal{I}$	A	B	C	$\mathcal{I}$	A	B	C
1	[3]	[3]	2	1	[2]	[2]	[2]'
2	[6]	5	3	2	[5]'	4	3
3	0	[2]	0	3	-1	[1]'	0
$p^5(k)$	3	5	0	$p^6(k)$	3	5	0

There are two properties of this algorithm which are important and need to be discussed. First, the algorithm is a variant of the Hungarian algorithm (Kuhn, 1955), which is a primal–dual algorithm. Using such algorithms for the design of multi-object auctions has been shown to be a powerful idea. Second, the minimal price vector in the core is equivalent to the VCG price vector for assignment markets (Leonard, 1983). The algorithm always ends up in the minimal price vector if bidders bid straightforwardly, and doing so creates an ex post Nash equilibrium. Incentive compatibility and the core property make the mechanism robust against deviations caused by coalitions as well. We will discuss these aspects further, in the context of greedy auctions, in section 8.2 but the ascending auctions of Demange *et al.* (1986) for unit-demand bidders and the deferred acceptance auction for single-minded bidders, who are interested only in a single package, are robust against coalitional deviations. Let's first discuss incentive compatibility.

Theorem 8.1.2 (Demange *et al.*, 1986) *Let P be the price vector obtained from the ascending auction mechanism and let Q be any other competitive price vector; then $p(k) \leq q(k)$ for all $k \in K$.*

Proof. The proof is by contradiction. Suppose that $P \leq Q$ at stage 0. Let t be the last stage where $P_t \leq Q$. Now let's look at stage $t + 1$. Define $S_1 = \{k \mid p_{t+1}(k) > q(k)\}$, and an overdemanded set S whose prices are raised at stage $t + 1$, i.e., $S = \{k \mid p_{t+1}(k) > p_t(k)\}$, such that $S_1 \subset S$. It can be shown that $S - S_1$ is non-empty and overdemanded, i.e., S cannot be a minimally overdemanded set, but this is not possible due to the price update rules of the auction.

Let's define $T = \{i | D_i(P_t) \subset S\}$. Since S is overdemanded, this means that $|T| > |S|$. Now, $T_1 = \{i | i \in T \text{ and } D_i(P_t) \cap S_1 \neq \emptyset\}$. We claim that $D_i(Q) \subset S_1$ for all $i \in T_1$. Let's choose $k \in S_1 \cap D_i(P_t)$. If $l \notin S$ then i prefers k to l at price P_t because $i \in T$. But $p_t(l) \leq q(l)$ and $p_t(k) = q(l)$, so i prefers k to l at price Q. If $l \in S - S_1$ then i likes k at least as much as l at price P_t. However, $p_t(l) < p_{t+1}(l) \leq q(l)$ and $p_t(k) = q(k)$. So, i prefers k to l at price Q, as claimed.

A price is called *competitive* if there exists an assignment μ such that $\mu(i) \in D_i(P)$. Since Q is competitive there are no overdemanded sets at prices Q, and $|T_1| \leq |S_1|$. Now, $T - T_1 = \{i \mid i \in T \text{ and } D_i(P_t) \in S - S_1\}$. But we have shown that $|T| > |S|$ and $|T_1| \leq |S_1|$, and so it follows that $|T - T_1| > |S - S_1|$; thus $S - S_1$ is overdemanded, which is a contradiction. $\qquad\qquad\square$

There is an equilibrium (P, μ) if P is competitive, and if $k \notin \mu(i)$ then $p(k) = r(k)$. It can also be shown that if P is a minimum CE price vector then there is an assignment μ^* such that (P, μ^*) is an equilibrium.

We now provide an extended example which illustrates that the ascending auction described above amounts to a primal–dual algorithm that solves the assignment problem AP. Primal–dual algorithms are often used to solve linear programs such as the assignment problem. Such algorithms can be interpreted as ascending auctions, where the auctioneer solves the primal problem, i.e., the AP, and the bidders solve the dual problem, the DAP. This interpretation is not obvious for other algorithms, such as the Simplex algorithm, which also solve a linear program.

At the start of a primal–dual algorithm, the dual is derived from the primal problem. Using the complementary slackness conditions, a second primal problem can be formulated, also known as the *restricted primal problem* (RP). If the restricted primal problem is feasible then the original primal problem is optimal. If this is not the case, the dual of the restricted problem is formulated and the dual prices are updated iteratively until optimality is achieved.

The following example illustrates how the algorithm works. Consider again the valuations in table 8.1, where the bidders 1, 2, and 3 are bidding on items A, B, and C. We will go through the iterations of a primal–dual algorithm and show that it is indeed equivalent to the ascending auction in example 8.1.2. Although the example is lengthy, it should aid our understanding of how algorithms can be interpreted as open auctions.

First Iteration, Step 0 (P)

We start by stating the relaxed primal LP for the example:

$$\max\{z = 5x_{1,A} + 7x_{1,B} + 2x_{1,C} + 8x_{2,A} + 9x_{2,B} + 3x_{2,C} + 2x_{3,A} + 6x_{3,B} + 0x_{3,C}\}$$

$$
\begin{aligned}
\text{s.t.} \quad & x_{1,A} + x_{1,B} + x_{1,C} = 1 & (\pi_1) \\
& x_{2,A} + x_{2,B} + x_{2,C} = 1 & (\pi_2) \\
& x_{3,A} + x_{3,B} + x_{3,C} = 1 & (\pi_3) \\
& x_{1,A} + x_{2,A} + x_{3,A} = 1 & (p(A)) \\
& x_{1,B} + x_{2,B} + x_{3,B} = 1 & (p(B)) \\
& x_{1,C} + x_{2,C} + x_{3,C} = 1 & (p(C)) \\
& x_{i,k} \geq 0 & \forall i \in \{1, 2, 3\} \text{ and } k \in \{A, B, C\}
\end{aligned}
$$

First Iteration, Step 1 (D)

Now we formulate the corresponding dual LP:

$$\min\{z = \pi_1 + \pi_2 + \pi_3 + p(A) + p(B) + p(C)\}$$

$$
\begin{aligned}
\text{s.t.} \quad & \pi_1 + p(A) \geq 5 & (x_{1,A}) \\
& \pi_1 + p(B) \geq 7 & (\boldsymbol{x_{1,B}}) \\
& \pi_1 + p(C) \geq 2 & (x_{1,C}) \\
& \pi_2 + p(A) \geq 8 & (x_{2,A}) \\
& \pi_2 + p(B) \geq 9 & (\boldsymbol{x_{2,B}}) \\
& \pi_2 + p(C) \geq 3 & (x_{2,C}) \\
& \pi_3 + p(A) \geq 2 & (x_{3,A}) \\
& \pi_3 + p(B) \geq 6 & (\boldsymbol{x_{3,B}}) \\
& \pi_3 + p(C) \geq 0 & (x_{3,C}) \\
& \pi_i, p(k) \text{ unrestricted}
\end{aligned}
$$

The solution with starting prices 0 is $p_k = (0, 0, 0)$, $\pi_i = (7, 9, 6)$. Given this solution, we want to find $x_{i,k} \neq 0$ in $\mathcal{J}$ such that $\pi_i + p_k = 0$, i.e., complementary slackness is satisfied. The following $x_{i,k}$ are in $\mathcal{J}$ and are non-zero: $\{x_{1,B}, x_{2,B}, x_{3,B}\}$ (shown in bold). This set $\mathcal{J}$ is the set of dual constraints which are tight, so the respective constraints are binding, i.e. $x_{i,k} \neq 0$. Even without knowing the valuations, the bidders in an auction can indicate at this stage for which items they maximize payoff.

First Iteration, Step 2 (RP)
In this step we formulate the restricted primal problem (RP) and solve it:

$$\max\{z = -s_1 - s_2 - s_3 - t_B\}$$

$$
\begin{aligned}
\text{s.t.} \quad & x_{1,B} + s_1 = 1 & (\pi_1) \\
& x_{2,B} + s_2 = 1 & (\pi_2) \\
& x_{3,B} + s_3 = 1 & (\pi_3) \\
& x_{1,B} + x_{2,B} + x_{3,B} + t_B = 1 & (p(B)) \\
& x_{i,k} \geq 0 & \forall (i, k) \in \mathcal{J} \\
& x_{i,k} = 0 & \forall (i, k) \in E \setminus \mathcal{J}
\end{aligned}
$$

This is the same problem as trying to find an assignment in the resulting subgraph. If $z = 0$ then terminate. The s_i are unsatisfied bidders, while t_B are unallocated items in the demand set of the bidders.

This RP has $z = -2$, which is the number of free nodes in the matching, i.e., $|z|$ is the number of unsatisfied bidders.

First Iteration, Step 3 (DRP) + Step 4 (dual variables update)
We next formulate the dual of the restricted primal (DRP):

$$\min\{z = \pi_1' + \pi_2' + \pi_3' + p'(B)\}$$

$$
\begin{aligned}
\text{s.t.} \quad & \pi_1' + p'(B) \geq 0 & (x_{1,B}) \\
& \pi_2' + p'(B) \geq 0 & (x_{2,B}) \\
& \pi_3' + p'(B) \geq 0 & (x_{3,B}) \\
& \pi_1' \geq -1 & (s_1) \\
& \pi_2' \geq -1 & (s_2) \\
& \pi_3' \geq -1 & (s_3) \\
& p(B) \geq -1 & (t_B)
\end{aligned}
$$

Now we need to find an optimal solution to the DRP. It can be shown that every basic solution has all its components equal to $+1$ or -1. Here $p' = (0, 1, 0)$ is the direction of price change for item k, and $\pi' = (-1, -1, -1)$ is the change in bidder i's payoff; $z = -3 + 1 = -2$. We then update the dual variables:

$$
\begin{aligned}
p^{new} &= (0, 0, 0) + (0, 1, 0) & = (0, 1, 0) \\
\pi^{new} &= (7, 9, 6) + (-1, -1, -1) & = (6, 8, 5)
\end{aligned}
$$

Therefore, the valuation matrix in table 8.1 changes to the following form, which is equivalent to $t = 1$ in table 8.2:

	A	B	C
1	5	6	2
2	8	8	3
3	2	5	0

Second Iteration, Step 1 (D)

Since $z \neq 0$ we need to reconsider the dual LP (D):

$$\min\{z = \pi_1 + \pi_2 + \pi_3 + p(A) + p(B) + p(C)\}$$

$$
\begin{aligned}
\text{s.t.} \quad & \pi_1 + p(A) \geq 5 & (x_{1,A}) \\
& \pi_1 + p(B) \geq 7 & (x_{1,B}) \\
& \pi_1 + p(C) \geq 2 & (x_{1,C}) \\
& \pi_2 + p(A) \geq 8 & (x_{2,A}) \\
& \pi_2 + p(B) \geq 9 & (x_{2,B}) \\
& \pi_2 + p(C) \geq 3 & (x_{2,C}) \\
& \pi_3 + p(A) \geq 2 & (x_{3,A}) \\
& \pi_3 + p(B) \geq 6 & (x_{3,B}) \\
& \pi_3 + p(C) \geq 0 & (x_{3,C}) \\
& \pi_i, p(k) \text{ unrestricted}
\end{aligned}
$$

The values $p = (0, 1, 0)$ and $\pi = (6, 8, 5)$ admit a feasible dual solution. Therefore, we need to find $x_{i,k} \neq 0$; in this case $\mathcal{J} = \{x_{1,B}, x_{2,A}, x_{2,B}, x_{3,B}\}$.

Second Iteration, Step 2 (RP)

We reformulate the RP for $\mathcal{J} = \{x_{1,B}, x_{2,A}, x_{2,B}, x_{3,B}\}$:

$$\max\{z = -s_1 - s_2 - s_3 - t_A - t_B\}$$

$$
\begin{aligned}
\text{s.t.} \quad & x_{1,B} + s_1 = 1 & (\pi_1) \\
& x_{2,A} + x_{2,B} + s_2 = 1 & (\pi_2) \\
& x_{3,B} + s_3 = 1 & (\pi_3) \\
& x_{2,A} + t_A = 1 & (p(A)) \\
& x_{1,B} + x_{2,B} + x_{3,B} + t_B = 1 & (p(B)) \\
& x_{i,k} \geq 0 & \forall (i, k) \in \mathcal{J} \\
& x_{i,k} = 0 & \forall (i, k) \in E \setminus \mathcal{J}
\end{aligned}
$$

The objective value z is equal to -1; this means that only one bidder is still unsatisfied.

Second Iteration, Step 3 (DRP) + Step 4 (dual variables update)

We now formulate the dual of the restricted primal (DRP):

$$\min\{z = \pi_1' + \pi_2' + \pi_3' + p'(A) + p'(B)\}$$

$$
\begin{aligned}
\text{s.t.} \quad & \pi_1' + p'(B) \geq 0 & (x_{1,B}) \\
& \pi_2' + p'(A) \geq 0 & (x_{2,A}) \\
& \pi_2' + p'(B) \geq 0 & (x_{2,B}) \\
& \pi_3' + p'(B) \geq 0 & (x_{3,B}) \\
& \pi_1' \geq -1 & (s_1) \\
& \pi_2' \geq -1 & (s_2) \\
& \pi_3' \geq -1 & (s_3) \\
& p'(A) \geq -1 & (t_A) \\
& p'(B) \geq -1 & (t_B)
\end{aligned}
$$

The direction of price change is $p' = (0, 1, 0)$ for item k and the change in bidder i's payoff is $\pi' = (-1, 0, -1)$; moreover $z = -2 + 1 = -1$. We then update the dual variables:

$$p^{new} = (0, 1, 0) + (0, 1, 0) \qquad = (0, 2, 0)$$
$$\pi^{new} = (6, 8, 5) + (-1, 0, -1) \qquad = (5, 8, 4)$$

Hence, the valuation matrix needs to be updated (see $t = 2$ in table 8.3):

$$
\begin{array}{c}
\quad A \quad B \quad C \\
\begin{array}{c} 1 \\ 2 \\ 3 \end{array}
\left(\begin{array}{ccc}
5 & 5 & 2 \\
8 & 7 & 3 \\
2 & 4 & 0
\end{array} \right)
\end{array}
$$

Third Iteration, Step 1 (D)

The value of the objective function z is still $\neq 0$ and therefore we start a new iteration. In the first step we reconsider the dual LP (D):

$$\min\{z = \pi_1 + \pi_2 + \pi_3 + p(A) + p(B) + p(C)\}$$

$$
\begin{array}{lll}
\text{s.t.} & \pi_1 + p(A) \geq 5 & (x_{1,A}) \\
 & \pi_1 + p(B) \geq 7 & (x_{1,B}) \\
 & \pi_1 + p(C) \geq 2 & (x_{1,C}) \\
 & \pi_2 + p(A) \geq 8 & (x_{2,A}) \\
 & \pi_2 + p(B) \geq 9 & (x_{2,B}) \\
 & \pi_2 + p(C) \geq 3 & (x_{2,C}) \\
 & \pi_3 + p(A) \geq 2 & (x_{3,A}) \\
 & \pi_3 + p(B) \geq 6 & (x_{3,B}) \\
 & \pi_3 + p(C) \geq 0 & (x_{3,C}) \\
 & \pi_i, p(k) \text{ unrestricted} &
\end{array}
$$

We see that $p = (0, 2, 0)$, $\pi = (5, 8, 4)$ is a feasible dual solution. We then find $\mathcal{J} = \{x_{1,A}, x_{1,B}, x_{2,A}, x_{3,B}\}$ with $x_{i,k} \neq 0$.

Third Iteration, Step 2 (RP)

We solve the (RP) for $\mathcal{J} = \{x_{1,A}, x_{1,B}, x_{2,A}, x_{3,B}\}$:

$$\max\{z = -s_1 - s_2 - s_3 - t_A - t_B\}$$

$$
\begin{array}{lll}
\text{s.t.} & x_{1,A} + x_{1,B} + s_1 = 1 & (\pi_1) \\
 & x_{2,A} + s_2 = 1 & (\pi_2) \\
 & x_{3,B} + s_3 = 1 & (\pi_3) \\
 & x_{1,A} + x_{2,A} + t_A = 1 & (p(A)) \\
 & x_{1,B} + x_{3,B} + t_B = 1 & (p(B)) \\
 & x_{i,k} \geq 0 & \forall (i, k) \in \mathcal{J} \\
 & x_{i,k} = 0 & \forall (i, k) \in E \backslash \mathcal{J}
\end{array}
$$

We see that $z = -1$, which means there is still one unsatisfied bidder.

Third Iteration, Step 3 (DRP) + Step 4 (dual variables update)

In the third step we reformulate the dual of the restricted primal (DRP):

$$\min\{z = \pi_1' + \pi_2' + \pi_3' + p'(A) + p'(B)\}$$

$$
\begin{aligned}
\text{s.t.} \quad & \pi_1' + p'(A) \geq 0 & (x_{1,A}) \\
& \pi_1' + p'(B) \geq 0 & (x_{1,B}) \\
& \pi_2' + p'(A) \geq 0 & (x_{2,A}) \\
& \pi_3' + p'(B) \geq 0 & (x_{3,B}) \\
& \pi_1' \geq -1 & (s_1) \\
& \pi_2' \geq -1 & (s_2) \\
& \pi_3' \geq -1 & (s_3) \\
& p'(A) \geq -1 & (t_A) \\
& p'(B) \geq -1 & (t_B)
\end{aligned}
$$

We then search for an optimal solution to the DRP. Now $p' = (1, 1, 0)$ is the direction of price change for item k and $\pi' = (-1, -1, -1)$ is the change in bidder i's payoff; $z = -3 + 2 = -1$. Finally, we update the dual variables:

$$
\begin{aligned}
p^{new} &= (0, 2, 0) + (1, 1, 0) & = (1, 3, 0) \\
\pi^{new} &= (5, 8, 1) + (-1, -1, -1) & = (4, 7, 3)
\end{aligned}
$$

We then update the valuation matrix (see $t = 3$ in table 8.3):

$$
\begin{array}{c|ccc}
 & A & B & C \\
\hline
1 & 4 & 4 & 2 \\
2 & 7 & 6 & 3 \\
3 & 1 & 3 & 0
\end{array}
$$

We skip the next iterations until iteration 6, for brevity.

Sixth Iteration, Step 1 (D)

Since $z \neq 0$ we again reconsider the dual LP (D):

$$\min\{z = \pi_1 + \pi_2 + \pi_3 + p(A) + p(B) + p(C)\}$$

$$
\begin{aligned}
\text{s.t.} \quad & \pi_1 + p(A) \geq 5 & (\boldsymbol{x_{1,A}}) \\
& \pi_1 + p(B) \geq 7 & (\boldsymbol{x_{1,B}}) \\
& \pi_1 + p(C) \geq 2 & (\boldsymbol{x_{1,C}}) \\
& \pi_2 + p(A) \geq 8 & (\boldsymbol{x_{2,A}}) \\
& \pi_2 + p(B) \geq 9 & (x_{2,B}) \\
& \pi_2 + p(C) \geq 3 & (x_{2,C}) \\
& \pi_3 + p(A) \geq 2 & (x_{3,A}) \\
& \pi_3 + p(B) \geq 6 & (\boldsymbol{x_{3,B}}) \\
& \pi_3 + p(C) \geq 0 & (x_{3,C}) \\
& \pi_i, p(k) \text{ unrestricted}
\end{aligned}
$$

Here $p = (3, 5, 0)$ and $\pi = (2, 5, 1)$ give a feasible solution. In this case $\mathcal{J} = \{x_{1,A}, x_{1,B}, x_{1,C}, x_{2,A}, x_{3,C}\}$ is the set of non-zero $x_{i,k}$.

Sixth Iteration, Step 2 (RP)

Once again, we reconsider the RP:

$$\max\{z = -s_1 - s_2 - s_3 - t_A - t_B - t_C\}$$

$$\begin{aligned}
\text{s.t.} \quad & x_{1,A} + x_{1,B} + x_{1,C} + s_1 = 1 & (\pi_1) \\
& x_{2,A} + s_2 = 1 & (\pi_2) \\
& x_{3,B} + s_3 = 1 & (\pi_3) \\
& x_{1,A} + x_{2,A} + t_A = 1 & (p(A)) \\
& x_{1,B} + x_{3,B} + t_B = 1 & (p(B)) \\
& x_{1,C} + t_C = 1 & (p(C)) \\
& x_{i,k} \geq 0 & \forall (i, k) \in \mathcal{J} \\
& x_{i,k} = 0 & \forall (i, k) \in E \backslash \mathcal{J}
\end{aligned}$$

We choose the allocation $(1, C)$, $(2, A)$, $(3, B)$ and therefore $z = 0$. This means that the solution is optimal and thus the algorithm terminates. Also, note that the payment vector p is equivalent to the VCG payments in this example.

8.2   Greedy Auctions and Matroids

Some auctions can be interpreted as simple greedy algorithms. Such algorithms greedily just make the locally optimal choice in each step. It is well known in algorithm design and combinatorics that greedy algorithms that find the global optimum constitute an optimization problem with an additive objective function if the problem is subject to constraints that have a matroid structure. A *matroid* is a structure that generalizes the notion of linear independence in vector spaces. In an allocation problem with a matroid structure in an auction, adding one bidder displaces at most one other bidder. A greedy algorithm is one that makes the locally optimal choice at each stage with the intention of finding a global optimum.

If an optimization problem has a matroid structure, the allocation is always optimal and, as was shown by Bikhchandani *et al.* (2011), such an auction implements the VCG outcome. Bikhchandani *et al.* (2011) proved the impossibility of an ascending auction (or a descending auction in procurement), which always yields the optimal solution for non-matroidal independence set-systems. In this sense matroids are relevant, as they define the boundaries, when simple greedy auctions implement the VCG outcome.

Let us revisit some definitions and theorems from matroid theory (Oxley, 1992).

Definition 8.2.1 (Matroid)   A matroid M is a pair of sets (E, I), where E is a finite set called the ground set and I is a collection of subsets of E called the independent sets, which satisfy the following properties:

1. $\emptyset \in I$;
2. for each $A \in I$, if $A' \subset A$ then $A' \in I$ (hereditary property);
3. $A, B \in I$ and $|A| > |B| \implies \exists j \in A \setminus B$ such that $B \cup \{j\} \in I$ (exchange property).

The first two criteria in the definition of a matroid define an *independence system*.

Example 8.2.1 Suppose that $M_1 = (S_1, I_1)$ is a matroid, where $S_1 = \{1, 2, 3\}$ and $I_1 = \{\{1, 2\}, \{2, 3\}, \{1\}, \{2\}, \{3\}, \emptyset\}$. Now look at $M_2 = (S_2, I_2)$, where $S_2 = \{1, 2, 3, 4, 5\}$ and $I_2 = \{\{1, 2, 3\}, \{3, 4, 5\}, \{1, 2\}, \{1, 3\}, \{2, 3\}, \{3, 4\}, \{3, 5\}, \{4, 5\}, \{1\}, \{2\}, \{3\}, \{4\}, \{5\}, \emptyset\}$. The set M_2 is not a matroid: consider $B = \{1, 3\}$ and $A = \{3, 4, 5\}$, which violate the exchange property.

Matroids can be found in linear algebra or in graph theory, for example. If E is any finite subset of a vector space V, then we can define a matroid M on E to be the linearly independent subsets of E. This is called a vector matroid. Similarly, a matrix A gives rise to a matroid M on its set of columns. The dependent sets of the columns in the matroid are those that are linearly dependent as vectors. This matroid is called the *column matroid* of A. To see this, let S be the set of columns of A, and let $F = \{C | C \subseteq S, C$ is a linearly independent subset$\}$. Then we have the following theorem:

Theorem 8.2.1 *The pair of sets (S, F) is a matroid.*

Proof. Clearly, F is not empty as it contains every column of A. Observe, that if B is a set of linearly independent columns of A then any subset D of B is linearly independent. Thus, F is hereditary. Also, if B and D are sets of linearly independent columns of A, and $|D| < |B|$, then the dimension of the span of D is less then the dimension of the span of B. Choose a column x in B that is not contained in the span of D; then $D \cup \{x\}$ is a linearly independent subset of columns of A. Hence, F satisfies the exchange property. $\square$

Definition 8.2.2 (Dependent set) If $A \subset E$ and $A \notin I$ then A is called a dependent set.

A maximally independent set, i.e., an independent set which becomes dependent on the addition of any element of E, is called a basis for the matroid.

Definition 8.2.3 (Basis) Let (E, I) be an independence system. For any $S \subset E$, a set $B \subset S$ is called a *basis* of S or maximal in S if $B \in I$ and $B \cup \{j\} \notin I$ for all $j \in S \setminus B$.

If (E, I) is an independence system, a set $S \subset E$ is called a *circuit* or minimally dependent if $S \notin I$ but $S \setminus \{j\} \in I$ for all $j \in S$. The circuits of graphic matroids are actually cycles in the corresponding graphs. It is a basic result of matroid theory that any two bases of a matroid M have the same number of elements.

Theorem 8.2.2 *If (E, I) is a matroid then every basis of $S \subset E$ has the same size. In other words, if B and B' are bases of S then $|B| = |B'|$.*

The theorem follows from the exchange property of a matroid. Suppose that there are two independent sets B and B' with $|B| > |B'|$; then B' is not a maximally independent set, because it can be augmented by an element from B.

The size of a basis of a matroid M is also called the *rank* of M. The rank of a subset $A \subset E$ is given by the rank function $r(A)$ of the matroid, which is known to be monotonic and submodular for two subsets $A, B \subset E$.

A *weighted matroid* is a matroid together with a function from its elements to the non-negative real numbers. The weight of a subset of elements is defined to be the sum of the weights of the elements in the subset. A greedy algorithm can be used to find a maximum-weight basis of the matroid, by starting from the empty set and repeatedly adding one element at a time, at each step choosing a maximum-weight element among the elements whose addition would preserve independence. More formally, consider the constrained optimization problem, where a weight w_k is assigned to every $k \in E$:

$$\max_{S \in I} \sum_{k \in S} w_k.$$

The weights w_k could be interpreted as the reported values of a bidder for item k, and $w(S) = \sum_{k \in S} v_k$ for all $S \in I$. A *greedy algorithm*, Algorithm 1, can be used to solve this optimization problem, as follows:

---

1. Order the elements of E by weight: $w_1 \geq w_2 \geq \cdots \geq w_n$;
2. $A_0 = \emptyset$; $k = 1$;
3. If $w_k \leq 0$, stop and return A_{k-1};
4. If $w_k > 0$ and $A_{k-1} \cup k \in I$, define $A_k = A_{k-1} \cup \{k\} \in S$;
5. If $w_k > 0$ and $A_{k-1} \cup k \notin I$; define $A_k = A_{k-1}$; $k = k+1$; goto step 3.

Algorithm 1 Greedy algorithm

This algorithm terminates, as E is finite, and it finds the optimum if and only if (E, I) is a matroid (with distinct values).

Theorem 8.2.3 *(E, I) is a matroid if and only if, for every possible set of weights w, the greedy algorithm solves the above optimization problem.*

In what follows, we show only that if (E, I) is a weighted matroid (and there are no ties) then the solution of the greedy algorithm results in the maximally independent set of maximal weight for every set of non-negative weights.

Proof. Call the weight function $w : E \to \mathbb{R}^{\geq 0}$, and suppose that the greedy algorithm picks elements $B = \{x_1, x_2, \ldots, x_r\} \in E$ in that order and that $w(x_1) \geq w(x_2) \geq \cdots \geq w(x_r)$. If there is any list of r independent elements $y_1, y_2, \ldots, y_r \in X$ that has $w(y_1) \geq \cdots \geq w(y_r)$, we claim that $w(x_i) \geq w(y_i)$ for all i. This proves what we want, because if there were a basis of size r with higher weight then sorting its elements by weight would give a list contradicting this claim. To prove the claim, suppose that it is false and that for some k we have $w(x_k) < w(y_k)$. Moreover, pick the smallest k for which this is true. Note that $k > 1$, and so we can look at the special sets $S = \{x_1, \ldots, x_{k-1}\}$ and $T = \{y_1, \ldots, y_k\}$. Now $|T| = |S| + 1$, so by the matroid property there is some j between 1 and r such that $S \cup \{y_j\}$ is an independent set (and y_j is not in S). But then $w(y_j) \geq w(y_k) > w(x_k)$, and so the greedy algorithm would have picked y_j before it picks x_k. This contradicts how the greedy algorithm works, and hence proves the claim. $\qquad\square$

If (E, I) does not satisfy the exchange property then there is some vector of weights such that the greedy algorithm does not find the optimal solution.

Note that spanning trees form a matroid (E, I), with E the set of edges and I the set of spanning trees. The spanning tree of each subset of vertices V or components is part of I, the set of trees. Let's discuss a network procurement application to illustrate how a greedy algorithm maximizes welfare and how the prices that are determined coincide with the VCG payments. In this example, a buyer needs to procure a minimal weight (or cost) spanning tree of a graph to achieve connectivity among all vertices of the graph (e.g., buildings in a city). Each supplier or bidder $i \in I$ in this auction is interested in a single edge $k \in K$ only. This means that the bidders are single-minded (see definition 10.2.1 in section 10.2, where this property is discussed in more detail). Note that v_i is the valuation of the agent on edge $i = k$. We assume that the graph G is complete and no single agent is in a position to prevent a spanning tree from forming. There is no competition for edges between agents, but there is competition between different bidders to be on the minimal spanning tree.

There are a number of greedy algorithms for the minimum spanning tree problem. The greedy-worst-out or reverse-delete algorithm works like a reverse Kruskal algorithm. Starting with the set of edges K, delete the edges in order of decreasing weight (or value) while keeping the graph connected. An edge is not deleted until all higher-weight edges that could cover the same cut have been deleted.

The algorithm can be interpreted as an auction that begins with a price p on each edge which is high enough that every agent would sell. Throughout the auction this price is decreased. At each point in time, an agent announces whether she is willing to sell her edge at the current price or build the link in our example. As the price decreases, agents drop out of the auction when the price falls below their value v_i for the edge, reducing the connectivity of the graph. At some price an agent becomes *critical*, because removing the agent would disconnect the graph. At this point the auctioneer sells the edge to the critical agent at the current price. This edge becomes part of the final minimum-weight spanning tree. The auction continues with other agents dropping out or becoming critical and ends when the last critical agent is awarded an edge and a tree is formed. The mechanism can be conducted as a sealed-bid or an open auction. Let's provide a small example with numbers.

Example 8.2.2 Suppose there is a network with seven nodes and 11 edges, as shown in figure 8.2. With a greedy-worst-out algorithm, the auctioneer would start at a price of \$15 and remove edges in the following sequence: (d, e), (f, g), (b, d), (b, c), (e, f). After (f, g) is rejected, the edge (e, g) becomes critical and is sold at a price of \$11. When (b, d) is rejected, no edge becomes critical. However, when (b, c) is rejected (e, c) becomes critical and is sold at a price of \$8. Finally, when (e, f) is rejected, (a, b), (b, e), (a, d), and (d, f) become critical and are also sold at a price of \$8.

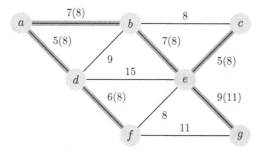

Figure 8.2 Example of a graph with a minimum spanning tree (shaded edges); the payments are in parentheses.

The algorithm in example 8.2.2 is just one variant of a greedy algorithm. They all optimize locally and find the global optimum, the minimum spanning tree in a weighted graph. Bikhchandani *et al.* (2011) showed that the auction yields Vickrey prices and therefore truthful bidding corresponds to an ex post equilibrium for agents. To see this, remove one edge from the minimum spanning tree in the previous example and check the value of the Vickrey payment; it coincides with the payments set by the algorithm.

The mechanism is a form of a clock auction and bidders need only to decide at which point to drop out. Some authors argue that such a simple clock auction has advantages over sealed-bid auctions. For example, the simple single-object clock auction is strategically equivalent to the Vickrey auction, because they both have the same reduced normal form. Nonetheless, laboratory subjects are substantially more likely to play the dominant strategy under a clock auction than under sealed bids (Kagel *et al.*, 1987).

Li (2015) introduced *obvious strategy-proofness* and argued that a clock auction as described in this section satisfies this property. A strategy *s* is obviously dominant if, for any deviating strategy *s'* in an extensive-form game, starting from the earliest information set where *s* and *s'* diverge, the best possible outcome from *s'* is no better than the worst possible outcome from *s*. A mechanism is obviously strategy-proof if it has an equilibrium in obviously dominant strategies. In the auction in example 8.2.2 there is no better strategy than to stay in the auction until the price is below cost. Obvious strategy-proofness implies weak group-strategy-proofness, a property that is desirable in many markets. A mechanism is *weakly group-strategy-proof* if there does not exist a coalition that could deviate in such a way that all members would be strictly better off ex post.

Definition 8.2.4 (Weak group-strategy-proofness) A mechanism $\mathcal{M} = (f, p)$ is weakly group-strategy-proof if, for every group of bidders $\mathcal{C} \subseteq \mathcal{I}$, every strategy profile $\sigma_{\mathcal{C}}$, and every profile of values $v_{\mathcal{C}}$, it holds that at least one bidder $i \in \mathcal{C}$ has a weakly higher payoff from the profile of truthful bids $v_{\mathcal{C}}$ than from the strategy profile of bidders in a set C playing according to the strategy profile $\sigma_{\mathcal{C}}$ with other bidders behaving truthfully.

That is, for any group deviation there is at least one seller who does not strictly gain from the group deviation. The discussion in this section is closely related to the design of deterministic approximation mechanisms for single-minded bidders, to be discussed in section 10.2.2.

8.3   Models of Open Combinatorial Auctions

In the previous subsections we considered markets where the valuations are severely restricted. Then bidders are interested in exactly one object and the constraints of the allocation problem have a matroid structure. For these environments we could implement the VCG outcome. There are also other environments where we can achieve ex post incentive-compatibility with ascending auctions. We've discussed the fact that the clinching auction for the sale of multiple units and bidders with *decreasing marginal valuations* is ex post incentive-compatible (see section 5.2.2). Also, for the sale of multiple units of a good to *unit-demand* bidders, there is a simple ascending auction which stops at the price where demand equals supply; this can be shown to be the VCG price. The same is true for purely *additive valuations* of all bidders, where we can run parallel or sequential clock auctions. Unfortunately, all these examples are very restricted and rarely happen in the field, where typically we have a richer set of valuation types and allocation problems.

First, we discuss conditions on the bidder valuations such that linear prices are possible. In this context we show that actually there is a need for non-linear and personalized prices. Second, we introduce algorithmic models of ascending combinatorial auctions and provide conditions on the valuations such that these algorithms yield an ex post equilibrium. This also proves that there cannot be ex post incentive-compatible ascending combinatorial auctions for general valuations. We provide an example of valuations where bidders have incentives to manipulate in an ascending combinatorial auction. Finally, we show that linear prices can work well if markets grow (very) large.

8.3.1   Limits of Linear Prices

Let's start out with linear prices and the conditions for which such prices are feasible. Kelso and Crawford (1982) showed that valuations need to satisfy the *gross-substitutes condition* for Walrasian equilibrium prices to exist. It is worth noting that their labor market model can be seen as a market with indivisible items, which is important as the prior literature often assumed divisibility. Interestingly, the auction they proposed is similar to a deferred accepted algorithm, which will be described in chapter 11 on matching markets (without money). Valuations which satisfy the gross-substitutes condition form a subclass of submodular valuations which encompasses additive and unit-demand valuations, as well as such with decreasing marginal values. Let's first introduce submodularity.

Definition 8.3.1 (Submodularity)   The values $v(A)$ and $v(B)$ of a bidder for objects A and B satisfy $v(A) + v(B) \geq v(A \cup B) + v(A \cap B)$ $\forall A, B \in E$, where E is the object set of interest. Also, there is an equivalent definition: $v(A \cup \{e\}) - v(A) \geq v(B \cup \{e\}) - v(B)$ $\forall A \subseteq B \subseteq E$ and $e \in E \setminus B$.

Submodularity implies subadditivity (i.e., $v(A) + v(B) \geq v(A \cup B)$), which can be seen from the definitions. The gross-substitutes condition requires that increasing the price of some item should not reduce the demand for item k, if the price on item k is fixed.

Definition 8.3.2 (Gross substitutes, GS) Let $P = (p(1), \ldots, p(k), \ldots, p(m))$ denote the prices on all items, with item k demanded by bidder i if there is some bundle S, with $k \in S$, for which S maximizes the utility $v_i(S') - \sum_{j \in S'} p(k)$ across all bundles. The gross substitutes condition requires that, for any prices $P' > P$ with $p'(k) = p(k)$, if item $k \in K$ is demanded at the prices P then it is still demanded at P'.

Gross substitutes means that the bidder regards the items as substitute goods or independent goods (i.e., additive valuations) but not complementary goods. For example, in a market for tea, increasing the price of Darjeeling tea is likely to increase the demand for Assam tea, as buyers substitute the cheaper tea for the more expensive tea. We also say that *goods are substitutes* when the GS condition is satisfied. The GS property of valuations is important in general equilibrium theory and it was first discussed by Arrow *et al.* (1959), who showed that with gross substitutes there is a unique competitive equilibrium price vector in a market with divisible goods and that the Walrasian price-adjustment procedure converges to these prices. Later, Kelso and Crawford (1982) analyzed markets with discrete goods and the gross substitutes property. It is of interest that an equivalent concept to GS was developed independently in discrete convex analysis and is referred to as $M^\natural$-convexity (Fujishige, 2005).

Unit demand means that the agent only wants a single good. Unit demand and additive valuations are gross substitutes but it does not follow that the gross substitutes property necessarily implies unit demand and additive valuations. The relationship of different types of valuations can be described as follows:

$$\text{unit demand} \subset \text{GS} \subset \text{submodular} \subset \text{subadditive} \subset \text{general}$$

Note, that if the valuations of a bidder i satisfy the gross substitutes property and are monotonic then they are submodular, but not vice versa (Gul and Stacchetti, 1999). Monotonicity (aka free disposal) means that, for $S \subseteq T$, $v(S) \leq v(T)$. Subadditivity and monotonocity do not imply the gross substitutes property. This is shown by the following counterexample, example 8.3.1.

Example 8.3.1 Consider the valuations v_i of a bidder i for items $1, 2, 3$ in table 8.5. It is easy to observe that the valuations are subadditive (in fact, submodular) and monotonic. For price vectors $P = (3, 3, 3)$ and $Q = (3, 4, 3)$ the demands (i.e., the payoff-maximizing packages) are $D(P) = \{\{1, 2\}\}$ and $D(Q) = \{\{3\}\}$. But the demand for item 1 has decreased after the price of item 2 increases and this contradicts the gross substitutes property.

As early as 1972, Hurwicz (1972) observed, for markets with divisible goods, that truthfully reporting preferences does not always give an equilibrium of a Walrasian mechanism. Kelso and Crawford (1982) argued that an ascending auction terminates naturally in a Walrasian equilibrium when the valuations are GS and bidders report true demands throughout the auction. Then, Gul and Stacchetti (1999) showed that, even if

Table 8.5 Valuations of a bidder i and payoffs π_i for price vectors P and Q.
The boxed values maximize payoff at the given prices

	Ø	{1}	{2}	{3}	{1, 2}	{1, 3}	{2, 3}	{1, 2, 3}
v_i	0	4	4	4.25	7.5	7	7	9
π_i^P	0	1	1	1.25	$\boxed{1.5}$	1	1	0
π_i^Q	0	1	0	$\boxed{1.25}$	0.5	1	0	−1

goods are substitutes, ascending auctions with item-level prices cannot implement the VCG outcome, and consequently they are not strategy-proof. They provided an ascending auction and showed that it terminated in a Walrasian equilibrium when valuations were GS.

So far, we have focused on Walrasian equilibria with item-level (i.e., linear) prices. We now focus on ascending combinatorial auctions with general preferences (including substitutes and complements) and show that

1. we need non-linear and personalized prices, so that straightforward bidding results in a competitive equilibrium which maximizes welfare, and
2. we need the *bidder submodularity* condition for straightforward bidding to always end up with VCG payments and therefore to be an ex post equilibrium for bidders.

Example 8.3.2 below shows that anonymous and linear CE prices are not always feasible.

Example 8.3.2 In this example, we have three items, A, B, C, and three bidders, whose values can be found in table 8.6. If bidders submitted their values truthfully, bidder 1 would win the package $\{A, B\}$, and bidder 3 would win C with a social welfare of $28. Now, the prices for the package $\{A, B\}$ should be less than or equal to $20, the winning bid of bidder 1, and less than or equal to $8 for C, the winning bid of bidder 3. At the same time, we can pick two losing bids, by bidder 2 and bidder 3, which are boxed in table 8.6. If we want linear and anonymous prices then these prices would need to be greater than $20 for $\{A, C\}$ and greater than $20 for the losing bid on $\{B, C\}$. Adding the constraints for both losing packages to a package $\{A, B, 2C\}$ would require the sum of the linear prices to be greater than $40 but less or equal to $36, according to the constraints for the winning bids.

Table 8.6 Example without linear ask prices

	{A}	{B}	{C}	{A, B}	{B, C}	{A, C}	{A, B, C}
Bidder 1	3	4	5	20*	8	11	24
Bidder 2	5	6	5	11	$\boxed{20}$	9	27
Bidder 3	4	5	8*	10	12	$\boxed{20}$	25

Prices are *linear* or *item-level* if the price of a bundle is equal to the sum of the prices of its items, and prices are *anonymous* if they are equal for every bidder. As we have seen that such prices cannot always yield a competitive equilibrium, we introduce additional types of price:

1. a set of linear anonymous prices $P = \{p(k)\}$;
2. a set of linear personalized prices $P = \{p_i(k)\}$;
3. a set of non-linear anonymous prices $P = \{p(S)\}$;
4. a set of non-linear personalized prices $P = \{p_i(S)\}$.

Non-anonymous ask prices are called *personalized* prices. In the next subsection, we use duality theory again to derive non-linear and personalized competitive equilibrium prices.

In our analysis of assignment markets in section 8.1, the dual variables were instrumental in finding market prices. So, let us start by looking at the winner determination problem with relaxed integrality constraints (and an XOR bidding language):

$$\max_{x_i(S)} \sum_{S \subseteq K} \sum_{i \in I} x_i(S) v_i(S) \qquad \text{(relaxed WDP)}$$

$$\text{s.t.} \quad \sum_{S \subseteq K} x_i(S) \leq 1 \qquad \forall i \in I \qquad (\pi_i)$$

$$\sum_{S:k \in S} \sum_{i \in I} x_i(S) \leq 1 \qquad \forall k \in K \qquad (p(k))$$

$$0 \leq x_i(S) \leq 1 \qquad \forall i, S$$

Our primal linear program has one constraint per bidder and per item. The dual of the relaxed WDP can now be written as:

$$\min \left\{ \sum_{i \in I} \pi_i + \sum_{k \in K} p(k) \right\} \qquad \text{(dual relaxed WDP)}$$

$$\text{s.t.} \quad \pi_i + \sum_{k \in S} p(k) \geq v_i(S) \qquad \forall S \subseteq K, \forall i \in I$$

$$\pi_i, p(k) \geq 0 \qquad \forall k \in K, \forall i \in I$$

There exists a Walrasian equilibrium if the relaxed WDP yields an optimal integer solution. The complementary slackness conditions can now be written as follows:

- $\pi_i - [v_i(S) - \sum_{k \in K} p(k)] = 0$ when $x_i(S) > 0$
- $\sum_{S \subseteq K} x_i(S) = 1$ when $\pi_i > 0$
- $\sum_{S:k \in S} \sum_{i \in I} x_i(S) = 1$ when $p(k) > 0$

The dual variables of the relaxed WDP have a natural interpretation as Walrasian prices, as in the assignment problem. Unfortunately, the relaxed WDP typically does not yield an integral solution, and there can be a significant integrality gap between the objective function value of the relaxed WDP and that of the optimal integer problem (WDP). The integrality gap refers to the differences in objective function values of the best solution of the integer program and the best solution of the corresponding LP relaxation. As a consequence, the dual variables $p(k)$ of the relaxed WDP in total overestimate prices.

It can be shown that if the gross substitutes condition is satisfied for all bidders then the LP-relaxation of the WDP has an integral optimal solution. Consequently, with gross subsitutes valuations we can achieve a Walrasian equilibrium (Bikhchandani and Mamer, 1997; Vohra, 2004). The proofs of this proposition are rather involved.

Unfortunately, the gross substitutes conditions rarely hold in the field.

By adding constraints for each set-partition of items and each bidder to the WDP the formulation can be strengthened, so that the integrality constraints on all variables can be omitted but the solution is still always integral (Bikhchandani and Ostroy, 2002; de Vries *et al.*, 2007). Such a formulation gives every feasible solution to an integer problem, and is solvable with linear programming. We refer to this formulation as strong WDP (SWDP):

$$\max \sum_{i \in \mathcal{I}} \sum_{S \subseteq \mathcal{K}} v_i(S) x_i(S) \tag{SWDP}$$

$$\text{s.t.} \quad x_i(S) = \sum_{x : x_i = S} \delta_x \qquad \forall i \in \mathcal{I}, \forall S \subseteq \mathcal{K} \tag{$p_i(S)$}$$

$$\sum_{S \subseteq \mathcal{K}} x_i(S) \le 1 \qquad \forall i \in \mathcal{I} \tag{π_i}$$

$$\sum_{x \in \Gamma} \delta_x = 1 \tag{π^s}$$

$$0 \le x_i(S) \qquad \forall S \subseteq \mathcal{K}, \forall i \in \mathcal{I}$$

$$0 \le \delta_x \qquad \forall x \in \Gamma$$

The dual variables $p_i(S)$ of the SWDP can now be interpreted as non-linear CE prices. In the first side constraint, $x_i(S)$ is equal to the sum of the weights δ_x over all allocations x where bidder i gets bundle S. The dual variables of this constraint are the personalized bundle prices $p_i(S)$. The second side constraint ensures that each bidder i receives at most one bundle, and the dual variable π_i describes bidder i's payoff. Finally, the total weight of all selected allocations $x \in \Gamma$ equals 1, since only one allocation can be selected; Γ describes the set of all possible allocations. The dual variable (π_s) for this side constraint describes the seller's payoff. Let us now look at the dual of the SWDP (the DSWDP):

$$\min \sum_{i \in \mathcal{I}} \pi_i + \pi_s \tag{DSWDP}$$

$$\text{s.t.} \quad \pi_s \ge \sum_{i \in \mathcal{I}} p_i(S_i) \qquad \forall x = (S_1, \cdots, S_n) \in \Gamma$$

$$\pi_i > v_i(S) - p_i(S) \qquad \forall S \subseteq \mathcal{K}, \forall i \in \mathcal{I}$$

$$\pi_i, \pi_s, p_i(S) \ge 0 \qquad \forall S \subseteq \mathcal{K}, \forall i \in \mathcal{I}$$

For an efficient allocation x^* there always exist personalized non-linear CE prices. To see this, let us revisit the definition of a CE (see definition 8.1.2). The prices P and allocation $x^* = (S_1^*, \ldots, S_n^*)$ are in CE if the allocation x^* maximizes the payoffs of the bidders π_i and of the seller π_s at the prices P. This is actually what the dual complementary slackness (DCS) conditions of the SWDP and the DSWDP require:

$$\delta(x)[\pi_s - \sum_{i \in \mathcal{I}} p_i(S_i)] = 0 \qquad \forall x \in \Gamma \tag{DCS}$$

$$x_i(S)[\pi_i - (v_i(S) - p_i(S))] = 0 \qquad \forall S \subseteq \mathcal{K}, \forall i \in \mathcal{I}$$

In words, if bidder i wins a package, i.e., $x_i(S) = 1$, then $\pi_i = v_i(S) - p_i(S)$. Also, if an allocation is chosen, i.e., $\delta(x) = 1$, then the seller maximizes her revenue and $\pi_s = \sum_{i \in \mathcal{I}} p_i(x_i)$. Therefore, no participant wants to change this allocation. A trivial example of such CE prices is given by the valuations of the bidders in the efficient allocation. Let us now prove the integrality of the SWDP. We mark the optimal solution with an asterisk in what follows.

Theorem 8.3.1 (Bikhchandani and Ostroy, 2002) *The pair (x^*, P^*) corresponds to a competitive equilibrium if and only if x^* is an integral optimal solution to the SWDP, and (π_i^*, π_s^*, P^*) is an optimal solution to the DSWDP, for all bids. That is, SWDP =* $\sum_{i \in \mathcal{I}} \pi_i^* + \pi_s^* = \sum_{i \in \mathcal{I}} v_i(S^*) = DSWDP.$

Proof sketch: If the solution to the SWDP is integral then we have a competitive equilibrium, which follows from the interpretation of the dual complementary slackness (DCS) conditions. From complementary slackness, we know that $\pi_i^* = v_i(S^*) - p_i^*(S^*) \geq v_i(S) - p_i^*(S)$. If we are in competitive equilibrium, then the SWDP is integral:

SWDP = DSWDP	owing to strong duality
$\leq \sum_{i \in \mathcal{I}} \pi_i^* + \pi_s^*$	follows from the feasibility of (π_i^*, π_s^*)
$= \sum_{i \in \mathcal{I}} [v_i(S^*) - p_i^*(S^*)] + \sum_{i \in \mathcal{I}} p_i^*(S^*)$	
$= \sum_{i \in \mathcal{I}} v_i(S^*)$	constitutes a feasible assignment
$\leq$ WDP	in the feasible set of WDP
$\leq$ SWDP	this always holds for maximization $\square$

Theorem 8.3.1 shows that if an allocation x^* is supported in competitive equilibrium by some set of prices P then x^* is an efficient allocation. This insight allows for the design of open combinatorial auctions which follow algorithms to solve the SWDP, a linear program. We will see in the next subsection that, with some assumptions on the bidder valuations, the VCG payments are in the core. In this case, one can devise a mechanism that is CE and has dominant strategies.

Note that our discussion in this section is restricted to markets with a single seller, where competitive equilibria always exist and fill out the *core*. The core is a solution concept from coalitional game theory and describes a form of stability. In combinatorial exchanges with multiple buyers and sellers the core may be empty (Bikhchandani and Ostroy, 2002). See example 8.3.3 below.

Example 8.3.3 Suppose that there is a combinatorial exchange with three sellers (s_1, s_2, and s_3) all selling one object (A, B, and C, respectively). There are three buyers (b_1, b_2, and b_3). Buyer b_1 is willing to pay \$3 for $\{A, B\}$ and \$4 for $\{A, B, C\}$, b_2 is willing to pay \$3 for $\{A, C\}$ and \$4 for $\{A, B, C\}$, and b_3 would pay \$3 for $\{B, C\}$ and \$4 for $\{A, B, C\}$. The efficient allocation is to sell $\{A, B, C\}$ to one of the three buyers.

Suppose that the three sellers sell their objects at a price of \$1.33 to b_1. Then buyer b_2 (or b_3) could approach two of the sellers and offer up to \$3 for package $\{A, C\}$ (or

Table 8.7 A combinatorial exchange with three buyers and three sellers selling A, B, and C, respectively

	{A}	{B}	{C}	{A, B}	{B, C}	{A, C}	{A, B, C}
Buyer b_1			3			4	
Buyer b_2				3		4	
Buyer b_3					3	4	

$\{B, C\})$. These two sellers would have an incentive to deviate as they would get $1.5 each. Suppose that the coalition of b_2, s_1 and s_3 deviates; then the allocation would not maximize welfare. Also, b_1 might approach s_1 and s_2 and offer $1.6 and $1.4 respectively, so that all participants could improve their utility. Next, bidder b_3 might approach s_2 and s_3, etc.

Let us now show that the core of this combinatorial exchange is empty. First, we require that the sum of the payoffs should equal the social welfare in the welfare-maximizing allocation: $\pi_{s_1} + \pi_{s_2} + \pi_{s_3} + \pi_{b_1} + \pi_{b_2} + \pi_{b_3} = 4$. A core allocation would also need to satisfy $\pi_{s_1} + \pi_{s_2} + \pi_{b_1} \geq 3$, $\pi_{s_1} + \pi_{s_3} + \pi_{b_2} \geq 3$, and $\pi_{s_2} + \pi_{s_3} + \pi_{b_3} \geq 3$. However, no payoff vector can satisfy these inequalities, and so the core is empty.

8.3.2   Algorithmic Models of Ascending Auctions

In section 8.1 we saw how a primal–dual algorithm to solve the assignment problem can be used as a model for an ascending auction. In this subsection we provide an overview of similar auction models for ascending combinatorial auctions which either follow a primal–dual algorithm or a subgradient algorithm. Then, we show under which conditions these algorithms terminate with VCG payments, so that straightforward bidding is an ex post equilibrium. Otherwise, there is no strong solution concept and we need to restrict our equilibrium analysis to Bayesian Nash equilibria.

The program *iBundle* (Parkes and Ungar, 2000) computes a provisional revenue-maximizing allocation at the end of every round and increases the prices on the basis of the bids of non-winning bidders. Three different versions of iBundle were suggested by Parkes and Ungar (2000): iBundle(2) has anonymous prices, iBundle(3) has personalized prices, and iBundle(d) starts with anonymous prices and switches to personalized prices for agents who submit bids for disjoint bundles. The *ascending proxy auction* (Ausubel and Milgrom, 2006a) is equivalent to iBundle(3) but the use of proxy agents is mandatory, which essentially leads to a sealed-bid auction format. The paper de Vries *et al.* (2007) showed that iBundle implements a subgradient algorithm to solve the underlying SWDP.

Algorithm 2 outlines the basic process of an iBundle(3) auction, in which an ask price $p_i(S)$ is available for each bundle S and each bidder i. Note that bidders see neither the identity nor the exact bids of other bidders, but only the ask prices. Ascending auctions consist of multiple rounds, each of which starts with new prices for the bidders, who then have the opportunity to submit new bids, i.e., for bundles in which they are interested, given the current prices. When all bidders have finished their bid submission, the round is closed. The mechanism then computes the currently best allocation along with new price feedbacks for the losing bidders and bundles, which are then reported back to the bidders at the beginning of the next round. We use $t \in \mathbb{N}_0$ to refer to the auction state after the first t rounds, B^t to describe the bids submitted in round t, and $\vec{x}^t$ to describe the revenue-maximizing allocation after this round, which is based on the set of all bids $b_i(S) \in B$ submitted in the auction so far. Note that a round could close after each newly submitted bid, so that round t is defined by a single bid. A bidder can submit multiple bids in a round. The set of all bids made by bidders who are losing after round t is B_l^t. The minimum bid increment is ε. The auction terminates when no new bid is submitted in a round, and the winning bidders then pay what they bid.

Result: allocation $\vec{x}^t$ and prices $p_i(S)$
Initialization
    for $i=1$ to n **do**
        foreach S **do** $p_i(S) \leftarrow 0$
        $x_i \leftarrow \emptyset, t \leftarrow 0$
    end
termination $\leftarrow$ false
while $(\neg\ termination)$ **do**
    $t \leftarrow t+1$
    Bidders submit bids $B^t \ni b_i(S) \geq p_i(S)$
    if $(B^t = \emptyset)$ **then** termination $\leftarrow$ true
    else
        $B \leftarrow B \cup B^t$
        Compute $\vec{x}^t \in \text{argmax}_x \sum_{i\in\mathcal{I}} b_i(x_i)$
        foreach $b_i(S) \in B_l^t$ **do** $p_i(S) \leftarrow p_i(S) + \varepsilon$
    end
end

Algorithm 2 The iBundle auction process

The *dVSV* auction design (de Vries et al., 2007) differs from iBundle in that it increases prices for one *minimally undersupplied set of bidders*. A set of bidders is minimally undersupplied if no bidder in this set receives a bundle from her demand set and if removing only one bidder from the set forfeits this property. This auction implements a primal–dual algorithm. Similarly to iBundle(3), it maintains non-linear personalized prices and increases the prices for all agents in a minimally undersupplied set on the basis of their bids in the last round.

Unfortunately, such primal–dual or subgradient auction designs do not always end up with VCG prices, as in the assignment market. In order to show that primal–dual algorithms can end up with VCG payments, we actually need a restriction on the bidders' valuations.

Definition 8.3.3 (Bidder submodularity, BSM) Bidder submodularity requires that for all $M \subseteq M' \subseteq N$ and all $i \in N$ the following condition holds:

$$w(M \cup \{i\}) - w(M) \geq w(M' \cup \{i\}) - w(M')$$

Under BSM bidders are more valuable when added to a smaller coalition. Furthermore, under BSM ascending combinatorial auctions yield VCG payments and straightforward bidding is an ex post equilibrium. Remember that the BSC condition (definition 7.3.2) is sufficient for VCG prices to be supported in CE. The slightly stronger *bidder submodularity condition* (BSM) is required for a purely ascending combinatorial auction to implement VCG payments (de Vries *et al.*, 2007).

Theorem 8.3.2 (Ausubel and Milgrom, 2002; Bikhchandani and Ostroy, 2002) *The ascending proxy auction terminates with VCG prices for BSM valuations and straightforward bidding.*

Proof. First, let $\overline{\pi}_i$ be the VCG payoff of bidder i and π_i^t the payoff of bidder i in round $t < T$. The social welfare or coalitional value of a coalition $C \subseteq \mathcal{I}$ is $w(C)$. Suppose there is some round t in which $\pi_i^t < \overline{\pi}_i$. Then we would have

$$w(C) - \sum_{i \in C} \pi_i^t < w(C) - \sum_{i \in C} \pi_i^t + (\overline{\pi}_j - \pi_j^t) \quad \text{since } \pi_j^t < \overline{\pi}_j$$

$$= w(C) - \sum_{i \in C \cup \{j\}} \pi_i^t + w(\mathcal{I}) - w(\mathcal{I} - j) \quad \text{since } \overline{\pi}_j = w(\mathcal{I}) - w(\mathcal{I} - j)$$

$$\leq w(C) - \sum_{i \in C \cup \{j\}} \pi_i^t + w(C \cup j) - w(C) \quad \text{since the BSM holds}$$

$$= w(C \cup j) - \sum_{i \in C \cup \{j\}} \pi_i^t$$

However, if this were the case then the coalition $C \cup j$ would win in round t and not coalition C. Second, straightforward bidding corresponds to an ex post Nash equilibrium since if all bidders follow this strategy then the auction leads to a Vickrey outcome. $\square$

Milgrom (2017) provides an elegant proof showing that if goods are substitutes then the coalitional value function is BSM and the VCG outcome is in the core. When the BSM condition does not hold, a straightforward strategy is likely to lead a bidder to pay more than the VCG price for the winning bundle; furthermore bidders have an incentive to shade their bids and deviate from straightforward bidding. In the case of non-straightforward bidding the outcome of such algorithms can deviate significantly from the efficient solution (Schneider *et al.*, 2010). We discuss issues with different auction formats in section 8.4.

8.3.3   Perfect Bayesian Equilibria with General Valuations

A simple situation, in which the BSM is violated, is the *threshold problem* with two local bidders competing against a global bidder. Its strategic complexity can best be understood if it is modeled as a complete information game.

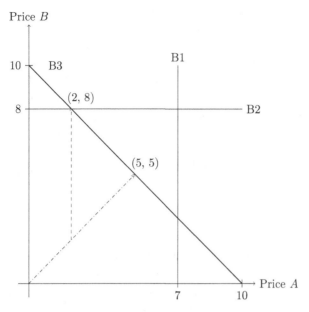

Figure 8.3 Example of a threshold problem.

Example 8.3.4 Suppose there are two items A, B and three bidders, B1 to B3. Bidder B1 is only interested in item A and has a value of $7, bidder B2 is only interested in item B with a value of $8, while bidder B3 has a value of $10 for a package consisting of both items. This situation is described in figure 8.3. In an ascending and core-selecting auction, bidders B1 and B2 compete against bidder B3. If they all bid truthfully in each round of the ascending auction, the prices would start at zero and then increase to $(5, 5)$ for both items. However, in the complete-information game the weaker local bidder $B1$ can drop out at a price of $2 + \varepsilon$ for item A. Then, she forces bidder $B2$ to bid up to his true valuation $8 - \varepsilon$, which is his dominant strategy. In other words, bidder $B1$ free-rides on bidder $B2$.

This problem is fundamental and, with the right set of prior distributions, similar problems arise in the corresponding Bayesian game. Goeree and Lien (2014) looked at a specific version of an ascending core-selecting auction where, if two or more local bidders want to drop out at the same time, one is selected to drop out while the others are allowed to continue. While this additional tie-breaking rule differs from some activity rules in the field, it allows the derivation of a pure perfect Bayesian strategy, one where all local bidders try to drop out at a null price. Sano (2011) characterized the results for ascending combinatorial auctions with the same tie-breaking rule and provided a condition for a non-bidding equilibrium for general continuous distribution functions and non-zero reserve prices. His models provide a characterization of the prior distributions when local bidders drop out straight away. This means that the perfect Bayesian equilibrium strategy is such that the small bidders drop out immediately in an effort to free-ride on each other, so that the outcome is actually inefficient: the local bidders should win in an efficient allocation but in equilibrium a global bidder interested in the package wins.

Guler *et al.* (2016) showed that inefficiencies of ascending auctions in a threshold model are also possible with risk-averse bidders. The impact of risk aversion on equilibrium bidding strategies is not obvious, since higher bidding by one local bidder can allow the other local bidder to drop out even earlier. This means that bidders cannot simply buy insurance against the possibility of losing by increasing their bids, and increasing bids may lead to a lower probability of winning. However, this shows that risk aversion reduces the scope of the non-bidding equilibrium in the sense that dropping out at the reserve price ceases to be an equilibrium as bidders become more risk averse.

8.3.4   Large Markets with Non-Convexities

In the previous subsections we have seen that, in markets with a finite number of bidders, indivisible objects, and quasi-linear preferences, a Walrasian equilibrium with linear and anonymous prices is possible in the assignment market but not with general preferences on bundles. Such markets lead to non-convex optimization problems such that LP duality, as in an assignment market, no longer holds. Farrell (1959) already showed that the impact of non-convexities in demand diminishes as the number of market participants increases. Consequently, even if individual demand is not convex, when there is an infinite number of consumers the aggregate demand does exhibit the convexity required to yield the existence of a Walrasian equilibrium price vector. Let's consider a simple market with two bidders and two objects to illustrate the point (Azevedo *et al.*, 2013).

Example 8.3.5   Suppose that there are two items and bidder 1 has a value of only $1 for the package of two items while bidder 2 values each item at $0.75 but has no additional value for two items. For bidder 1 to demand the package of two items, the price for each item would need to be less than $1. However, then one of the two prices must be strictly less than $0.75, so bidder 2 will demand one item. Assigning one item to bidder 2 would not be efficient, however.

Now consider a market in which there are many units of the two items and many bidders like bidder 1 (type 1) and bidder 2 (type 2) and there is enough of each item for half the bidders. The efficient allocation is to assign the bidders of type 2 an item each and the remaining items, in packages, to bidders of type 1. The reason is that each bidder of type 1 effectively has a value of $0.5 for an item. Consequently, bidders of type 2 should be satisfied before the type 1 bidders. This efficient allocation is supported by a Walrasian price vector ($0.5, $0.5) for both items. At these prices bidders of type 2 prefer to receive an item while bidders of type 1 are indifferent as to whether they receive their desired package or not.

In summary, non-convexities become less of a concern in large markets, and, with some assumptions, a Walrasian (linear-price) equilibrium exists regardless of the nature of the bundle preferences. Unfortunately, markets are rarely large enough that non-convexities can be ignored. For example, there are many buyers and sellers in day-ahead energy markets, as described in section 7.6, but the non-convexities matter and typically one cannot find linear prices for the welfare-maximizing allocation.

The existence of Walrasian prices does not mean that in such markets truthful bidding is necessarily a dominant strategy. Hurwicz (1972) observed, for markets with divisible goods, that truthfully reporting preferences does not always give an equilibrium for a Walrasian mechanism. However, in large markets with many bidders the possibilities for manipulation are typically much reduced and bidders become *price-takers*; that is, they do not bid strategically because they do not think that they can affect the price. Roberts and Postlewaite (1976) showed that in large markets the ability of an individual player to influence the market is minimal, so agents should behave as price-taking agents. Jackson and Manelli (1997) identified conditions under which, as the size of the market increases, the market-clearing prices and allocations of the reported economy approximate the competitive equilibria of a market with true preferences.

Azevedo and Budish (2015) introduced *strategy-proofness in the large* (SP-L), which is also referred to as *approximate strategy-proofness*, to generalize the idea; SP-L means that, for any bidder and any full-support i.i.d. probability distribution of the other bidders' reports, and for any $\varepsilon > 0$, in a large enough market the agent maximizes her expected payoff to within ε by reporting her preferences truthfully. They showed that envy-freeness is a sufficient condition for SP-L and proved that the Walrasian mechanism satisfies SP-L by showing that these mechanisms are envy-free. *Envy-freeness* is a form of fairness where the expected utility (i.e., value $-$ price) of the allocation of one agent is not less than the expected utility of every other allocation.

8.4   Overview of Open Combinatorial Auction Formats

In this section we extend the discussion of algorithmic models for ascending combinatorial auctions in section 8.3.2, where we introduced iBundle and dVSV. In addition, we discuss alternative designs, which are often based on heuristics, to determine prices. Such designs can be simple clock auctions and auctions where the prices are derived from the duals of the linear programming relaxation of the WDP.

8.4.1   Auction Formats with Non-Linear Prices

We have already discussed iBundle and dVSV as two auction designs implementing algorithms to solve the SWDP. For full efficiency they require non-linear and personalized prices, and therefore we refer to them as non-linear personalized price auctions. Full efficiency comes at a cost. These auction formats implement exact algorithms to solve an optimization problem, they incur a very large number of auction rounds, and they are not very robust to deviations from straightforward bidding (Schneider *et al.*, 2010). Also, they exhibit an ex post Nash equilibrium only if bidder valuations are bidder submodular, which is not necessarily the case. Finally, there are some markets where non-linear and personalized prices are just not acceptable. If BSM is not given, as in the local–local–global model, bidders can manipulate and the auction can even be inefficient, as discussed in section 8.3.3.

There are a number of extensions of these basic auction formats. The *credit–debit auction* is an extension to the dVSV design which achieves the VCG outcome for general valuations (not only BSM) by determining payments or discounts from the auctioneer to the bidders at the end. Similarly, *iBEA* can be described as an extension of iBundle. Both approaches are based on universal competitive equilibrium (UCE) prices, which are CE prices for the main economy as well as for every marginal economy, i.e., an economy where a single buyer is excluded (Mishra and Parkes, 2007). These auctions terminate as soon as UCE prices are reached and VCG payments are dynamically determined as one-time discounts during the auction. Truthful bidding is an ex post equilibrium in the credit–debit auction and in iBEA. There are no restrictions on the valuations, but there are discounts at the end. This means that these auction formats also differentiate between prices and payments.

Deadness levels (DLs) and winning levels (WLs) were first suggested as pricing rules for bidders in combinatorial auctions with an OR bidding language (Adomavicius *et al.*, 2013; Adomavicius and Gupta, 2005), and they lead to another open combinatorial auction format. Deadness levels are the lowest prices above which a bid can become winning in any future auction state.

Definition 8.4.1 (Deadness level)   The *deadness level* (DL) of a bundle S for bidder i at auction state t is the minimal price that bidder i has to overbid to maintain a chance of winning S at some future auction state $t' > t$.

Winning levels are prices above which a bid would win immediately if no further bid was submitted from any other bidder. Deadness levels can also be computed in the presence of an XOR bid language. Then the auction is equivalent to iBundle(3) with a different price update rule (Petrakis *et al.*, 2012). While iBundle increases prices only by a minimum bid increment, DLs are computed in such a way that no lower bid can ever be winning in a future auction state. Such DLs can be much higher than the minimum bid increment in iBundle, thus saving on unnecessary auction rounds. Unfortunately, this reduction in the number of auction rounds has a downside: the computation of DLs with an XOR bid language is a computationally very hard problem, i.e., a Π_2^P-complete problem. However, the strategic properties are identical to those of iBundle(3). If the bidders' valuations satisfy BSM, straightforward bidding is an ex post Nash equilibrium in such a DL auction.

While linear-price auction formats, discussed in the next section, reveal some information about those items for which there is a lot of demand and those items for which there is little competition, personalized and non-linear prices just reveal that a bidder has lost or won. In contrast with single-object auctions, bidders in open multi-object auctions need to decide not only at which price they will drop out. They also need to decide for which packages to bid. If there are several objects, they need to coordinate on a specific allocation of the packages to bidders. In other words, bidders try to agree on a partition of the items to be allocated to them. This is not an easy task, because the number of possible allocations is huge.

The Stirling number of the second kind counts the number of ways to partition a set of m items into k non-empty subsets:

$$S(m, k) = \frac{1}{k!} \sum_{j=0}^{k} (-1)^j \binom{k}{j} (k - j)^m.$$

If the number of items is less then the number of bidders, $m \leq n$, then the number of coalitions grows as $C(m, n) = \sum_{k=1}^{m} S(m, k) n!/(n - k)!$, as there are $n!/(n - k)!$ ways to distribute n bidders among k bundles.

If $m \geq n$ then $C(m, n)$ is an upper bound consisting of a sum of the following two parts:

$$\sum_{k=1}^{n} S(m, k) \frac{n!}{(n - k)!} \qquad \forall k \in \{1, \ldots, n\} \qquad (1)$$

$$\sum_{k=n+1}^{m} S(m, k) \frac{k!}{(k - n)!} \qquad \forall k \in \{n + 1, \ldots, m\} \qquad (2)$$

While $C(m, n)$ describes the worst case, there can be thousands of possible allocations even for small combinatorial auctions. Therefore, it is a key strategic challenge for bidders to coordinate on one of these allocations in an auction. Auctions with *coalitional winning levels* (CWLs) leverage the information that an auctioneer collects during the auction about the preferences of bidders for specific packages: the auctioneer then proposes prices to coalitions of bidders, whose bundles complement each other (Bichler et al., 2017b). Such auctions extend the idea of a DL to a coalition of losing bidders to help them find bidders with complementary interests with whom they could form a winning coalition. The auctioneer selects losing coalitions and proposes, to the members of such coalitions, CWLs as ask prices which would allow them to jointly outbid the currently winning coalition. The semantics of CWLs is intuitive for bidders and provides guidance in what is arguably a central problem that bidders face in ascending combinatorial auctions with many items: the selection of promising bundles in each round which stand a chance of becoming a winner together with the bids of other bidders. Let's look at a simple example to highlight the difference between DLs, CWLs, and WLs.

Example 8.4.1 Consider the sale of 18 pieces of land $A, \ldots, R$ on a shoreline. One developer (bidder 1) needs three adjacent pieces of land for a small hotel, while the other developer (bidder 2) plans for a large resort and needs 15 adjacent pieces. Both compete against bidder 3, who is interested in all 18 pieces of land. Let's assume that, in the first round, bidder 1 submits XOR bids of €3 on $\{A, B, C\}$, $\{D, E, F\}$, $\{G, H, I\}$, $\{J, K, L\}$, $\{M, N, O\}$ and $\{P, Q, R\}$, for which he has the same preference, while bidder 2 bids on $\{A, \ldots, O\}$ for €9, and bidder 3 on $\{A, \ldots, R\}$ for €20. The CWL for bidder 1's bid on $\{P, Q, R\}$ will be €7 (€3 + €4), while that of bidder 2 will be €13 (€9 + €4) (using a uniform-distribution sharing rule for simplicity). In contrast, the CWL for all other bundle bids for bidder 1 will be €20. Therefore, the CWL information can serve as a signal that, right now, bidder 1 can focus on bundle $\{P, Q, R\}$. In contrast, with only DLs available, bidder 1 would not be able to see the difference between $\{P, Q, R\}$ and his other five bundles of interest and might bid on other bundles which cannot become winning given the valuations. She could be trying to bid on these other packages over multiple rounds and increase the ask prices, but the allocation would not change. Furthermore, if WL information is available, the WL for $\{P, Q, R\}$ on the other hand would be €11 (€20 + €9), which indicates the entire cost that is needed to outbid bidder 3 without taking into account possible coalitions.

In examples with many items and bidders interested in many bundles, CWLs can give bidders useful information about bundles for which complementary bids exist. In addition, they can help bidders focus on a few (rather than all) bundles with positive valuations.

8.4.2   Auction Formats with Linear Ask Prices

It has been shown that the *gross substitutes* property is a sufficient condition for the existence of exact linear CE prices (Kelso and Crawford, 1982), as the LP-relaxation of the WDP is integral and dual variables can be interpreted as prices. The substitutes condition is, however, very restrictive and is not satisfied in most combinatorial auctions, which are often used when there are complements (i.e., a set of items whose combined value is greater than the sum of the individual item values). In spite of these negative aspects, some combinatorial auction designs with linear prices have achieved high levels of efficiency in the laboratory, even for auctions with up to 18 items (Bichler *et al.*, 2013b; Brunner *et al.*, 2010; Goeree and Holt, 2010; Kagel *et al.*, 2010; Porter *et al.*, 2003; Scheffel *et al.*, 2012). The main auction formats, which were tested for selling spectrum in the USA, used linear ask prices (Brunner *et al.*, 2010; Goeree and Holt, 2010). Linear ask prices have been shown to be a good guideline to bidders in finding an efficient solution, even though no formal equilibrium analysis is available for any of these auction formats.

8.4.2.1   Combinatorial Clock Auctions

The single-stage combinatorial clock auction, SCCA (Porter *et al.*, 2003) utilizes anonymous linear ask prices called *item clock prices*. In each round bidders express the quantities they desire for certain bundles of items at the current prices. As long as demand exceeds supply for at least one item (each item is counted only once for each bidder) the price clock "ticks" upwards for those items (the item prices are increased by a fixed price increment), and the auction moves on to the next round. If there is no excess demand and no excess supply, the items are allocated according to the last round bids and the auction terminates. If there is no excess demand but there is excess supply (all active bidders on some item did not resubmit their bids in the last round), the auctioneer solves the winner determination problem by considering all bids submitted during the auction. If the computed allocation does not displace any bids from the last round, the auction terminates with this allocation; otherwise the prices of the respective items are increased and the auction continues. Note that, owing to winner determination, the final payments can deviate from the ask prices.

The SCCA can suffer from demand reduction, and no equilibrium strategies are known for general valuations. Consider an example with six identical spectrum licenses for sale and two bidders who both want to win four licenses for technical reasons. In the initial phase they might try to bid for three licenses and see whether the other player agrees, so that they both get the spectrum licenses for a low price. However, an efficient allocation might be to award four licenses to one bidder and two licenses to the other. A two-stage version of the CCA was designed to address these inefficiencies, and it has been used in spectrum auctions around the world. In the first phase, bidders participate in a version of the SCCA where they can submit only a single package bid per round. The second phase is a sealed-bid phase where bidders can submit bids for every possible package. Because of their practical importance, we provide a more detailed analysis of combinatorial clock auctions in section 9.1.

8.4.2.2 Auctions with Pseudo-Dual Prices

Resource allocation design (RAD) and *approximate linear prices* (ALPS) are two examples of *pseudo-dual linear ask prices*. These prices are based on a restricted dual of the LP relaxation of the WDP (Rassenti *et al.*, 1982). The dual price of each item measures the cost of not awarding the item to the bidder whom it was allocated in the previous round. In each round the losing bidders have to bid the sum of ask prices for a desired bundle plus a fixed minimum increment. Resource allocation design suggests the use of an OR bidding language and that only winning bids remain in the auction, in the original form of this design. The approximate linear prices auction (Bichler *et al.*, 2009) is also based on ideas in Rassenti *et al.* (1982) but modifies the termination rules and the ask-price calculation to balance prices across items better and avoid cycles in the auction. Note that, in RAD and ALPS, prices can also decrease if the competition shifts to different items. This non-monotonicity makes a game-theoretical analysis challenging. The following LP describes the basic ideas of pseudo-dual prices:

$$\min_{p(k),\delta_b} \{\max\{\delta_b\}, \max\{p(k)\}\} \tag{1}$$

$$\text{s.t.} \quad \sum_{k \in S} p(k) = b_i(S) \qquad \forall \text{ winning bids } b = b_i(S)$$

$$\sum_{k \in S} p(k) + \delta_b \geq b_i(S) \qquad \forall \text{ losing bids } b = b_i(S)$$

$$\delta_b \geq 0 \qquad \forall \text{ losing bids } b = b_i(S)$$

$$p(k) \geq 0 \qquad \forall k \in \mathcal{K}$$

The first constraint sets the bid prices of the winning bids equal to the sum of the item-level ask prices $p(k)$ for $k \in \mathcal{K}$. The second constraint enforces that prices are higher than the losing bids. This is not always possible, and distortions δ_b represent the deviations from the ideal. The schematically defined objective function $\min\{\max\{\delta_b\}, \max\{p(k)\}\}$ indicates a balanced minimization of all slack variables δ_b and also of the prices. This typically incurs solving multiple linear programs, where the price distortions and the prices are determined sequentially. If the competition shifts,

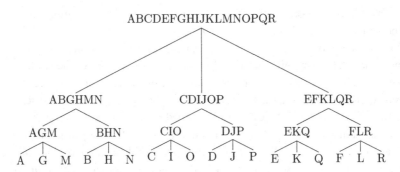

Figure 8.4 Example hierarchy of 18 objects.

such prices can also decrease, similarly to the prices set by the famous Walrasian auctioneer in equilibrium theory.

8.4.2.3 Hierarchical Package Bidding

Hierarchical package bidding (HPB) imposes a hierarchical structure of allowed package bids (see figure 8.4). The US Federal Communications Commission used this auction format in 2008 (Goeree and Holt, 2010). The hierarchy and an OR bidding language reduce the winner determination problem to a computationally simple problem that can be solved in linear time (Rothkopf *et al.*, 1998). Note that this computational simplicity breaks down if an XOR bid language is used or when additional allocation constraints are required. If the hierarchy meets the bidders' preferences, this auction has advantages. In particular, it is easier for bidders to coordinate in a threshold problem, and the predefined packages on a level complement each other. In fully combinatorial auctions that allow bidders to submit bids on all packages, bidders often submit only a few package bids, which leads to inefficiencies (Scheffel *et al.*, 2012). This is no problem in HPB.

Goeree and Holt (2010) introduced a simple and transparent pricing mechanism. They proposed a recursive algorithm for computing new ask prices which starts with the highest bid on every individual item as a lower bound, adding a surcharge if the next-level package received a bid higher than the sum of the individual-item bids contained in the package. The difference is distributed uniformly across the respective item prices. The algorithm ends by evaluating the package(s) at the top level, resulting in new ask prices for each item.

Note that the ask prices in HPB can be non-monotonic, as in auctions with pseudo-dual ask prices. Consider the following example. In the first round only one bid on package $\{A, B\}$ is placed at a price of 20. The price calculation of HPB sets new prices for A and B at 10 each. In the second round a bidder bids 10 on A and no other bids are made. The prices for the third round are calculated as the difference of 20 and 10 divided by 2 and added to the highest bid on each item. This results in new prices for the third round of 15 for item A and 5 for item B. Thus the prices on B fluctuate in the course of the auction from 0 to 10 to 5 in the third round.

Table 8.8 Example with six bids, five bundles, and different ask prices. The subscript on an ask price identifies the bidder

	$\{A, B\}$	$\{B, C\}$	$\{A, C\}$	$\{B\}$	$\{C\}$
Bids	$22^*_1, 16_2$	24_3	20_4	7_5	8^*_6
DL	$22_1, 16_2$	24_3	20_4	7_5	8_6
WL	$22_1, 22_2$	30_3	23_4	10_5	8_6
iBundle	$22_1, 17_2$	25_3	21_4	8_5	8_6
RAD	22	24	14	16	8
CWL	$22_1, 22_2$	30_3	$\mathbf{21.5_4}$	$\mathbf{8.5_5}$	8_6

A few other combinatorial auction designs have been suggested which use linear and non-linear prices. For example, progressive adaptive user selection environment (PAUSE) combines a simultaneous multi-round auction with bidding on bundles in later stages. Here, the burden of evaluating a combinatorial bid is transferred to the bidder. We do not discuss such designs further in this book but refer the interested reader to Kelly and Steinberg (2000).

Example 8.4.2 The following illustrative example extends the one used by Petrakis *et al.* (2012) to illustrate DLs. We compare CWLs with iBundle, DLs, WLs, and an auction format with linear ask prices, RAD (Kwasnica *et al.*, 2005).

The first row of table 8.8 shows six bids from different bidders (i.e., bidders 1 to 6, indicated by the subscripts), submitted on five subsets of three items (*A*, *B*, and *C*). At this point in the auction, bidders are interested only in those bundles for which they have submitted bids so far.

The lower five rows of table 8.8 give the ask prices in different auction formats. The ask prices have subscripts only if they differ among bidders. The asterisks denote the provisional winning bids. In this example, we assume a XOR bid language. For such languages, it is known that the DLs and WLs for a given bundle may have different values for different bidders, i.e., their computation needs to be personalized (Petrakis *et al.*, 2012). Losing bidders need to bid higher than the DL or the WL by a minimum bid increment. As mentioned earlier, the WL for a given bundle is the lowest bid price above which a submitted bid would instantly become winning, i.e., it would not need any new complementary bids from other bidders. However, it should be clear from the example that the bids from bidders 4 and 5 could possibly become winning even at lower prices than their current WLs if they coordinated and formed a coalition, indicated by prices in bold type. The ask prices in iBundle (Parkes and Ungar, 2000) are in line with DLs, but they add a bid increment (€1) for losing bids.

Linear-programming-based heuristics for computing item-level prices such as resource allocation design (RAD) (Kwasnica *et al.*, 2005) are an alternative. Unfortunately, RAD prices can be lower than a losing bid (see the RAD ask price on $\{A, C\}$ for bidder 4) or unnecessarily much higher than the sufficient winning bid (see the RAD ask price on $\{B\}$ for bidder 5) (Bichler *et al.*, 2009). We have not included HPB in this example, as we would then require a hierarchical structure of the items, and some package bids might not be feasible in such a hierarchy.

8.5   Empirical Results

A number of experimental studies have focused on open combinatorial auctions and their comparison with simultaneous or sequential auctions. Initial experiments analyzed small markets with a few items only, while more recently experiments with 18 items have been conducted. Overall, they suggest that in the presence of super-additive valuations, i.e., complementarities, combinatorial auctions achieve a higher efficiency. Later experiments considered larger combinatorial auctions and highlighted that a restricted package selection of bidders had the biggest impact on efficiency, much more than the auction format used. This is an issue that can potentially be addressed with the use of a compact bid language, as discussed in section 7.5. The package selection of individuals and the use of an XOR bid language were also reasons for low efficiency in experiments with the combinatorial clock auction; these are discussed below.

8.5.1   Experiments with Small Markets

Banks *et al.* (1989) analyzed various mechanisms and found that combinatorial auctions exhibited higher efficiency than traditional auctions, in the presence of super-additivity. In line with this research, Ledyard *et al.* (1997) compared the SMRA, sequential ascending auctions, and a simple combinatorial auction format and found that, in the case of exposure problems, the combinatorial auction led to a significantly higher efficiency than the other two formats. Banks *et al.* (2003) did another analysis on the SMRA and ascending auctions allowing package bidding and also found that package bidding achieved higher efficiency for superadditive valuations.

Porter *et al.* (2003) compared the SMRA with the combinatorial clock auction and found that the latter achieved the higher efficiency and in addition was simpler for bidders. Kwasnica *et al.* (2005) described the resource allocation design (RAD) and compared it with the SMRA. They found that in environments with complementarities RAD significantly increased efficiency; also, RAD had a lower number of auction rounds. In additive environments without complementarities, package bidding rarely occurred and no significant differences in efficiency and seller revenue could be found.

Kazumori (2005) analyzed the SMRA, the VCG mechanism, and the clock proxy auction. He conducted experiments with students and professional traders and confirmed the results of previous studies that, when there are significant complementarities, bundle bidding leads to higher efficiency than the SMRA. He also found, however, that when there are coordination problems, package bidding may be less powerful. The clock-proxy auction outperformed both the SMRA and the VCG auctions, while the SMRA outperformed the clock-proxy auction for additive value structures. Kazumori (2005) also found that professional traders had higher payoffs than students on average. In another study Chen and Takeuchi (2010) compared the VCG auction and iBEA in experiments in which humans competed against artificial bidders. Here, the sealed-bid VCG auctions generated significantly higher efficiency and revenue than the iBEA auctions. Participants in the VCG auctions either underbid or bid their true values.

8.5.2   Experiments with Larger Markets

Goeree and Holt (2010) performed experiments for the US Federal Communications Commission (FCC) in which they compared the SMRA and a modified version of RAD against hierarchical package bidding (HPB), a design for large combinatorial auctions where the auctioneer restricts bidders to bidding on a few preselected bundles. The value model in these experiments included 18 items, which allows for 262 143 possible bundle bids, while the tested HPB design reduced this set to bids on the 18 individual licenses and only four bundle bids, which needed to be hierarchically structured. In these experiments, which were focused on the allocation problem of the FCC, HPB achieved the highest efficiency and revenue, followed by RAD and then SMRA. Hierarchical package bidding is designed for large-scale combinatorial auctions, in which it is possible for the auctioneer to suggest a hierarchical structuring of bundles that fits the bidders' preferences. If this is not done, the design can lead to exposure problems. Additional results of related experiments for the FCC can be found in Brunner *et al.* (2010).

Scheffel *et al.* (2012) partly replicated the experiments of Goeree and Holt (2010) but extended them with the CC auction. They added experiments with a new value model that has different synergy characteristics and captures the local synergies of licenses, which can be well motivated from observations in the field (Ausubel *et al.*, 1997; Moreton and Spiller, 1998). Scheffel *et al.* (2012) found that restricted package selection of bidders, not the auction design, is the biggest barrier to full efficiency. Their conjecture is that satisficing behavior is an explanation for bidders to select a subset out of the many possible packages in larger combinatorial auctions. Scheffel *et al.* (2012) found only a few statistically significant differences in efficiency and revenue among the different open combinatorial auction formats. They replicated important findings of Goeree and Holt (2010) in their value model with global synergies, namely that HPB achieves higher efficiency than RAD. The results of HPB and RAD were not significantly different in a second value model with local synergies, which is less suitable for hierarchical prepackaging. Interestingly, they found a significantly higher efficiency for single-stage CCA compared with HPB in the value model with local synergies. In HPB, regional bidders had to take an exposure risk more often and, in a significantly higher number of cases, they failed to outbid the national bidder in a threshold problem.

Another set of experiments compared auctions with linear and non-linear prices. Scheffel *et al.* (2011) analyzed the single-stage CCA, a version of RAD, and iBundle with the VCG auction. They compared small auctions, with three or six items, and medium-sized auctions, with nine or 18 items, and their impacts on auction performance metrics. Bidders did not seem to bid straightforwardly in any of the auction formats, not even in iBundle, where there are incentives to do so. This motivates the issue of the robustness of the combinatorial auction formats to non-best response bidding (Schneider *et al.*, 2010). Also, the experiments confirmed that the number of auction rounds in iBundle can be prohibitive in practical settings, even for auctions with only six items. As in previous studies (Bichler *et al.*, 2009; Porter *et al.*, 2003), linear-price auctions achieved high levels of efficiency.

8.6   Summary

Open auctions have advantages in multi-object markets, as they do not require bidders to reveal their valuations in a single step and bidders can eventually identify efficient packages in a series of auction rounds. Formal models of open auctions are rare, probably owing to the revelation principle. Interestingly, algorithms have served as models for ascending auctions. In particular, primal–dual algorithms have a nice interpretation as a distributed system where both the bidders and the auctioneer optimize in each step until they eventually identify a welfare-maximizing solution. This can be seen as a design recipe for ascending auctions. For assignment markets where each bidder wants to win at most one item, not only do such processes end up with the optimal outcome; also, the prices charged at the end of the process coincide with VCG prices. This serves as a proof that such auctions satisfy an ex post equilibrium. There are other (restricted) environments, such as allocation problems, which have a matroid structure, where even simple greedy algorithms achieve the above properties. Overall, much of the theory on ascending multi-object auctions is rooted in the theory of linear and integer linear optimization and the corresponding algorithms.

Unfortunately, ascending combinatorial auctions with general valuations constitute an impossibility. Ascending auctions implement a VCG outcome only if the valuations of bidders satisfy the bidder submodularity condition. If bidders have complementary valuations, this condition is violated. However, combinatorial auctions are often used when bidders have complementary valuations. A number of heuristics have been developed for ask prices in ascending auctions. Some use anonymous and linear prices, others non-linear prices. Overall, the efficiency of these auctions in the laboratory is surprisingly high, even though one cannot prove strong game-theoretical solution concepts such as an ex post equilibrium. One might argue that, in the field, bidders rarely have reliable prior distributional information about the preferences of competitors for various packages, so that manipulation is hard. In particular, simple combinatorial clock auction formats have been used in many cases in the field, which is why we discuss these auction formats in more detail in the next chapter.

8.7   Comprehension Questions

1. Define the assignment problem. How is it related to combinatorial auctions in general?
2. Explain the primal–dual method for solving linear programs.
3. Define different types of ask prices and explain why ask prices are required in an ascending auction.

4. Enumerate four desirable properties for ascending combinatorial auctions.
5. Is it always possible to implement an ascending combinatorial auction which satisfies an ex post equilibrium?
6. Define the bidder submodularity (BSM) property and its importance for ascending combinatorial auctions.

8.8 Problems

Linear Prices

Given the bids shown in table 8.9, compute anonymous and linear ask prices for every bundle.

Table 8.9 Bidder valuations

	{A}	{B}	{C}	{A, B}	{A, C}	{B, C}	{A, B, C}
Bidder 1	1	3	2	5	5	5	11
Bidder 2	2	2	1	6	4	7	8

Assignment Market

Consider the valuation matrix shown in table 8.10 and compute the allocation and prices using the algorithm of Demange *et al.* (1986). Let $p = (0, 0, 0)$ be the initial price vector.

Table 8.10 Valuation matrix

	A	B	C
Bidder 1	5	2	3
Bidder 2	7	1	4
Bidder 3	9	5	8

Bidder Valuations

Consider an auction with two bidders, 1, 2, and three items, A, B, C (see table 8.11).

Table 8.11 Bidder valuations

	{A}	{B}	{C}	{A, B}	{A, C}	{B, C}	{A, B, C}
Bidder 1	5.5	8.5	0.5	10	5.5	5.5	15.5
Bidder 2	4.5	5.5	6.5	10	10	10	13

(a) Analyze whether the valuations from both bidders are subadditive.
(b) Analyze whether the valuations from both bidders are submodular.
(c) Analyze whether the valuations from both bidders fulfill the gross substitutes condition.

iBundle

Consider the valuations of three bidders, 1, 2, 3, for three items, A, B, C (see table 8.12).

Table 8.12 Bidder valuations

	$\{A\}$	$\{B\}$	$\{C\}$	$\{A, B\}$	$\{A, C\}$	$\{B, C\}$	$\{A, B, C\}$
Bidder 1	30	0	50	80	100	90	110
Bidder 2	0	50	60	90	80	150	160
Bidder 3	60	40	0	110	70	40	130

Conduct the iBundle(2) mechanism with a minimum increment of 25 and the following bidder strategy: *bidders bid on all bundles with maximum positive utility.* (Remember that utility = value – price.)

9 The Combinatorial Clock Auction Formats

Combinatorial clock auctions (CCAs) have been adopted in spectrum auctions (Bichler and Goeree, 2017) and in other applications for their simple price-update rules. There are single-stage and two-stage versions, which have been used in spectrum auctions worldwide. We devote a chapter to CCAs because of their practical relevance, as for chapter 6 on the SMRA. We will discuss both versions and a practical example of a market mechanism that includes a discussion of activity rules, which are sometimes ignored in theoretical treatments.

9.1 The Single-Stage Combinatorial Clock Auction

The single-stage combinatorial clock auction (SCCA) is easy to implement and has therefore found application in spectrum auctions and in procurement. In this section we provide a more detailed discussion of the SCCA, as introduced by Porter *et al.* (2003), and give an algorithmic description in algorithm 3.

9.1.1 Auction Process

In this type of action, prices for all items are initially zero or at a reserve price r. In every round bidders identify a package of items, or several packages, which they offer to buy at current prices. If two or more bidders demand an item then its price is increased by a fixed bid increment in the next round. This process iterates. The bids which correspond to the current ask prices are called *standing* bids, and a bidder is standing if she has at least one standing bid. In a simple scenario in which supply equals demand, the auction terminates and the items are allocated according to the standing bids.

If at some point there is an excess supply of at least one item and no item is over-demanded, the auctioneer determines the winners to find an allocation of items that maximizes his revenue by considering all submitted bids. If the solution displaces a standing bidder, the prices of items in the corresponding standing bids rise by the bid increment and the auction continues. The auction ends when no prices are increased and bidders finally pay their bid prices for the winning packages. We will analyze a version that uses an XOR bidding language.

Data: package bids $p_i(S)$
Result: allocation $\bar{x}$ and prices $p_i(\bar{x}_i)$
initialization
    for $k = 1$ **to** m **do** $p_k \leftarrow r$
    for $i = 1$ **to** n **do** $x_i \leftarrow \emptyset$
repeat
    overdemand $\leftarrow$ *FALSE*
    oversupply $\leftarrow$ *FALSE*
    for $i = 1$ **to** n **do** bidders submit bids $p_i(S)$

        for $k = 1$ **to** m **do**
            if ≥ 2 bidders $i \neq j$ demand item k **then**
                $p_k \leftarrow p_k + \epsilon$
                overdemand $\leftarrow$ *TRUE*
        end
        if item k is not part of a bid $p_i(S)$ **then**
            oversupply $\leftarrow$ *TRUE*
        end
    if *overdemand* = *TRUE* **then** continue with next iteration
    else if *oversupply* = *FALSE* **then** break
    else

        for $k = 1$ **to** m **do**
            Assign $p_i(S)$ with $k \in S$ to the set of standing bids B
            Calculate $\bar{x}$ based on all bids submitted in the auction
            if a bidder holding a bid in B is displaced, i.e. no bid by this bidder
            is in $\bar{x}$, **then**
                foreach item k which was displaced: **do**
                    $p_k \leftarrow p_k + \epsilon$
                end
            else $\bar{x}$ is the final allocation;
    until stop

Algorithm 3 Pseudo-code of the single-stage combinatorial clock auction

9.1.2   Efficiency of the SCCA

Traditionally, auction theorists first derive an equilibrium strategy for an auction and then analyze whether the auction terminates in an efficient solution if all bidders follow their equilibrium strategy.

If bidders have substitute valuations then straightforward bidding already leads to an efficient allocation in an auction with item prices, such as the SCCA. But, even with this strong restriction on the valuations, no ascending auction can always impute

Vickrey prices (Gul and Stacchetti, 1999). This implies that bidders have no incentive to bid straightforwardly and indeed they might have incentives to engage in demand reduction in order to impact prices favorably, as we described for the case of multi-unit auctions in section 5.2. This can actually lead to inefficiency. If valuations do not even satisfy the gross substitutes property, ascending core-selecting auctions can also lead to inefficient outcomes in equilibrium as described in section 8.3.3.

Depending on prior information about the competitors' valuations, various types of strategy might be possible. An equilibrium analysis of the SCCA is therefore challenging and as a consequence not much has been published about the SCCA although it has found application in high-stakes auctions worldwide.

Neverthless, one can ask under what conditions such an auction ends in an efficient allocation. Even if straightforward bidding does not constitute an equilibrium in such an auction, sometimes there is so little prior information about competitors available that one could expect bidders to follow a simple straightforward bidding strategy, and so demand reduction is unlikely. Can we expect the SCCA to be at least efficient, if bidders follow a straightforward bidding strategy? Unfortunately this is not the case, as we will show in this chapter. We also evaluate a powerset strategy, which describes the situation in which bidders reveal all packages with a positive valuation at the current prices.

Definition 9.1.1 A *powerset* bidder bids on all packages S with a non-negative value $v_i(S) - \sum_{k \in S} p(k) \geq 0$ at the current set of ask prices $p_1, \ldots, p_m$.

This could be considered a best-case strategy to achieve efficiency. However, even a powerset strategy would not always lead to full efficiency. Nevertheless, there are some possible ways to address the inefficiencies arising in a SCCA.

We start with a general theorem by Kagel *et al.* (2010), which describes when (i.e., with which strategies) an ascending combinatorial auction will end in an efficient allocation. Such an ascending combinatorial auction is defined in such a way that it selects an allocation $\bar{x}$ to maximize the auctioneer's revenue $\bar{x} \in \text{argmax}_x \sum_{i \in \mathcal{I}} p_i(x_i)$ and has bidder i pay $p_i(x_i)$, where $p_i(x_i)$ denotes the highest price that i bids for a package $x_i \subseteq \mathcal{K}$ during the course of the auction.

An ascending combinatorial auction can be modeled as a cooperative game with transferable utility, in which the payoff vector or *imputation* π is given by the auctioneer's revenue $\pi_0 = \sum_{i \in \mathcal{I}} p_i(x_i)$, and bidder i's payoff $\pi_i = v_i(x_i) - p_i(x_i)$. The value of a coalition including the auctioneer and the bidders in $T \subseteq \mathcal{I}$ is $w(T) = \sum_{i \in T} v_i(x_i)$.

A feasible allocation x with prices P and a corresponding imputation π is a *core allocation* if, for every set of bidders $T \subseteq \mathcal{I}$, the imputation satisfies $\pi_0 + \sum_{i \in T} \pi_i \geq w(T)$. A set of bidders T is *relevant* if there is some imputation such that $\pi_0 + \sum_{i \in T} \pi_i = w(T)$. The package $x_i(\mathcal{I})$ is the respective efficiency-relevant package with $\pi_0 + \sum_{i \in \mathcal{I}} \pi_i \geq w(\mathcal{I})$.

Theorem 9.1.1 (Kagel *et al.*, 2010) *In an ascending combinatorial auction, let P denote the final bids and $\bar{x} \in \text{argmax}_x \sum_{i \in \mathcal{I}} p_i(x_i)$ the final allocation in the auction.*

Table 9.1 Example of a demand-masking set of bidder valuations and the SCCA process, assuming straightforward bidders

	$P_{(1)}$	$P_{(2)}$	$P_{(3)}$	...	(1)	(2)	(3)	...	(1, 2)	(1, 3)	...
v_1					10*						
v_{2_a}						4*			10		
v_{2_b}									10		
v_{3_a}							4*			10	
v_{3_b}										10	
...							...				...
$t = 1$	1	1	1	...	1_1				$2_{2_a,2_b}$	$2_{3_a,3_b}$	...
$t = 2$	2	2	2	...	2_1				$4_{2_a,2_b}$	$4_{3_a,3_b}$	...
$t = 3$	3	3	3	...	3_1				$6_{2_a,2_b}$	$6_{3_a,3_b}$	...
$t = 4$	4	4	4	...	4_1				$8_{2_a,2_b}$	$8_{3_a,3_b}$	...
$t = 5$	5	5	5	...	5_1				$10_{2_a,2_b}$	$10_{3_a,3_b}$	...
$t = 6$	6	6	6	...	6_1						
$t = 7$	7	6	6	...	7_1						
...											
$t = 10$	10	6	6	...	10_1						

If, for all bidders $i \in \mathcal{I}$, $v_i(x_i(\mathcal{I})) - p_i(x_i(\mathcal{I})) \le v_i(\bar{x}_i) - p_i(\bar{x}_i)$ then the allocation $\bar{x}$ is efficient: $\sum_{i \in \mathcal{I}} v_i(\bar{x}_i) = w(\mathcal{I})$.

Proof sketch:

$$\sum_{i \in \mathcal{I}} v_i(\bar{x}_i) = \sum_{i \in \mathcal{I}} p_i(\bar{x}_i) + \sum_{i \in \mathcal{I}} [v_i(\bar{x}_i) - p_i(\bar{x}_i)]$$

$$\ge \sum_{i \in \mathcal{I}} p_i(x_i(\mathcal{I})) + \sum_{i \in \mathcal{I}} [v_i(\bar{x}_i) - p_i(\bar{x}_i)]$$

$$\ge \sum_{i \in \mathcal{I}} v_i(x_i(\mathcal{I})) = w(\mathcal{I})$$

The first inequality is based on the definition of a total-bid-maximizing package auction. The second inequality follows from the hypothesis of the theorem, and the final equality follows from the definition of $x_i(\mathcal{I})$. $\square$

To promote these results, the auction mechanism must encourage bidders to bid aggressively all the way up to their full values $v_i(x_i(\mathcal{I}))$ if necessary for *efficiency-relevant packages*, i.e., packages that may become winning packages. We will now analyze, if this is possible for straightforward bidders in the SCCA. Unfortunately, if a bidder follows the straightforward strategy in the SCCA, she does not necessarily bid on all relevant packages in the course of the auction.

The example in table 9.1 illustrates a characteristic situation where efficiency-relevant packages are not revealed by straightforward bidders. The upper part of the table describes the valuations of $2m - 1$ bidders for m items, while the lower part shows both

Table 9.2 Demand-masking set of bidder valuations

	$\{R\}$	$\{S_h\}$	$\{R \dot{\cup} S_h\}$
v_1	ξ	0	ξ
$\{v_{h_a}\}$	0	v_h	μ
$\{v_{h_b}\}$	0	0	μ

the ask prices for items and the corresponding package bids in individual rounds t. The indices of the bid prices for different packages indicate which straightforward bidder submits the bid on the respective package. There is a single bidder 1 and for each $h \in \{2, \ldots, m\}$ there are two bidders h_a and h_b. Bidder 1 values item (1) at a value of 10 and does not value any other item. For $h = 2, \ldots, m$, bidders h_a and h_b value the package $(1, h)$ at 10 and bidder h_a values the item (h) at 4; neither bidder is interested in any other package. Without loss of generality, we can assume an item-level bid increment of 1.

The straightforward bidders h_a and h_b demand the package $(1, h)$ until round 6, at which point they demand nothing. After round 6 there is therefore excess supply and the auctioneer solves the winner determination problem, which displaces the sole remaining standing bidder, who bids on item (1). Thus the price on item (1) increases further until bidder 1 wins this item in round 10, and the auction terminates with a social surplus of 10.

However, the efficient allocation assigns item (1) to bidder 1 and item (h) to bidder h_a for a social welfare of $10 + 4(m - 1)$. The bidders $h \geq 2$ never revealed their preference for single items only. As a result, $10/(10 + 4(m - 1))$ converges to 0 as $m \to \infty$.

We now describe the specific type of valuations in our example more formally as a *demand-masking set*.

Definition 9.1.2 (Demand-masking set) A *demand-masking set* of bidder valuations is given if the following properties are fulfilled. There is a set of bidders $\mathcal{I}$ with $|\mathcal{I}| \geq 3$, a set of items $\mathcal{K} = \{1, \ldots, m\}$ with $R \subseteq \mathcal{K}$, and a partition $\mathcal{H}$ of $\mathcal{K} \backslash R$. Let S_h be the elements of $\mathcal{H}$ with $h \in \{2, \ldots, |\mathcal{H}| + 1 = g\}$. For each S_h there are two bidders h_a and h_b. Bidder 1 values package R at ξ. For $h \in \{2, \ldots, g\}$ the bidders h_a value the packages S_h at v_h and $R \dot{\cup} S_h$ at μ, and the bidders h_b value only the package $R \dot{\cup} S_h$ at μ (the symbol $\dot{\cup}$ implies the union of R with all the S_h). No bidders are interested in the other packages, i.e., the marginal value of winning any item additional to the positively valued packages is zero.

Note that the valuations of zero, as shown in table 9.2, do not in fact need to be strictly zero but rather sufficiently small as not to influence the allocation. The result illustrates that it is difficult to recommend a strategy to bidders in these auctions. It is also relevant for the two-stage CCA in the next section, because activity rules in this auction format set incentives for straightforward bidding in the clock phase.

Theorem 9.1.2 *If bidder valuations are demand masking and all bidders follow the straightforward strategy in the SCCA then the efficiency converges to $2/(m+1)$ in the worst case.*

The proof draws on the example in table 9.2. Obviously if the number of items m and the corresponding number of bidders increase to fulfill the requirements of a demand masking set, the efficiency converges to 0% in the worst case.

Different versions of the SCCA have been used in the field. The differences involve the bid language (OR or XOR), the termination rule (with or without optimization), and the activity rules. We discuss the latter in more detail in the following section on the two-stage CCA.

9.2   The Two-Stage Combinatorial Clock Auction Format

In the previous section we discussed why there is no equilibrium strategy for the single-stage CCA (SCCA) and why we cannot expect this auction to be efficient if bidders follow a simple straightforward bidding strategy.

It is also the case that in the two-stage CCA, straightforward bidding is not an equilibrium strategy, but the auction can be shown to be efficient if bidders follow a straightforward strategy in the first stage and bid truthfully in the second stage. This auction format has been used worldwide to sell spectrum licenses.

9.2.1   Auction Process

The auction process consists of a clock phase (or primary-bids rounds) and a supplementary-bids phase. In the *clock phase* the auctioneer announces ask prices for all licenses at the beginning of each round. In every round bidders communicate their demand for each item at the current prices. At the end of a round, the auctioneer determines a set of over-demanded licenses for which the bidders' demand exceeds the supply. The price for all over-demanded items is increased by a bid increment for the next round. This clock phase continues until there are no over-demanded items left. If all bidders follow a straightforward strategy and all licenses were sold after the clock phase terminated, then the auction outcome is efficient (Ausubel *et al.*, 2006).

The *supplementary phase* is designed to eliminate inefficiency arising from the single-stage clock phase. In this sealed-bid stage, bidders are able to increase bids from the clock phase or submit bids on bundles on which they have not bid in the clock phase. Bidders can submit as many bids as they want, but the bid price is restricted, being subject to the CCA activity rule (see the next subsection). Finally, all bids from both phases of the auction are taken into account in the winner determination and the computation of payments for the winners. The bids by a single bidder are mutually exclusive (i.e., the CCA uses an XOR bidding language). For the computation of payments, a Vickrey-nearest bidder-optimal core-pricing rule (Day and Cramton, 2012) is used in spectrum auctions, although there have been proposals for other types of core-payments (Erdil and Klemperer, 2010). The computation of core-selecting payments as in the CCA is described in section 7.3.3.

9.2.2 Activity Rules

The CCA combines two auctions, an ascending auction in the clock phase and a sealed-bid auction in the supplementary phase. This requires additional rules setting incentives to bid consistently throughout the two phases. Without activity rules, bidders might not bid in the clock phase but wait for the other bidders to reveal their preferences and only bid in the supplementary phase.

9.2.2.1 Activity Rules in the Clock Phase

Originally, the clock phase of the CCA employed a simple activity rule which does not allow increases in the size of packages in later rounds, as prices increase. It has been shown that, with substitute preferences, straightforward bidding is impossible with such an activity rule (Bichler *et al.*, 2011b, 2013a). Later versions use a hybrid activity rule that combines a monotonicity rule and a revealed preference rule (Ausubel *et al.*, 2006). Revealed-preference rules allow bidders to bid straightforwardly in the clock phase. If they do, then bidders are able to bid on all possible packages up to their true valuation in the supplementary stage (Bichler *et al.*, 2013a).

First, an eligibility-points rule is used in the clock phase to enforce activity in the primary bid rounds. The number of a bidder's eligibility points is non-increasing between rounds, so that bidders cannot bid on more licenses when the prices rise. A bidder may place a bid on any package that is within her current eligibility. Second, in any round, the bidder is also permitted to bid on a package that exceeds her current eligibility provided that the package satisfies her revealed preference with respect to each prior eligibility-reducing round. Bidding on a larger package does not increase the bidder's eligibility in subsequent rounds.

The revealed-preference rule works as follows. A package in clock round t satisfies the revealed preference, with respect to an earlier clock round s, of a given bidder if the bidder's package x_t has become relatively less expensive than the package on which she bid x_s in clock round s, as clock prices have progressed from those in clock round s to those in clock round t; x_s and x_t are vectors whose components are the numbers of licenses demanded in the respective category, e.g., a spectrum band. For example, in a market with three types of item or three spectrum bands with licenses of the same quality, a bidder who is interested in a package with two licenses in the first band and one license in the third band has the bid $x_t = (2, 0, 1)$ at prices p_t. The revealed preference constraint is:

$$\sum_{i=1}^{m} [x_{t,i} \times (p_{t,i} - p_{s,i})] \leq \sum_{i=1}^{m} [x_{s,i} \times (p_{t,i} - p_{s,i})]$$

where:

- i indexes the licenses;
- m is the number of licenses;

- $x_{t,i}$ is the quantity of the ith license bid in clock round t;
- $x_{s,i}$ is the quantity of the ith license bid in clock round s;
- $p_{t,i}$ is the clock price of the ith license bid in clock round t; and
- $p_{s,i}$ is the clock price of the ith license bid in clock round s.

A bidder's package x_t in clock round t is consistent with her revealed preference in the clock rounds if it satisfies the revealed-preference constraint with respect to all eligibility-reducing rounds prior to clock round t for the given bidder.

9.2.2.2   Activity Rules in the Supplementary Phase

Under the activity rule for the supplementary round, there is no limit on the supplementary-bids amount for the final clock package. All supplementary bids on packages other than the final clock package must satisfy the bidder's revealed preference with respect to the final clock round, regardless of whether the supplementary-bids package is smaller or larger, in terms of eligibility points, than her eligibility in the final clock round. This is referred to as the *final cap rule*.

In addition, supplementary bids for packages that exceed the bidder's eligibility in the final clock round must satisfy her revealed preference with respect to the last clock round in which the bidder was eligible to bid on the package and every subsequent clock round in which the bidder reduced her eligibility. This is called the *relative cap rule*.

Let x denote the package on which the bidder wishes to place a supplementary bid. Let x_s denote the package on which the bidder bid in clock round s and let b_s denote the bidder's highest monetary amount bid in the auction on package x_s, whether the highest amount was placed in a clock round or the supplementary round.

A supplementary bid b on package x satisfies the bidder's revealed preference with respect to a clock round s if b is less than or equal to the highest monetary amount bid on the package in clock round s, that is, b_s plus the price difference in the respective packages x and x_s, using the clock prices of clock round s. Algebraically, the revealed-preference limit on b is expressed as the condition

$$b \leq b_s + \sum_{i=1}^{m} [p_{s,i} * (x_i - x_{s,i})]$$

where:

- x_i is the quantity of the ith license in package x;
- b is the maximum monetary amount of the supplementary bid on package x; and
- b_s is the highest monetary amount bid on package x either in a clock round or in the supplementary round.

In addition, for supplementary-bids package x, let $t(x)$ denote the last clock round in which the bidder's eligibility was at least equal to the number of eligibility points associated with package x.

A given bidder's collection of supplementary bids is consistent with her revealed-preference limit if the supplementary bid of the given bidder for package x with monetary amount b satisfies the following condition: for any package x, the monetary amount b must satisfy the revealed-preference constraint, as specified above, with respect to the final clock round and with respect to every eligibility-reducing round equal to $t(x)$ or later.

Note that, in the application of the above formula, the package x_s may itself be subject to a revealed-preference constraint with respect to another package. Thus, the rule may have the effect of creating a chain of constraints on the monetary amount of a supplementary bid for a package x relative to the monetary amounts of other clock bids or supplementary bids.

Theorem 9.2.1 *If a bidder follows a straightforward bidding strategy in the primary bid rounds of a CCA then the activity rule will not restrict her to bid her maximum valuation on every bundle in the supplementary-bids round.*

Proof. Let's assume that the bidder bids straightforwardly, i.e., she submits a bid on her payoff-maximizing bundle in every round. Throughout the clock rounds she might have switched from a bundle x_s to a bundle x_t in a round t, when $v(x_t) - p_t(x_t) > v(x_s) - p_t(x_s)$, where $p_t(x_s)$ is the price of bundle x_s in round t. For the bundle x_s the bidder did not necessarily bid up to her true valuation in the clock round. On the basis of the activity rule, in supplementary-bids round s the bidder can submit a maximum bid of $p_s^{max}(x_s) = v(x_t) + p_t(x_s) - p_t(x_t)$ if she bids her true valuation $p_s(x_t) = v(x_t)$. As a result, $p_s^{max}(x_s) > v(x_s)$, so that the bidder can bid up to her true valuation on x_s in the supplementary-bids phase. Note that the same argument applies for bundle bids submitted in the primary-bid rounds before x_s, after the bidder has revealed her true valuation $v(x_s)$ in the supplementary-bids round. The proof also applies to bundles x_c on which the bidder has never submitted a bid in the clock rounds, as long as $v(x_t) - p_t(x_t) > v(x_c) - p_t(x_c)$ in a round t where the bidder had sufficient eligibility points to bid on this bundle. □

9.2.3 A Note on Revealed Preference Theory

Ausubel and Baranov (2014) used the theory of revealed preference as a rationale for the activity rules used in spectrum auctions. They showed that some versions of the activity rule in the CCA are based on the weak axiom of revealed preference (WARP), while future versions should be based on the general axiom of revealed preference (GARP) and so eliminate eligibility-point-based activity rules. In what follows we will revisit important concepts of revealed-preference theory and then discuss how they relate to straightforward bidding in an auction.

The concept of revealed preferences was originally introduced by Samuelson (1938) in order to describe the rational behavior of an observed individual without knowing the underlying utility function. He made the simple observation that "if an individual selects batch one over batch two, he does not at the same time select two over one". The term "select over" relates to a concept which is nowadays known as "revealed preferred to" and can be defined as follows.

Definition 9.2.1 (Directly-revealed preferred bundle)   Given vectors of prices and chosen bundles (p_t, x_t) for $t = 1, \ldots, T$, x_t is directly-revealed preferred to a bundle x
$(x_t R_D x)$ if $p_t x_t \geq p_t x$. Furthermore, x_t is strictly directly-revealed preferred to x $(x_t P_D x)$
if $p_t x_t > p_t x$. The relations R and P are the transitive closures of R_D and P_D, respectively.

Intuitively, a selected bundle x_1 is directly-revealed preferred to bundle x_2 if, given
x_1 and x_2, both at price p, x_1 is chosen. Definition 9.2.1 implies some sort of budget
(or income) for each observation. Consider a world with only two bundles x_1 and x_2, x_1
being the more expensive. If nevertheless, an individual chooses to consume x_1, then we
know that she prefers it over x_2, so that $(x_1 R_D x_2)$ holds. This implies that, as a rational
utility maximizer, she will never strictly prefer x_2 when x_1 is affordable at the same
time. More formally, this is known as the weak axiom of revealed preference (WARP).
If $x_t R_D x_s$ then it must not be the case that $x_s P_D x_t$ for WARP to be satisfied. If she chooses
x_2, though, we do not know if that decision is due to an actual preference or to a budget
constraint below the price of x_1. Hence, there is also no way to predict which choice
would be made in another observation where she might have a higher income or face
different prices, as we have learned nothing about the relation R_D.

In a setting with more than two bundles, WARP is not enough to determine whether
a consumer is a rational utility maximizer. A set of choices $\{x_1 R_D x_2, x_2 R_D x_3, x_3 R_D x_1\}$
does not violate WARP but is possibly irrational. In order to detect this inconsistency,
we need to consider that the transitive closure R, which includes $x_1 R_D x_3$, possibly contradicts $x_3 R_D x_1$. Therefore, in a world with more than two bundles the consumption data
of a rational utility maximizer needs to satisfy the strong axiom of revealed preference
(SARP). If $x_t R x_s$ then it must not be the case that $x_s R x_t$ for SARP to be satisfied or,
if indifference between distinct bundles is valid, for the generalized axiom of revealed
preference (GARP) to be satisfied. Varian (2006) provided an extensive discussion of
WARP, SARP, and GARP.

Applying these axioms to the clock phase of the CCA is straightforward. In each
clock round (observation), there is a single known price vector for which each bidder
submits a single demand vector. Hence, we can easily build the revealed-preference
relation R_D and its transitive closure R for every bidder. For supplementary round S we
know the bundle bid prices $p^S x$ even without an explicit price vector p^S, as bidders bid
on bundles instead of single items. As only at most one of the bidder's bids will win, for
any pair of supplementary bids $\{x_1^S, x_2^S\}$, the bidder reveals her preference for the higher
bid. This allows us to infer $x_1^S R_D x_2^S$ if the bid on x_1^S is higher or equal to the bid x_2^S, or
vice versa.

Table 9.3 provides a simple example of CCA bidding data for items A, B in an auction
with three clock rounds and a supplementary phase. In each round of the clock phase,
the bidder under consideration reveals her preference for the chosen bundle over all
other affordable bundles. The given data are consistent with a set of valuations such as
$(75, 60, 55)$ for the three bundles. However, the data are not consistent with the actual
valuations $(100, 100, 100)$ that would require a bidder always to choose the cheapest
of the three packages. The resulting revealed-preference relation violates GARP in this
case, but this violation cannot be detected without knowing the true valuations.

Table 9.3 Applying the revealed-preference theory to a bidder's CCA bids. The chosen bundles x_t are marked with an asterisk; the bundles in parentheses are assumed non-affordable

Round t	Price p_t A	B	Bundle price $p_t x$ $x_1 = (2, 2)$	$x_2 = (2, 1)$	$x_3 = (1, 1)$	Revealed preference
1	10	10	40*	30	20	$x_1 P_D x_2, x_1 P_D x_3$
2	20	20	(80)	60*	40	$x_2 P_D x_3$
3	30	20	(100)	(80)	50*	
S			75		55	$x_1 P_D x_3$
Valuations			100	100	100	

Afriat's theorem says that a finite set of data is consistent with utility maximization (i.e., straightforward bidding) if and only if it satisfies GARP (Afriat, 1967). However, GARP allows for changes in income or budget across different observations (see table 9.4), as traditional revealed-preference theory is based on the assumption of an idealized individual who "confronted with a given set of prices and with a given income [...] will always choose the same set of goods" (Samuelson, 1938).

The auction literature typically assumes that bidders have quasi-linear utility functions such that they maximize their payoff given the prices. For quasi-linear utility functions there are no binding budget constraints, i.e., "infinite income". Ausubel and Baranov (2014) argued that a GARP-based activity rule would require GARP and also quasi-linearity. Also, the efficiency results for the CCA in Ausubel and Milgrom (2002) and Ausubel et al. (2006) only hold if bidders are quasi-linear and bid straightforwardly. Unfortunately, table 9.4 shows that the traditional definition of GARP allows for changes in income and therefore substantial deviations from straightforward bidding, if we assume quasi-linear utility functions.

Therefore, we aim for a stronger definition of revealed preference with non-binding budgets, as they are assumed to be in theory. With this assumption, the different bids in an auction also reveal by how much one bundle is preferred to another.

Definition 9.2.2 (Revealed-preferred bundle) Given vectors of prices and chosen bundles (p_t, x_t) for $t = 1, \ldots, T$ and a constant income, we say x_t is revealed-preferred to a bundle x by amount c (written $x_t R_c x$) if $p_t x_t \geq p_t x + c$.

Table 9.4 Example of non-straightforward bidding behavior with GARP. This example does not violate GARP. It can be explained by an increase in income from round $t = 1$ to round $t = 2$

Round t	Price p_t A	B	Bundle price $p_t x$ $x_1 = (1, 0)$	$x_2 = (0, 1)$	Revealed preference
1	10	50	10*	(50)	–
2	30	80	30	80*	$p_2 x_2 > p_2 x_1 \Rightarrow x_2 P_D x_1$

Intuitively, $x_t R_c x$ can be interpreted as "x_t is chosen over x if it costs no more than the price of x plus c". Note that c will be negative in all cases where x is more expensive than x_t; this would be ignored in the traditional definition of revealed preferences (see definition 9.2.1). The result of applying definition 9.2.1 to a set of bid data is a family of relations R_c instead of a single revealed preference relation R. The family R_c has several properties:

- $x_1 R_c x_2$ implies $x_1 R x_2$ if $c \geq 0$ (definition);
- $x_1 R_c x_2$ implies $x_1 P x_2$ if $c > 0$ (definition);
- $x R_c x$ for all $c \leq 0$ (reflexivity);
- $x_1 R_{c_1} x_2$ and $x_2 R_{c_2} x_3$ imply $x_1 R_{c_1+c_2} x_3$ (transitivity);
- $x_1 R_{c_1} x_2$ implies $x_1 R_{c_2} x_2$ if $c_1 > c_2$ (derived from the transitivity and reflexivity of $R_{c_1-c_2}$).

These properties are sufficient to derive a contradiction $x R_c x$ with $c > 0$ ("$u(x) > u(x)$") for any non-straightforward bidding behavior that can be detected without knowing the actual utility function u. For example, it is easy to see that the choices in table 9.4 do not describe straightforward bidding because they are not consistent under the above properties of R_c: ($x_1 R_{-40} x_2 \wedge x_2 R_{50} x_1 \Rightarrow x_1 R_{10} x_1$). In order to enforce straightforward bidding among bidders, one could use an activity rule based on definition 9.2.2. Overall, there is a close relationship between the activity rules in the CCA and revealed-preference theory.

9.2.4   Strategies in the Two-Stage CCA

Game-theoretical models of general core-selecting auctions were described in section 7.4. An equilibrium analysis of a CCA with all its detailed rules is difficult. However, there are a number of papers that have analyzed simplified environments game-theoretically. Levin and Skrzypacz (2017) showed that truthful bidding is not dominant in an environment with homogeneous goods and that there is a wide range of ex post equilibria with demand expansion and also demand reduction. In the following we focus on possibilities to raise rivals' costs in a CCA. These possibilities can arise because of the payment rule, which charges bidders differential payments, and because safe supplementary bids can be submitted, i.e., bids which will definitely be losing but could possibly impact the payments of competitors (Bichler et al., 2011b, 2013a). Janssen and Karamychev (2016) provide motivation for spiteful bidding behavior and a game-theoretical model with complete information, where bidders raise rivals' cost.

9.2.4.1   Non-Anonymous Payments

Neither the two-stage CCA nor the VCG mechanism have anonymous prices. Although this has been discussed extensively in sections 7.3.2 and 7.3.3, it might be helpful to look at a simple example.

Example 9.2.1 Suppose that there are two bidders and two homogeneous units of one item. Bidder 1 submits a bid of $5 for one unit, while bidder 2 submits a bid of $5 for one unit and a bid of $9 for two units. Each bidder wins one unit, but bidder 1 pays $4 and bidder 2 pays zero.

This difference is due to the asymmetry of bidders, and this asymmetry leads to a violation of the law of one price, a criterion which is often seen as desirable in market design. Although arbitrage is avoided, as bidders typically cannot sell licenses to one another immediately after a spectrum auction, different prices for the same spectrum are difficult to justify to the public and also violate the anonymity of prices. This has become a topic of debate in relation to a Swiss auction in 2012, where two bidders payed substantially different prices for almost the same allocation (see section 9.2.4.4 below).

9.2.4.2   Safe Supplementary Bids

After the clock rounds, if a bidder has a standing bid on his most preferred bundle, she might not have an incentive to bid truthfully in the supplementary phase because she can submit a bid price which is sufficient to win this standing bid with certainty. The following two theorems define "safe supplementary bids", which on the basis of the CCA activity rules cannot become losing if the bidders have a standing bid after the primary-bids rounds. These bids also, however, introduce the possibility of riskless spiteful bidding, as we will see later. Note that we assume a CCA with a final cap rule, which was not used in early applications of this auction format in certain countries.

We first introduce some necessary notation. Let $\mathcal{K}$ denote the supply of items or licenses, and $b_j^p(x_j) \in B$ denote the standing bid of bidder $j \in \mathcal{I}$ on bundle $x_j \subseteq \mathcal{K}$ after the clock phase. In addition, let $r^s(\mathcal{K})$ denote the auctioneer's revenue for the optimal allocation after the supplementary-bids phase including all bids B in both phases; $r^p(\mathcal{K})$ describes his revenue with only standing bids in the last round of the clock phase; $r_{-b_j}^s(\mathcal{K})$ denotes the auctioneer's revenue in the optimal allocation without any bid of bidder $j \in \mathcal{I}$ for the bundle x_j; $x_j^C = \mathcal{K} \backslash x_j$ is the set of licenses complementary to x_j. We refer to α as the ask price vector in the last clock round.

Theorem 9.2.2 *If demand equals supply in the last clock round, any single supplementary bid* $b_j^s(x_j) > b_j^p(x_j)$ *cannot become losing in a CCA with a final cap rule.*

Proof. In the last clock round, there is a demand of exactly $\mathcal{K}$ licenses if demand equals supply. Bidder $j \in \mathcal{I}$ submits a bid $b_j^p(x_j)$ in the last clock round; this is her standing bid after the primary bid rounds. Let $b_j^s(x_j) > r_{-b_j}^s(\mathcal{K}) - r_{-b_j}^s(x_j^C)$ be the bid price that bidder j needs to submit in order to win x_j after the supplementary-bids round. Owing to the activity rule, j's competitors $k \in \mathcal{I}$ with $k \neq j$ can increase their bids without limit only on bundles $x_k \subseteq x_j^C$ which were submitted in the last primary-bids round. Any high supplementary bid $b_k^s(x_k^p)$ on a bundle x_k^p from k's standing bid after the primary-bids rounds will increase $r_{-b_j}^s(\mathcal{K})$ as well as $r_{-b_j}^s(x_j^C)$ and cannot impact $b_j^s(x_j)$. Supplementary bids on packages different from the standing bid of bidder k are restricted by the activity rule in such a way that $b_k^s(x_k^s \cup Z) \leq b_k^s(x_k^s) + \alpha Z$

and $b_k^s(x_k^s \backslash Z) \leq b_k^s(x_k^s) - \alpha Z$, with $Z \subseteq \mathcal{K}$. As a result, any supplementary bid $b_j^s(x_j) > b_j^p(x_j) = \alpha x_j$ must be winning. $\qquad\square$

The intuition is that the supplementary bids of her competitors on their standing bundle bid from the final primary-bids round do not impact the safe supplementary bid of a bidder $j \in \mathcal{I}$. Any additional items added by competitors to their standing bundle bids cannot increase the supplementary-bids price by more than the ask price in the last of the clock rounds. If the bidder submits additional supplementary bids on packages not containing x_j, his bid $b_j^s(x_j)$ could well become losing, as can easily be shown by examples. The activity rule also applies to bundles which are smaller than the standing bid of the last clock round.

If there is excess supply in the last round of the clock phase, a last primary-round bid b_j^p can become losing because, even if no supplementary bids were submitted, the auctioneer will conduct an optimization with all bids submitted at the end, which might displace b_j^p. This raises the question what is a safe supplementary bid $b_j^s(x_j^p)$ which ensures that the bidder j wins the bundle x_j^p of his standing bid from the last clock round after the supplementary-bids phase?

Theorem 9.2.3 *If there is zero demand on bundle M after the last clock round, a single supplementary bid of a standing bidder $b_j^s(x_j) > b_j^p(x_j) + \alpha M$ cannot become a losing bid in the CCA with a final cap rule.*

Proof. Let's assume a bidder j bidding on a bundle x_j^p in the last primary-bids round and two other competitors, who bid on a bundle of licenses $\mathcal{K}$ in the previous to last round of the primary-bids phase. In the last round the two competitors reduce their demand to zero, so that x_j^C licenses have zero demand after the last primary-bids round. Now, at least one of these competitors submits a supplementary bid on the bundle $\mathcal{K}$ at the prices $\alpha \mathcal{K}$ of the last primary round. Therefore bidder j can only win if she increases her bid to $b_j^s(x_j) > b_j^p(x_j) + \alpha x_j^C$.

Here, αx_j^C is the maximum markup that bidder j has to pay to become winning with certainty. To see this, note that the bid by any competitor $k \in \mathcal{I}$ with $k \neq j$ on any subset of x_j^C in this example is limited to α, owing to the activity rule. Now, even if there were another standing bid by a competitor k on any subset of x_j^C after the last primary-bids round, the maximum markup of j would not increase. Owing to the activity rule, j's competitors k can only increase their bids without limit on bundles $x_k \subseteq x_j^C$ which were submitted in the last primary-bids round. Such bids will increase $r_{-b_j}^s(\mathcal{K})$ as well as $r_{-b_j}^s(x_j^C)$ and cannot impact $b_j^s(x_j)$. Supplementary bids on packages different from the standing bid of bidder k are restricted by the activity rule in such a way that $b_k^s(x_k^s \cup Z) \leq b_k^s(x_k^s) + \alpha Z$ and $b_k^s(x_k^s \backslash Z) \leq b_k^s(x_k^s) - \alpha Z$.

Similarly, if the other bidders reduce their demand, so that a package M with $|M| < |x_j^C|$ licenses remains unsold after the primary-bids rounds, bidder j has to increase her standing bid by no more than αM to become winning after the supplementary-bids round with certainty. $\qquad\square$

Table 9.5 Example with supplementary-bids phase (S)

	B1	B2	B3	B4
Round 1 (80)	2	2	3	3
Round 2 (90)	2	2	3	3
Round 3 (100)	2	0	0	0
Round S	2(200)		3(300)	3(300)

Let's take an example with four bidders (B1 to B4), described in table 9.5, to illustrate this point. There is a supply of six units of a single license. The number in brackets after rounds 1 to 3 is the ask price for the licenses in this round. There is overdemand until round 3, when bidders 2, 3, and 4 reduce to a demand of zero. In the supplementary-bids round (S) these two bidders increase their last bid to a maximum of $300 for three licenses. They then become winning, while the standing bid of bidder 1 after the primary-bids rounds is displaced. In the example, bidder B1 needs to increase his bid price only by $100 and not by $\alpha \times 4 = \$400$. This is the difference between the allocation with B3 and B4, and the best allocation with B1's bid winning, which is B1's bid on two licenses for $200 and the bid by bidders B3 or B4 on three units.

9.2.4.3 Possibilities for Spiteful Bidding

As a consequence of safe supplementary bids, bidders can submit spiteful bids to drive up the payments of other bidders. Bidders in spectrum markets may spitefully prefer that their rivals earn a lower surplus. This is different from the expected utility maximizers typically assumed in the literature.

Spiteful bidding was analyzed by Morgan *et al.* (2003) and Brandt *et al.* (2007), who showed that the expected revenue in second-price auctions is higher than the revenue in first-price auctions in a Bayesian Nash equilibrium. While spiteful bidding is possible in any auction, the two-stage CCA provides the possibility of submitting spiteful supplementary bids with no risk of actually winning such a bid, if all licenses are sold after the primary-bids rounds and the standing bidders want to win their standing bid in the supplementary-bids round with only a small bid increment. The latter is a relatively mild assumption.

In the following, we will provide a brief example of a CCA in which a bidder can submit a spiteful bid that increases the payments of other bidders with little risk of that bidder's winning such a bid. If there is no excess supply after the primary-bids rounds and bidders do not submit additional smaller bundle bids in the supplementary-bids round, such bids would not stand a chance of winning.

Consider one region in which three licenses A (1 unit) and B (2 units) are up for auction and another region in which three licenses C (1 unit) and D (2 units) are up for auction, each with one national and several regional bidders. The start prices are $1 for all licenses, and prices for over-demanded licenses are increased by $1 per round. Each license corresponds to one eligibility point.

Table 9.6 Bids in the clock rounds

	Bidder N	Bidder R_{11}	Bidder R_{21}	Bidder R_{12}	Bidder R_{22}
Round 1	(AC) = \$2	(A) = \$1	(AB) = \$2	(CD) = \$2	(CD) = \$2
...					
Round 15	(AC) = \$30	(A) = \$15	**(AB) = \$16**	(CD) = \$16	(CD) = \$16
Round 16	(AC) = \$32	(A) = \$16	**(2B) = \$2**	(CD) = \$17	(CD) = \$17
...					
Round 20	**(AC) = \$40**	(A) = \$20	(2B) = \$2	(CD) = \$21	(CD) = \$21
Round 21		(A) = \$21	(2B) = \$2	(CD) = \$22	(CD) = \$22
...					
Round 40		(A) = \$21	(2B) = \$2	(CD) = \$41	**(CD) = \$41**
Round 41		(A) = \$21	(2B) = \$2	(CD) = \$42	**(D) = \$1**
		– Termination –			

The national bidder N is only interested in winning licenses A and C in each of the two regions for at most \$40, i.e. she is not willing to switch to other packages. Regional bidder R_{11} is only interested in obtaining license A in his region. Regional bidder R_{21} prefers AB over 2B. However, she is willing to switch from AB to 2B if their prices differ by at least \$15. Regional bidders R_{12} and R_{22} would like to obtain CD, but bidder R_{22} is weaker and willing to bid on just D if he is overbid.

Table 9.6 illustrates the clock rounds, while table 9.7 gives the payments if no supplementary-round bid was submitted. Finally, table 9.8 gives the payments if bidder R_{21} submitted a spiteful bid on AB for \$22, the package price in the final round for which she would still be eligible according to the activity rule; consequently, the payment of the regional competitor increases by \$6. Such bids are possible owing to the initial eligibility-points rule, which might not reflect the market value of the different items appropriately.

The example suggests that there are situations where the clock auction reveals enough information for a bidder to increase the Vickrey price of other bidders, by losing bids, and therefore also to increase the Vickrey-closest core-selecting payment of all bidders. Not revealing excess supply after the clock rounds can mitigate the problem, but, depending on the history of primary-round bids, there might still be a risk of spiteful bids.

Table 9.7 Payments after the supplementary-bids round without additional supplementary bids

	Bid price	VCG payment	CCA payment
National N (AC)	(\$40)	–	–
Regional R_{11} (A)	\$21	\$14	\$14
Regional R_{21} (2B)	\$2	\$0	\$0
Regional R_{12} (CD)	\$42	\$40	\$40
Regional R_{22} (D)	\$1	\$0	\$0
	\$66	**\$54**	**\$54**

Table 9.8 Payments after the supplementary bids round with an additional supplementary bid by bidder R_{21} on AB for $22

	Bid price	VCG payment	CCA payment
National N (AC)	($40)	–	–
Regional R_{11} (A)	$21	**$20**	**$20**
Regional R_{21} (2B)	$2	$0	$0
Regional R_{12} (CD)	$42	$40	$40
Regional R_{22} (D)	$1	$0	$0
	$66	**$60**	**$60**

9.2.4.4   Evidence From the Field

The Swiss auction in 2012 was remarkable, because one bidder paid almost 482 million Swiss francs, while another one paid around 360 million Swiss francs, for almost the same allocation. While it is easy to explain such an outcome using the VCG payment rule, it could well be seen as unfair by participants. Combined with the possibility of safe supplementary bids discussed in this section, bidders can try to raise rivals' costs. The Austrian auction in 2013 is interesting for this reason. In this auction bidders could potentially submit up to 12 810 package bids (taking into consideration caps) on the 800 MHz, 900 MHz, and 1800 MHz bands, but they were limited to 2000 bids in the supplementary phase. The regulator reported that the three bidders actually submitted 4000 supplementary bids in total. The regulator also disclosed that most of these bids were submitted on very large packages up to the price limits imposed by the activity rule. This large number of supplementary bids can be seen as one reason for the high prices paid in Austria. The attempt to drive up the prices paid by other bidders and avoid having to pay more for an allocation than one's competitors, as happened in Switzerland, can serve as an explanation for this bidding behavior. Of course, if all bidders followed this strategy, it would lead to a strategic situation similar to a Prisoner's Dilemma. If none of the bidders had submitted high supplementary bids on these large packages, they would all have had to pay less (see Kroemer *et al.*, 2014). Some implementations of the CCA do not reveal the level of excess supply in the last clock rounds, so that it is harder to determine safe supplementary bids.

9.3   Experiments on the Two-Stage CCA

We have already discussed experiments on the single-stage CCA and other open combinatorial auction formats, in section 8.5. Some authors have also analyzed the two-stage CCA. Bichler *et al.* (2013a) analyzed the performance of the CCA and SMRA with value models similar to those in spectrum auctions. The first set of experiments shared the main characteristics of the spectrum sale in the 2.6 GHz band in Europe, with 48 possible bundles in two bands of identical items (the base-value model). The second-value model described a multiband setting (four bands of identical items), which allowed for 2 400 different bundles. The authors showed that the efficiency in the CCA in the base-value model was not higher than that of the SMRA. In the multiband-value model the efficiency was actually significantly lower than in the SMRA, owing to the low number of bundle bids and unsold items. Auctioneer revenue was considerably lower than in the SMRA, which could be explained by the CCA second-price payment rules. However, the auctioneer revenue in the CCA was also significantly lower than in CCA simulations with artificial bidders submitting bids on all possible combinations truthfully with the same-value models.

Important reasons for inefficiency in the laboratory and probably also in the field are the result of deviations from truthful bidding in the supplementary stage. Bidders submitted only a small subset of the thousands of packages they could bid for, both in the laboratory and in the field. This might have had strategic but certainly also practical reasons. In larger combinatorial spectrum auctions, with 100 licenses and more, it is only possible to submit bids on a small subset of all possible packages. All other packages are treated by the winner determination in the CCA as if bidders had no valuation for these packages, which is unlikely. In contrast, the SMRA uses an "OR" bidding language, where bidders can have multiple winning bids. During the winner determination, bids on different items provide an estimate for the value that a bidder has for every possible combination of bids on individual items. Such "missing bids" can be a significant source of inefficiency in any larger combinatorial auction with an XOR bid language.

Apart from missing bids in the supplementary phase, deviating from straightforward bidding in the clock phase is also a significant source of inefficiency. The revealed-preference activity rule in the CCA prohibits bidders from revealing their valuations truthfully in the supplementary phase if they do not bid straightforwardly in the clock phase, and this can lead auctioneers to select an inefficient solution (Kroemer et al., 2014).

The missing-bids problem in the CCA was addressed in Bichler et al. (2014a). The authors analyzed a bid language that drastically reduced the number of possible bids that could be submitted, a compact bid language. This reduced the number of possible bids from 2400 to 12 in the multiband value model introduced by Bichler et al. (2013a). Overall, the experiments analyzed the impact of two main design choices on efficiency and revenue: simple "compact" bid languages versus complex "fully expressive" bid languages and simple "pay-as-bid" payment rules versus complex "core-selecting" payment rules. They considered these design choices both for ascending and sealed-bid formats. The study found that simplicity of the bid language had a substantial positive impact on the auction's efficiency and simplicity of the payment rule had a substantial positive impact on the auction's revenue. The single-stage CCA, which uses a complex bid language and payment rule, achieved the lowest efficiency and revenue among all treatment combinations. Recent versions of the CCA allow for a more compact bid language in the supplementary stage, in order to combat the missing-bids problem.

There are also field data available for some CCAs; this was is discussed by Kroemer et al. (2014). The British regulator Ofcom was the first to publish bid data on a CCA, in 2008 and 2013. In addition, data on the Canadian 700 MHz auction in 2014, which was a large-scale application with around 100 regional licenses, has been published.

9.4   Summary

Combinatorial clock auctions are appealing for their simple linear prices. We first analyzed the single-stage CCA and found that a straightforward and truthful bidding strategy can yield low welfare. Interestingly, in the laboratory, bidders do not follow a purely straightforward bidding strategy and efficiency of the single-stage CCA is high on average. The two-stage CCA was designed to avoid the inefficiencies of the single-stage CCA and provide incentives for truthful bidding. The design uses a bidder-optimal core payment rule and a sophisticated activity rule based on revealed preferences. The auction format is based on a number of innovative ideas and has been used for spectrum auctions worldwide. Depending on the version of the activity rules used there might be possibilities for spiteful bidding, and the missing-bids problem with an XOR bid language can lead to inefficiencies. The design of robust auction formats to be used in spectrum auctions is still a topic of much ongoing research.

9.5   Comprehension Questions

1. Explain the single-stage combinatorial clock auction (CCA).
2. Describe the activity rule of the two-stage CCA for the clock and the supplementary stage.
3. Decide whether these statements are true or false for the two-stage CCA.
   (a) A bidder can submit multiple package bids in a round of the clock phase.
   (b) Bids in the supplementary phase are not restricted.
   (c) Bids in the supplementary phase can be placed on any bundle.
   (d) Prices of the CCA are always in the core with respect to the bids.

9.6   Problems

Bidder-Optimal Core Prices
Determine the core and the VCG prices graphically using the valuations in table 9.9. Can a winning bidder decrease his payment?

Table 9.9 Bidder valuations

	$\{A\}$	$\{B\}$	$\{A, B\}$
Bidder 1		11	
Bidder 2	22		
Bidder 3	8		
Bidder 4			27
Bidder 5		21	

CCA

Conduct the clock phase of a CCA with the valuations shown in table 9.10:

Table 9.10 Bidder valuations

	{A}	{B}	{C}	{A, B}	{A, C}	{B, C}	{A, B, C}
Bidder 1	4				6		11
Bidder 2		7		8			9
Bidder 3			3			7	8

1. Model the first stage of the CCA under the following conditions: assume all bidders bid straightforwardly on the package maximizing their utility; prices start at 1 for all items and in each round the price of each overdemanded item increases by 1; every item requires one activity point.
2. What would be the allocation after the first stage of the CCA? Is this allocation efficient?

Part III

Approximation and Matching Markets

10 Approximation Mechanisms

Many real-world markets require the solving of computationally hard allocation problems, and realistic problem sizes are often such that they cannot be solved optimally. For example, there have been spectrum auctions using the combinatorial clock auction with 100 licenses. The allocation problems are modeled as integer programs intended to produce an exact solution (see section 7.2), but this cannot always be guaranteed without restrictions. Actually, the number of bids in combinatorial spectrum auctions is typically restricted to a few hundred. Section 7.5 provides examples of allocation problems in other domains, sometimes using compact bid languages, which also cannot be solved optimally for larger instances. Sometimes it is acceptable to settle for suboptimal solutions. Often, heuristics are used to solve computationally hard problems. However, with heuristics we do not have worst-case bounds on the quality of the solution. In contrast, approximation algorithms provide worst-case bounds on the solution quality and a polynomial runtime. For this discussion, we expect the reader to have some basic familiarity with approximation algorithms; we provide an overview of the field and the necessary terminology and concepts in appendix B.4.

In this section, we analyze approximation mechanisms which provide good approximation ratios, which run in polynomial time, and which are also incentive-compatible. This leads to new notions of incentive compatibility beyond strategy-proofness (i.e., dominant-strategy incentive compatibility) and new types of mechanism. We often talk about *truthfulness* instead of *incentive compatibility*, both terms referring to different solution concepts setting incentives to reveal preferences truthfully.

One can think of the VCG mechanism as a black-box transformation from exact algorithms solving the allocation problem to a strategy-proof mechanism. A central question in this chapter is whether there is a similar black-box transformation, from approximation algorithms to truthful approximation mechanisms, which maintains the approximation ratios of non-truthful approximation algorithms. We show that black-box transformations for quite general allocation problems are possible with strong forms of truthfulness, when we use randomization.

Approximation algorithms are typically only available for idealized models such as knapsack problems or bin-packing problems. In practice, many allocation problems are quite messy and have many complicating side constraints that make it hard to find an approximation algorithm with a good performance guarantee. Examples of realistic allocation problems are discussed in section 7.5. Although some approaches discussed in this chapter might not be directly applicable, they may give us some idea of how to devise mechanisms with good computational and incentive properties. Linear programming plays a central role in the design and analysis of approximation algorithms, and we will focus on such techniques for their versatility and applicability to different types of allocation problems.

10.1   Approximation and Truthfulness

Approximation algorithms have provided a very active field of research in the past few decades (see appendix B.4 for a brief introduction of the key concepts). Approximation algorithms do not take into consideration incentive constraints. The goal of *approximation mechanisms* is the design of computationally efficient algorithms which take into account the incentives of participants as well. These mechanisms should run in polynomial time and satisfy strong game-theoretical solution concepts such that bidders have incentives to reveal their valuations truthfully and the auctioneer can determine the optimal allocation or one that approximates the optimal solution. Part of the research in this field is aimed at finding dominant strategies in the case of deterministic mechanisms, but some mechanisms also use randomization. For randomized approximation mechanisms *truthfulness in expectation* or *universal truthfulness* have been introduced as alternative solution concepts, which we discuss below.

If we drop the requirement of computational efficiency then we could solve the allocation problem optimally and use a VCG payment rule to achieve truthfulness. However, computational efficiency is important in many allocation problems, as we have seen. It is worth noting that the VCG mechanism is no longer truthful if the allocation does not maximize social welfare exactly (Nisan and Ronen, 2007). The proof showing that the VCG mechanism leads to a dominant-strategy equilibrium for each individual bidder (see section 3.4.2) relies on the argument that the auctioneer will choose the allocation that maximizes the social welfare on the basis of the reported bids of all bidders. So, if the allocation cannot be computed optimally then the VCG mechanism loses this strong game-theoretical property. For example, assume a single-object auction, where the object is assigned to the second highest bidder as an approximation of the optimal allocation, and the auctioneer charges the price of the third highest bid. The highest bidder might try to bid below the second-highest bidder in this case, and truthful bidding is no longer an equilibrium.

It is of interest to understand whether truthful approximation mechanisms can always match the approximation guarantee of the best (non-truthful) polynomial-time approximation algorithm with public input data. Understanding the power of truthful approximation mechanisms is a central goal of *algorithmic mechanism design*.

Unfortunately, the approximation ratios of algorithms for combinatorial optimization problems are sometimes low, and often no such approximation algorithms are available for specific problems. For example, the algorithmic problem of finding the optimal social welfare for general valuations in combinatorial sales auctions (equivalent to the weighted-set packing problem) is $O(\sqrt{m})$, where m is the number of items (Halldórsson *et al.*, 2000), which is a natural upper bound on the approximation ratio of truthful approximation mechanisms. This means that, in an auction with 25 items only, in the worst case the solution can be five times worse than the optimal solution. Of course, the average approximation might be much better, so that approximation mechanisms can be an interesting alternative in the case of computationally hard allocation problems. Let's briefly provide an overview of deterministic and randomized mechanisms for *combinatorial auctions*, before we give more details about specific types of mechanism.

10.1.1 Deterministic Approximation Mechanisms

A general recipe for the design of truthful and deterministic approximation mechanisms is a *maximal-in-range (MIR)* allocation rule, which computes the welfare-maximizing outcome over a restricted set of allocations (its range). These MIR mechanisms are equivalent to VCG mechanisms for this range and hence are strategy-proof. The range should be such that it allows for efficient computation of the maximum welfare. Note that the range must not depend on the valuations of the bidders as this would make it manipulable.

Unfortunately, there is no known general black-box reduction, from approximation algorithms to deterministic truthful approximation mechanisms, which would maintain the approximation ratios achieved for the best non-truthful approximation algorithms and that does not involve a strong restriction of the type of valuations allowed (e.g., to single-minded bidders or bidders with submodular valuations). Truthful and deterministic mechanisms seem to be at odds with the approximation ratio and communication complexity (Daniely *et al.*, 2015; Lavi *et al.*, 2003; Papadimitriou *et al.*, 2008). The best deterministic and truthful approximation guarantee known for general combinatorial auctions is $O(m/\sqrt{\log m})$ (Holzman *et al.*, 2004). If the types of valuation are further restricted then one can find better approximation ratios. For example, there is a simple and strategy-proof approximation mechanism for combinatorial auctions with single-minded bidders with an $O(\sqrt{m})$ approximation ratio, which we discuss later in section 10.2. However, it is unknown whether there is a deterministic approximation mechanism which yields an $O(\sqrt{m})$ ratio for general valuations. These negative results do not apply to randomized mechanisms, which we discuss next.

10.1.2 Randomized Approximation Mechanisms

The MIR principle can be extended to randomized mechanisms, where it is called *maximal-in-distributional-range* (MIDR). Instead of committing to a specific set of allocations, we commit upfront to a set of distributions over allocations, which must be independent (aka *oblivious*) of the valuations of bidders. Once this distribution is chosen, the corresponding MIDR allocation rule chooses the distribution that is best for the bidders in the sense of maximizing expected welfare with respect to the bids. Interestingly, there are *black-box reductions*, generic methods that invoke an approximation algorithm polynomially many times and achieve truthfulness without degrading the approximation ratio (Dobzinski *et al.*, 2012b; Lavi and Swamy, 2011). These frameworks can also be applied to the combinatorial auction problem with general (unrestricted) valuations and quasi-linear bidders.

Lavi and Swamy (2011) showed how any approximation algorithm witnessing an LP integrality gap for a packing problem can be transformed into an algorithm that is *truthful in expectation* (TIE), a solution concept for randomized mechanisms, which is introduced in definition 10.3.2. Their framework first optimizes the LP relaxation of the allocation problem and then uses a rounding technique called *randomized meta-rounding*, proposed earlier by Carr and Vempala (2000), which yields a convex decomposition of the scaled-down fractional solution into polynomially many integer solutions. We refer to this as the *relax-and-round framework* and will discuss it in section 10.3.1. For the multi-unit auction problem the integrality gap is 2 and, hence, the relax-and-round framework is said to give a 2-approximation.

Dughmi *et al.* (2011) proposed an approach (*convex rounding*) which optimizes directly the outcome of the rounding algorithm rather than the outcome of the relaxation algorithm. Since the rounding procedure is embedded into the objective function this approach is not always computationally tractable. Yet, assuming that the optimization problem can be solved efficiently, the approach always leads to an MIDR algorithm which is truthful-in-expectation. In general, the two frameworks by Lavi and Swamy (2011) and Dughmi *et al.* (2011) rely on the idea of *relaxation and rounding*.

Dobzinski *et al.* (2012b) proposed a general framework for randomized mechanisms which achieves *universal truthfulness*, an even stronger notion of truthfulness for randomized mechanisms that is independent of the risk attitude of bidders. This randomized framework yields an $O(\sqrt{m})$ approximation ratio. The framework distinguishes two cases: either there is a dominant bidder such that allocating all items to that bidder gives a good approximation to the revenue or there is no such bidder. In the first case all items will be assigned to the bidder. In the second case the items are either allocated via a first-price auction or via a fixed-price auction, depending on statistics gathered from the bid data from a subset of the bidders. The relax-and-round framework of Lavi and Swamy (2011), the convex rounding approach of Dughmi *et al.* (2011), and the universally truthful framework of Dobzinski *et al.* (2012b) are general and are applicable to a broad class of mechanism design problems.

Bayesian Nash incentive compatiblility has also been explored in the context of approximation mechanisms. There are a number of results on Bayesian Nash incentive-compatible approximation mechanisms for markets where bidders have restricted valuation functions. There are even black-box reductions from approximation algorithms to Bayesian Nash incentive-compatible mechanisms (Hartline *et al.*, 2015). This means that if there is an approximation algorithm for an allocation problem then it can be transformed into a Bayesian Nash incentive-compatible approximation mechanism.

There is a significant literature on deterministic and randomized approximation mechanisms for specific allocation problems beyond that which we can describe in this chapter. Overall, such research is aimed at understanding to what extent truthful algorithms are less powerful than algorithms ignoring truthfulness. Note that approximation mechanisms are a very active area of research in theoretical computer science and this chapter will provide only an introduction to some of the most prominent approaches. In what follows we introduce approximation mechanisms for combinatorial auctions with single-minded bidders, i.e., bidders only interested in a single package. Then we discuss the relax-and-round framework of Lavi and Swamy (2011), as it provides a very general method allowing for a broad class of allocation problems with arbitrary allocation constraints, as the latter are almost always important in the field.

10.2   Deterministic Mechanisms for Single-Minded Bidders

We start our discussion of approximation mechanisms with a deterministic approximation mechanism for combinatorial auctions where bidders are only interested in a single package, so-called single-minded bidders.

Definition 10.2.1 (Single-minded bidder)   A bidder with a valuation v is called single-minded if there exists a bundle of items S^* and a value $v^* \in \mathbb{R}^+$ such that $v(S) = v^*$ for all $S \supseteq S^*$ and $v(S) = 0$ for all other S.

A single-minded bidder wants to get one specific good or package and cares only about this good or package. Although this is a strong restriction, it is relevant in some applications and interesting to analyze. If only a single parameter of a bid can be manipulated by bidders, we also refer to such problems as *single-parameter* mechanism design problems. Such restricted environments allow for simple strategy-proof mechanisms but, unfortunately, mechanisms for these restricted domains cannot easily be extended to multi-parameter domains. Still, these mechanisms are a good starting point to learn about approximation mechanisms.

Interestingly, single-minded bidders, monotonicity and critical payments are sufficient for a truthful mechanism. A critical payment c_i is such that for all $v_i(S) < c_i$ the mechanism assigns $\emptyset$, and for all $v_i(S) > c_i$ the mechanism assigns S, to bidder i.

Theorem 10.2.1 (Nisan, 2007)   *A mechanism* $\mathcal{M}(f, p_1, \ldots, p_n)$ *for single-minded bidders in which losers pay 0 is strategy-proof if and only if it satisfies the following two conditions.*

1. *Monotonicity: f is monotonic in every $v_i(S)$, i.e., a bidder who wins with bid (v_i^*, S^*) keeps winning for any $v_i' > v_i^*$ and for any $S_i' \subset S_i^*$.*
2. *Critical payment $p_i = c_i$: a bidder i who wins pays the minimum value c_i needed for winning, i.e., the infimum of all values v_i' such that a bid (v_i', S^*) still wins.*

Proof sketch: We make the analysis for a specific bidder i, but will drop the subscript i for brevity. A truthful bidder cannot receive negative utility. She has a zero utility while losing and her value must be at least the critical value, which equals her payment. We show that the bidder cannot improve her utility by reporting some bid (v', S') instead of her true value (v, S). If (v', S') is losing or S' does not contain S then a bid (v, S) is preferred. Therefore, we assume that (v', S') is a winning bid and that $S \subseteq S'$.

We first show that a bidder is never worse off by reporting (v', S) rather than (v', S'). We denote the payment for (v', S') as c', and the payment for (v', S) as c. For every

$x < c$, bidding x on package S will lose since c is a critical value. By monotonicity, a bid of (x, S') will also be losing for every $x < c$, and therefore the critical value c' is at least c. It follows that by bidding (v', S) instead of (v', S') the bidder still wins and her payment will not increase.

Next, the bid (v, S) is not worse than the winning bid (v', S). Assume that (v, S) is a winning bid with a critical payment $\hat{c}$. As long as v' is greater than $\hat{c}$, the bidder still wins with the same payment, thus misreporting her value would not increase utility. With $v' < \hat{c}$ the bidder will lose.

If (v, S) is a losing bid, v must be smaller than the corresponding critical value. Therefore, the payment for any winning bid (v', S) will be greater than v, which is unprofitable. □

Let us now take a look at a simple greedy-acceptance mechanism for combinatorial auctions which is monotonic and charges the critical value as a payment.

10.2.1　Greedy-Acceptance Auctions

A family of greedy-acceptance algorithms for combinatorial auctions with single-minded bidders put forward by Lehmann et al. (2002) satisfies monotonicity and computes critical payments and is therefore strategy-proof. Algorithm 4 provides pseudo-code for a simple greedy algorithm, which is a truthful auction for single-minded bidders as it is monotonic and charges bidders a critical payment. A *greedy algorithm* is an algorithm that follows the problem-solving heuristic of making the locally optimal choice at each stage.

Data: Bundle bids $b_i(S)$
Result: Winners $\mathcal{W}$ and prices $p_i(S)$
Phase 1: $\mathcal{W} \leftarrow \emptyset$. Bids are sorted by some scoring rule, e.g., $b_i(S_i)/|S_i|$, resulting in a list L of bids.
Phase 2: Accept top-down each bid in L, which does not overlap with already accepted bids: if $S_i^* \cap (\bigcup_{j \in \mathcal{W}} S_j^*) = \emptyset$ then $\mathcal{W} \leftarrow \mathcal{W} \cup \{i\}$.
Phase 3: Each winner $i \in \mathcal{W}$ pays $|S_i|$ times $p_i = b_j^*/|S_j^*|$ for the first bid j that is rejected exclusively due to this bid, with j being the smallest index in L such that $S_i^* \cap S_j^* \neq \emptyset$.

Algorithm 4 Pseudo code of a greedy-acceptance algorithm for single-minded bidders, following Lehmann et al. (2002)

The use of such a greedy algorithm is straightforward and runs in polynomial time. Phase 1 requires $O(n \log n)$, where n is the number of bidders, while phases 2 and 3 require linear time only. It can also be shown that the scheme using a scoring rule $b_i(S)/\sqrt{|S|}$ approximates the optimal allocation within a factor $O(\sqrt{m})$, where m is the number of items, which is equal to the best known approximation algorithm for the weighted-set packing problem.

Example 10.2.1 Suppose that there is the following list of bids by single-minded bidders, sorted by $b_i(S)/|S|$:

- $b_1(\{a\}) = 11$
- $b_2(\{b, c\}) = 20$
- $b_3(\{a, d\}) = 18$ (losing to b_1)
- $b_4(\{a, c\}) = 16$ (losing to b_1)
- $b_5(\{c\}) = 7$ (losing to b_2)
- $b_6(\{d\}) = 6$

Algorithm 4 proceeds top down and accepts the bids of bidder 1 and bidder 2. The bids of bidders 3, 4, and 5 overlap with those already accepted and therefore will be rejected, but the bid of bidder 6 can be accepted. Phase 3 of the algorithm determines the payments of the three winning bidders, 1, 2, and 6. Bidder 1 forced out bidder 3, whose bid has an average price of $\$18/2 = \$9$ for each item. As a result, bidder 1 pays $\$9$. Bidder 2 makes the bid of bidder 5 losing with an average price of $\$7$, which makes bidder 2 pay $\$14$ for her package with two items. Finally, bidder 6 does not make any other bidder losing and therefore he pays $\$0$.

Unfortunately the mechanism cannot be extended to multi-minded bidders without losing truthfulness, as illustrated in the next example.

Example 10.2.2 Consider a simple example where bidder 1 has a valuation of $\$14$ for item a, which is her bid, $b_1(a) = 14$. Bidder 2 is multi-minded. He has a valuation of $\$9$ for the individual items a and b respectively and a value of $\$30$ for the package. If both bidders are truthful, bidder 2 wins the package and pays $\$28$, i.e., he has a payoff of $\$2$. However, bidder 2 can do better by bidding only $b_2(\{a, b\}) = 27$. Now, bidder 1 wins a and bidder 2 wins b but his payoff is $\$10$. Note that, in a VCG mechanism, bidder 2 would pay only $\$12$ for the package when bidding truthfully.

There is actually no payment scheme that would make a greedy algorithm truthful, and we already know that the VCG mechanism is the unique truthful mechanism given multi-minded bidders. While single-mindedness might seem a very strong assumption, there are markets in which the bidders have too little information and too few resources to be able to analyze the global strategic situation. If bidders can be assumed to bid straightforwardly in each round, then the auction will be efficient. With single-minded bidders one could even aim for stronger properties such as group-strategy-proofness as defined in our section on greedy auctions (see definition 8.2.4). The greedy-acceptance algorithm, however, is strategy-proof but not group-strategy-proof as we show in the following example.

Example 10.2.3 There are four items a, b, c, d and four single-minded bidders 1–4. Bidder 1 has a value of $\$1$ for $\{a, b\}$, bidder 2 has a value of $\$4$ for $\{b, c\}$, bidder 3 has a value of $\$6$ for $\{c, d\}$, and bidder 4 has a value of $\$2$ for $\{a, d\}$:

- $b_3(\{c, d\}) = 6$
- $b_2(\{b, c\}) = 4$

- $b_4(\{a, d\}) = 2$
- $b_1(\{a, b\}) = 1$

The greedy-acceptance algorithm would accept the bids of bidders 3 and 1 and charge prices of $4 and $0. If bidders 2 and 4 submitted bids of $7 or higher then they would both pay zero. This means that the mechanism is not group-strategy-proof. To see this, take a look at a new ranking of bids:

- $b_2'(\{b, c\}) = 7$
- $b_4'(\{a, d\}) = 7$
- $b_3(\{d, c\}) = 6$
- $b_1(\{a, b\}) = 1$

In this case bidders 2 and 4 are both responsible for the rejection of bidders 3 and 1. Owing to the fact that not a single bidder but two bidders are responsible for the bids of bidder 3 and 1 being rejected, the payments of bidders 2 and 4 are zero.

We now look at a variation of the greedy-acceptance algorithm which is even group-strategy-proof.

10.2.2   Deferred-Acceptance Auctions

Let us now define a broad class of auctions, in which allocations are chosen by an iterative process of greedily rejecting the least attractive bids instead of greedily accepting bids in each iteration, which was the case in the greedy-acceptance algorithm in the previous section. Milgrom and Segal (2014) proposed the term *deferred acceptance auctions* (DAAs) for such auctions, which are reminiscent of the deferred acceptance algorithms used in stable matching without money (see chapter 11).

This difference in the allocation rule has a significant impact on the incentives of bidders, and DAAs possess a number of desirable properties. They can be conducted as sealed-bid, but also as open clock, auctions. A DAA with critical payments (aka threshold payments) is strategy-proof and, what is more, such a DAA is also *weakly group-strategy-proof*. This means that the auction is robust against the collusion of bidders. Let us revisit example 10.2.3 to illustrate a DAA.

Example 10.2.4   With the reported valuations of bidders the auctioneer would first remove $b_1(\{a, b\}) = 1$. There is still a feasible allocation after removing this bid. The bids of bidder 2 and 4 cannot be rejected, because otherwise one of the items in these bids could no longer be sold. Consequently, only $b_3(\{c, d\}) = 6$ can be rejected next. The allocation arising from this deferred-acceptance algorithm is one where bidders 2 and 4 have a social welfare of 6, which is not fully efficient. Now, the threshold payment for bidders 2 and 4 would be $1 + \epsilon$, because with this price they would still be awarded their desired packages. If bidder 1 submitted a high bid, $2 + \epsilon$, to become winning then she would also have to pay $2, which is more than her valuation. Also, she cannot collude with the other losing bidder, 3, to become winning in the DAA.

A DAA is a mechanism which selects the winning bids by iteratively rejecting the active bid with the highest score after each round. In the first round, all bids are *active*.

When a bid gets rejected, it becomes *inactive*. Let's define deferred-acceptance auctions more formally.

Definition 10.2.2 (Deferred-acceptance auction (DAA); Milgrom and Segal, 2014) A DAA operates in stages $t \geq 1$. In each stage t a set of bidders $\Lambda_t \subseteq \mathcal{I}$ is active. In iteration 1, $\Lambda_1 = \mathcal{I}$. The DAA is fully defined by a collection of deterministic scoring rules $\sigma_i^{\Lambda_t}(b_i, b_{\mathcal{I} \setminus \Lambda_t})$ which are non-increasing in their first argument. Stage t proceeds as follows:

- if Λ_t is feasible, the bidders in Λ_t are accepted and each bidder $i \in \Lambda_t$ receives her critical payment $p_i(b_i) = \sup\{b_i' | i \in \Lambda(b_i', b_{-i}), \}$, where $\Lambda(b_i', b_{-i})$ is the set of bidders that would have been accepted if the reported bids were (b_i', b_{-i}) instead of (b_i, b_{-i});
- otherwise set $\Lambda_{t+1} = \Lambda_t \setminus \{i\}$, where bidders $i \in \operatorname{argmax}_{i \in \Lambda_t} \{\sigma_i^{\Lambda_t}(b_i, b_{\mathcal{I} \setminus \Lambda_t})\}$ are the active bidders with the worst scores.

The term DAA describes a family of auctions, and the scoring function can differ. The scoring rule can just return the bid of a bidder, it can compute the ratio of a bid and the size of a package in a combinatorial auction (as in section 10.2.1), or it can assume the form of any other function of the bids. The design of DAAs was motivated by the design of the US government's effort to reallocate the channels used by television broadcasting stations to wireless broadband services from 2016 to 2017, also known as the *US FCC incentive auction*.

Example 10.2.5 The US FCC incentive auction involved purchasing television broadcast rights from TV stations and reassigning the remaining broadcasters to a smaller set of channels. The cleared spectrum was used to create licenses suitable for wireless broadband and to sell these licenses, to cover the costs of acquiring broadcast rights. Conceptually, this is a double auction with multiple buyers and sellers, but it was organized as a DAA reverse auction for TV stations which was linked with a forward auction for telecom operators who wanted to buy spectrum. Single-mindedness was an appropriate assumption in the reverse auction, where TV stations owned a particular set of spectrum licenses. The auction proceeded in stages where a reverse auction was followed by a forward auction. The auctioneer set different clearing targets in each stage and repeated the stages until the demand exceeded supply.

In each step of the reverse auction, the auctioneer needed to make sure that a feasible allocation was possible, taking into consideration many interference constraints. This is an NP-complete vertex-coloring problem and it was so big that the auctioneer could not hope to solve it optimally. If no feasible solution was found within a certain time frame, the scoring function $\sigma_i^{\Lambda_t}(b_i, b_{\mathcal{I} \setminus \Lambda_t})$ returned 0. This guaranteed that the algorithm terminated and returned a feasible set of acceptable bids. In the simplest case, a scoring function takes into account only the amount bid. However, it can also take into account characteristics of a bid which lead to infeasibility of the solution, such as the interference of a TV station with many others.

Bidding in the auction closed on 30 March 2017, repurposing 84 MHz of spectrum. The auction yielded $19.8 billion in revenue, including $10.05 billion for winning broadcast bidders and more than \$7 billion to be deposited to the US Treasury for deficit reduction.

There are environments where simple greedy algorithms such as those discussed in this section implement the welfare-maximizing allocation; those problems have a matroid structure as discussed in section 8.2. The scoring function in the network procurement example was $\sigma_i^{\Lambda_t}(b_i, b_{\mathcal{I}\setminus\Lambda_t}) = b_i$ if $\Lambda \setminus \{i\}$ was feasible, otherwise it was 0. Typically, allocation problems do not have a matroid structure and the scoring functions are more complicated. This raises the question which approximation bounds we can expect for different types of problems in a DAA. Dütting *et al.* (2014) derived an approximation bound $O(\sqrt{m \log m})$ for DAAs for combinatorial auctions with single-minded bidders using multiple scoring functions. They also proposed a DAA for a knapsack auction with an approximation factor $O(\log m)$.

Single-mindedness might be too strong an assumption for most markets. Unfortunately, neither greedy acceptance nor deferred acceptance algorithms have a straightforward extension to multi-minded bidders. Also, no general deterministic scheme to achieve truthfulness for allocation problems is known. However, randomization has been shown to be very useful and there are general schemes for randomized mechanisms which achieve truthfulness in expectation, which we discuss in the next section.

10.3   Randomized Mechanisms

Randomized mechanisms $\mathcal{M}^R = (f^R, p^R)$ are a probabilistic extension of deterministic mechanisms (chapter 3), which compute outcomes and prices according to some internal random process. As a result $f^R(w)$ and $p_i^R(w)$ are both random variables.

Definition 10.3.1 (Randomized mechanism)   A randomized quasi-linear mechanism $\mathcal{M}^R = (f^R, p^R)$ is defined by a random social choice function $f^R : V \to \Gamma$ and a random pricing scheme $p_i^R : V \to \mathbb{R}$ for each bidder i.

Both the random functions f^R and p_i^R are usually assumed to follow discrete probability distributions. For a randomized mechanism we need a different concept of truthfulness, which can be defined with respect to the bidders' expected utilities. A randomized mechanism is called *truthful in expectation* if each bidder optimizes her expected utility by declaring her valuation truthfully.

Definition 10.3.2 (Truthful in expectation (TIE) mechanism)   A mechanism $\mathcal{M}^R = (f^R, p^R)$ is truthful in expectation if, for every bidder i, her (true) valuation function v_i, the (reported) valuation function v_i', and the (reported) valuation functions v_{-i} of the other bidders satisfy

$$E\left[f_i^R(v_i, v_{-i}) - p_i^R(v_i, v_{-i})\right] \geq E\left[f_i^R(v_i', v_{-i}) - p_i^R(v_i', v_{-i})\right].$$

This is a weaker notion of truthfulness, different from that for dominant strategies as it relies on randomization and therefore a bidder's risk attitude matters. In other words, a TIE mechanism sets incentives for truthful bidding if bidders are risk neutral. Universal truthfulness is a stronger concept, not requiring risk neutrality.

Definition 10.3.3 (Universal truthfulness) A mechanism is universally truthful if it is a probability distribution over truthful deterministic mechanisms. That is, even when a bidder knows all random decisions in advance, reporting the true valuation is a dominant strategy.

A randomized mechanism $\mathcal{M}^R = (f^R, p^R)$ is called individually rational if, for every result $f^R(v)$ and $p_i^R(v)$, the utility of player i is never negative with respect to her reported valuation v.

The most general approach known for designing randomized TIE mechanisms is via *maximal-in-distributional range* (MIDR) algorithms. An MIDR algorithm fixes a set of distributions over feasible solutions, the distributional range, independently of the valuations reported by the self-interested participants and outputs a random sample from the distribution that maximizes the expected (reported) welfare.

Definition 10.3.4 (Maximal-in-distributional range (MIDR) algorithm; Dobzinski and Dughmi, 2009) Given reported valuations $v_1, \ldots, v_n$, and a previously defined probability distribution over feasible sets $\mathcal{R}$, an MIDR algorithm returns an outcome that is sampled randomly from a distribution $D^* \in \mathcal{R}$ that maximizes the expected welfare $E_{x \sim D}[\sum_i v_i(x)]$ over all distributions $D \in \mathcal{R}$.

An analogue of the payments of the VCG mechanism can be used to extend an MIDR algorithm to a mechanism that is truthful in expectation. Because of the revelation principle, the literature focuses on direct revelation mechanisms.

10.3.1   The Relax-and-Round Framework

The relax-and-round framework of Lavi and Swamy (2011) is a general framework for designing MIDR approximation mechanisms which are truthful in expectation. The basic idea of Lavi and Swamy (2011) is to move to a fractional domain and use the VCG mechanism to obtain a *truthful fractional mechanism*. The LP relaxation of the underlying problem can be solved exactly in polynomial time. Now we can scale down this solution into the constraint polytope in such a way that we can compute a convex decomposition of the scaled-down fractional solution into polynomially many feasible integer solutions. We can do this via the ellipsoid method and by using an α-approximation algorithm $\mathcal{A}$ that proves an integrality gap of at most α for the LP relaxation.

It is important to note that the approximation algorithm needs to be able to handle all types of valuation because it can be called with an arbitrary valuation vector. However, the approximation algorithm used in the relax-and-round framework does not need to be truthful. By treating the factors of the convex combination as probabilities, a randomized mechanism with a probability distribution over integer solutions that is truthful in expectation is obtained. The social welfare in expectation is now equivalent to the optimal social welfare of the fractional solution of the LP relaxation, scaled down by α. With this equivalence and a respective scaled-down payment function one can show also that the resulting randomized mechanism is truthful.

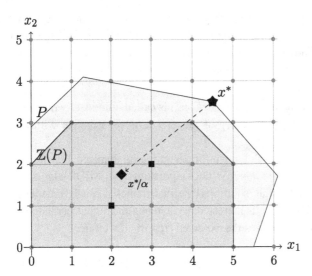

Figure 10.1 Graphical explanation of the relax-and-round framework.

The illustration in figure 10.1 provides an example. The underlying problem is expressed as an IP with feasible region given by the polytope $\mathbb{Z}(P)$. Note that only the integer-valued points in the darker gray area are feasible solutions of the IP. By relaxing the integrality constraint of the LP we obtain the polytope P. The LP relaxation can be solved to get the fractional solution $x^* = \left(\begin{smallmatrix} 4.5 \\ 3.5 \end{smallmatrix}\right)$ (the black star). We assume that an approximation algorithm with an integrality gap of $\alpha = 2$ is given. The fractional solution is scaled down to get $x^*/\alpha = \left(\begin{smallmatrix} 2.25 \\ 1.75 \end{smallmatrix}\right)$ (the black diamond). Now we calculate the convex decomposition of x^*/α into polynomially many integer solutions. In the example, we obtain three integer solutions (the black squares) using the approximation algorithm, leading to the following convex combination: $\left(\begin{smallmatrix} 2.25 \\ 1.75 \end{smallmatrix}\right) = \frac{1}{4}\left(\begin{smallmatrix} 2 \\ 1 \end{smallmatrix}\right) + \frac{1}{4}\left(\begin{smallmatrix} 3 \\ 2 \end{smallmatrix}\right) + \frac{1}{2}\left(\begin{smallmatrix} 2 \\ 2 \end{smallmatrix}\right)$. The factors $\frac{1}{4}$, $\frac{1}{4}$ and $\frac{1}{2}$ are treated as probabilities that the corresponding integer solutions occur. This probability distribution over the allocations leads, in expectation, to the fractional solution scaled down by α. The same holds for the expected social welfare.

One may note that, in most allocation problems, the variables which indicate whether an item or a package is assigned to a bidder are binary. A fractional solution, however, has values in between 0 and 1. In an example with only two dimensions, this restriction to binary variables would lead to a low number of possible integer solutions, which is why we used integer-variable solutions in our example, in order to better illustrate the overall idea. Since a scaled-down fractional VCG mechanism is truthful, so also is a randomized mechanism where the expected outcome exactly equals that of the scaled-down fractional VCG mechanism.

After computation of the allocation, it is necessary to compute the VCG payments for each integer solution. The VCG prices are scaled down by dividing them by α; this is described in more detail in the next subsection. Following all these steps, a general technique to convert any α-approximation algorithm into a randomized and truthful in expectation mechanism is obtained.

10.3.2 Combinatorial Auctions via Relax-and-Round

We now analyze how combinatorial auctions are implemented in the relax-and-round framework. The first step is to formulate the WDP as an IP (see section 7.2) and relax the integrality constraint:

$$\max \sum_{i,S \neq \emptyset} v_i(S) x_i(S) \qquad \text{(WDP-LP)}$$

$$\text{s.t.} \quad \sum_{S \neq \emptyset} x_i(S) \leq 1 \qquad \forall i \in \mathcal{I}$$

$$\sum_{i} \sum_{S:k \in S} x_i(S) \leq 1 \qquad \forall k \in \mathcal{K}$$

$$x_i(S) \geq 0 \qquad \forall i \in \mathcal{I}, S \subseteq \mathcal{K}$$

The LP relaxation can be solved using any algorithm or solver which finds an exact solution in polynomial time. An optimal fractional solution to WDP-LP is obtained.

Next, the convex decomposition of the fractional solution scaled down by α is computed. We denote P as the feasible region of WDP-LP and $\mathbb{Z}(P) = \{x^l\}_{l \in \mathbb{I}}$ as the set of all integer solutions to WDP-LP; here, the index set for the integer solutions is represented by $\mathbb{I}$. The optimal fractional solution is denoted as x^*. We introduce $E = \{(i, S) : x_i^*(S) > 0\}$ as the set of all indices i and S that belong to the optimal solution x^*. It is important to mention that the size of this set (denoted as $|E|$) is polynomial because the maximum number of non-zero components in a solution is at most the number of constraints of the LP (Chvatal, 1983). The number of constraints is $m + n$ in our case. The goal is to express x^*/α as a convex combination $\sum_{l \in \mathbb{I}} \lambda_l x^l$. A convex combination is defined as follows.

Definition 10.3.5 (Convex combination) A convex combination of vectors y^1, $y^2, \ldots, y^k$ is:

$$y = \lambda_1 y^1 + \lambda_2 y^2 + \cdots + \lambda_k y^k,$$

where $\lambda_j \geq 0$ are real numbers that satisfy $\sum_{j=1}^{k} \lambda_j = 1$.

Since the factors $\lambda_1, \ldots, \lambda_k$ are treated as probabilities, it is necessary that they add up to exactly 1. The decomposition technique (called randomized meta-rounding) is based on Carr and Vempala (2000) and was modified by Lavi and Swamy (2011) to ensure that an exact decomposition is obtained. The solution of the following LP provides the desired convex combination:

$$\min \sum_{l \in \mathbb{I}} \lambda_l \qquad \text{(Primal)}$$

$$\text{s.t.} \quad \sum_{l} \lambda_l x_i^l(S) = \frac{x_i^*(S)}{\alpha} \qquad \forall (i, S) \in E$$

$$\sum_{l} \lambda_l \geq 1$$

$$\lambda_l \geq 0 \qquad \forall l \in \mathbb{I}$$

Unfortunately, the objective function constitutes a sum over all integer solutions. Thus, we need an exponential number of variables and cannot solve the LP efficiently. To overcome this problem, one can convert the variables to an exponential number of constraints by taking the dual. The dual LP is solvable with the *ellipsoid method* since the latter can handle an exponential number of constraints using a separation oracle, i.e., without having to fully describe all constraints. One can use an approximation algorithm as a separation oracle to learn whether the center of the ellipsoid is in the polytope. The dual solved by the ellipsoid method is defined as follows:

$$\max \left\{ \frac{1}{\alpha} \sum_{(i,S) \in E} x_i^*(S) w_i(S) + z \right\} \qquad \text{(Dual)}$$

$$\text{s.t.} \quad \sum_{(i,S) \in E} x_i^l(S) w_i(S) + z \leq 1 \qquad \forall l \in \mathbb{I}$$

$$z \geq 0$$

$$w_{i,S} \text{ unconstrained} \qquad \forall (i, S) \in E$$

The ellipsoid method generates integer points in each iteration. It makes use of the α-approximation algorithm $\mathcal{A}$ to find integer solutions by treating the current center of the ellipsoid as the valuation vector, i.e., the parameters for calling $\mathcal{A}$.

The use of the ellipsoid method is computationally expensive and alternatives have been developed to obtain a convex decomposition more effectively (see Kraft *et al.* (2014) or the lottery algorithm used in section 11.4.2.2). After solving the dual, a polynomial number of integral solutions is available. Inserting these solutions into the primal LP, its solution can be obtained in polynomial time. The result is the desired convex combination over integer solutions.

Finally, it is necessary to compute the payment rules for each integer solution with the VCG mechanism. This is done taking into account the VCG payments of the fractional solution and scaling them down by dividing them by α as well. This results in a randomized mechanism that is truthful in expectation. The expected social welfare is the optimal social welfare scaled down by α.

Example 10.3.1 We provide a brief example of a convex decomposition in a simple multi-unit auction with three bidders and four identical items. An approximation algorithm with an integrality gap of $\alpha = 2$ is available for this problem, which can be used with the ellipsoid method to solve the dual. We assume the following valuation vectors $v_i(j)$ for each player i and quantity j:

j	1	2	3	4
$v_1(j)$	(6	6	6	6)
$v_2(j)$	(2	4	4	6)
$v_3(j)$	(0	0	1	1)

Solving the LP relaxation using any LP solver, one can obtain the following fractional solution: $x_{1,1} = 1, x_{2,2} = 0.5, x_{2,4} = 0.5$; otherwise, $x_{i,j} = 0$. This can also be written as follows:

$$x_{i,S}^* = \begin{pmatrix} 1.0 \\ 0.5 \\ 0.5 \end{pmatrix} \quad \text{for } (i, S) \in E \quad \text{with}$$

$$E = \{(1, 1), (2, 2), (2, 4)\}$$

Next, the ellipsoid method is run for the dual problem of the convex decomposition described above. The values $(w_{1,1}, w_{2,2}, w_{2,4}) = (0, 0, 0)$ and $z = 1$ can be used to initialize the ellipsoid method. During the iterations the ellipsoid method generates new feasible integer solutions by calling the approximation algorithm $\mathcal{A}$. This integer solution is added to the set of feasible integer solutions, but is also used in the ellipsoid method to start the next iteration. With a small threshold the ellipsoid method terminates after 145 iterations and finds five integer solutions: $\{(1, 1, 0), (0, 0, 1), (1, 0, 0), (0, 1, 0), (0, 0, 0)\}$. By solving the primal LP of the decomposition using these solutions, the following convex combination is computed:

$$\frac{x^*}{\alpha} = \sum_{l \in \mathbb{I}} \lambda_l x^l$$

$$\Rightarrow \begin{pmatrix} 0.5 \\ 0.25 \\ 0.25 \end{pmatrix} = \frac{1}{4}\begin{pmatrix} 1 \\ 1 \\ 0 \end{pmatrix} + \frac{1}{4}\begin{pmatrix} 0 \\ 0 \\ 1 \end{pmatrix} + \frac{1}{4}\begin{pmatrix} 1 \\ 0 \\ 0 \end{pmatrix} + 0\begin{pmatrix} 0 \\ 1 \\ 0 \end{pmatrix} + \frac{1}{4}\begin{pmatrix} 0 \\ 0 \\ 0 \end{pmatrix}$$

In words, bidder 1 will get one item with probability 0.5 (2×0.25) and nothing with probability 0.5, bidder 2 will get two items with probability 0.25, four items with probability 0.25, and nothing with probability 0.5. Bidder 3 will get nothing at all as this bidder was not part of the optimal fractional solution. Now the mechanism randomly selects one of these allocations.

Note that the truthfulness of the relax-and-round framework crucially depends on the bidders' inability to influence the polytope, and it implements the MIDR principle. For combinatorial auctions or multi-unit combinatorial auctions the relax-and-round framework provides a general framework to achieve truthfulness in expectation. The main difference is the approximation algorithm $\mathcal{A}$, which is different for each of these auctions. The relax-and-round framework is a nice example of a black-box reduction, which invokes an approximation algorithm polynomially many times and achieves truthfulness without degrading the approximation ratio. It is important to note, however, that if the fractional solution is scaled down by the worst-case approximation ratio α, then this worst case will become the average-case solution quality of the randomized mechanism. Often this average-case solution quality might not be acceptable.

10.4   Summary

The winner determination problem in combinatorial auctions and many other resource allocation problems is NP-hard. In the chapters in Part II of the book, we have largely assumed that we can solve these allocation problems exactly. Actually, with modern algorithms and computing hardware, large instances of the WDP can be solved to optimality. Of course, there are limits. The allocation problem of the procurement auction with volume discount bids in section 7.5.1 can already lead to a substantial integrality gap with 40 bidders and a similar number of items of commodity hardware. While research in combinatorial optimization is constantly pushing the boundaries of the problem sizes that can be solved to optimality, it is also easy to find examples of resource allocation problems where the designer cannot hope to compute exact solutions in the near future. Approximation algorithms run in polynomial time and often provide good approximation ratios to the optimal solution of an optimization problem. Unfortunately, the VCG mechanism assumes exact solutions to the winner determination problem, and applying the VCG mechanism to approximations is not straightforward. However, there are possibilities for designing truthful approximation mechanisms. For single-minded bidders, simple deterministic greedy algorithms are strategyproof. The relax-and-round framework of Lavi and Swamy (2011) introduces a blackbox framework which turns any packing problem with an approximation algorithm into a randomized mechanism that is truthful in expectation. Although the approach is quite general and strategies for bidders are simple, the resulting mechanisms are fairly complex.

Alternatively, some authors impose *simplicity* of the auction format as a hard constraint and then seek conditions when a format performs well. For example, it was shown that, in every (asymmetric) first-price auction, every Bayesian Nash equilibrium has an expected welfare that is at least 63% of the maximum possible (Syrgkanis and Tardos, 2013). This is the price-of-anarchy of this simple auction format. Lucier and Borodin (2010) used the price-of-anarchy to characterize simple mechanisms which are robust even if they are not truthful. They demonstrate that a broad class of greedy approximation algorithms can be implemented as mechanisms for which the price-of-anarchy nearly matches the performance of the original algorithm, even in Bayesian settings, where the agents' valuations are drawn from a common prior distribution. They provided a simple deterministic mechanism for combinatorial auctions with $O(\sqrt{m})$ price-of-anarchy. Dütting *et al.* (2015) did a similar analysis for relax-and-round approximation algorithms. Overall, the literature in algorithmic mechanism design is developing rapidly, and many new concepts and approaches to designing economic mechanisms for hard resource allocation problems are being introduced.

10.5   Comprehension Questions

- What are the necessary and sufficient conditions for a mechanism to be truthful in a setting with single-minded bidders?

- Suppose that we have a setting in which all bidders are single-minded and we can only approximate the winner determination problem. Why can we not use VCG techniques directly to get a truthful mechanism?
- What is MIR, and what are the MIDR allocation rules? Explain their significance in finding truthful approximation mechanisms.
- Explain why a relax-and-round framework can be viewed as a MIDR mechanism.

11 Matching Markets

So far, we have assumed that monetary transfers among market participants are possible. This is not always the case and in many situations resources need to be allocated on the basis of the preferences of the market participants but we cannot use a payment rule to incentivize truthfulness. Gibbard (1973) proved that any non-dictatorial voting scheme with at least three possible outcomes cannot have dominant strategies for all agents (see section 3.1).

Rather than deterministic rules, one might hope for randomized and truthful rules. However, Gibbard (1977) showed that every strategy-proof mechanism is a lottery over deterministic mechanisms, each of which either has not more than two alternatives or is dictatorial. This implies that random dictatorships are the only strategy-proof and ex post efficient probabilistic social choice functions. In random dictatorships one voter is picked at random and her most preferred alternative is implemented as the social choice. Random dictatorship is known to be the only rule satisfying strategy-proofness and ex post efficiency. When indifferences are also allowed, random serial dictatorship (RSD) is a well-known generalization of random dictatorship that retains both properties (Aziz *et al.*, 2013). In RSD, dictators are invoked sequentially and ties between most preferred alternatives are broken by subsequent dictators. For the assignment of objects, the agents are ordered randomly and the most preferred package of items is assigned to one agent after the other in this order. Random serial dictatorship can be unfair in the sense that all objects could be assigned to a single agent. However, one can put a cap on the maximum number of objects allocated to each agent, a modification which does not compromise strategy-proofness. We define the mechanism in more detail in the context of two-sided matching (see section 11.2.1), although it is normally used for voting or one-sided matching problems.

Non-dictatorial mechanisms are possible for more restricted environments even without monetary transfers, as the theory of matching with preferences shows. This theory has found many applications and we discuss the key concepts in this chapter.

11.1 Overview of Matching Problems

In 2012 the Royal Swedish Academy of Sciences awarded Alvin E. Roth and Lloyd S. Shapley the Nobel Memorial Prize in Economic Science for "The theory of stable allocations and the practice of market design" (Nobel Prize, 2012). Many algorithms

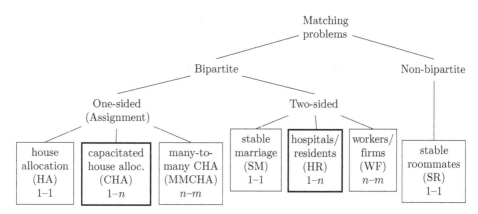

Figure 11.1 Overview of widespread matching problems (based on a classification in Manlove (2013)). This chapter focuses on the problems with a bold frame.

have been developed in this field, starting with the seminal work by Gale and Shapley (1962). They introduced the *deferred acceptance* (DA) algorithm for the one-to-one *stable marriage problem* (SM). The problem is two-sided, as men and women have preferences about each other. The one-to-many generalization of SM is known as the *hospitals/residents problem* (HR), because the assignment of residents or students to hospitals has become an influential application. The one-to-many version of the DA algorithm, where students propose assignments to hospitals, is also referred to as *student-optimal stable mechanism* (SOSM). Gale and Shapley (1962) showed that a DA algorithm yields a unique stable matching that weakly Pareto-dominates any other stable matching from the viewpoint of the students when the preferences of both sides are strict in a student-proposing version. A matching is *stable* if every individual is matched with an acceptable partner and if there is no student–hospital pair each member of which would prefer to match with the other rather than their assigned partner. The algorithm has a number of additional properties if priorities are strict: it is *strategy-proof for students* (the proposing side) and it is not Pareto-dominated by any other Pareto-efficient mechanism that is strategy-proof. The DA algorithm is also favorable from a computational point of view, because the worst-case complexity is only quadratic.

Apart from two-sided matching problems, a large variety of other matching problems have been discussed in the literature. Figure 11.1 classifies common matching problems under preferences. In contrast with two-sided matching problems, in *one-sided matching problems* only one set of agents has preferences. One-sided matching problems are also referred to *assignment problems* in the literature. In the one-to-one *house allocation problem* (HA) only applicants have preferences over houses. The one-to-many version, where multiple applicants can be assigned to one house, is called the *capacitated house allocation problem* (CHA) and houses have a fixed capacity. In addition to these widespread problems, many-to-many versions of the bipartite matching problem under preferences have been studied as well as problems which are not based on a bipartite graph, such as the *stable roommates* problem. For example, in the *workers/firms* problem both workers and firms can have capacities greater than one and can be assigned to several agents of the other side.

The *stable roommates* (SR) *problem* is similar to the stable matching problem, but differs in that there is only one set of entities and not a bipartite graph. Unlike the stable marriage problem, the stable roommates problem may not admit a stable solution (Irving, 1985; Teo and Sethuraman, 2000). An examples of the stable roommates problem is a kidney exchange involving an incompatible patient–donor pair (Manlove and O'Malley, 2012; Roth *et al.*, 2005). In this chapter, we will discuss only bipartite matching problems. We also restrict ourselves to static problems, although there is much recent research on *dynamic matching problems*, where demand and supply arrive gradually over time. Online ride-sharing services, for example, match drivers and customers dynamically.

11.2   Two-Sided Matching

Matching under preferences has found widespread application for *school choice, college admission*, or the *assignment of junior doctors to hospitals*. All these problems are examples of the hospitals residents problem. In the school choice problem, for example, public school districts give parents the opportunity to choose which public school their child will attend. The problem of finding a stable matching is solved by considering the preferences of both families and schools. The assignment of students to courses at universities is probably even more widespread. Such problems can be found in almost every university, although they are often solved via first-come first-served mechanisms in spite of the advantages that recent matching mechanisms provide. In contrast with the matching of hospitals to residents, schools are considered as agents who have not preferences but priorities. In the assignment of residents to hospitals both types of agents have preferences that they could manipulate. All these prominent applications are versions of the HR or the CHA problems. Properties such as efficiency, incentives to report preferences truthfully, and stability of the outcome in two-sided markets are crucial success factors in practical applications (Roth, 2002).

In this chapter, we focus on the HR problem in the context of *course allocation* as this application will be familiar to most readers. In course allocation problems, the students and the course organizers have preferences over each other, and each student needs to be assigned to one course. A variety of non-stable matching methods, such as first-come first-served policies and course bidding, are in use in practice. In course bidding systems (Budish and Cantillon, 2012; Krishna and Ünver, 2008) students get equal budgets of an artificial currency, and then they bid on different courses. This currency does not have a value outside the matching market. The highest bidders for each course get a place. Course bidding has a number of strategic problems. For example, on the one hand bidders might be tempted to submit all their budget on their top preferences. Let's assume there is a very popular course and everybody bids their budget on this course. Only a few students can win, and the others might get courses which are very low on their preference list. On the other hand, students might preemptively bid on courses with lower preference because they believe they have a higher probability to win. So, various types of manipulation are possible.

We first introduce two well-known mechanisms: random serial dictatorship (RSD) and the Gale–Shapley deferred acceptance algorithm, often referred to as student-optimal stable matching (SOSM) in the context of the HR problem. In fact RSD considers the preferences of only one side of the market, but it is a simple mechanism to start with. The SOSM mechanism might lead to inefficiencies for the students in particular, and also in general, in the presence of ties. The efficiency adjusted deferred acceptance mechanism (EADAM) recovers these inefficiencies at the expense of strategy-proofness. Diebold *et al.* (2014) provides an extended discussion of the SOSM and EADAM with results from a field experiment.

11.2.1   Definitions and Notation

A *one-to-many matching problem* (or *course allocation problem*) consists of a finite set of students (or agents) $S = \{s_1, s_2, \ldots, s_n\}$ and a finite set of courses (or objects) $C = \{c_1, c_2, \ldots, c_m\}$ with *maximum capacities* $q = (q_{c_1}, q_{c_2}, \ldots, q_{c_m})$. To ensure that a feasible matching exists we assume $q_c \geq 0$ for all $c \in C$ and $n \leq \sum_{c \in C} q_c$. Each student has a *preference relation* $\succeq_s$ over the courses C (called a student preference) and each course (organizer) has a *preference relation* $\succeq_c$ over the students S (called a course priority).

The *preferences* of the students and courses $(\succeq_s, \succeq_c)$ do not have to be strict in general; they could also contain *indifferences*. The vectors for these relations are denoted $\succeq_S = (\succeq_s)_{s \in S}$ and $\succeq_C = (\succeq_c)_{c \in C}$. Let $\mathcal{P}$ denote the set of all possible preference relations over C and $\mathcal{P}^{|S|}$ the set of all preference vectors for all students. Similarly, $\mathcal{P}^{|C|}$ is the set of all preference vectors for all course organizers.

Definition 11.2.1 (Matching) A *matching* is a mapping μ of students S and courses C that satisfies:

(i) $\mu(s) \in C$ for all $s \in S$,
(ii) $\mu(c) \subseteq S$ for all $c \in C$, and
(iii) for any $s \in S$ and $c \in C$, $\mu(s) = c$ if and only if $s \in \mu(c)$.

A matching is *feasible* if $|\mu(c)| \leq q_c$ for all $c \in C$, which means that no course is overcrowded. Let M denote the set of all feasible matchings. One desirable property of matchings is *Pareto efficiency*, which is such that no student can be made better off without making any other student worse off. In school choice (and similarly in course allocation) problems, it is often assumed that schools have priorities but that they are not strategic. Also, Pareto efficiency is typically analyzed from the students' point of view.

Definition 11.2.2 (Pareto efficiency of matchings (for students)) A matching μ is *Pareto efficient* with respect to the students if there is no other feasible matching μ' such that $\mu'(s) \succeq_s \mu(s)$ for all students $s \in S$ and $\mu'(s) \succ_s \mu(s)$ for some $s \in S$, where $\succ_s$ describes a strict preference.

Stability means that there should be no unmatched pair of a student and a course (s, c) where student s prefers course c to her current assignment and she has a higher priority than some other student who is assigned to course c. Stability can be seen as a property of a solution that has *no justified envy*. In other words, stability means that there are no incentives for some pair of participants to undermine an assignment by joint action.

Definition 11.2.3 (Stability) A matching μ is *stable* if $\mu(s') \succ_s \mu(s)$ implies $s' \succ_{\mu(s')} s$ for all s, s'.

The stability of a matching is closely connected to competitive equilibria in assignment markets (with money) as discussed in section 8.1 (see also Milgrom, 2017). Stable matchings, in which no pair of players would prefer to switch partners, are a subset of Pareto-optimal matchings considering both sides. Note that the notion of Pareto efficiency introduced above *concerns only the students*. A stable matching is Pareto optimal for both sides taken together but not necessarily for the students only. In section 11.2.3 we discuss Pareto improvements for students, which are possible for an SOSM outcome.

Matching is related to assignment markets (see section 8.1), and we can also formulate the stable matching problem as a linear program. For the following linear program of the course assignment (CA) problem, we assume that each course has a capacity of only one and students need to be assigned to at most one course:

$$\max \sum_{(s,c) \in A} x_{s,c} \qquad\qquad\qquad\qquad \text{(CA)}$$

$$
\begin{aligned}
\text{s.t.} \quad & \sum_{s \in S} x_{s,c} \leq 1 & & \forall c \in C \\
& \sum_{c \in C} x_{s,c} \leq 1 & & \forall s \in S \\
& x_{s,c} = 0 & & \forall (s, c) \in (S \times C)\backslash A \\
& \sum_{j \in C: j \succ_s c} x_{s,j} + \sum_{i \in S: i \succ_c s} x_{i,c} + x_{s,c} \geq 1 & & \forall (s, c) \in A \\
& x_{s,c} \geq 0 & & \forall (s, c) \in (S \times C)
\end{aligned}
$$

The variables $x_{s,c}$ describe the assignment μ of a student s to a course c if they assume the value 1 and are 0 otherwise; A denotes the set of acceptable pairs. A matching μ is called *individually rational* if no student or course organizer prefers being unmatched (the third constraint in CA). A matching μ is *stable* if it is individually rational and there is no pair (s, c) in A such that student s prefers course c to $\mu(s)$ and course organizer c prefers student s to $\mu(c)$. We also say that an individually rational matching μ is stable if there is no pair (s, c) in A such that both $s \succ_c \mu(c)$ and $c \succ_s \mu(s)$ hold (the fourth constraint in CA). It can be shown that the solution x to the CA problem is a stable matching if and only if it is an integer solution of CA. This means that the vertices of the CA polytope are exactly stable matchings.

We describe a fractional solution to CA as a *fractional matching* or *random matching*. The Birkhoff–von Neumann theorem says that each random matching for the assignment problem can be represented as a convex combination of deterministic matchings (Birkhoff, 1946; Von Neumann, 1953). So, every lottery over feasible integral allocations corresponds to a feasible fractional solution on setting $x_{s,c}$ equal to the probability that student s obtains course c. Consequently, a random matching x can be decomposed

Table 11.1 (a) Course priorities ($\succ_c$) and (b) student preferences ($\succ_s$)

(a)	$\succ_{c_1}$	$\succ_{c_2}$	$\succ_{c_3}$	(b)	$\succ_{s_1}$	$\succ_{s_2}$	$\succ_{s_3}$
	$\underline{s_1}$	$\underline{s_2}$	s_2		c_2	c_1	c_1
	s_3	s_1	s_1		$\underline{c_1}$	$\underline{c_2}$	c_2
	s_2	s_3	$\underline{s_3}$		c_3	c_3	$\underline{c_3}$

into a convex combination of deterministic matchings. This will also be important when we discuss a randomized mechanism for one-sided matching with complementarities in section 11.4.

Next we discuss mechanisms to compute matchings and their properties. A mechanism is an algorithm which computes a matching for given preferences of students and courses. More formally, a *two-sided matching mechanism* χ is a function $\chi : \mathcal{P}^{|S|} \times \mathcal{P}^{|C|} \rightarrow M$ that returns a feasible matching of students to courses for every preference profile of the students. We assume that course organizers have public priorities which are not manipulable. For a submitted preference profile $\succeq = (\succeq_S, \succeq_C)$, $\chi(\succeq)$ is the associated matching. For a student s the assigned course is $\chi_s(\succeq_S) \in C$. For a course c the set of assigned students is $\chi_c(\succeq_S) \subseteq S$.

A mechanism is *Pareto efficient* if it always selects a Pareto-efficient matching. Also, a mechanism is *stable* if it always selects a stable matching. Another important property of a mechanism is *strategy-proofness*: there is no incentive for any student not to submit her truthful preferences, no matter which preferences the other students report.

Definition 11.2.4 (Strategy-proofness) A mechanism χ is *strategy-proof* if for any $\succ_S \in \mathcal{P}^{|S|}$ with $s \in S$ and $\succ'_s \in \mathcal{P}$ we have $\chi_s(\succ_S) \succeq_s \chi_s(\succ'_s, \succ_{S \setminus \{s\}})$.

Unfortunately, matching mechanisms cannot always be Pareto efficient for students and also stable, as the following example shows.

Example 11.2.1 Consider the course allocation problem with three students $S = \{s_1, s_2, s_3\}$ and three courses $C = \{c_1, c_2, c_3\}$, each course having one place. The course priorities ($\succ_c$) and the student preferences ($\succ_s$) are given in table 11.1.

The matching

$$\mu_1 = \begin{pmatrix} c_1 & c_2 & c_3 \\ s_1 & s_2 & s_3 \end{pmatrix}$$

is the only stable matching; it is underlined in table 11.1. However, the matching is Pareto dominated by

$$\mu_2 = \begin{pmatrix} c_1 & c_2 & c_3 \\ s_2 & s_1 & s_3 \end{pmatrix}$$

Stability forces students s_1 and s_2 to share the courses in an inefficient way. If these students, s_1 and s_2, were assigned the courses c_2 and c_1 respectively, then student s_3 would prefer course c_1 to her assignment c_3 and she has a higher priority for course c_1 than student s_2. As a result, stability may conflict with Pareto efficiency.

Table 11.2 (a) Course priorities ($\succ_c$) and (b) student preferences ($\succ_s$)

(a)	$\succ_{c_1}$	$\succ_{c_2}$	$\succ_{c_3}$	$\succ_{c_4}$
	s_4	s_2	s_3	$\underline{s_1}$
	$\underline{s_1}$	$\underline{s_3}$	$\underline{s_4}$	$\vdots$
	$\underline{s_2}$	$\vdots$	$\vdots$	$\vdots$

(b)	$\succ_{s_1}$	$\succ_{s_2}$	$\succ_{s_3}$	$\succ_{s_4}$
	c_1	$\underline{c_1}$	$\underline{c_2}$	$\underline{c_3}$
	$\underline{c_4}$	c_2	c_3	c_1
	$\vdots$	$\vdots$	$\vdots$	$\vdots$

We now use the concept of *serial dictatorship* (SD) discussed in the introduction to this chapter to illustrate some definitions introduced above. Serial dictatorship can be used for one-sided or two-sided matching problems. For random serial dictatorship (RSD, aka random priority), the students are ordered with a lottery. As a randomized mechanism RSD is *universally truthful* (see section 10.3). The SD algorithm proceeds as follows.

Consider a particular ordering of the students S, i.e., a particular permutation ϕ of $\{1, 2, \ldots, n\}$. We assume strict student preferences.

For x from 1 to $n = |S|$ do:

Assign student $s_{\phi(x)}$ to her top choice among the remaining slots.

Algorithm 5 The SD algorithm

The following example illustrates the serial dictatorship mechanism.

Example 11.2.2   Consider the course allocation problem with four students $S \equiv \{s_1, s_2, s_3, s_4\}$ and four courses $C \equiv \{c_1, c_2, c_3, c_4\}$, each course having one place. The course priorities ($\succ_c$) and the student preferences ($\succ_s$) are given in table 11.2; the ellipses indicate that the ranking is arbitrary from the point where they begin. Consider the permutation

$$\phi = \begin{pmatrix} 1 & 2 & 3 & 4 \\ 2 & 1 & 3 & 4 \end{pmatrix}$$

which could be the result of a lottery. This would lead to the following ordering of the students: (s_2, s_1, s_3, s_4). Then the mechanism would work as described in table 11.3. The matching

$$\mu_1 = \begin{pmatrix} c_1 & c_2 & c_3 & c_4 \\ s_2 & s_3 & s_4 & s_1 \end{pmatrix}$$

would be the result. The table entries corresponding to this result are underlined in table 11.2.

The SD mechanism is *Pareto efficient* for students with strict preferences, because no student can be made better off without hurting another student. One disadvantage is that *course-specific priorities* are not considered. Furthermore, the SD mechanism is *not stable*, as the following example shows. Student s_1 and course c_1 are unmatched, in

Table 11.3 Example of the serial dictatorship mechanism. The boxes describe an assignment

Step	Student to be assigned	c_1	c_2	c_3	c_4
1	s_2	$\boxed{s_2}$			
2	s_1	$\vdots$			$\boxed{s_1}$
3	s_3	$\vdots$	$\boxed{s_3}$		$\vdots$
4	s_4	$\vdots$	$\vdots$	$\boxed{s_4}$	$\vdots$

that student s_1 would prefer course c_1 to her current assignment (c_4) and she has higher priority to c_1 than student s_2, who is actually assigned to course c_1. Assuming $s = s_1$ and $s' = s_2$ we obtain

$$c_1 = \mu(s_2) = \mu(s') \succ_{s_1} \mu(s) = \mu(s_1) = c_4 \qquad \text{and} \qquad s_2 = s' \prec_{c_1} s = s_1$$

which contradicts the definition of stability.

11.2.2 The Gale–Shapley Student-Optimal Stable Mechanism

The *Gale–Shapley student-optimal stable mechanism* (SOSM) is a modified version of the Gale–Shapley deferred acceptance algorithm of Gale and Shapley (1962), which allows for one-to-many assignments. This "student-proposing" deferred acceptance algorithm works as follows.

Step 1: Each student proposes her first-choice course. For each course c with a capacity q_c, those q_c proposers who have the highest priority for c are tentatively assigned to c; the remaining proposers are rejected.
In general,
at *step k, $k \geq 2$:* Each student who was rejected in the previous step, $k - 1$, proposes her next-choice course. For each course c, from the new proposers and those who were tentatively assigned at a previous step, the q_c with the highest priority are tentatively assigned to c; the rest are rejected.

Algorithm 6 The Gale–Shapley SOSM algorithm

The algorithm terminates when there are no further rejections of students or proposals.

Example 11.2.3 Consider the problem in Example 11.2.2 with $q_c = 1$ (see table 11.4). The steps of the algorithm applied to this problem are shown in the table 11.5. Students tentatively assigned to a course are boxed; rejected students are not.

Table 11.4 (a) Course priorities ($\succ_c$) and (b) student preferences ($\succ_s$)

(a) $\succ_{c_1}$	$\succ_{c_2}$	$\succ_{c_3}$	$\succ_{c_4}$
$\underline{s_4}$	$\underline{s_2}$	$\underline{s_3}$	$\underline{s_1}$
s_1	s_3	s_4	$\vdots$
s_2	$\vdots$	$\vdots$	$\vdots$

(b) $\succ_{s_1}$	$\succ_{s_2}$	$\succ_{s_3}$	$\succ_{s_4}$
c_1	c_1	c_2	c_3
$\underline{c_4}$	$\underline{c_2}$	$\underline{c_3}$	$\underline{c_1}$
$\vdots$	$\vdots$	$\vdots$	$\vdots$

The resulting matching is

$$\mu_2 = \begin{pmatrix} c_1 & c_2 & c_3 & c_4 \\ s_4 & s_2 & s_3 & s_1 \end{pmatrix}$$

and the corresponding entries are underlined in table 11.4.

11.2.2.1 Properties of the SOSM

The student-optimal stable mechanism is widespread because it satisfies a number of desirable properties such as strategy-proofness for the students (since in SOSM students do the proposing) and stability. In addition, it weakly Pareto-dominates any other stable matching mechanism for students.

Theorem 11.2.1 (Gale and Shapley, 1962) *There always exists a stable matching for the two-sided matching problem.*

Proof. Existence can be proved by using the deferred-acceptance algorithm to find a stable set. Let each student propose to her favorite course. Each course organizer who receives more proposals than there are course places available rejects all but his favorite students from among those who have proposed to him. However, he does not actually accept these students yet but puts them "on a string" and allows for the possibility that a preferred student may come along later.

Table 11.5 Example of the Gale–Shapley student-optimal stable mechanism. The boxes describe intermediate results of the algorithm

Step	c_1	c_2	c_3	c_4
1	$\boxed{s_1}, s_2$	$\boxed{s_3}$	$\boxed{s_4}$	
2	$\vdots$	$\boxed{s_2}, s_3$	$\vdots$	
3		$\vdots$	$\boxed{s_3}, s_4$	
4	$\boxed{s_4}, s_1$		$\vdots$	
5	$\boxed{s_4}$	$\boxed{s_2}$	$\boxed{s_3}$	$\boxed{s_1}$

In the second stage, those students who were rejected propose their second choices. Again, each course organizer receiving proposals chooses his favorite student from the group consisting of the new proposers and the students on his string, if any. The course organizer rejects all the rest but again keeps the favorite student in suspense. We proceed in the same manner.

Suppose student s_i and course c_j are not matched to each other but s_i prefers c_j to her own course c_l. Then s_i must have proposed c_j at some stage and subsequently must have been rejected in favor of someone that the organizer of course c_j liked better. Therefore, the organizer of course c_j must prefer his favorite student to s_i and there is no instability.   □

The above mechanism is used in several public school systems in the USA, and its stability is often used as an explanation for its popularity.

Theorem 11.2.2 (Gale and Shapley, 1962) *The SOSM Pareto-dominates any other stable matching mechanism.*

Proof. Let us call a course "possible" for a particular student if there is a stable matching that assigns her to this course. The proof is by induction. Assume that up to a given point in the algorithm no student has yet been turned away from a course that is possible for her. At this point suppose that course organizer c_j, having received proposals from $q = q_{c_j}$ of his preferred students s'_l with $0 < l \le q_{c_j}$, rejects student s_i. We must show that c_j is impossible for s_i. We know that each s'_l prefers course c_j to all the others, except for those that have previously rejected her and hence are impossible for her. Consider a hypothetical assignment that sends s_i to c_j and everyone else to courses that are possible for them. At least one of the s'_l will have to go to a less desirable place than c_j. But this assignment is unstable, because s'_l and c_j could both benefit by being assigned to each other. Therefore, c_j is impossible for s_i. As a consequence, a stable matching mechanism only rejects students from courses which they could not possibly be assigned to in any stable matching. The resulting matching is therefore Pareto optimal.   □

Let us now discuss incentives. Although no stable matching mechanism can be strategy-proof for all agents, the SOSM is strategy-proof for the proposing side (the students in our examples).

Theorem 11.2.3 (Roth, 1982a) *No stable matching procedure for the general matching problem exists for which the truthful revelation of preferences is a dominant strategy for all participants.*

Proof. We aim to show that there is a matching problem for which no stable matching procedure has truthful revelation as a dominant strategy. Suppose there are students $S = s_1, s_2, s_3$ and courses $C = c_1, c_2, c_3$. Let μ be an arbitrary stable matching procedure which, for any reported preference profile $\succeq = (\succeq_S, \succeq_C)$ selects some outcome $\chi(\succeq)$ from the set of stable outcomes with respect to the reported preference profile $\succeq$. Suppose that the preferences of the participants are given in table 11.6. There are two

Table 11.6 (a) Course priorities ($\succ_c$) and (b) student preferences ($\succ_s$)

(a)	$\succ_{c_1}$	$\succ_{c_2}$	$\succ_{c_3}$	(b)	$\succ_{s_1}$	$\succ_{s_2}$	$\succ_{s_3}$
	s_1	s_3	s_1		c_2	c_1	c_1
	s_3	s_1	s_2		c_1	c_2	c_2
	s_2	s_2	s_3		c_3	c_3	c_3

stable outcomes, μ_1 and μ_2:

$$\mu_1 = \begin{pmatrix} s_1 & s_2 & s_3 \\ c_2 & c_3 & c_1 \end{pmatrix} \qquad \mu_2 = \begin{pmatrix} s_1 & s_2 & s_3 \\ c_1 & c_3 & c_2 \end{pmatrix}$$

Note that the students prefer μ_1 while the course organizers prefer μ_2. Since $\chi(\succeq)$ is a stable matching procedure, one of the two matchings is selected.

Suppose that c_1 reports $s_1 \succ s_2 \succ s_3$ instead of $s_1 \succ s_3 \succ s_2$. The new preference profile is referred to as $\succeq'$. Now, the outcome μ_2 is the unique stable outcome with respect to the preference profile $\succeq'$ and any stable matching mechanism can only select $\succeq'$.

In a similar way, $\succeq''$ is the preference profile which differs from $\succeq$ only in that $\succeq''$ replaces the report by s_1 with $c_2 \succ c_3 \succ c_1$. Then the outcome μ_1 is the unique stable outcome with respect to $\succeq''$.

As a consequence, if in the original problem μ_1 is selected by $\chi(\succeq)$ then c_1 has an incentive to state the preference relation $\succeq'$ instead of the true preference $\succeq$ in order to change the outcome from μ_1 to μ_2. If, however, $\chi(\succeq)$ selects μ_2 then s_1 has an incentive to report $\succeq''$ to change the outcome from μ_2 to μ_1. ☐

The proof also shows that the set of agents favored by a stable matching procedure has no incentive to misreport preferences. In the SOSM, no student can be matched with a course that is better than the course assigned. We only state the theorem and leave the proof as an exercise.

Theorem 11.2.4 (Roth, 1982a) *The SOSM is strategy-proof for the students.*

In the literature on school choice, schools are typically assumed to have publicly known priorities but they are assumed not to be strategic, while the relevant students are possibly strategic. While these are positive results, SOSM is not without problems. There are potential tradeoffs between stability and Pareto efficiency for the students, and tie-breaking is an issue. Both problems led to new developments, which we discuss in what follows.

11.2.2.2 Ties and Pareto Improvements for Students

Let us first discuss Pareto improvements for students in the SOSM. For this, it is of interest that the matching μ_2 in example 11.2.3 is not *Pareto efficient* for the students. If the students s_2, s_3, and s_4 were instead assigned to their first choice course and s_1's allocation didn't change then three students would be better off.

Table 11.7 (a) Course priorities ($\succeq_c$) and (b) student preferences ($\succ_s$)

(a)	$\succeq_{c_1}$	$\succeq_{c_2}$	$\succeq_{c_3}$		(b)	$\succ_{s_1}$	$\succ_{s_2}$	$\succ_{s_3}$
	s_1	s_2	s_3			c_2	c_3	c_2
	s_2, s_3	s_1, s_3	s_1, s_2			c_1	c_2	c_3
						c_3	c_1	c_1

The SOSM is stable and it is "constrained efficient" for students in the sense that the outcome is not Pareto dominated by any other stable matching. If there are ties, independently of how the ties are broken the outcome is still stable; however, it is no longer guaranteed to be constrained efficient (Erdil and Ergin, 2008).

In most applications, however, preferences include ties. For example, course organizers might be indifferent between all students in a particular semester. Also, in school choice, school priorities are typically determined according to criteria that do not provide a strict ordering of all students and there are often large indifference classes. We refer to the two-sided version of the HR problem with ties as HRT, or HRTI if incomplete preference lists are included. Such ties in preferences are typically broken randomly to achieve a fixed strict ordering. Although random tie-breaking procedures preserve the stability and strategy-proofness of the matching, they adversely affect the efficiency of the outcome, as is illustrated in the example in table 11.7.

Example 11.2.4 Consider three course organizers c_1, c_2, and c_3 and three students s_1, s_2, and s_3 with the preferences given in table 11.7. Course organizer c_1 in table 11.7 is indifferent between s_2 and s_3, etc.

If the ties are broken in such a way that s_1 is preferred to s_2, and s_2 is preferred to s_3, then the student-optimal stable matching μ would assign c_1 to s_1, c_2 to s_2, and c_3 to s_3. However, considering the original course-organizer preferences with indifferences, there are Pareto improvements by assigning student s_3 to course c_2 and student s_2 to course c_3. The new matching Pareto-dominates μ from the student-optimal point of view and it is stable with respect to the original preferences of the course organizer.

11.2.3 The Efficiency-Adjusted Deferred-Acceptance Mechanism

The problems with ties in the previous article led to a number of extensions of SOSM, which try to get rid of inefficiencies. We discuss an example, the *efficiency-adjusted deferred-acceptance mechanism* (EADAM) of Kesten (2010). This mechanism eliminates welfare losses on the student side in the way described above, but it gives up on strategy-proofness. The outcome of EADAM is only stable if all students consent to waive their preferences.

If we again look at example 11.2.3, we can see that there is a *rejection chain* from step 1 to 4, which is initiated by student s_1 as course c_1 prefers s_1 over s_2 in step 1. This rejection induces the rejections at steps 2, 3, and 4, where s_1 is rejected from course c_1. Student s_1 does not benefit from being tentatively assigned to course c_1 from step 1

Table 11.8 (a) Course priorities ($\succ_c$) and (b) updated student preferences ($\succ_s$)

(a)	$\succ_{c_1}$	$\succ_{c_2}$	$\succ_{c_3}$	$\succ_{c_4}$	(b)	$\succ_{s_1}$	$\succ_{s_2}$	$\succ_{s_3}$	$\succ_{s_4}$
	s_4	s_2	s_3	$\boxed{s_1}$		c_1	$\boxed{c_1}$	c_2	c_3
	s_1	$\boxed{s_3}$	$\boxed{s_4}$	$\vdots$		$\boxed{c_4}$	c_2	c_3	c_1
	$\boxed{s_2}$	$\vdots$	$\vdots$	$\vdots$		$\vdots$	$\vdots$	$\vdots$	$\vdots$

to step 4 and this also adversely affects the other students (s_2, s_3, and s_4). Hence, any student like s_1 is called an *interrupter* and a pair like (s_1, c_1) an *interrupting pair*. If student s_1 waived his priority for the critical course c_1 then the other students would be assigned to their first-choice course. We refer to student s_1 in this case as a *consenting interrupter*.

Definition 11.2.5 (Interrupter) Given a problem to which the DA algorithm is applied, let s be a student who is tentatively placed on a course c at some step t and rejected from it at some later step t'. If there is at least one other student who is rejected from course c after step $t - 1$ and before step t', then we call student s an *interrupter* for course c and the pair (s, c) an *interrupting pair* at step t'.

Algorithm 7 describes EADAM.

Round 0: Run the DA algorithm.

Round k, k $\geq$ 1: Find the last step, of the DA algorithm run in round $k - 1$, at which a consenting interrupter is rejected from the course for which she is an interrupter. Identify all interrupting pairs of that step each of which contains a consenting interrupter. If there are no interrupting pairs then stop. For each identified interrupting pair (s, c), remove course c from the preferences of student s without changing the relative order of the remaining courses. Rerun the DA algorithm with the new preference profile.

Algorithm 7 The efficiency-adjusted deferred-acceptance mechanism.

Example 11.2.5 Again, we look at the problem given in example 11.2.2 (adapted from Kesten, 2010), assuming for simplicity that all students consent to their allocations.

Round 0: See example 11.2.3.

Round 1: Since student s_1 is rejected from course c_1 at step 4 and since student s_2 has been rejected from course c_1 while student s_1 was tentatively assigned to course c_1, we identify (s_1, c_1) as the last and the only interrupting pair. Suppose student s_1 consents to her allocation. Then we remove course c_1 from student s_1's preferences and rerun the DA algorithm with the new preference profile shown in table 11.8. The resulting

Table 11.9 Example of the efficiency-adjusted deferred-acceptance mechanism

Step	c_1	c_2	c_3	c_4
1	s_2	s_3	s_4	s_1

matching is (see table 11.9)

$$\mu_3 = \begin{pmatrix} c_1 & c_2 & c_3 & c_4 \\ s_2 & s_3 & s_4 & s_1 \end{pmatrix}$$

The outcomes of SOSM (underlined) and EADAM (in boxes) are shown in table 11.8.

While EADAM is not strategy-proof, manipulation is arguably difficult in many larger course-assignment problems. Truth telling is an ordinal Bayesian Nash equilibrium in EADAM, i.e., it is a Bayesian Nash equilibrium for every von Neumann–Morgenstern utility function of students' true preferences. Alternatives to EADAM are discussed in section 11.6.1.

11.3   One-Sided Matching

Apart from two-sided matching markets, one-sided matching problems (aka assignment problems), where only one side of the market has preferences, can also often be found. In course assignment problems students often need to be assigned to tutor groups at different times of the week. The material discussed in these tutor groups is identical within a week and tutors do not have preferences, but students do have preferences for different times in their weekly schedule. This is an example of a one-sided one-to-many matching problem. Other applications are the assignment of students to dormitories or volunteers to tasks.

Two subtypes of assignment problems are the house allocation problem and the housing market. In the *house allocation problem* each of a set of agents is assigned to an object (or house). In a *housing market* each agent owns an object (or house) and the objects are reallocated. Peer-to-peer exchanges for collectables can be seen as housing markets.

We introduced random serial dictatorship (RSD) at the beginning of the previous section because of its simplicity. It is actually a mechanism for house allocation problems as it does not take into account the preferences of course organizers, and it is truthful and Pareto efficient. As we saw in section 11.2.1, agents are randomly ordered and then, in the realized order, they successively pick their favorite objects from those available.

Unfortunately, the outcomes of RSD can be very unfair ex post, in particular when multiple objects are assigned. Consider an example with two agents, two diamonds, and two rocks. Each agent prefers diamonds to rocks and is assigned at most two objects. RSD will assign both diamonds to the first agent, who is allowed to select her package. Such an outcome would be considered unfair. Alternatively, each agent could have received one diamond and one rock.

The top trading cycle is strategy-proof, efficient, and in the core (see definition 11.3.1) for situations where there is an initial allocation of objects to agents. It was originally designed for housing markets, where each agent owns an object, but it can be adapted to two-sided matching markets. It is actually also used for school choice programs like SOSM. Another alternative is the probabilistic serial (PS) mechanism of Bogomolnaia and Moulin (2001) for the HA problem, which satisfies ex ante fairness and efficiency properties defined for randomized mechanisms.

11.3.1   The Top Trading Cycle Mechanism

The top trading cycle (TTC) mechanism was described in the context of housing markets by Shapley and Scarf (1974), who attributed it to David Gale. It is a deterministic mechanism and applicable when the number of objects equals the number of agents. The algorithm starts with an assignment $\hat{\mu}$ of agents to objects. This assignment, which is called the initial endowment of agents, is independent of the preference orders of the agents. Subsequently, the agents trade among themselves and return the final allocation. The algorithm proceeds in rounds (see algorithm 8).

Step 0: Each agent i reports her preferences $\succ_i$ on objects. All agents are marked active.

Step 1: Each agent i points to her most preferred house (possibly her own); each house points back to its owner.

Step 2: This creates a directed graph. In this graph, cycles are identified. Each agent has an out-degree (i.e., the number of directed edges departing from a vertex) equal to 1, so that there exists at least one directed cycle in the graph. With strict preferences each agent is in at most one cycle.

Step 3: Each agent in a cycle is given the object she points at, and she is then removed from the market with her assigned house.

Step 4: If unmatched agents remain, jump to step 1 and iterate.

Algorithm 8 The TTC algorithm

If an agent prefers her own object to all others then this is a self-loop, i.e., an agent trading with herself and leaving the market with her own object. A cycle with n agents involves all these agents trading with each other.

Example 11.3.1 To illustrate the TTC algorithm, consider the preference profile of four agents for the objects a, b, c, and d in table 11.10.

The first round of the TTC algorithm with these preferences is illustrated in figure 11.2. The dashed lines mark a cycle. Object c is assigned to agent 1 and object a is assigned to agent 3. Then these objects and agents are removed. In the second round

Table 11.10 Example preferences for TTC

$\succ_1$	$\succ_2$	$\succ_3$	$\succ_4$
c	d	a	c
b	a	d	b
d	b	c	a
a	c	b	d

there remains a bipartite graph with the nodes $2, 4, b$, and d. Agent 2 points to object d, and agent 4 to object b. These nodes form a new cycle and are assigned accordingly. The final matching is $(1, c), (2, d), (3, a), (4, b)$.

The TTC algorithm terminates in at most n rounds, where n is the number of agents, because in each round at least one agent gets assigned. It satisfies a number of desirable properties. First, the outcome is in the (weak) core, when agents have actual endowments in a housing market. We have already discussed the core concept in the context of payment rules for combinatorial auctions (see section 7.3.2.1), where we used payoff vectors for cardinal utility and transferable utility via payments. We now look at the core from the perspective of ordinal preferences and non-transferable utilities.

Definition 11.3.1 (Core) The *core* is the set of feasible assignments that cannot be improved upon by a subset (a coalition) of the agents by exchanging the houses they initially own in a different way.

If there were an alternative assignment μ' in which all agents are at least as happy as in μ but at least one agent is strictly better off, then μ is not in the core. The coalition of agents who can make themselves better off in μ' is called a blocking coalition. If an assignment is in the core then no coalition wants to deviate from that assignment.

The outcome of the TTC algorithm is a unique core assignment in the housing market. We do not provide the formal proof, but it proceeds straightforwardly via induction. A blocking coalition cannot involve those agents matched at round 1, because all agents

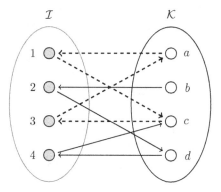

Figure 11.2 Illustration of the first round of the TTC algorithm for the example in table 11.10. The dashed lines describe the first cycle to be removed.

get their first choice. A blocking coalition also cannot involve those agents matched in the first two rounds. One cannot improve the situation for agents from round 1 and, in order to effect such an improvement in round 2, one would need to displace agents from round 1, etc. Each core assignment is also Pareto optimal and individually rational. Individual rationality means in this context that every agent is at least as happy with the resulting allocation as with the object she initially owns. It holds, because an agent can also trade with herself. Strategy-proofness follows from the fact that no agent can trade any of the objects that, with her true reports, are matched on cycles before the round in which she trades. Also, no objects assigned in a later round will make her better off.

Theorem 11.3.1 (Roth, 1982b) *The TTC mechanism is strategy-proof.*

Proof. Suppose that an agent i reports his true preferences and trades in round t of the TTC algorithm. For any such report of agent i, the agents matched in round t' with $t' < t$ will trade with each other in round t' and none of these items can be assigned to agent i. The preferred objects of the agents on cycles in round 1 do not change, and the same cycles trade in round 1. This holds for the agents on cycles in round 2, etc. Truthfulness follows because by reporting her true preference order, the agent receives her most preferred item of all the items owned by the agents other than those in rounds 1 to $t - 1$.   □

The TTC algorithm can also be adapted for one-to-many and *two-sided matching problems*, such as the course allocation problem discussed in section 11.2.1, where students and course organizers have preferences and more than only a single course place is available.

Step 1: Assign a counter for each course, which keeps track of how many places are still available on the course. Initially set the counters equal to the capacities of the courses. Each student points to her favorite course under her reported preferences. Each course points to the student who has the highest priority for the school. Since the number of students and schools are finite, there is at least one cycle. Moreover, each student and each course can be part of at most one cycle. Every student in a cycle is assigned a place in a course she points to and is then removed. The counter of each school in a cycle is reduced by 1 and, if it thus reduces to zero, the school is also removed.

Step $k > 1$: Each remaining student points to her favorite course among the remaining courses and each remaining course points to the student with its highest priority among the remaining students. There is at least one cycle. Every student in a cycle is assigned a seat at the course that she points to, and is removed. The counter of each school in a cycle is reduced by 1 and, if it reduces to zero, the school is also removed.

Algorithm 9 The TTC algorithm for two-sided matching markets

Table 11.11 (a) Course priorities ($\succ_c$) and (b) student preferences ($\succ_s$)

(a)	$\succ_{c_1}$	$\succ_{c_2}$	(b)	$\succ_{s_1}$	$\succ_{s_2}$	$\succ_{s_3}$
	s_1	s_3		c_2	c_1	c_1
	s_2	s_1		c_1		c_2
	s_3					

Note that the TTC algorithm used for two-sided matching problems is efficient and strategy-proof but not stable.

Example 11.3.2   Consider a course allocation problem with three students $S \equiv \{s_1, s_2, s_3\}$ and two courses $C \equiv \{c_1, c_2\}$, each course having one place. The course priorities ($\succ_c$) and the student preferences ($\succ_s$) are given in table 11.11.

In the first round there is a cycle $s_1 \to c_2 \to s_3 \to c_1 \to s_1$ which leads to a matching

$$\mu = \begin{pmatrix} c_1 & c_2 \\ s_3 & s_1 \end{pmatrix}$$

and leaves s_2 unmatched. The outcome is Pareto efficient for the students but not stable. For example, if c_1 were assigned to s_2 and not to s_3 then c_1 and s_2 would be better off.

Overall, strategy-proofness, efficiency, and stability are desirable properties for two-sided matching problems. Unfortunately, a well-known negative result for two-sided matching is the incompatibility of these properties. Remember that a matching is Pareto efficient (for students) if there is no other matching at which all students are at least as well off, and at least one student is better off. A matching is stable if there is no student–course pair such that student s_i prefers course c_j to the course she is placed in, and course c_j prefers student s_i to at least one other student who is assigned to it. A mechanism is strategy-proof (for students) if no student can ever gain by mis-stating his preferences. A Pareto-efficient and fair matching may not always exist but, if it does exist, it is unique (Roth, 1982a). There is also no strategy-proof mechanism (for students) that selects the Pareto-efficient (for students) and stable matching whenever it exists (Kesten, 2010). For this reason EADAM (see section 11.2.3) relaxed the incentive constraints.

This TTC algorithm for two-sided matching markets has actually been used for school choice in US school districts. Ties also matter in the TTC mechanism, because core stability does not imply Pareto optimality anymore. We discuss mechanisms addressing ties in housing markets in section 11.6.2.

11.3.2   The Probabilistic Serial Mechanism

The probabilistic serial (PS) mechanism is a *randomized matching mechanism* ψ : $\mathcal{P}^{|S|} \mapsto \Delta(C)$ which yields a lottery $p \in \Delta(C)$ on a set of course places C. Randomization can be useful to address impossibility results in social choice and mechanism design, as we saw in the previous chapter, on approximation mechanisms. In this section we again use the course allocation application as an example, although the students S

Table 11.12 Example preferences for PS

$\succ_{s_1}$	$\succ_{s_2}$	$\succ_{s_3}$
a	a	b
c	b	a
b	c	c

can be any type of agents $i \in \mathcal{I}$ and the course seats any type of objects $k \in \mathcal{K}$. Randomized ordinal mechanisms require a redefinition of many concepts which are well-defined for deterministic mechanisms. For example, it needs to be defined exactly what it means if one agent prefers one lottery to another. Stochastic orderings are typically used to describe such preference relationships formally. Also, various notions of stability are possible.

We briefly discussed random matchings in section 11.2.1. A *randomized matching mechanism* $\psi(\succeq_S) = p$ is *ex ante Pareto optimal* if no agent prefers p to any other lottery $q \in \Delta(C)$. We call ψ *ex post Pareto optimal* if p is a convex combination of Pareto-optimal matchings. A fair allocation is one where all agents are treated equally. We call a randomized matching mechanism ψ *symmetric* if, for every pair of students s_i and s_j with $\succeq_{s_i} = \succeq_{s_j}$, $p_{s_i} = p_{s_j}$. This means that two students who have the same preference profile also have the same outcome in expectation.

Zhou (1990) showed that no random mechanism for assigning objects to agents can satisfy strong notions of strategy-proofness, Pareto optimality, and symmetry simultaneously for more than three objects and agents. Note that RSD does satisfy weaker notions of these concepts. The PS mechanism produces an envy-free assignment with respect to the reported preferences, but it is not strategy-proof. Each of these properties requires a careful definition in the context of randomized matching (Brandl *et al.*, 2016).

In the following, we provide an example of PS (see also example 11.3.3) to get an understanding of how it differs from deterministic mechanisms.

Step 1: Suppose each object is divisible and is divided into probability shares, and there is a time interval $[0, 1]$.

Step 2: Each agent "eats" the object she prefers the most among all the objects that have not yet been eaten, with speed 1.

Step 3: Once the agent's favorite object is gone, she turns to her next favorite object, and so on.

Step 4: The amount of an object eaten by an agent at time $t = 1$ is interpreted as the probability with which she is assigned this object.

Algorithm 10 The PS algorithm

Example 11.3.3   To illustrate how to compute a PS outcome, consider the preference profile of three students s_1, s_2, and s_3 for three courses (each with only one place), or objects a, b, and c, shown in table 11.12.

In step 1, students 1 and 2 are each awarded their favorite object a with probability 0.5, while student 3 is awarded her favorite object b with probability 0.5. At time $1/2$, a is exhausted and 0.5 of b is available. Then, in step 2, all three students turn to their next favorite among the remaining objects b, c. This means that student 1 is awarded his object c with probability 0.25, while students 2 and 3 receive are awarded object b each with probability 0.25. At time $t = 0.25 + 0.5 = 0.75$, b is exhausted and 0.75 of c is available. In the last step, all students are awarded the remaining object c with probability 0.25. Thus student 1 receives a lottery $\{0.5, 0, 0.5\}$ for the three objects $\{a, b, c\}$, student 2 gets $\{0.5, 0.25, 0.25\}$, and student 3 gets $\{0, 0.75, 0.25\}$. After determining the probabilities, a deterministic matching can be drawn from the lottery.

In each moment, every student is "eating" her favorite available object. So, if a student would prefer a probability share of a different good rather than the one she is eating at this point in time, then that preferred good must have already been partly eaten away. This leads to a form of ordinal efficiency, given the reported preferences. The procedure is envy-free because everyone eats an object they prefer to the object others are eating, so no one envies the random assignment of anyone else. While RSD has better incentive properties (universal truthfulness), it is worse than PS in terms of fairness.

11.4   One-Sided Matching with Complementarities

In many situations market participants have preferences for multiple objects or even packages of objects. This observation has been a main motivation for the combinatorial auctions discussed in Part II of the book. Many-to-many CHA problems are a super-class for various types of problem, including multi-unit assignment problems or combinatorial assignment problems. Two-sided many-to-many matching problems are sometimes referred to as worker–firms problems. In all of these problems complementarities might matter as agents could have preferences for packages of objects. For example, Nguyen and Vohra (2014) proposed a two-sided matching mechanism which allows for bundle preferences.

In this section, we focus on one-sided matching, i.e., many-to-many CHA problems. First, we provide an overview of problem types, before we discuss a specific mechanism for assignment problems with complementarities in more detail.

11.4.1   Multi-Unit and Combinatorial Assignments

In *multi-unit assignment problems* agents desire multiple objects. The literature typically assumes that preferences are ordinal and responsive. *Responsiveness* describes a form of separability of preferences about different objects: if an agent prefers one object k over the other, k', she also prefers the bundle of objects $S \cup \{k\}$ to the bundle of objects $S \cup \{k'\}$. Again, serial dictatorships are the only strategy-proof and efficient mechanisms for multi-unit assignments (Ehlers and Klaus, 2003; Pápai, 2001). As discussed earlier, dictatorships can lead to unfair distributions of outcomes in which some agents get all the objects they like whereas others get nothing. Alternative assignment methods, as used in the field of multi-unit assignment problems, are not strategy-proof. For example, in the *draft mechanism*, used at the Harvard Business School, students (agents) report their preferences over individual courses (objects) to a computer, which then chooses courses for them one at a time over a series of rounds. The order of choosing is random in the first round and then reverses in subsequent rounds (Budish and Cantillon, 2012).

The *combinatorial assignment problem* can be seen as a generalization of the multi-unit assignment problem, where a set of indivisible objects is allocated amongst a set of agents with preferences over bundles, monetary transfers not being allowed. Again each student wants to get 0 or 1 place in a given course but her preferences for particular bundles of courses might be substitutes or complements, as opposed to the responsive preferences assumed in the multi-unit assignment problem. This is similar to a combinatorial auction, where no monetary transfers are allowed.

There are a few recent mechanisms for assignment problems with complementarities. Budish (2011) proposed a variation of the competitive equilibrium with equal incomes (CEEI) mechanism of Hylland and Zeckhauser (1979) for matching with complementarities assuming ordinal preferences of the agents. Nguyen *et al.* (2016) provided two randomized mechanism for one-sided matching problems, one with cardinal and one with ordinal preferences for bundles of objects. In what follows, we describe the MAXCU mechanism for cardinal valuations proposed by Nguyen *et al.* (2016). This is an interesting example, which provides the reader with an understanding of the randomized algorithms used to address such challenging problems.

11.4.2   Cardinal Assignment Problems with Complementarities

The MAXCU mechanism of Nguyen *et al.* (2016) maximizes the social welfare under envy-freeness constraints. The allocation problem is modeled as a linear program where variables describe bundles; the LP then is solved in three steps. First, an optimal fractional solution to a welfare-maximization problem with envy-freeness constraints is computed. The reported utilities are perturbed before computing the welfare-optimal solution, because the welfare-maximizing problem may be sensitive to the reported valuations of the agents. Then the fractional solution is decomposed into a set of integer solutions each of which over-allocates no object to more than $l - 1$ agents, where l is the maximum size of the packages. The fractional solution represents a random matching, and each integer solution derived from the random matching is a deterministic matching. The integer solutions are used to construct a lottery that is equivalent to the optimal fractional solution in expectation. The MAXCU mechanism satisfies envy-freeness and asymptotic strategy-proofness. In what follows, we describe the method in more detail. We abstract from the course allocation problem and talk about agents and objects instead.

11.4.2.1   The Fractional Allocation Problem

Let us first introduce the fractional allocation problem in MAXCU. We assume that, for each object $k \in \mathcal{K}$, the available supply of object k is an integer c_k. A bundle is a non-negative vector $S \in \mathbb{N}^{|\mathcal{K}|}$ whose component S_k indicates the number of copies of object k in bundle S. The size of a bundle S is denoted as $size(S)$, defined as the total number of objects in S, i.e., $\sum_{k \in \mathcal{K}} S_k$. Agent i wants to win at most one bundle, and we assume that the maximum size of a bundle is at most l. In course allocation problems students require at most $l = 5$ places per semester, while the course capacities c_k are 30 places or more. We denote the utility of an agent i for a package S as $u_i(S)$. The linear program MAXCU is as follows:

$$\max \sum_{i \in \mathcal{I}} \sum_{S} u_i(S) x_i(S) \qquad \text{(MAXCU)}$$

$$\text{s.t.} \quad \sum_{S} x_i(S) \leq 1 \qquad \forall i \in \mathcal{I} \qquad (1)$$

$$\sum_{i \in \mathcal{I}} \sum_{k:k \in S} S_k x_i(S) \leq c_k \qquad \forall k \in \mathcal{K} \qquad (2)$$

$$\sum_{S} u_i(S)(x_i(S) - x_{i'}(S)) \geq 0 \qquad \forall i, i' \in \mathcal{I} \qquad (3)$$

$$x \in \mathbb{R}_{\geq 0}^{|\mathcal{I}||\mathcal{K}|^l}$$

Constraint (1) in this linear MAXCU program is referred to as a demand constraint, i.e., no bidder can win more than one bid. The supply constraint (2) specifies the available capacities for each object, while constraint (3) describes envy-freeness. After the optimal solution x^* to this linear program is computed, we need to implement x^* as a lottery over integral matchings satisfying the demand and supply constraints. A fractional solution x^* is *implementable* if it can be expressed as a convex combination of feasible integer solutions, and it can be interpreted as a lottery over feasible assignments of bundles.

For unit-demand assignment problems, the equivalence between probability shares and lotteries is given by the Birkhoff–von Neumann theorem, which was mentioned in section 11.2.1. Remember, the theorem says that every lottery over feasible integral allocations corresponds to a feasible fractional allocation on setting $x_i(S)$ equal to the probability that agent i obtains bundle S. For $l > 1$ this is no longer true, unless the demand and supply constraints are relaxed. Nguyen *et al.* (2016) showed that any fractional solution of MAXCU considering only demand and supply constraints can be implemented as a lottery over integral allocations that satisfy a supply constraint relaxed by $l - 1$ copies of each object.

There are different algorithms to decompose the fractional solution x^* into a convex combination of integer solutions. We discuss the iterative rounding algorithm below. Note that the problem is related to the convex decomposition used in the TIE framework described in section 10.3, where a scaled-down fractional allocation is decomposed into integer solutions. However, the rounding process for integer solutions is different.

11.4.2.2 The Lottery Algorithm

After we have solved MAXCU, we implement the optimal fractional solution x^* of MAXCU as a lottery over integer matchings satisfying the above constraints (1) and (2). As indicated earlier, we need to relax the right-hand side by $l - 1$ to be able always to implement the fractional solution as a lottery: $\sum_{i \in \mathcal{I}} \sum_{k:k \in S} S_k x_i(S) \leq c_k + l - 1$.

In the polynomial time *lottery algorithm* (see algorithm 12 below) we find at most $d + 1$ integer points, the convex hull of which is arbitrarily close to the fractional solution x^*. The lottery algorithm then returns a lottery over these $d + 1$ integer vectors, which is close to x^* in expectation. The variable d describes the dimensions of the problem. In this lottery algorithm, we use a subroutine to return an integer point $\bar{x}$ such that $u\bar{x} \geq ux^*$. This subroutine is called an *iterative rounding algorithm* (IRA) and proceeds as follows (see algorithm 11).

1a. Delete all $x_i = 0, x_i = 1$, update the constraints and go to 1b.
1b. If there is no $x_i \in \{1, 0\}$ one can find at least one supply constraint:

$$\sum_{i \in I} \sum_{S:k \in S} S_k \lceil x_i(S) \rceil \leq c_k + l - 1$$

Delete these constraints and go to step 2.
2. Solve $\max\{u^t x \mid (1), (2), x \in \mathbb{R}_{\geq 0}\}$; **if**(all $x_i \in \{0, 1\}$) return x. **else** go to step 1a.

Algorithm 11 Pseudo-code for the iterative rounding algorithm

Now we can discuss the lottery algorithm (see algorithm 12). Let $B(x^*, \delta) = \{x \mid |x^* - x| \leq \delta\} \subseteq \{x \in \mathbb{R}_{\geq 0} \mid \sum_S x_i(S) \leq 1\}$ with $\delta > 0$. The parameter δ in $B(x^*, \delta)$ determines some space around x^* such that the demand constraint $\sum_S x_i(S) \leq 1$ is not violated. Here, $|x - y|$ describes the Euclidean distance between two vectors x and y.

---

1. Set $Z = \{IRA(x^*)\}$, i.e., find an integer solution z' via the IRA.
2. Set $y = \text{argmin}\{|x^* - y| \mid y \in \text{conv}(Z)\}$; **if** $|x^* - y| < \varepsilon$ **end**
3. Choose $Z' \subset Z$ of size $|Z'| \leq d$ and $y \in \text{conv}(Z')$. Set $z = x^* + \delta \frac{x^* - y}{|x^* - y|}$.
   Find optimal integer z' s.t. (1), (2) in MAXCU hold, and we have
   $(x^* - y)^t z' \geq (x^* - y)^t z$
   via the IRA.
4. Set $Z = Z' \cup \{z'\}$ and go back to step 1.

Output: Convex combination of final y values

Algorithm 12 Pseudo-code for the lottery algorithm

Step 3 of the lottery algorithm determines a new point z by moving a distance δ in the direction $(x^* - y)/|x^* - y|$. Starting from z, IRA is used to determine a nearby integer solution z', which is then added to Z; $(x^* - y)^t z' \geq (x^* - y)^t z$ is a new hyperplane introduced when searching for z'. Figure 11.3 illustrates the variables in the lottery algorithm.

Example 11.4.1 Let's look at an example with two bidders 1, 2 and two items A, B only (see table 11.13).

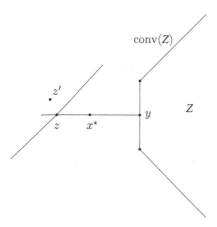

Figure 11.3 Graphical illustration of the variables in the lottery algorithm

First, we solve MAXCU so that the demand (1), supply (2), and envy-freeness constraints (3) hold:

$$\max(1 \quad 2 \quad 3)^t x$$

$$\text{s.t.} \begin{pmatrix} 1 & 1 & 0 \\ 0 & 0 & 1 \\ 1 & 1 & 1 \\ 0 & 1 & 1 \\ -1 & -2 & 2 \\ 0 & 3 & -3 \end{pmatrix} x \leq \begin{pmatrix} 1 \\ 1 \\ 1 \\ 1 \\ 0 \\ 0 \end{pmatrix}$$

$$(x_{1,A}; x_{1,AB}; x_{2,AB})^t \in \mathbb{R}^3_{\geq 0}$$

The optimal solution is $x^* = (0, 0.5, 0.5)^t$. Let $B(x^*, \delta) = \{x \mid |x^* - x| \leq \delta\} \subseteq \{x \in \mathbb{R}_{\geq 0} \mid \sum_S x_i(S) \leq 1\}$ with $\delta > 0$ be a small area around the optimal solution. With $x^* = (0, 0.5, 0.5)^t$ we can have $\delta \leq 0.5$. We set $\delta = 0.25$ and $\varepsilon = 0.1$.

Iteration 1 of the Lottery Algorithm
In the initial step 1 of the lottery algorithm, we find an integer solution z' via IRA. We do not need to consider constraint (3) in MAXCU; we set $x_{1,A} = 0$ and, as a first solution, we get an allocation where the package $\{A, B\}$ is assigned to bidder 2, with $z' = (0, 0, 1)^t$. The convex set of $Z_0 = \{z'\}$ consists of a single point, z'.

Table 11.13 Example valuations for the algorithm MAXCU

$w_i = 1$	$\{A\}$	$\{A, B\}$
Bidder 1	1	2
Bidder 2	0	3

In step 2 of the lottery algorithm, we minimize the distance between the optimal solution x^* and the convex set Z_0, with $y = \text{argmin}\{|x^* - y| \mid y \in \text{conv}(Z)\}$. If $|x^* - y| < \varepsilon$ then the algorithm ends. In our example, $|x^* - y| = 1/\sqrt{2} > 0.1$, $Z' = Z$.

In step 3 of the lottery algorithm, we choose Z', with $|Z'| \le d$ and $y \in \text{conv}(Z')$. Then we determine a new point $z = x^* + \delta(x^* - y)/|x^* - y|$. Now we find the optimal integer z' such that (1), (2) hold and $(x^* - y)^t z' \ge (x^* - y)^t z$, via the IRA:

$$z = \begin{pmatrix} 0 \\ 0.5 \\ 0.5 \end{pmatrix} + \frac{\sqrt{2}}{4} \begin{pmatrix} 0 \\ 0.5 \\ -0.5 \end{pmatrix} = \begin{pmatrix} 0 \\ 0.6768 \\ 0.3232 \end{pmatrix}.$$

Note that $x^* - y = (0, 0.5, -0.5)^t$, $\delta = 1/4$, and $|x^* - y| = 1/\sqrt{2}$ in this equation. Now $(x^* - y)^t z = 0.1768$, and $(x^* - y)^t z' \ge (x^* - y)^t z$ translates to $(0, -0.5, 0.5)z' \le -0.1768$, which is added as a constraint (ζ) to MAXCU without the envy-freeness constraints.

Iteration 2 of the Lottery Algorithm

In the next iteration of the lottery algorithm, we first need to run the IRA. Step 1 in the IRA solves $\max\{u^t x \mid (1), (2), (\zeta) \in \mathbb{R}_{\ge 0}\}$. If (all $x_i \in \{0, 1\}$) holds we could return x:

$$\max(1 \quad 2 \quad 3)^t z'$$

$$\text{s.t.} \quad \begin{pmatrix} 1 & 1 & 0 \\ 0 & 0 & 1 \\ 1 & 1 & 1 \\ 0 & 1 & 1 \\ 0 & -0.5 & 0.5 \end{pmatrix} z' \le \begin{pmatrix} 1 \\ 1 \\ 1 \\ 1 \\ -0.1768 \end{pmatrix}$$

$$z_1', z_2', z_3' \in \mathbb{R}_{\ge 0}$$

The solution of the first IRA iteration is IT1: $z'^1 = (0, 0.6767, 0.3232)^t$. We delete the first component z_1', which is zero, and repeat the optimization:

$$\max(2 \quad 3)^t z'$$

$$\text{s.t.} \quad \begin{pmatrix} 1 & 0 \\ 0 & 1 \\ 1 & 1 \\ 1 & 1 \\ -0.5 & 0.5 \end{pmatrix} z' \le \begin{pmatrix} 1 \\ 1 \\ 1 \\ 1 \\ -0.1768 \end{pmatrix}$$

$$z_2', z_3' \in \mathbb{R}_{\ge 0}$$

This second IRA iteration results in IT2: $z'^2 = (0.6767, 0.3232)^t$. In order to get an integer solution, we try to find at least one unviolated relaxed supply constraint. Constraints (3) and (4) are not violated, $z_2' + z_3' \le 1 + 2 - 1 = 2$, and deleted. This leads to the third IRA iteration:

$$\max(2 \quad 3)^t z'$$

$$\text{s.t.} \quad \begin{pmatrix} 1 & 0 \\ 0 & 1 \\ -0.5 & 0.5 \end{pmatrix} z' \le \begin{pmatrix} 1 \\ 1 \\ -0.1768 \end{pmatrix}$$

$$z_2', z_3' \in \mathbb{R}_{\ge 0}$$

The solution to this LP leads to IT3: $z'^3 = (1, 0.6464)^t$, so z_2' can be deleted. Then we have

$$\max(3)^t z'$$

$$\text{s.t.} \quad \begin{pmatrix} 1 \\ 0.5 \end{pmatrix} z' \le \begin{pmatrix} 1 \\ -0.1768 \end{pmatrix}$$

$$z_3' \in \mathbb{R}_{\ge 0}$$

This IRA iteration leads to IT4: $z'^4 = 0.6464$. We round z'^4 to 0, leading to $z'^* = (0, 1, 0)^t$ as the result of the IRA.

The set of integer points is now $Z = \{(0, 0, 1)^t; (0, 1, 0)^t\}$, and $y = 0.5(0, 0, 1)^t + 0.5(0, 1, 0)^t$. Since $|x^* - y| = 0$ we can end the lottery algorithm, and return Z and $\lambda = (0.5, 0.5)$. The solution $\lambda = (0.5, 0.5)$ is the result of minimizing the Euclidean distance between $x^* = (0, 0.5, 0.5)$ and $(\lambda_1(0, 0, 1) + \lambda_2(0, 1, 0))$. Finally, one of the two integer solutions is determined randomly, with λ the probability distribution.

The MAXCU mechanism is based on cardinal valuations. The second mechanism for ordinal preferences is a generalization of the probabilistic serial mechanism (see section 11.3.2), called the bundled probabilistic serial (BPS) mechanism. Informally, in BPS all agents "eat" their most preferred bundle in $[0, 1]$ simultaneously, with the same speed, as long as all included objects are available. As soon as one object is exhausted, every bundle containing this object is deleted and the agents continue eating the next available bundle in their preference list. The duration for which every bundle is eaten by an agent specifies the probability for assigning this bundle to this agent. In this way BPS yields probability shares of bundles, which again are implemented as lotteries over bundles. Nguyen *et al.* (2016) showed that BPS is approximately Pareto optimal, envy-free, and strategy-proof.

11.5   Applications and Empirical Results

Matching markets have found widespread adoption. In particular, the school choice problem has drawn a lot of attention; it is similar to the course allocation problem discussed in this chapter. In order to give parents the opportunity to choose the public school their child will attend, many US states provide school choice systems. Each prospective student submits a list of school preferences to the central placement authority of the school district. On the other hand each school has a priority ordering of all students and a maximum capacity. This information is used to determine which student will be assigned to which school. Abdulkadiroğlu and Sönmez (2003) showed that the matching mechanisms in use in the USA did not perform well in terms of efficiency, incentives, and stability. As a consequence, the Boston public schools replaced a priority mechanism (the Boston mechanism) with a deferred-acceptance mechanism. The Boston mechanism does not exhibit a dominant-strategy equilibrium and it is not stable.

Some experimental work has focused on school choice, comparing these two approaches. For example, in Chen and Deng (2006) experimental subjects played a one-shot game of incomplete information, in which each participant was informed only about her own preferences, schools' capacities, and the matching mechanism. They found that, from the perspective of students, the SOSM outperforms both the Boston mechanism and other alternatives. Featherstone and Niederle (2008) confirmed this but also discussed settings with only private information of subjects, where the Boston mechanism has advantages.

In Germany, the assignment of students to universities via the Zentralstelle für die Vergabe von Studienplätzen (ZVS) is a large-scale application of matching. One part of the capacity is reserved for excellent students and students with long waiting times, via a Boston mechanism. The remaining places are allocated on the basis of universities' preferences via a university-proposing Gale–Shapley deferred-acceptance mechanism. The two parts are administered sequentially in the aforementioned order (Westkamp, 2013). Braun *et al.* (2010) presented evidence from the field that some applicants behave strategically and not truthfully in this combined mechanism.

Another widely cited application of one-to-many stable matching is the assignment of graduating medical students to their first hospital appointments by the National Resident Match Program in the USA (Roth, 1984). A number of other applications can be found online (www.matching-in-practice.eu). Roth (2002) argued, on the basis of empirical observations, that stability is a key feature of successful matching mechanisms in practice.

Although the course allocation problem is similar to school choice it has not received as much attention, and in practice different mechanisms are being used. Typically, monetary transfers are not allowed in relation to course assignment in higher education, so that auctions are not an option. However, some business schools in the USA use course bidding, where students are given a bid endowment in a virtual currency to allocate across the courses they consider taking. This virtual currency does not have outside value and there are various possibilities for manipulation (Sönmez and Ünver, 2010). ? reported on a field experiment with 535 students, comparing course bidding with the Gale–Shapley stable matching mechanism, and found that the latter could vastly improve efficiency.

Diebold *et al.* (2014) compared SOSM and EADAM with a first-come first-served (FCFS) system. They used average rank, rank distribution, and popularity to compare matchings empirically. Popularity simply measures how many students prefer one matching over another. Overall, the outcomes of stable matching mechanisms were preferable to FCFS in both experiments; however, the differences were not substantial. Actually, the number of unmatched students was lower in FCFS throughout. Still, one of the biggest advantages of SOSM and EADAM, beyond stability outcome, might be the fact that there are strong incentives for telling the truth and there are no benefits of being first during the registration period. If there were a benefit to being first then this might lead to unfair outcomes, as some students just cannot be first owing to circumstances beyond their control.

11.6   Summary

Matching with preferences is a field of research that has yielded remarkable mechanisms, which are nowadays used for school choice, course allocation, kidney exchanges, or the assignment of residents to hospitals, and other such cases where monetary transfers are not allowed. Some problems allow for preferences on two sides of the market, while others are one-sided. Random serial dictatorship, the Gale–Shapley student-optimal stable mechanism, and Gale's top trading cycle allow for dominant strategies, at least for one side of the market. While original contributions to this field have often assumed strict preferences, much recent work has focused on ties in preferences. There is also some literature on approximation algorithms for hard stable matching problems (Halldórsson et al., 2003).

This chapter could only provide an introduction into some of the main questions and techniques used. We refer the interested reader to Manlove (2013) for an excellent survey of the algorithmic aspects of matching problems. A full discussion of the many matching mechanisms discussed in the literature is beyond this chapter. However, the following two subsections provide an overview of further mechanisms, their properties, and references to the literature.

11.6.1   Two-Sided Matching Mechanisms

We have primarily discussed SOSM and EADAM as mechanisms for two-sided matching problems. A main motivation for EADAM is possible Pareto improvements in the case of indifference in preferences (see section 11.2.3). This topic has led to a number of developments. Abdulkadiroğlu et al. (2009) showed that every student-optimal stable matching can be obtained with "single tie breaking", but the outcome might not be Pareto efficient. Single tie breaking means that a single tie-breaking rule is used for all courses in the course assignment problem. These authors also showed that there exists no strategy-proof mechanism (stable or not) that Pareto-improves on the DA algorithm with single tie breaking. This means that no other strategy-proof mechanisms such as RSD or TTC Pareto dominate the DA algorithm with single tie breaking.

A summary of the properties of two-sided mechanisms in HRTI problems, i.e., hospital/residents problems with ties and indifferences, is given in table 11.14. The SOSM mechanism with random tie breaking is not Pareto efficient for students. The EADAM mechanism takes an SOSM matching and identifies student–course pairs (interrupting pairs) that may harm the welfare when the SOSM matching is constructed. Therefore,

Table 11.14 Summary of two-sided matching mechanisms for HRTI

Matching mechanism	Stability	Pareto efficiency	Strategy-proofness	Maximum size	Polynomial time
SOSM	✓	✗	✓	✗	✓
EADAM	✗	✓	○	✗	✓
ESMA	✓	○	○	✗	✓
WOSMA	✓	○	○	✗	✓
TTC	✗	✗	✓	✗	✓
IP MAX HRT	✓	✗	✗	✓	✗

the preferences of the student can be modified if she consents to waive her preferences, and SOSM is executed on the updated preferences. This procedure is repeated until there are no longer any interrupting pairs. The algorithm only discovers Pareto improvements such that no student would be worse off compared with the SOSM matching even if she waives her preferences. There is no other fair matching that Pareto-dominates the EADAM outcome. A similar algorithm can be used to handle inefficiency due to ties. One can combine the EADAM algorithm proposed for the case when priority orders are strict with the case handling ties, as a way to achieve full Pareto efficiency. The EADAM algorithm achieves Pareto efficiency in the presence of ties regarding students, but it relaxes strategy-proofness and stability; the matching may become unstable concerning the original preferences. EADAM is not strategy-proof, but truth telling is an ordinal Bayesian Nash equilibrium in this algorithm. The circles in the column for strategy-proofness in table 11.14 refer to those mechanisms for which ordinal Bayesian Nash incentive compatibility is shown.

Leaving aside EADAM, Erdil and Ergin (2008, 2006) developed an *efficient and stable matching algorithm* (ESMA) to address ties in the preferences. The algorithm also takes an SOSM matching and performs Pareto improvements which preserve stability by exchanging course places in the presence of ties. ESMA is not Pareto efficient for students, but it is stable. However, it does not necessarily lead to a maximum matching, and it is not strategy-proof. The authors showed that truth telling is also an ordinal Bayesian Nash equilibrium in ESMA in an environment with symmetric information. Erdil and Ergin (2008, 2006) also suggested a *worker optimal stable matching algorithm* (WOSMA), which is similar to ESMA. It computes a student-optimal stable matching by carrying out *stable resident improvement* chains and cycles based on an SOSM matching. WOSMA is again stable but not Pareto efficient for students (Erdil and Ergin, 2008, 2006). Like ESMA, WOSMA does not necessarily lead to a maximum matching and it is not strategy-proof. ESMA and WOSMA compute stable outcomes which are not Pareto dominated. We also add TTC in our summary in table 11.14; this can be adapted for two-sided matching problems as described in section 11.3.1. The TTC mechanism does not yield a stable two-sided matching; however, it is efficient except in the presence of ties.

When preferences involve ties, there is a non-empty set of stable matchings that are Pareto optimal for students. These stable matchings have different sizes and one might

Table 11.15 Summary of one-sided matching mechanisms for CHATI

Matching mechanism	Pareto efficiency	Strategy proofness	Polynomial time	Other properties
RSD	✓	✓	✓	
PS	✓	✗	✓	envy-free
Pop-CHAT	✓	✗	✓	popular
MPO CHAT	✓	✗	✓	max. size

want to find the *maximum stable matching* even if the respective mechanisms are not strategy-proof. Manlove *et al.* (2002) showed that ties can lead to computationally hard problems. Kwanashie and Manlove (2013) proposed an integer program to find the *maximum-cardinality stable matching* for the HR problem with ties (IP MAX HRT). The solution of this integer program is a stable and maximum cardinality matching. Even though the problem is NP-hard, in practice instances with hundreds of students can typically be solved to optimality.

Note that additional constraints can make two-sided matching problems complex. A non-trivial constraint in the course assignment problem is the incorporation of minimum quotas for courses. This is practically relevant if course organizers want to avoid situations where they have only a few students in their class. It is known that there is no strategy-proof mechanism that completely eliminates "justified envy" when minimum quotas are imposed (Hamada *et al.*, 2011). Ueda *et al.* (2012) proposed strategy-proof mechanisms which allow for minimum quotas and achieve efficiency and a modified definition of stability.

11.6.2 One-Sided Matching Mechanisms

Table 11.15 provides an overview of selected mechanisms for one-sided one-to-many assignment problems and selected properties. We refer to the problem as CHAT (capacitated house allocation with ties), if ties are included, or CHATI if there are also incomplete preference lists. Stability is not an issue in these settings, but Pareto efficiency is.

The *popular-CHAT* mechanism (Pop-CHAT) (Manlove and Sng, 2006) aims to find the largest popular matching in a CHAT instance. A matching is popular if there is no other matching that is preferred by a majority of the agents. The *maximum Pareto-optimal CHAT* (MPO CHAT) mechanism of Sng (2008) aims to find a maximum matching which is Pareto optimal. It proceeds in three phases satisfying three conditions for a Pareto-optimal matching (Manlove, 2013) but it is not strategy-proof. Note that this is an active field of research and several variants and extensions of existing mechanisms for agents with single-unit demand have been proposed (see for example Ehlers and Erdil (2010); Ergin (2002); Pycia and Ünver (2015)).

Table 11.16 concerns housing markets as an interesting subcategory of CHA where agents have an initial endowment of objects. The TTC mechanism satisfies individual rationality, Pareto efficiency, and strategy-proofness and the outcome is in the core.

Table 11.16 Summary of one-sided matching mechanisms for housing markets with indifferences

Matching mechanism	Pareto efficiency	Strategy proofness	Polynomial time	Core
TTC	✗	✓	✓	✓
TCR	✓	✓	✓	✓
TTAS	✓	✓	✗	✓

However, in the presence of indifferences the core does not imply Pareto optimality. A few articles have addressed housing markets with indifferences. *Top trading absorbing sets* (TTAS) (Alcalde-Unzu and Molis, 2011) and the *top cycle rules* (TCR) (Jaramillo and Manjunath, 2012) are strategy-proof, core selecting, and Pareto optimal. While TCR is a polynomial-time algorithm, TTAS can take exponential time to terminate. In this chapter, we have also described PS, which is a randomized alternative to RSD satisfying *envy-freeness*. Aziz and de Keijzer (2012) and Saban and Sethuraman (2013) provide a more general framework of housing markets with indifferences.

11.7   Comprehension Questions

- Which side of the market has dominant strategies to reveal preferences truthfully in SOSM? Describe the mechanism.
- Which types of inefficiency arise in SOSM, and how are they addressed in EADAM?
- Why is TTC a strategy-proof mechanism?
- How does the MAXCU mechanism decompose an optimal fractional solution into feasible assignments?

11.8   Problems

SOSM

Consider the course allocation problem with three students $S \equiv \{s_1, s_2, s_3\}$ and three courses $C \equiv \{c_1, c_2, c_3\}$, each course having one place. The course priorities ($\succ_c$) and the student preferences ($\succ_s$) are given in table 11.17. Find a student-optimal and a course-optimal allocation with SOSM.

Table 11.17 Preferences of (a) course organizers and (b) students

(a)	$\succ_{c_1}$	$\succ_{c_2}$	$\succ_{c_3}$	(b)	$\succ_{s_1}$	$\succ_{s_2}$	$\succ_{s_3}$
	s_2	s_1	s_1		c_1	c_2	c_2
	s_1	s_2	s_2		c_2	c_1	c_3
	s_3	s_3	s_3		c_3	c_3	c_1

TTC

Apply TTC to the following sets of preferences of house owners 1 to 5 over their respective houses:

1. $h_5 \succ h_2 \succ h_1 \succ h_3 \succ h_4$
2. $h_5 \succ h_4 \succ h_3 \succ h_1 \succ h_2$
3. $h_4 \succ h_2 \succ h_3 \succ h_5 \succ h_1$
4. $h_2 \succ h_1 \succ h_5 \succ h_3 \succ h_4$
5. $h_2 \succ h_4 \succ h_1 \succ h_5 \succ h_3$

12 Outlook

There has been substantial progress in market design in the past few decades. The advent of the Internet and the availability of fast algorithms to solve computationally hard allocation problems has considerably extended the design space and has led to new types of markets which would have been impossible only 20 years ago. The theoretical models discussed in this book help one to understand when markets are efficient and when they are not. Many recent models for multi-object markets draw on the theory of linear programming and combinatorial optimization, at the same time adding to this theory in a fundamental way. This is one reason why market design has also found much attention in computer science and operations research lately.

Most models of markets in this book are normative and describe efficient markets with rational decision makers having independent and private values with quasi-linear utility functions. In the natural sciences models are evaluated by their predictive accuracy in the laboratory and in the field. Unfortunately, the predictive accuracy of some auction models is low (see for example section 4.8). For example, Bayesian Nash equilibrium strategies require strong assumptions about a common-prior type distribution. Even if this distributional information is provided by a laboratory experiment, bidders do not always maximize payoff. Loss aversion, risk aversion, spite, or ex post regret can all affect the decision making of individuals. It is even less likely that bidders would follow a Bayesian Nash equilibrium strategy in the field, where the prior information of bidders is typically asymmetric and different between bidders.

Auction designs satisfying stronger solution concepts such as dominant strategies or ex post equilibrium strategies are promising, because they don't require a common prior assumption. However, such solution concepts are quite limiting in the design. In the standard independent-private-values model, the VCG mechanism is unique and, even if we allow the social welfare to be approximated, the scope of strategy-proof approximation mechanisms is narrow. Also, the VCG mechanism is strategy-proof for independent and private values. Jehiel *et al.* (2006) showed the impossibility of ex post implementation with interdependent values in multi-parameter settings. What is more, often the characteristics of market participants and the design goals are quite different from those assumed in the academic literature.

12.1 Challenges in Market Design

Whenever a theory appears to you as the only possible one, take this as a sign that you have neither understood the theory nor the problem which it was intended to solve.

Karl Popper, 1972

In what follows we summarize a number of considerations which require us to adapt or extend existing models to provide robust market design solutions for the field.

Design goals: In the academic literature we almost always assume a utilitarian social choice function maximizing the sum of the valuations of all participants. Thus the welfare-maximizing solution might well be an allocation where all objects are assigned to a single bidder, but there are many situations where this is not a desired allocation. For example, in spectrum auctions the regulator typically wants to have sufficient competition in the downstream end-consumer market. Also, in procurement, a buyer might prefer to have multiple suppliers rather than only one and a manager has allocation constraints on the number of winners or the quantity awarded to bidders.

  The impact of such *allocation constraints* on auction designs has received little attention so far. *Revenue maximization* of the auctioneer is yet another design goal, which is much less well understood than the maximization of social welfare except for situations with a single object only. Apart from this, there are design goals, such as the anonymity of prices or the transparency of the allocation process, that are sometimes at odds with incentives for truthful bidding.

Value models: In many markets, the value of an object or a package cannot be easily assessed by a bidder. In spectrum auctions bidders spend a substantial time estimating the net present value of certain packages of licenses. Such estimates are highly uncertain, because they are based on assumptions about technological development. *Common value models* have been introduced as another extreme assumption for single-object auctions, but such models are less well understood in general compared with the independent-private-values model.

  Also, in some markets *the entire allocation matters* to a bidder and not only her allocation. Suppose that a bidder in a spectrum auction wins a third of all the licenses. If the three other competitors share the remaining spectrum licenses equally, or if all the remaining licenses go to one bidder, this has a substantial impact on the valuations. In the first case the original bidder will be the market leader in terms of spectrum; in the other, she will be the second out of two. Similarly, if car manufacturers compete for advertisement slots in sponsored search auctions then there is a negative *externality* if another car manufacturer is awarded an adjacent ad slot (Krysta *et al.*, 2010; Papadimitriou and Garcia-Molina, 2011).

  It is important to understand how bidders should bid in standard auction formats if there are allocative externalities, and also how to design auctions considering these externalities. While the VCG mechanism can still be used as a recipe in theory, it is less clear how bidders would express their preferences for many possible allocations in a succinct way using this mechanism.

In game-theoretical models, valuations are typically modeled as some function of the objects without specifying these functions further. In market design it is important to understand such value or cost models in much greater detail and then to derive appropriate bid languages. For example, in procurement markets, economies of scale and scope play a role in the cost functions of suppliers and bid languages are needed to express these cost functions succinctly (see section 7.5.1.1).

The specifics of the valuation and cost models are different across markets and carefully designed bid languages are necessary to allow bidders to express their preferences with a low number of parameters.

Utility models: A quasi-linear utility function is almost always assumed in mechanism design theory. However, often a quasi-linear utility function might not provide an appropriate model of the bidders' preferences. We have already discussed how spite, loss aversion, or ex post regret can influence bidder behavior and how models assuming payoff maximization with risk-neutral bidders might not describe bidder behavior in the field well. In many situations bidders have binding budget constraints, which makes bidding even in a VCG auction strategically difficult (Dobzinski *et al.*, 2012a). Often the model of a bidder as a single individual might be wrong: bidders in bidding firms often act on behalf of a principal.

Principal–agent relationships in bidding firms can be hard to control via budget constraints, and agents bidding in auctions might maximize value, not payoff (Bichler and Paulsen, 2017). There is also a literature on display-ad auctions and keyword-ad auctions, where bidders get a budget and their task is to spend the budget as well as possible (e.g., maximizing the number of page impressions), which differs from pure payoff maximization (Zhang *et al.*, 2014). *Non-quasi-linear utility functions* have become a topic of interest only recently and they can lead to very different strategies.

Dynamic allocation: Most models of markets consider single isolated events where all buyers and sellers are present at the same time. On the Internet there are competing markets for substitutes and often markets are run repeatedly. For example, the outcome and prices of one procurement auction might have an impact on the reservation prices of the next auction. More importantly, the matching of supply and demand is often done dynamically over time and an allocation decision at one point in time has an impact on later decisions. Dynamic mechanism design is a field of research that deals with the resulting challenges. However, models of dynamic allocation mechanisms as they are used to analyze display-ad auctions or dynamic matching markets are still in their infancy.

12.2   Going Forward

In the long term, the real test of our success will be not merely how well we understand the general principles which govern economic interactions, but how well we can bring this knowledge to bear on practical questions of microeconomic engineering.

Alvin Roth, 1991

Fundamentally, market design is a modeling exercise which requires an in-depth understanding of auction design goals, bidders' value models, and utility functions. A market design based on the wrong assumptions will most likely lead to bad outcomes. Understanding the allocation problem with the assumption of truthful bidders is an important first step in market design and, not surprisingly, it is similar to the types of mathematical programming problem found in other areas of operations research and computer science. On this level, there is no "one size that fits all", and the bid languages and allocation problems required are quite different across markets.

The question is, if and when we can draw on general principles to incentivize truthfulness among bidders. The VCG mechanism might often not be acceptable, for reasons discussed earlier. In such situations we need to restrict ourselves to weaker solution concepts. Depending on the type of prior information available to bidders, some market designs might be robust against manipulation even though they are not strategy-proof. For example, the amount of prior information about competitors that is necessary to manipulate strategically in large combinatorial auctions can be prohibitive. It is important to characterize alternative notions of stability and of robustness against manipulation in situations where strategy-proof mechanisms might not be feasible.

Although a market designer can draw on a number of principles developed in theory, each market has its own requirements. In some cases market participants insist on an open and transparent auction process, and in other cases they need anonymous clearing prices (as is the case in day-ahead electricity markets). There can be good reasons for these requirements, and a market designer often needs to strike a balance between different design goals.

This does not mean that every instance of a market is different. It is quite possible to develop robust market designs for certain types of markets which can be characterized by a set of assumptions on the bidder's value and utility functions, the auctioneer's design goals, and the procedural requirements. The challenge is to elicit and categorize these requirements and come up with good market designs for the various classes of market design problems that we can find in the field.

With new technology available, market-based coordination becomes a reality in new domains where previously a centralized decision maker had to allocate resources based on incomplete information, which often led to inefficient or unfair assignments of scarce resources. In particular, algorithmic advances in combinatorial optimization, combined with the possibility to elicit complex preferences online, allow for new types of markets, which need to be explored. The way in which we match supply and demand is a central question in the digital economy. Market design is an ongoing journey, with many interesting and intellectually challenging problems lying ahead.

Part IV

Appendices: Mathematical Optimization

A Linear Optimization

In the appendices we provide a succinct summary of relevant results from mathematical optimization, with a focus on linear and integer linear programming. Similar but more extensive treatments can be found in standard textbooks on linear programming and mathematical optimization such as Chvatal (1983), Nemhauser and Wolsey (1988), or Bertsimas and Tsitsiklis (1997).

A.1 Geometry of Linear Programs

Linear optimization (aka linear programming) refers to the problem of optimizing a linear objective function with the decision variables, $x_1, \ldots, x_n$, subject to linear equality or inequality constraints. In *canonical form* a *linear program* (LP) is given as:

$$\max \sum_{j=1}^{n} c_j x_j \qquad \text{(objective function)}$$

$$\text{s.t.} \ \sum_{j=1}^{n} a_{ij} x_j \leq b_i \qquad i = 1, \ldots, m \qquad \text{(constraints)}$$

$$x_j \geq 0, \qquad j = 1, \ldots, n \quad \text{(non-negativity conditions)}$$

where $\{a_{ij}, b_i, c_j\}$ are parameters.

A linear program can be expressed succinctly using matrices:

$$\max\{c^T x\} \quad \text{s.t.} \quad \begin{cases} Ax \leq b \\ x \geq 0 \end{cases}$$

where

$$x = \begin{pmatrix} x_1 \\ \vdots \\ x_n \end{pmatrix} \in \mathbb{R}^{n \times 1}, \qquad b = \begin{pmatrix} b_1 \\ \vdots \\ b_m \end{pmatrix} \in \mathbb{R}^{m \times 1}, \qquad c = \begin{pmatrix} c_1 \\ \vdots \\ c_n \end{pmatrix} \in \mathbb{R}^{n \times 1}$$

$$A = \begin{pmatrix} a_{11} & & \\ & \ddots & \\ & & a_{mn} \end{pmatrix} \in \mathbb{R}^{m \times n}$$

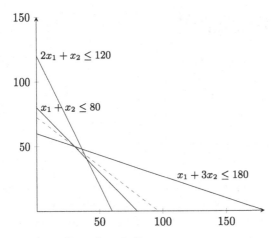

Figure A.1 Illustration of a linear program.

Note that $b \geq 0$ in canonical form. With additional slack variables the canonical form can be transformed into the normal form, $\max\{c^T x : Ax = b, x \geq 0\}$, of the LP. Note that the normal form has equality constraints and all variables are non-negative. Let's introduce some additional terminology.

Definition A.1.1 If x satisfies $Ax = b, x \geq 0$, then x is a *feasible* solution.

Definition A.1.2 A linear program (LP) is feasible if there exists a feasible solution; otherwise it is said to be *infeasible*.

Definition A.1.3 An *optimal solution* x^* is a feasible solution s.t. $c^T x^* = \max\{c^T x : Ax = b, x \geq 0\}$.

A linear program can be modeled in several forms. We can maximize or minimize an objective function and have a combination of equality and inequality constraints. Two forms are said to be equivalent if they have the same set of optimal solutions or are both infeasible or both unbounded. The linear program in example A.1.1 below is illustrated in figure A.1.

Example A.1.1 Consider the following problem:

$$\max\{3x_1 + 4x_2\}$$
$$\text{s.t.} \quad 2x_1 + 1x_2 \leq 120$$
$$1x_1 + 3x_2 \leq 180$$
$$1x_1 + 1x_2 \leq 80$$
$$x_1, x_2 \geq 0$$

The optimal solution of this LP is $(30, 50)$ with objective function value 290 (see figure A.1).

Let $P = \{x : Ax = b, \ x \geq 0\} \subseteq \mathbb{R}^n$ be the polytope defined by the constraints; then we can define a vertex of this polytope.

Definition A.1.4 The point x is a *vertex* of P if there does not exist a $y \neq 0$ s.t. $x + y$, $x - y \in P$.

We can now show that there is a vertex $x \in P$ which minimizes $c^T x$.

Theorem A.1.1 *Assume that* $\min\{c^T x : x \in P\}$ *is finite; then* $\forall x \in P$ *there exists a vertex* x' *such that* $c^T x' \leq c^T x$.

Proof. If x is a vertex, then take $x' = x$. If x is not a vertex then there exists a $y \neq 0$ such that $x + y$, $x - y \in P$. Since $A(x + y) = b$ and $A(x - y) = b$, we have $Ay = 0$. Suppose that $c^T y \leq 0$. Without loss of generality take y as positive (otherwise take $-y$). If $c^T y = 0$, choose the components of y such that $\exists j$ with $y_j < 0$. Since $y \neq 0$ and $c^T y = c^T(-y) = 0$, this must be true for either y or $-y$.

Consider $x + \lambda y$, $\lambda > 0$. We have $c^T(x + \lambda y) = c^T x + \lambda c^T y \leq c^T x$, since $c^T y$ is assumed non-positive.

Case 1: $\exists j$ such that $y_j < 0$

   As λ increases, the component y_i decreases until $x + \lambda y$ is no longer feasible. Choose $\lambda = \min_{\{j : y_j < 0\}}\{x_j / -y_j\} = x_k / -y_k$. This is the largest λ such that $x + \lambda y \geq 0$. Since $Ay = 0$, $A(x + \lambda y) = Ax + \lambda Ay = Ax = b$. So $x + \lambda y \in P$, and moreover $x + \lambda y$ has one more zero component, $(x + \lambda y)_k$, than x. Replace x by $x + \lambda y$.

Case 2: $y_j \geq 0 \ \forall j$

   By assumption, $c^T y < 0$ and $x + \lambda y$ is feasible for all $\lambda \geq 0$, since $A(x + \lambda y) = Ax + \lambda Ay = Ax = b$, and $x + \lambda y \geq x \geq 0$. But $c^T(x + \lambda y) = c^T x + \lambda c^T y \to -\infty$ as $\lambda \to \infty$, implying that the LP is unbounded, a contradiction.

Case 1 can happen at most n times, since x has n components. By induction on the number of non-zero components of x, we obtain a vertex x'.   □

The following corollaries show that every LP in standard form with a finite objective value has an optimal solution, x^*, which is a vertex.

Corollary A.1.1 *If* $\min\{c^T x : Ax = b, x \geq 0\}$ *is finite then there exists an optimal solution,* x^*, *which is a vertex.*

Proof. Suppose this is not the case. Take an optimal solution x^*. By theorem A.1.1 there exists a vertex costing no more than the vertex x^*, which must be optimal as well.   □

It can be shown that, for a linear program in standard form, if the objective function has a maximum value on the feasible region then it has this value on (at least) one of the extreme points.

A vertex of the polytope P can be computed with a submatrix A_x of A. Here A_x is a set of linearly independent columns of A as in the following example.

Example A.1.2 $A = \begin{bmatrix} 2 & 1 & 3 & 0 \\ 7 & 3 & 2 & 1 \\ 0 & 0 & 0 & 5 \end{bmatrix}$, $x = \begin{bmatrix} 2 \\ 0 \\ 1 \\ 0 \end{bmatrix}$, $A_x = \begin{bmatrix} 2 & 3 \\ 7 & 2 \\ 0 & 0 \end{bmatrix}$, and x is a vertex.

Theorem A.1.2 *Let $P = \{x : Ax = b, x \geq 0\}$. For $x \in P$, let A_x be a submatrix of A corresponding to j s.t. $x_j > 0$. Then x is a vertex iff A_x has linearly independent columns.*

Proof. Assume that x is not a vertex. Then, by definition, $\exists y \neq 0$ s.t. $x + y$, $x - y \in P$. Let A_y be the submatrix corresponding to the non-zero components of y.

As in the proof of theorem A.1.1,

$$\left.\begin{array}{r} Ax + Ay = b \\ Ax - Ay = b \end{array}\right\} \Rightarrow Ay = 0$$

Therefore, A_y has linearly dependent columns since $y \neq 0$.

Moreover,

$$\left.\begin{array}{r} x + y \geq 0 \\ x - y \geq 0 \end{array}\right\} \Rightarrow y_j = 0 \text{ whenever } x_j = 0$$

Therefore A_y is a submatrix of A_x. Since A_y is a submatrix of A_x, A_x also has linearly dependent columns.

Suppose A_x has linearly dependent columns. Then $\exists y$ such that $A_x y = 0$, $y \neq 0$. Extend y to $\mathbb{R}^n$ by adding zeros. Then $\exists y \in \mathbb{R}^n$ s.t. $Ay = 0$, $y \neq 0$ and $y_j = 0$ wherever $x_j = 0$.

Consider $y' = \lambda y$ for small $\lambda \geq 0$. Claim that $x + y'$, $x - y' \in P$, by an argument analogous to that in case 1 of the proof of theorem A.1.1 above. Hence, x is not a vertex. $\qquad\square$

Now let x be a vertex of $P = \{x : Ax = b, x \geq 0\}$. Suppose first that $|\{j : x_j > 0\}| = m$ (where A is $m \times n$). In this case we denote $B = \{j : x_j > 0\}$. Also let $A_B = A_x$; we use this notation not only for A and B but also for x and for other sets of indices. Then A_B is a square matrix whose columns are linearly independent (by theorem A.1.2), so it is non-singular. Therefore we can express x as $x_j = 0$ if $j \notin B$ and, since $A_B x_B = b$, it follows that $x_B = A_B^{-1} b$. The variables corresponding to B will be called *basic*. The others will be referred to as *non-basic*. The set of indices corresponding to non-basic variables is denoted by $N = \{1, \ldots, n\} \setminus B$. Thus, we can write the above as $x_B = A_B^{-1} b$ and $x_N = 0$.

Without loss of generality we will assume that A has full row rank: $\mathrm{rank}(A) = m$. Otherwise either there is a redundant constraint in the system $Ax = b$ (and we can remove it) or the system has no solution at all.

If $|\{j : x_j > 0\}| < m$, we can augment A_x with additional linearly independent columns until it is an $m \times m$ submatrix of A of full rank, which we will denote A_B. In other words, although there may be fewer than m positive components in x, it is convenient always to have a *basis* B such that $|B| = m$ and A_B is non-singular. This enables us always to express x as we did before, $x_N = 0$, $x_B = A_B^{-1} b$.

Thus x is a vertex of P iff there is a $B \subseteq \{1, \ldots, n\}$ such that $|B| = m$ and

1. $x_N = 0$ for $N = \{1, \ldots, n\} - B$,
2. A_B is non-singular,
3. $x_B = A_B^{-1} b \geq 0$.

In this case we say that x is a *basic feasible solution*. Note that a vertex can have several basic feasible solutions corresponding to it (by augmenting $\{j : x_j > 0\}$ in different ways). However, a basis might not lead to any basic feasible solution since $A_B^{-1}b$ is not necessarily non-negative.

Example A.1.3 Consider the system of relations

$$x_1 + x_2 + x_3 = 5$$
$$2x_1 - x_2 + 2x_3 = 1$$
$$x_1, x_2, x_3 \geq 0$$

We can select as a basis $B = \{1, 2\}$. Thus, $N = \{3\}$ and

$$A_B = \begin{pmatrix} 1 & 1 \\ 2 & -1 \end{pmatrix}, \qquad A_B^{-1} = \begin{pmatrix} \frac{1}{3} & \frac{1}{3} \\ \frac{2}{3} & -\frac{1}{3} \end{pmatrix}, \qquad A_B^{-1}b = \begin{pmatrix} 2 \\ 3 \end{pmatrix}$$
$$x = (2, 3, 0)$$

An upper bound on the number of vertices of the polytope P is of the constraints $\binom{n}{m}$. This number is exponential and upper-bounded by n^m. However, the number of basic feasible solutions is much smaller because most basic solutions of the system $Ax = b$ (which we have counted) are not feasible, that is, they do not satisfy $x \geq 0$.

A.2   Feasibility

An important question is the feasibility of linear programs of the form $Ax = b$, $x \geq 0$. As the objective function has no effect on the feasibility of the program, we ignore it for now. We restrict our attention to systems of equations and ignore the non-negativity constraints.

Example A.2.1 Consider the following system of equations:

$$x_1 + x_2 + x_3 = 6$$
$$2x_1 + 3x_2 + x_3 = 8$$
$$2x_1 + x_2 + 3x_3 = 0$$

and the linear combinations

$$-4 \times (x_1 + x_2 + x_3 = 6)$$
$$+1 \times (2x_1 + 3x_2 + x_3 = 8)$$
$$+1 \times (2x_1 + x_2 + 3x_3 = 0)$$

The linear combinations result in the equation

$$0x_1 + 0x_2 + 0x_3 = -16$$

which means that the system of equations has no feasible solution.

Actually, if a system has no solution, there is always a vector y, as in our example, $y = (-4, 1, 1)$, which proves that the system has no solution. In other words, one of the following is true for the system $Ax = b$:

1. there is an x such that $Ax = b$;
2. there is a y such that $A^T y = 0$ but $y^T b < 0$.

Farkas' lemma establishes an equivalent result for $Ax = b, x \geq 0$, which we state without a proof.

Lemma A.2.1 (Farkas' lemma) *Exactly one of the following is true for the system $Ax = b, x \geq 0$:*

1. *there is an x such that $Ax = b, x \geq 0$;*
2. *there is a y such that $A^T y \geq 0$ but $b^T y < 0$.*

One can show the same for the canonical form:

Theorem A.2.1 *Exactly one of the following is true for the system $Ax \leq b$:*

1. *there is an x such that $Ax \leq b$;*
2. *there is a $y \geq 0$ such that $A^T y = 0$ but $y^T b < 0$.*

The intuition behind part 2 of theorem A.2.1 lies in the proof that both cannot happen. The contradiction $0 = 0x = (y^T A)x = y^T (Ax) = y^T b < 0$ is obtained if $A^T y = 0$ and $y^T b < 0$.

A.3   Duality Theory

Let us now discuss duality in linear programming. Duality can be motivated by the problem of trying to find lower bounds on the value of the optimal solution to a linear programming problem (if the problem is a maximization problem then we would like to find upper bounds). We consider problems in the following standard form:

$$\min\{c^T x\}$$
$$\text{s.t.} \quad Ax = b$$
$$x \geq 0$$

Suppose we wanted to obtain the best possible upper bound on a cost function. By multiplying each equation $A_m x = b_m$ by some number y_m and summing the resulting equations, we obtain $y^T Ax = b^T y$. If we impose that the coefficient of x_j in the resulting inequality is less or equal to c_j then $b^T y$ must be a lower bound on the optimal value, since x_j is constrained to be non-negative. To get the best possible lower bound, we want to solve the following problem:

$$\max\{b^T y\}$$
$$\text{s.t.} \quad A^T y \leq c$$

This is another linear program. We call this the *dual* of the original LP, the *primal*. As we have just argued, solving this dual LP will give us a lower bound on the optimum value of the primal problem. *Weak duality* says precisely this: if we denote the optimum value of the primal by z, $z = \min(c^T x)$, and the optimum value of the dual by w then $w \leq z$. We can use Farkas' lemma to prove *strong duality*, which says that these quantities are in fact equal. We will also see that, in general, the dual of the dual is the primal problem.

Example A.3.1 Consider

$$z = \min\{x_1 + 2x_2 + 4x_3\}$$
$$\text{s.t.} \quad x_1 + x_2 + 2x_3 = 5$$
$$2x_1 + x_2 + 3x_3 = 8$$

The first equality gives a lower bound of 5 on the optimum value z, since $x_1 + 2x_2 + 4x_3 \geq x_1 + x_2 + 2x_3 = 5$ because of non-negativity of the x_i. We can get an even better lower bound by taking three times the first equality minus the second equality. This gives $x_1 + 2x_2 + 3x_3 = 7 \leq x_1 + 2x_2 + 4x_3$, implying a lower bound of 7 on z. For $x = \begin{pmatrix} 3 \\ 2 \\ 0 \end{pmatrix}$, the objective function is precisely 7, implying optimality. The mechanism of generating lower bounds is formalized by the dual linear program:

$$\max\{5y_1 + 8y_2\}$$
$$\text{s.t.} \quad y_1 + 2y_2 \leq 1$$
$$y_1 + y_2 \leq 2$$
$$2y_1 + 3y_2 \leq 4$$

Here y_1 represents the multiplier for the first constraint and y_2 the multiplier for the second constraint, This LP's objective function also achieves a maximum value of 7, at $y = \begin{pmatrix} 3 \\ -1 \end{pmatrix}$.

We now formalize the notion of duality. Let (P) and (D) be the following pair of dual linear programs:

$$(P) \quad z = \min\{c^T x : Ax = b, x \geq 0\}$$
$$(D) \quad w = \max\{b^T y : A^T y \leq c\}.$$

The *primal* linear program is (P) and the *dual* linear program is (D).

If one formulates (D) as a linear program in standard form (i.e., in the same form as (P)), the dual of (D) can be seen to be equivalent to the original primal (P). In any statement, we may thus replace the roles of primal and dual without affecting the statement. We have the following results relating w and z.

Lemma A.3.1 (Weak duality) *If x is a feasible solution for the primal minimization problem with objective function value z, and y is a feasible solution for the dual maximization problem with objective function value w, then weak duality implies $z \geq w$.*

Proof. Suppose that x is primal feasible and y is dual feasible. Then, $c^T x \geq y^T A x = y^T b$; thus $z = \min\{c^T x : Ax = b, x \geq 0\} \geq \max\{b^T y : A^T y \leq c\} = w.$ $\square$

Note that both the primal and the dual might be infeasible. To prove a stronger version of the *weak duality lemma,* let's revisit a corollary of *Farkas' lemma* (lemma A.2.1):

Corollary A.3.1 *Exactly one of the following is true:*

1. $\exists x' : A'x' \leq b'$;
2. $\exists y' \geq 0 : (A')^T y' = 0$ *and* $(b')^T y' < 0$.

Theorem A.3.1 (Strong duality) *If* (P) *and* (D) *are feasible then* $z = w$.

Proof. We need to show only that $z \leq w$. Assume without loss of generality (by duality) that P is feasible. If (P) is unbounded then, by *weak duality*, we have that $z = w = -\infty$. Suppose (P) is bounded, and let x^* be an optimal solution, i.e., $Ax^* = b$, $x^* \geq 0$, and $c^T x^* = z$. We claim that $\exists y$ s.t. $A^T y \leq c$ and $b^T y \geq z$. If so, we are done. Suppose no such y exists. Then, by the preceding corollary, with $A' = \left(\begin{smallmatrix} A^T \\ -b^T \end{smallmatrix} \right)$, $b' = \left(\begin{smallmatrix} c \\ -z \end{smallmatrix} \right)$, $x' = y$, $y' = \left(\begin{smallmatrix} x \\ \lambda \end{smallmatrix} \right)$, $\exists x \geq 0$, $\lambda \geq 0$ such that

$$Ax = \lambda b \qquad \text{and} \qquad c^T x < \lambda z$$

We have two cases.

- Case 1: $\lambda \neq 0$. Since we can normalize by λ we can assume that $\lambda = 1$. This means that $\exists x \geq 0$ such that $Ax = b$ and $c^T x < z$. But this contradicts the optimality of x^*.
- Case 2: $\lambda = 0$. This means that $\exists x \geq 0$ such that $Ax = 0$ and $c^T x < 0$. If this is the case then $\forall \mu \geq 0$, $x^* + \mu x$ is feasible for (P), and its cost is $c^T(x^* + \mu x) = c^T x^* + \mu(c^T x) < z$, which contradicts the optimality of (P). ☐

With a number of rules a primal (P) can be transformed to the dual (D). If (P) is a minimization problem then (D) is a maximization problem. If (P) is a maximization problem then (D) is a minimization problem. In general, using the rules for transforming a linear program into standard form, we have that the dual of the problem (P) defined by

$$z = \min \left\{ c_1 x_1 + c_2 x_2 + c_3 x_3 \right\}$$
$$\begin{aligned} \text{s.t.} \quad & A_{11} x_1 + A_{12} x_2 + A_{13} x_3 = b_1 & (y_1) \\ & A_{21} x_1 + A_{22} x_2 + A_{23} x_3 \geq b_2 & (y_2) \\ & A_{31} x_1 + A_{32} x_2 + A_{33} x_3 \leq b_3 & (y_3) \\ & x_1 \geq 0, x_2 \leq 0, x_3 \in \mathbb{R} \end{aligned}$$

is (D), given by

$$w = \max \left\{ b_1 y_1 + b_2 y_2 + b_3 y_3 \right\}$$
$$\begin{aligned} \text{s.t.} \quad & A_{11} y_1 + A_{21} y_2 + A_{31} y_3 \leq c_1 & (x_1) \\ & A_{12} y_1 + A_{22} y_2 + A_{32} y_3 \geq c_2 & (x_2) \\ & A_{13} y_1 + A_{23} y_2 + A_{33} y_3 = c_3 & (x_3) \\ & y_1 \in \mathbb{R}, y_2 \geq 0, y_3 \leq 0 \end{aligned}$$

Table A.1 Rules for constructing a dual

Primal (P)	$\rightarrow$	Dual (D)
max	$\rightarrow$	min
constraint i	$\rightarrow$	variable y_i
$\leq$	$\rightarrow$	$y_i \geq 0$
$\geq$	$\rightarrow$	$y_i \leq 0$
$=$	$\rightarrow$	$y_i \in \mathbb{R}$
variable x_j	$\rightarrow$	constraint j
$x_j \geq 0$	$\rightarrow$	$\geq$
$x_j \leq 0$	$\rightarrow$	$\leq$
$x_j \in \mathbb{R}$	$\rightarrow$	$=$

Complementary slackness conditions are convenient for thinking about the optimality of linear programs. Again, let (P) and (D) be as follows:

$$(P) \qquad z = \min\{c^T x : Ax = b, x \geq 0\}$$
$$(D) \qquad w = \max\{b^T y : A^T y \leq c\},$$

and let x be feasible in (P) and y be feasible in (D). Then, by weak duality, we know that $c^T x \geq b^T y$. We call the difference $c^T x - b^T y$ the *duality gap*. Then we have that the duality gap is zero iff x is optimal in (P) and y is optimal in (D). That is, the duality gap can serve as a good measure of how close a feasible x and y are to the optimal solutions for (P) and (D).

A few simple rules to convert (P) into (D) and vice versa are summarized in table A.1. It is convenient to write the dual of a linear program as

$$(D) \qquad w = \max\{b^T y : A^T y + s = c \quad \text{for some} \quad s \geq 0\}$$

Then we can write the duality gap as follows:

$$c^T x - b^T y = c^T x - x^T A^T y$$
$$= x^T (c - A^T y)$$
$$= x^T s$$

since $A^T y + s = c$.

The following theorem, A.3.2, allows us to check the optimality of a primal and/or a dual solution.

Theorem A.3.2 (Complementary slackness) *Let x^*, (y^*, s^*) be feasible for (P), (D) respectively. The following are equivalent:*

1. *x^* is an optimal solution to (P) and (y^*, s^*) is an optimal solution to (D);*
2. *$(s^*)^T x^* = 0$;*
3. *$x_j^* s_j^* = 0, \forall j = 1, \ldots, n$;*
4. *if $s_j^* > 0$ then $x_j^* = 0$.*

Proof. Suppose part 1 holds; then, by strong duality, $c^T x^* = b^T y^*$. Since $c = A^T y^* + s^*$ and $Ax^* = b$, we get $(y^*)^T Ax^* + (s^*)^T x^* = (x^*)^T A^T y^*$ and thus $(s^*)^T x^* = 0$ (i.e., part 2 holds). It follows, since x_j^*, $s_j^* \geq 0$, that $x_j^* s_j^* = 0$, $\forall j = 1, \ldots, n$ (i.e., part 3 holds). Hence, if $s_j^* > 0$ then $x_j^* = 0$, $\forall j = 1, \ldots, n$ (i.e., part 4 holds). It can be shown that the converse holds as well, which completes the proof. □

In example A.3.1, the complementary slackness equations corresponding to the primal solution $x = (3, 2, 0)^T$ would be:

$$y_1 + 2y_2 = 1$$
$$y_1 + y_2 = 2$$

Note that this implies that $y_1 = 3$ and $y_2 = -1$. Since this solution satisfies the other constraint of the dual, y is dual feasible, proving that x is an optimum solution to the primal (and therefore y is an optimum solution to the dual).

A.4   Integrality of Linear Programs

In this book, integer linear programs are typically used to model discrete resource allocation problems. Integer variables are used to determine whether an object or a set of objects is allocated to a bidder. Linear programs do not yield integer solutions in general; we discuss algorithms for linear and integer linear programs in Appendix B.1. Integer linear programs are non-convex and usually much harder to solve. Sometimes, however, the linear programming relaxation of an integer linear program does yield integer solutions. For example, this is the case for the assignment problems discussed in section 8.1. A sufficient condition for a linear program to yield integer solutions is the total unimodularity of the constraint matrix A and the integrality of b.

Definition (Unimodular matrix)   A square integer matrix A is called *unimodular* if $|\det(A)| = 1$. A matrix A is called *totally unimodular* if every square non-singular submatrix of A is unimodular.

Theorem A.4.1   *Let A be an integer $m \times n$ matrix. If A is totally unimodular then, for all integer m-vectors b, all vertices of the convex polytope defined by $Ax = b$, $x \geq 0$, are integer.*

The following lemma provides a convenient means to check for total unimodularity.

Lemma A.4.1   *Let A be an integer matrix with coefficients from $\{-1, 0, 1\}$. Assume that the rows of A can be partitioned into two sets R_1 and R_2, such that the following hold:*

- *if a column has two entries of the same sign, their rows are in different sets;*
- *if a column has two entries of different signs, their rows are in the same set.*

Then, A is totally unimodular.

A few remarks follow.

- The total unimodularity of the constraint matrix A is a *sufficient* (and, for inequality constraints, also *necessary*) condition for a linear program to give integer solutions, provided that the constraint vector b is integer.
- A class of graphs, called *flow networks*, has the property that their incidence matrix A is *totally unimodular*. Therefore, integral solutions for this class of graphs can be obtained using an LP. This is an alternative to specialized graph-theoretic algorithms, such as min-cut/max-flow, min-cost flow, matching, transportation problem, multi-commodity flow, linear assignments, and many others.

B   Algorithms and Complexity

Most allocation problems in part III of the book can be modeled as mixed integer linear programs. We now discuss algorithms for pure linear programs and integer linear programs. While pure LPs can be solved in polynomial time, integer linear programs are computationally hard, as we will see. First, though, we introduce computational complexity and important complexity classes.

B.1   Computational Complexity

Complexity theory is important for market design, because many allocation and payment rules are computationally hard integer programming problems. For very practical reasons, it is important to understand whether a problem is tractable and we can hope to find exact solutions in a reasonable time. Sorting a series of bids by price for a single-object auction is a computationally simple task. In contrast, the WDP of a combinatorial auction or some allocation problems described in section 7.5 are computationally hard problems, where we cannot hope for a fast and exact algorithm. A complexity class is a set of problems of related complexity (see Papadimitriou (1993) for an extensive treatment). Here, we introduce basic terminology and restrict ourselves to the two well-known complexity classes P and NP.

A *decision problem* is a question in a formal system with a yes-or-no answer. For example, the decision version of the WDP in a combinatorial auction refers to a WDP in which the auctioneer wants to know only if there is an allocation with a revenue larger than a particular amount. In contrast, an *optimization problem* is the problem of finding the best solution from all feasible solutions. There are techniques for transforming optimization problems into decision problems, and vice versa, that do not significantly change the computational difficulty of these problems. For this reason, complexity theory has typically focused on decision problems.

For decision problems in the class P, there are algorithms where the "yes" instances can be accepted in polynomial time by a deterministic Turing machine. The worst-case running time of a polynomial algorithm is of order $\mathcal{O}(g)$ for some polynomial g. The *big-O notation* $\mathcal{O}(g(x))$ is used to indicate an asymptotic upper bound $g(x)$ for some function $f(x)$ of the input size x, up to a constant factor, and describes the worst-case run time of an algorithm. In other words, the complexity class P comprises those computational tasks that admit an efficient algorithm, one that runs in polynomial time.

Definition B.1.1 (Big-O notation) Let x describe the size of the input, and $f(x)$ the time complexity. We write $f(x) \in \mathcal{O}(g(x))$ if there exists a positive real number $r > 0$ and an input size x_0 such that $f(x) \leq rg(x)$ for all $x > x_0$.

The abbreviation NP refers to "non-deterministic polynomial time". The class of problems in NP can be described as the set of decision problems where "yes" answers can be verified in polynomial time by a deterministic Turing machine, and the "yes" instances can be accepted in polynomial time by a non-deterministic Turing machine.

A non-deterministic Turing machine is a Turing machine with an added feature of non-determinism, which allows it to have multiple possible future actions from a given state. It is a theoretical entity, not available as a computing device today. Since deterministic Turing machines are special non-deterministic Turing machines, each problem in P is also member of the class NP. Often NPO is used to describe the class of optimization problems corresponding to the decision problems in NP.

The complexity class NP contains many problems that we would like to solve efficiently but for which no efficient algorithm is known, such as the Boolean satisfiability problem (SAT), the Hamiltonian path problem, and the vertex cover problem. Actually, SAT was the first problem for which Cook (1971) showed that any problem in NP can be reduced in polynomial time by a deterministic Turing machine to the problem of determining whether a Boolean formula is satisfiable. A problem p is NP-hard if every other problem in NP can be transformed into p in polynomial time. Such a problem is at least as hard as the hardest problems in NP. A problem is NP-complete if it is in NP and NP-hard. The class of NP-complete problems contains the hardest problems in NP. Whether a problem is NP-hard can be shown via polynomial reduction from a known NP-complete problem. A polynomial-time reduction is a method of solving one problem by means of a subroutine for solving a different problem, which uses polynomial time.

A problem is said to be strongly NP-complete (NP-complete in the strong sense), if it remains so even when all its numerical parameters are bounded by a polynomial in the length of the input. A problem is said to be strongly NP-hard if a strongly NP-complete problem has a polynomial reduction.

It is generally believed, but has not been proven, that the class of polynomial-time algorithms P is different from the class NP. In other words, there are problems in NP which cannot be solved in polynomial time unless P = NP. The question of whether P $\neq$ NP is one of the most important open questions in theoretical computer science. These two complexity classes help us to characterize linear and integer linear programming problems. Linear programs can be solved in polynomial time using the ellipsoid method, while general integer linear programs are NP-hard.

B.2   Algorithms for Linear Programs

A number of algorithms for solving linear programming problems have been suggested. The *Simplex algorithm* (Dantzig, 1998) solves linear programming problems by focusing on basic feasible solutions. The basic idea is to start from some vertex and look at the adjacent vertices. If an improvement in cost is possible by moving to an adjacent vertices then we do so. Otherwise, the algorithm can be terminated.

In each iteration of the Simplex algorithm, we need a partition (B, N) of the index set $\{1, 2, \ldots, n\}$, with m indices in B, such that the basis matrix A_B is non-singular and $A_B^{-1} b \geq 0$. Then we let the m basic variables be $x_B = A_B^{-1} b$ and the rest of the (non-basic) variables be zeros. This gives us the basic feasible solution needed.

The main constraint $Ax \leq b$ is equivalent to $Ax + Is = b$ for $s \geq 0$. By adding the slack variable s, we convert the LP into the standard form with m equations and $n + m$ variables. The coefficient matrix becomes $\hat{A} = [A \ I]$, which is $m \times (n + m)$. It is often easy to construct an initial basic feasible solution by simply setting $x = 0$ as the non-basic variables and $s = b \geq 0$ as the m basic variables. In this way, we satisfy the equation $Ax + Is = b$ and in fact obtain a basic feasible solution. This is true because the corresponding basis matrix is the identity matrix and $\hat{A}_B^{-1} b = I * b = b \geq 0$.

We can start with such a basic feasible solution, corresponding to a basis B, and, at each iteration, try to improve the cost of the solution by removing one variable from the basis and replacing it by another until no further improvement is possible. A detailed description of the Simplex algorithm can be found in Bertsimas and Tsitsiklis (1997).

The Simplex algorithm was actually proposed in the 1940s and, although it has performed very well in practice, is known to run in exponential time in the worst case. The first polynomial-time algorithm solving linear programs was the *ellipsoid algorithm* of Khachiyan (1980). Though it has a polynomial runtime in the worst case, the algorithm is inefficient compared with the Simplex algorithm, on average, and is rarely used in practice.

In 1984, Karmarkar (1984) presented another polynomial-time algorithm for linear programming. His algorithm avoids the combinatorial complexity (inherent in the Simplex algorithm) of the vertices, edges, and faces of the polyhedron by staying inside the polyhedron. His algorithm led to a variety of algorithms for linear programming based on similar ideas; these are known as *interior point methods*.

B.3   Algorithms for Integer Linear Programs

A computationally hard class of linear optimization problems arises from applications in which some decision variables are required to take on integer values. An integer programming problem is a mathematical optimization or feasibility program in which some of or all the variables are restricted to be integers (see Nemhauser and Wolsey (1988) for an extensive treatment). Combinatorial optimization deals with finding an optimal set of objects from a finite set of objects, and such problems can typically be modeled as integer programs. An important subclass is the mixed integer (linear) programming problem (MIP), which has the following form:

$$\min \left\{ c^T x + d^T y \ : \ Ax + By \leq g, \ x \in \mathbb{Z}_+^n, y \in \mathbb{R}_+^p \right\} \tag{1}$$

Possibly the most widespread and effective methodology for solving MIPs is the *branch-and-bound* method. In a branch-and-bound algorithm we form relaxed versions of the MIP, in which some integer variables are fixed at certain integer values while the others are allowed to vary as continuous, real-valued, variables. Since the number of different ways in which we can fix some variables and relax others is exponential in the number of integer variables, it is clear that we cannot examine all possible relaxations for any but the smallest cases. Binary programs (with only binary variables) can be seen as a subclass of MIPs, and it is straightforward to reduce the satisfiability problem (SAT) in polynomial time to binary programs, proving that binary programs are NP-hard to solve (see section B.1). Binary integer programming belongs to the class of NP-complete problems, although there are subclasses of problems which can be solved in polynomial time.

Branch-and-bound is a strategy for performing a systematic search of the set of possible relaxations, recursively partitioning the solution space and calculating an upper/lower bound on all solutions in the partitions. These bounds avoid exploring a large part of the potential search space. They keep track of the best feasible solution found to date. If the algorithm finds that the solution of a particular relaxation is not feasible but decides that some variant on this relaxation could lead to a feasible solution that beats the best one found so far, it breaks up its feasible set into separate regions and formulates a relaxed version for each subproblem so generated. This is the "branching" part of the procedure.

The branch-and-bound algorithm can be illustrated by means of a tree, in which the nodes correspond to different relaxations of the problem. The root node is the relaxed problem, in which all integrality restrictions are ignored, while other nodes may have child nodes, generated by the branching procedure just described.

To give more details on the branch-and-bound approach, we introduce some notation. Let z_U denote an upper bound on the optimal objective value z_P of the integer program P. The highest objective value (z_L) in a maximization problem is obtained among all feasible points (x, y) of the MIP that have been encountered so far in the search process. For a given node N in the branch-and-bound tree, we use $F(N)$ to denote the feasible set for the subproblem at node N. This will be a subset of the feasible set for an MIP and will include the integrality constraints. We use $R(N)$ to denote the *relaxed* feasible region for node N, which is specified by the same set of constraints as $F(N)$ except that the integrality requirements are discarded.

Let z_{RP}^N be the optimal objective value calculated by solving the relaxation at node N (i.e., maximizing the objective over $R(N)$ and z_P^N be the objective values of the non-relaxed problem (i.e., the maximum over $F(N)$). Since $F(N) \subset R(N)$, we certainly have that $z_P^N \leq z_{RP}^N$. Let z_L^N be a lower bound on z_P^N that is known prior to solving the problem at node N. If the feasible region for the relaxation at node N is empty, we set $z_{RP}^N = 0$.

The *active set* Q is a list of relaxed problems that have been generated by the branching procedure but not yet solved. We use (x^*, y^*) to denote the current guess at the solution of an MIP. Using this notation, we give pseudo-code for the branch-and-bound procedure in algorithm 13.

---

0. *Initialize:* $Q \leftarrow P$, with integrality constraints ignored; $z_U \leftarrow 0$; $z_L \leftarrow 0$.
1. *Select:* Choose problem $N \in Q$ and delete it from Q.
2. *Evaluate:* Solve the relaxation of N (that is, maximize $f(x, y)$ over $R(N)$) to obtain z_{RP}^N. If the problem is infeasible ($z_{RP}^N = 0$), go to step 1, else let (x^N, y^N) be the solution obtained at this node.
3. *Prune:* If $z_{RP}^N \leq z_L$, go to step 1. If $x^N \notin Z_+^n$, go to step 4, else set $z_L \leftarrow z_{RP}^N (= z_P^N)$, $(x^*, y^*) \leftarrow (x^N, y^N)$, and delete from Q all relaxed problems M for which $z_U^M \leq z_L$. Go to step 1.
4. *Divide:* Form k new problems $N^1, N^2, \ldots, N^k$ by dividing the feasible region $F(N)$ into k parts such that $\cup_{i=1}^k F(N^i) = F(N)$. Assign a value of $z_U^{N^i}$ for each $i = 1, 2, \ldots, k$; for example, $z_U^{N^i} = z_{RP}^N$. Add the problems N^1, $N^2, \ldots, N^k$ to the active set Q. Go to step 1.

Algorithm 13 The branch-and-bound algorithm (for maximization problems)

The *Divide* step is commonly handled by simple branching, in which we select a component x_i^N of the solution of the relaxed problem at node N that is not integral, and define the child problems N^i as having the same constraints as N except that x_i is restricted to certain integer values.

Example B.3.1 Let's look at a simple maximization problem to see how the *Divide* step works:

$$\max\{8x_1 + 5x_2\}$$
$$\text{s.t.} \quad x_1 + x_2 \leq 6$$
$$9x_1 + 5x_2 \leq 45$$
$$x_1, x_2 \geq 0$$
$$x_1, x_2 \in \mathbb{Z}$$

The associated LP is

$$\text{LP}(1): \quad \max\{8x_1 + 5x_2\}$$
$$\text{s.t.} \quad x_1 + x_2 \leq 6$$
$$9x_1 + 5x_2 \leq 45$$
$$x_1, x_2 \geq 0$$

The optimal solution of LP(1) is $x^1 = (3.75, 2.25)$ with $z_{RP}^1 = 41.25$; $z_{RP}^1 > z_L$, and x^1 does not satisfy the integer restrictions. We can choose any variable either x_1 or x_2 (neither satisfies the integer restriction at present) for branching. Let us choose x_1.

Then

$$LP(2): \quad \max\{8x_1 + 5x_2\}$$
$$\text{s.t.} \quad x_1 + x_2 \le 6$$
$$9x_1 + 5x_2 \le 45$$
$$x_1 \le \lfloor x_1^k \rfloor = 3$$
$$x_1, x_2 \ge 0$$

and

$$LP(3): \quad \max\{8x_1 + 5x_2\}$$
$$\text{s.t.} \quad x_1 + x_2 \le 6$$
$$9x_1 + 5x_2 \le 45$$
$$x_1 \ge \lceil x_1^k \rceil = 4$$
$$x_2 \ge 0$$

The optimal solution of LP(2) is $x^2 = (3, 3)$ with $z_{RP}^2 = 39$. Since $\lfloor z_{RP}^2 \rfloor > z_L = 0$ and x^2 satisfies the integer restriction, update z_L by 39 and "fathom" the node 2 (i.e., fully explore it so that it can then be abandoned). The next node in the list is node 3. The optimal solution of LP(3) is $x^3 = (4, 1.8)$ and $z_{RP}^3 = 41$.

Now $z_{RP}^3 > z_L = 39$ and x^3 is not integer, so we branch node 3 to yield two new candidate problems. The branching is done via the variable x_2, as this time it is not integer-valued in the optimal solution of LP(3). The branch-and-bound continues by solving the new candidate problems.

Sophisticated algorithms for MIPs include a number of enhancements over the branch-and-bound algorithm. These algorithms add additional constraints (aka cutting planes or cuts) during the process (*branch-and-cut*) or they generate columns dynamically without having to set up the full problem from the start (*branch-and-price*).

Cutting planes are constraints which can be added to the LP relaxation without excluding any integer feasible solutions. Cutting planes are useful because they reduce the gap between the LP relaxation and the integer optimal solution. Branch-and-cut involves running a branch-and-bound algorithm and using cutting planes to tighten the linear programming relaxations. The method is a hybrid of branch-and-bound and column generation methods.

Branch-and-price is a branch-and-bound method in which, at each node of the search tree, columns may be added to the LP relaxation. The approach is based on the observation that, for large problems, most columns will be non basic and have their corresponding variable equal to zero in any optimal solution. Thus, the large majority of the columns are irrelevant for solving the problem. A branch-and-price algorithm often begins by reformulating the problem, in a way which gives better bounds in the relaxation. The so-called pricing problem is solved to find columns that can enter the basis and improve the objective function value. Most branch-and-price algorithms are specific to a problem. If cutting planes are used to tighten the LP relaxations within a branch-and-price algorithm, the method is known as branch-price-and-cut.

B.4   Approximation Algorithms

Approximation algorithms are algorithms to find suboptimal solutions to optimization problems (see Vazirani (2003) for an extensive treatment). They are often associated with NP-hard problems, because it is unlikely that there will be polynomial-time exact algorithms solving such problems. Unlike in an heuristic approach, one wants provable lower bounds on the solution quality and provable runtime bounds.

Definition B.4.1 (Approximation algorithm) A ρ-approximation algorithm $\mathcal{A}$ is an algorithm for which it can be proven that the solution of $\mathcal{A}$ is not further away from the optimal value OPT than a factor ρ.

Let's provide a simple greedy algorithm for the well-known 0/1 knapsack problem, which provides a 2-approximation.

Definition B.4.2 (The 0/1 knapsack problem) A thief robbing a store finds n items. The ith item a_i is worth v_i and weighs w_i, where v_i and w_i are integers. He wants to take as valuable a load as possible, but he can carry at most W pounds in his knapsack for some integer W. He can either take a given item or not. Which items should he take?

In a simple greedy algorithm, we can sort the items in non-increasing order of the ratio v_i/w_i. The complexity is in $\mathcal{O}(n \log n)$ for sorting and $\mathcal{O}(n)$ for the linear search, and therefore $\mathcal{O}(n \log n)$ is the overall complexity. The algorithm is optimal if fractional assignments are allowed but it can be arbitrarily bad for integer assignments.

To see this, consider an item with weight 1 and value 2, and another item with size 100 and profit 100, for a knapsack with size 100. The algorithm would pick the first item, because the ratio $v_i/w_i = 2$, while the optimal solution would have a value of 100.

A simple extension of the algorithm gives an approximation ratio of $\rho = 2$ (see algorithm 14):

---

1. Sort the items in non-increasing order of the ratio v_i/w_i.
2. Add items until we find an item i such that $\sum_{k=1}^{i} w_i > W$.
3. Pick the better of the two sets $\{a_1, a_2, \ldots, a_{i-1}\}$ and $\{a_i\}$.

Algorithm 14 Greedy knapsack algorithm

Theorem B.4.1 *The greedy knapsack algorithm is a 2-approximation for the 0/1 knapsack problem.*

Proof. The greedy knapsack algorithm selects a set of items with total weight W_a. The quantity OPT is the sum of the values in the optimal solution to the 0/1 knapsack problem. If the solution of the greedy knapsack algorithm is suboptimal then we must have some leftover space $W - W_a$ in the knapsack. If one could also assign fractions of an item then, by adding $(W - W_a)v_i/a_i$ to the knapsack value from the greedy algorithm, we would either match or exceed OPT. Therefore, either $\sum_{k=1}^{i-1} v_k \geq \frac{1}{2}OPT$ or $p_i \geq (W - W_a)v_i/a_i \geq \frac{1}{2}OPT$. $\square$

The approximation ratio $\rho = 2$ is not the best performance guarantee for the knapsack problem, though. The factor ρ is called a *relative* performance guarantee. In contrast, an *absolute* performance guarantee is described as $(OPT - c) \le f(x) \le (OPT + c)$. Some NP-hard problems can be approximated within any factor ρ, while others are impossible to approximate within any constant or even polynomial factor unless P = NP. Problems that are NP-hard are often modeled as integer programs, and many approximation algorithms emerge from the linear programming relaxation of the integer program. Note that some approximation algorithms have polynomial but impractical run times, and for some the approximation ratio is very low.

B.4.1 Complexity Classes

In complexity theory (see also appendix section B.1) the class APX is the set of NPO optimization problems that allows polynomial-time approximation algorithms with approximation ratio (aka approximation factor) bounded by a constant (aka *constant-factor approximation algorithm*). In simple terms, problems in this class have efficient (i.e., polynomial-time) algorithms that can find a solution within some fixed percentage ρ of the optimal solution.

MAX-3SAT is an example of an APX-complete problem. It is a variation of the boolean satisfiability problem in which we have a boolean formula in conjunctive normal form and every clause contains at most three variables. The problem is to find the maximum number of clauses that can be simultaneously satisfied by a single assignment of true and false values. The randomized Karloff–Zwick algorithm runs in polynomial time and satisfies $\ge 7/8$ of the clauses (Karloff and Zwick, 1997). Similarly, the maximum-independent-set problem and minimum-vertex-cover problem are APX-complete.

If there is an algorithm for solving an optimization problem which is polynomial in the input size within every fixed percentage ε greater than zero, then the problem is said to have a *polynomial-time approximation scheme* (PTAS). The PTAS is a subset of APX. Unless P $\ne$ NP, it can be shown that there are problems that are in APX but not in PTAS, i.e., problems that can be approximated within some constant factor but not every constant factor.

Definition B.4.3 (Polynomial-time approximation scheme) A polynomial-time approximation scheme (PTAS) is a family of algorithms $\{\mathcal{A}_\varepsilon\}$ where there is an algorithm for each $\varepsilon > 0$ such that $\mathcal{A}_\varepsilon$ is a $(1 + \varepsilon)$-approximation algorithm for minimization problems or a $(1 - \varepsilon)$-approximation algorithm for maximization problems, with a polynomial runtime in the input size n.

For example, the Euclidean traveling salesman problem has a PTAS. A problem is said to be APX-hard if there is a PTAS reduction from every problem in APX to that problem, and to be APX-complete if the problem is APX-hard and also in APX.

Even more restrictive, but useful in practice, is the *fully polynomial-time approximation scheme* or FPTAS, which requires the algorithm to be polynomial in both the problem size n and $1/\varepsilon$. An example of a problem that has an FPTAS is the knapsack problem. The algorithm is based on a dynamic programming approach. Any strongly NP-hard optimization problem cannot have an FPTAS unless $P = NP$.

Some problems which do not have a PTAS may admit a randomized algorithm with similar properties, a *polynomial-time randomized approximation scheme* or PRAS. A randomized algorithm is one that employs a degree of randomness. A PRAS is an algorithm which takes an instance of an optimization problem and a parameter $\varepsilon > 0$ and, in polynomial time, produces a solution that has a high probability of being within a factor ε of optimal.

B.4.2　LP-Based Approximation Algorithms

Some deterministic approximation algorithms include *rounding* of the LP relaxation or rounding of the dual of the LP relaxation. This is sometimes referred to as the *relax-and-round* approach. Also, primal–dual algorithms, as we have seen in section 8.1, are regularly used to design approximation algorithms. For randomized approximation algorithms, randomized rounding is often used, where the fractional value of a decision variable from the LP relaxation is interpreted as a probability.

Let us briefly discuss deterministic rounding. We refer to x^* as the solution to the LP relaxation, and x^I as a feasible solution to the integer program. $OPT(\text{IP})$ and $OPT(\text{LP})$ are the objective function values of the IP and the LP relaxation solved to optimality, respectively. The objective function value of the feasible (not necessarily optimal) integer solution x^I is $z(x^I)$.

The approximation ratio of a minimization problem (such as in a combinatorial procurement auction) using rounding is as follows:

$$z(x^I) = \frac{z(x^I)}{OPT(\text{LP})} \times OPT(\text{LP}) \le \frac{z(x^I)}{OPT(\text{LP})} \times OPT(\text{IP})$$

In a maximization problem the fraction is reversed to $OPT(\text{LP})/z(x^I)$.

Any upper bound of $z(x^I)/OPT(\text{LP})$ is an approximation ratio of the rounding algorithm, which rounds x^* to x^I. The best approximation ratio possible for an approximation algorithm is

$$\frac{z(x^I)}{OPT(\text{LP})} \le \frac{OPT(\text{IP})}{OPT(\text{LP})}$$

The supremum of $OPT(\text{IP})/OPT(\text{LP})$ across all parameters of the objective function is called the *integrality gap* (α). In other words, the *integrality gap* of an IP formulation for this problem gives an upper bound for the approximation ratio ρ.

Example B.4.1 Figure B.1 illustrates the integrality gap of a maximization problem. Note that $\mathbb{Z}(P)$ looks like a convex polytope, but the only feasible solutions are the integer solutions in the medium gray area. Let's assume that $OPT(\text{LP}_1)$ is the fractional objective function value for a particular valuation vector associated with x_1^{LP} and

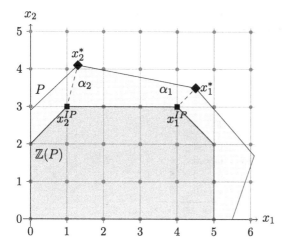

Figure B.1 Graphical illustration of the integrality gap.

$OPT(\text{IP}_1)$ is the integral objective function value for the same vector associated with the variables x_1^{IP}.

The integrality gap α is the supremum of all integrality gaps over all possible valuation vectors of all bidders: $\alpha = \sup_{v=(v_1,\ldots,v_n)}\{\alpha_1, \ldots, \alpha_n\}$, computed as $\alpha = OPT(\text{LP})/OPT(\text{IP})$ for this maximization problem. Consequently, $OPT(\text{LP}_1) = \alpha_1 \times OPT(\text{IP}_1)$.

We now take a look at a specific combinatorial optimization problem, the *weighted set cover problem*.

Definition B.4.4 (Weighted-set cover) Given a universe $\mathcal{K} = \{1, \ldots, m\}$, a collection $\mathcal{S} = \{S_1, \ldots, S_n\}$ of subsets in $\mathcal{K}$, and a weight function $v_i : \mathcal{S} \mapsto \mathbb{Q}^+$, find a minimum weight subcollection $\mathcal{C}$ of sets from $\mathcal{S}$ such that $\mathcal{C}$ covers all elements of $\mathcal{K}$.

The WDP in a combinatorial procurement auction can be modeled as a weighted-set cover problem (WSC); we assume for simplicity that one bidder submits only a single package bid S_i:

$$\min \sum_{i \in \mathcal{I}} v_i x_i \tag{WSC}$$

$$\text{s.t.} \sum_{i:k \in S_i} x_i \geq 1 \qquad \forall k \in \mathcal{K}$$

$$x_i \in \{0, 1\} \qquad \forall i \in \mathcal{I}$$

If we relax the last set of integrality constraints to $0 \leq x_i \leq 1$ then we get the LP relaxation WSC-LP of the set covering problem, which we can compute in polynomial time using the ellipsoid method. Now we can perform deterministic rounding and approximate the optimal solution of the LP relaxation x^* by x^I, a feasible integer solution to the WSC. Of course, if we round in such a way that all fractional solutions $x^* > 0 \mapsto x^I = 1$

Table B.1 Example of a deterministic rounding algorithm

k/S_i	1	2	3	4	5	6	7	f_k
1	1	0	0	1	0	0	0	2
2	0	1	1	0	0	1	0	3
3	1	1	0	0	1	1	1	5
4	1	0	0	1	0	0	1	3
5	0	0	1	0	1	1	0	3
v_i	5	2	3	1	2	6	2	
x^{LP}	0	0.5	0.5	1	0.5	0	0	4.5
x^{IP}	0	1	0	1	1	0	0	5
x^I	0	1	1	1	1	0	0	8

then the allocation will be feasible but we will obtain too many subsets or package bids, resulting in a low approximation ratio.

Let us provide an algorithm showing how a better approximation ratio can be gained. We define a function $f_k = |i : k \in S_i|$, which denotes the number of subsets S_i, which cover an element, i.e., the number of times an element or item appears in subsets or package bids respectively. Let's define $f = \max_{\{k=1,\ldots,m\}} f_k$. We round the fractional solution x^* to an integer solution x^I and include the subset S_i in our solution x^I by setting $x_k^I = 1$ if $x_k^* \geq 1/f$, and $x_k^I = 0$ otherwise.

Example B.4.2 In the example in table B.1, we show the constraint matrix for the integer program of a set cover problem. Each row represents an item k and each column a subset S_i; v_i gives the coefficients of the objective function, i.e., the bid prices in a procurement auction. The last three lines represent the optimal solutions of the LP relaxation, of the IP, and of the result of the rounding procedure with the corresponding objective function values in the last column.

Theorem B.4.2 *The collection of subsets S_i with $i \in \mathcal{I}$ is a feasible set cover.*

Proof. Let's call an element k covered if a solution to the deterministic rounding algorithm contains some subset containing k. Next, we show that each element k is covered. The optimal solution x^* is a feasible solution to the linear program, and consequently we know that $\sum_{i:k\in S_i} x_i^* \geq 1$ for element k. By the definitions of f_k and of f, there are $f_k \leq f$ terms in the sum so at least one variable x_i^* for a subset must be at least $1/f$. Thus, for some i such that $k \in S_i$, $x_i^* \geq 1/f$ and the subset will be rounded to 1. Therefore, at least one subset $i \in \mathcal{I}$ will be selected, and element k is covered. □

One can also show that the *rounding procedure* yields an approximation algorithm.

Theorem B.4.3 *The deterministic rounding algorithm is an f-approximation algorithm for the set cover problem.*

Proof. The algorithm has a polynomial runtime. It holds that $1 \leq fx_i^*$ for each $i \in \mathcal{I}$. Each term $f v_i x_i^*$ is non-negative for $i = 1, \ldots, n$, and one can show that

$$\sum_{i \in \mathcal{I}} v_i \leq \sum_{i \in \mathcal{I}} v_i(fx_i^*)$$

$$= f \sum_{i \in \mathcal{I}} v_i x_i^*$$

$$= f \times OPT(\text{LP})$$

$$\leq f \times OPT(\text{IP}) \qquad \qquad \square$$

A rounding can also be derived for the dual of the relaxed WSC-LP:

$$\max \sum_{k \in \mathcal{K}} y_k \qquad\qquad\qquad \text{(Dual WSC-LP)}$$

$$\text{s.t.} \quad \sum_{k:k \in S_i} y_k \leq v_i \qquad \forall i \in \mathcal{I}$$

$$y_k \geq 0 \qquad\qquad \forall k \in \mathcal{K}$$

Randomized rounding is often based on the procedure described for deterministic approximation mechanisms using the fractional solution of the *LP* relaxation. The difference is the rounding procedure. Let x^* again be the optimal solution to the *LP* relaxation. In randomized rounding, we interpret the fractional value x_i^* as the probability that x_i' is set to 1. As a consequence, each subset S_i is included in our allocation with probability x_i^*, and all n variables are treated as independent.

Let X_i be a random variable that is 1 if package S_i is included in the allocation and 0 otherwise. The expected value of the solution is the value of the LP relaxation:

$$E\left(\sum_{i \in \mathcal{I}} v_i X_i\right) = \sum_{i \in \mathcal{I}} v_i \Pr(X_i = 1) = \sum_{i \in \mathcal{I}} v_i x_i^* = OPT(\text{LP})$$

It might happen, however, that the solution is not a feasible set cover. This probability can be reduced by repeated coin flips. If heads comes up in any coin toss then a set S_i will be included in the allocation. There are several rounding procedures, and a specific example in the context of a randomized approximation mechanism is discussed in chapter 10.

Primal–dual algorithms are another recipe for fast approximation algorithms, because they do not require one to fully solve the primal or dual WSC-LP. We do not discuss the dual rounding or primal–dual approximation algorithms further, and refer the interested reader to Vazirani (2003).

References

Abdulkadiroğlu, A., T. Sönmez. 2003. School choice: a mechanism design approach. *American Economic Review* **93**(3) 729–747.

Abdulkadiroglu, A., P. Pathak, A. Roth. 2009. Strategy-proofness versus efficiency in matching with indifferences: redesigning the NYC high school match. *American Economic Review* **99**(5) 1954–1978.

Adomavicius, G., A. Gupta. 2005. Toward comprehensive real-time bidder support in iterative combinatorial auctions. *Information Systems Research (ISR)* **16** 169–185.

Adomavicius, G., S. Curley, A. Gupta, P. Sanyal. 2013. Impact of information feedback in continuous combinatorial auctions: an experimental study of economic performance. *MIS Quarterly* **37** 55–76.

Afriat, S. N. 1967. The construction of utility functions from expenditure data. *International Economic Review* **8**(1) 67–77.

Alcalde-Unzu, J., E. Molis. 2011. Exchange of indivisible goods and indifferences: the top trading absorbing sets mechanisms. *Games and Economic Behavior* **73**(1) 1–16.

Allais, M. 1953. Le comportement de l'homme rationnel devant le risque: critique des postulats et axiomes de l'école américaine. *Econometrica* **21** 503–546.

Alt, F. 1936. Ueber die Messbarkeit des Nutzens. *Zeitschrift fuer Nationaloekonomie* **7** 161–169.

Anderson, R. 1978. An elementary core equivalence theorem. *Econometrica* **46**(6) 1483–1487.

Anton, J., D. A. Yao. 1992. Coordination in split award auctions. *Quarterly Journal of Economics* **107** 681–707.

Ariely, D. 2008. *Predictably Irrational*. HarperCollins New York.

Arrow, K. J. 1950. A difficulty in the concept of social welfare. *Journal of Political Economy* **58** 328–346.

Arrow, K. J., H. D. Block, L. Hurwicz. 1959. On the stability of the competitive equilibrium, ii. *Econometrica* **27** 82–109.

Arrow, K. J., A. Sen, K. Suzumura. 2010. *Handbook of Social Choice & Welfare*, vol. 2. Elsevier.

Ashlagi, I., D. Monderer, M. Tennenholtz. 2008. On the value of correlation. *Journal of Artificial Intelligence Research (JAIR)* **33** 575–613.

Athey, S., I. Segal. 2013. An efficient dynamic mechanism. *Econometrica* **81**(6) 2463–2485.

Aumann, R. J. 1987. Correlated equilibrium as an expression of Bayesian rationality. *Econometrica* **55**(1) 1–18.

Ausubel, L. 2004. An efficient ascending-bid auction for multiple objects. *American Economic Review* **94** 1452–1457.

Ausubel, L., O. Baranov. 2014. Market design and the evolution of the combinatorial clock auction. *American Economic Review: Papers & Proceedings* **104**(5) 446–451.

Ausubel, L., P. Milgrom. 2002. Ascending auctions with package bidding. *Frontiers of Theoretical Economics* **1** 1–42.

Ausubel, L., P. Milgrom. 2006a. Ascending proxy auctions. In P. Cramton, Y. Shoham, R. Steinberg, eds., *Combinatorial Auctions*, chapter 3. MIT Press, 79–98.

Ausubel, L., P. Milgrom. 2006b. The lovely but lonely Vickrey auction. In P. Cramton, Y. Shoham, R. Steinberg, eds., *Combinatorial Auctions*, chapter 1. MIT Press, 17–40.

Ausubel, L. M., P. Cramton, R. P. McAfee, J. McMillan. 1997. Synergies in wireless telephony: evidence from the broadband pcs auctions. *Journal of Economics and Management Strategy* **6**(3) 497–527.

Ausubel, L., P. Cramton, P. Milgrom. 2006. The clock-proxy auction: a practical combinatorial auction design. In P. Cramton, Y. Shoham, R. Steinberg, eds., *Combinatorial Auctions*. MIT Press.

Ausubel, L., P. Cramton, M. Pycia, M. Rostek, M. Weretka. 2014. Demand reduction and inefficiency in multi-unit auctions. *Review of Economic Studies* **81**(4) 1366–1400.

Azevedo, E., E. Budish. 2015. Strategy-proofness in the large. *Chicago Booth Research Paper* 13–35.

Azevedo, E., E. Weyl, A. White. 2013. Walrasian equilibrium in large, quasilinear markets. *Theoretical Economics* **8**(2) 281–290.

Aziz, H., B. de Keijzer. 2012. Housing markets with indifferences: a tale of two mechanisms. In *Proc. 26th AAAI Conference on Artificial Intelligence*, 1249–1255.

Aziz, H., F. Brandt, M. Brill. 2013. The computational complexity of random serial dictatorship. *Economics Letters* **121**(3) 341–345.

Baisa, B. 2016. Efficient multi-unit auction design for normal goods. University of Michigan Working Paper.

Banks, J., J. Ledyard, D. Porter. 1989. Allocating uncertain and unresponsive resources: an experimental approach. *RAND Journal of Economics* **20** 1–25.

Banks, J., M. Olson, D. Porter, S. Rassenti, V. Smith. 2003. Theory, experiment and the fcc spectrum auctions. *Journal of Economic Behavior & Organization* **51** 303–350.

Bergemann, D., S. Morris. 2005. Robust mechanism design. *Econometrica* **73**(6) 1771–1813.

Bergemann, D., M. Said. 2011. Dynamic auctions. In *Encyclopedia of Operations Research and Management Science*. Wiley.

Bergemann, D., J. Välimäki. 2010. The dynamic pivot mechanism. *Econometrica* **78** 771–790.

Bergson, A. 1938. A reformulation of certain aspects of welfare economics. *Quarterly Journal of Economics* **52** 310–334.

Bernheim, B. D., M. D. Whinston. 1986. Menu auctions, resource allocation, and economic influence. *The Quarterly Journal of Economics* **101**(1) 1–31.

Bertsimas, D., J. Tsitsiklis. 1997. *Introduction to Linear Optimization*, vol. 6. Athena Scientific.

Bhattacharya, S., V. Conitzer, K. Munagala, L. Xia. 2010. Incentive compatible budget elicitation in multi-unit auctions. In *Proc. 21st Annual ACM-SIAM Symposium on Discrete Algorithms*. Society for Industrial and Applied Mathematics, 554–572.

Bichler, M. 2010. Combinatorial auctions: complexity and algorithms. In J. Cochran, L. Cox, P. Keskinocak, Kharoufeh, J. Smith, eds., *Encyclopedia of Operations Research and Management Science*. Wiley.

Bichler, M., A. Davenport, G. Hohner, J. Kalagnanam. 2006. Industrial procurement auctions. In P. Cramton, Y. Shoham, R. Steinberg, eds., *Combinatorial Auctions*. MIT Press.

Bichler, M., J. Goeree. 2017. *The Handbook of Spectrum Auction Design*. Cambridge University Press.

Bichler, M., J. Kalagnanam. 2005. Configurable offers and winner determination in multi-attribute auctions. *European Journal of Operational Research* **160**(2) 380–394.

Bichler, M., P. Paulsen. 2017. A principal–agent model of bidding firms in multi-unit auctions. Social Science Research Network (2775170).

Bichler, M., P. Shabalin, A. Pikovsky. 2009. A computational analysis of linear-price iterative combinatorial auctions. *Information Systems Research* **20**(1) 33–59.

Bichler, M., A. Gupta, W. Ketter. 2010. Designing smart markets. *Information Systems Research* **21**(4) 688–699.

Bichler, M., S. Schneider, K. Guler, M. Sayal. 2011a. Compact bidding languages and supplier selection for markets with economies of scale and scope. *European Journal of Operational Research* **214** 67–77.

Bichler, M., P. Shabalin, J. Wolf. 2011b. Efficiency, auctioneer revenue, and bidding behavior in the combinatorial clock auction. In *Proc. 2nd Conference on Auctions, Market Mechanisms and Their Applications*. New York.

Bichler, M., P. Shabalin, J. Wolf. 2013a. Do core-selecting combinatorial clock auctions always lead to high efficiency? An experimental analysis of spectrum auction designs. *Experimental Economics* **16**(4) 1–35.

Bichler, M., P. Shabalin, G. Ziegler. 2013b. Efficiency with linear prices? A game-theoretical and computational analysis of the combinatorial clock auction. *Information Systems Research* **24**(2) 394–417.

Bichler, M., J. Goeree, S. Mayer, P. Shabalin. 2014a. Simple auctions for complex sales: bid languages and spectrum auction design. *Telecommunications Policy* **38** 613–622.

Bichler, M., K. Guler, S. Mayer. 2014b. Split-award procurement auctions: can Bayesian equilibrium strategies predict human bidding behavior in multi-object auctions? *Production and Operations Management* **24** 1012–1027.

Bichler, M., V. Gretschko, M. Janssen. 2017a. Bargaining in spectrum auctions: a review of the German auction in 2015. *Telecommunications Policy*, to appear.

Bichler, M., Z. Hao, G. Adomavicius. 2017b. Coordination vs. free-riding: coalition-based pricing in ascending combinatorial auctions. *Information Systems Research* **28**(1) 159–179.

Bikhchandani, S., J. W. Mamer. 1997. Competitive equilibrium in an exchange economy with indivisibilities. *Journal of Economic Theory* **74** 385–413.

Bikhchandani, S., J. M. Ostroy. 2002. The package assignment model. *Journal of Economic Theory* **107**(2) 377–406.

Bikhchandani, S., S. de Vries, J. Schummer, R. Vohra. 2011. An ascending Vickrey auction for selling bases of a matroid. *Operations Research* **59**(2) 400–413.

Birkhoff, G. 1946. Three observations on linear algebra. *Rev. Univ. Nac. Tucumán. Revista A* **5** 147–151.

Black, D. 1948. On the rationale of group decision-making. *Journal of Political Economy* **56**(1) 23–34.

Boergers, T., C. Dustmann. 2003. Rationalizing the umts spectrum bids: the case of the UK auction. In G. Illing, U. Kuehl, eds., *Spectrum Auctions and Competition in Telecommunications*. CESifo Seminar Series.

Bogomolnaia, A., H. Moulin. 2001. A new solution to the random assignment problem. *Journal of Economic Theory* **100**(2) 295–328.

Borgers, T., D. Krahmer, R. Strausz. 2015. *An Introduction to the Theory of Mechanism Design*. Oxford University Press.

Boutilier, C., H. H. Hoos. 2001. Bidding languages for combinatorial auctions. In *Proc. 17th International Joint Conference on Artificial Intelligence 2001*, 1211–1217.

Brandl, F., F. Brandt, H. Seedig. 2016. Consistent probabilistic social choice. *Econometrica* **84**(5) 1839–1880.

Brandt, F., T. Sandholm, Y. Shoham. 2007. Spiteful bidding in sealed-bid auctions. In *Proc. 20th International Joint Conference on Artificial Intelligence*, 1207–1214.

Brandt, F., V. Conitzer, U. Endriss. 2012. Computational social choice. In G. Weiss, *Multiagent Systems*. MIT Press, 213–283.

Brandt, F., M. Brill, P. Harrenstein. 2015. Computational social choice. In F. Brandt, V. Conitzer, U. Endriss, J. Lang, A. Procaccia, eds., *Handbook of Computational Social Choice*, chapter 3. Cambridge University Press.

Braun, S., N. Dwenger, D. Kübler. 2010. Telling the truth may not pay off: an empirical study of centralized university admissions in Germany. *BE Journal of Economic Analysis & Policy* **10**(1) 1935–1982.

Brunner, C., J. K. Goeree, Ch. Holt, J. Ledyard. 2010. An experimental test of flexible combinatorial spectrum auction formats. *American Economic Journal: Micro-Economics* **2** 39–57.

Brusco, S., G. Lopomo. 2009. Simultaneous ascending auctions with complementarities and known budget constraints. *Economic Theory* **38** 105–124.

Budish, E. 2011. The combinatorial assignment problem: approximate competititve equilibrium from equal incomes. *Journal of Political Economy* **119** 1061–1103.

Budish, E., E. Cantillon. 2012. The multi-unit assignment problem: theory and evidence from course allocation at Harvard. *American Economic Review* **102** 2237–2271.

Bulow, J., P. Klemperer. 1996. Auctions versus negotiations. *The American Economic Review* 180–194.

Bulow, J. I., J. Levin, P. Milgrom. 2009. Winning play in spectrum auctions. National Bureau of Economic Research Working Paper No. 14765.

Bulow, J. I., D. J. Roberts. 1989. The simple economics of optimal auctions. *Journal of Political Economy* **97** 1060–1090.

Cantillon, E., M. Pesendorfer. 2006. Auctioning bus routes: the London experience. In P. Cramton, Y. Shoham, R. Steinberg, eds., *Combinatorial Auctions*. MIT Press.

Caplice, C., Y. Sheffi. 2006. Combinatorial auctions for truckload transportation. In P. Cramton, Y. Shoham, R. Steinberg, eds., *Combinatorial Auctions*. MIT Press.

Carr, R., S. Vempala. 2000. Randomized metarounding. In *Proc. 32nd Annual ACM Symposium on the Theory of Computing*. ACM, 58–62.

Chekuri, Ch., S. Khanna. 2006. A polynomial time approximation scheme for the multiple knapsack problem. *SIAM Journal of Computing* **35** 713–728.

Chen, X., X. Deng. 2006. Settling the complexity of two-player Nash equilibrium. *FOCS*, **6** 261–272.

Chen, Y., K. Takeuchi. 2010. Multi-object auctions with package bidding: an experimental comparison of Vickrey and iBEA. *Games and Economic Behavior* **68** 557–579.

Chvatal, V. 1983. *Linear Programming*. Macmillan.

Clarke, E. H. 1971. Multipart pricing of public goods. *Public Choice* **XI** 17–33.

Cook, S. A. 1971. The complexity of theorem-proving procedures. In *Proc. 3rd Annual ACM Symposium on the Theory of Computing*. ACM, 151–158.

Cox, J., B. Roberson, V. L. Smith. 1982. Theory and behavior of single object auctions. In V. L. Smith, ed., *Research in Experimental Economics*. JAI Press.

Cox, J., V. Smith, J. Walker. 1988. Theory and individual behavior of first-price auctions. *Journal of Risk and Uncertainty* **1**(1) 61–99.

Cramton, P., A. Ockenfels. 2016. The German 4G spectrum auction: design and behavior. *Economic Journal* (to appear).

Cramton, P., Y. Shoham, R. Steinberg, eds. 2006. *Combinatorial Auctions*. MIT Press.

Crawford, V. P., E. M. Knoer. 1981. Job matching with heterogeneous firms and workers. *Econometrica* **49**(2) 437–450.

Cremer, J., R. McLean. 1988. Full extraction of the surplus in Bayesian and dominant strategy auctions. *Econometrica* **56** 1247–1257.

Daniely, A., M. Schapira, G. Shahaf. 2015. Inapproximability of truthful mechanisms via generalizations of the vc dimension. In *Proc. 47th Annual ACM Symposium on the Theory of Computing*. ACM, 401–408.

Dantzig, G. B. 1998. *Linear Programming and Extensions*. Princeton University Press.

Dasgupta, P., P. Hammond, E. Maskin. 1979. The implementation of social choice rules: some general results on incentive compatibility. *The Review of Economic Studies* **46**(2) 185–216.

Daskalakis, C., P. Goldberg, C. Papadimitriou. 2009. The complexity of computing a Nash equilibrium. *SIAM Journal of Computing* **39**(1) 195–259.

d'Aspremont, C., L. Gérard-Varet. 1979. Incentives and incomplete information. *Journal of Public Economics* **11**(1) 25–45.

Davenport, A., J. Kalagnanam. 2000. Price negotiations for procurement of direct inputs. In *Proc. IMA "Hot Topics" Workshop: Mathematics of the Internet: E-Auction and Markets*, vol. 127. Minneapolis, USA, 27–44.

Day, R. 2013. The division of surplus in efficient combinatorial exchanges. Technical report, University of Connecticut.

Day, R., P. Cramton. 2012. Quadratic core-selecting payment rules for combinatorial auctions. *Operations Research* **60**(3) 588–603.

Day, R., P. Milgrom. 2008. Core-selecting package auctions. *International Journal of Game Theory* **36** 393–407.

Day, R., S. Raghavan. 2007. Fair payments for efficient allocations in public sector combinatorial auctions. *Management Science* **53** 1389–1406.

de Vries, S., J. Schummer, R. Vohra. 2007. On ascending Vickrey auctions for heterogeneous objects. *Journal of Economic Theory* **132** 95–118.

Debreu, G., H. Scarf. 1963. A limit theorem on the core of an economy. *International Economic Review* **4**(3) 235–246.

Demange, G., D. Gale, M. Sotomayor. 1986. Multi-item auctions. *Journal of Political Economy* **94** 863–872.

Diebold, F., H. Aziz, M. Bichler, F. Matthes, A. Schneider. 2014. Course allocation via stable matching. *Business & Information Systems Engineering* **6**(2) 97–110.

Dobzinski, S., S. Dughmi. 2009. On the power of randomization in algorithmic mechanism design. In *Foundations of Computer Science, FOCS'09, Proc. 50th Annual IEEE Symposium*. IEEE, 505–514.

Dobzinski, S., R. Lavi, N. Nisan. 2012a. Multi-unit auctions with budget limits. *Games and Economic Behavior* **74**(2) 486–503.

Dobzinski, S., N. Nisan, M. Schapira. 2012b. Truthful randomized mechanisms for combinatorial auctions. *Journal of Computer and System Sciences* **78**(1) 15–25.

Dughmi, S., T. Roughgarden, Q. Yan. 2011. From convex optimization to randomized mechanisms: toward optimal combinatorial auctions. In *Proc. 43rd Annual ACM Symposium on the Theory of Computing*. ACM, 149–158.

Dütting, P., V. Gkatzelis, T. Roughgarden. 2014. The performance of deferred-acceptance auctions. In *Proc. 15th ACM Conference on Economics and Computation*. ACM, 187–204.

Dütting, P., T. Kesselheim, E. Tardos. 2015. Algorithms as mechanisms: the price of anarchy of relax-and-round. In *Proc. 16th ACM Conference on Economics and Computation*. ACM, 187–201.

Edelman, B., M. Ostrovsky, M. Schwarz. 2007. Internet advertising and the generalized second-price auction: selling billions of dollars worth of keywords. *American Economic Review* **97**(1) 242–259.

Ehlers, L., B. Klaus. 2003. Coalitional strategy-proof and resource-monotonic solutions for multiple assignment problems. *Social Choice and Welfare* **21**(2) 265–280.

Ehlers, L., A. Erdil. 2010. Efficient assignment respecting priorities. *Journal of Economic Theory* **145**(3) 1269–1282.

Engelbrecht-Wiggans, R., E. Katok. 2008. Regret and feedback information in first-price sealed-bid auctions. *Management Science* **54**(4) 808–819.

Erdil, A., H. Ergin. 2006. Two-sided matching with indifferences. Unpublished mimeo, Harvard Business School.

Erdil, A., H. Ergin. 2008. What's the matter with tie-breaking? Improving efficiency in school choice. *American Economic Review* **98**(3) 669–689.

Erdil, A., P. Klemperer. 2010. A new payment rule for core-selecting package auctions. *Journal of the European Economic Association* **8**(2–3) 537–547.

Ergin, H. 2002. Efficient resource allocation on the basis of priorities. *Econometrica* **70**(6) 2489–2497.

Fadaei, S., M. Bichler. 2017. Truthfulness with value-maximizing bidders: on the limits of approximation in combinatorial markets. *European Journal of Operational Research* **260**(2) 767–777.

Fang, H., S. Morris. 2006. Multidimensional private value auctions. *Journal of Economic Theory* **126**(1) 1–30.

Farrell, M. J. 1959. The convexity assumption in the theory of competitive markets. *Journal of Political Economy* 377–391.

Featherstone, C., M. Niederle. 2008. Ex ante efficiency in school choice mechanisms: an experimental investigation. Technical report, National Bureau of Economic Research.

Fujishige, S. 2005. *Submodular Functions and Optimization*, vol. 58. Elsevier.

Gale, D., L. S. Shapley. 1962. College admissions and the stability of marriage. *American Mathematical Monthly* **69**(1) 9–15. doi:10.2307/2312726.

Garey, M. R., D. S. Johnson, eds. 1972. *Computers and Intractability – A Guide to the Theory of NP-Completeness*. W. H. Freeman.

Georgescu-Roegen, N. 1979. Methods in economic science. *Journal of Economic Issues* **13** 317–328.

Gibbard, A. 1973. Manipulation of voting schemes: a general result. *Econometrica* **41** 587–601.

Gibbard, A. 1977. Manipulation of schemes that mix voting with chance. *Econometrica* **45** 665–681.

Gilboa, I., A. Postlewaite, L. Samuelson, D. Schmeidler. 2014. Economic models as analogies. *Economic Journal* **124**(578) F513–F533.

Goeree, J., C. Holt. 2002. Quantal response equilibrium and overbidding in private-value auctions. *Journal of Economic Theory* **104** 247–272.

Goeree, J., C. Holt. 2010. Hierarchical package bidding: a paper & pencil combinatorial auction. *Games and Economic Behavior* **70**(1) 146–169.

Goeree, J., Y. Lien. 2014. An equilibrium analysis of the simultaneous ascending auction. *Journal of Economic Theory* **153**(153) 506–533.

Goeree, J., Y. Lien. 2016. On the impossibility of core-selecting auctions. *Theoretical Economics* **11** 41–52.

Goetzendorff, A., M. Bichler, P. Shabalin, R. Day. 2015. Compact bid languages and core pricing in large multi-item auctions. *Management Science* **61**(7) 1684–1703.

Goossens, D. R., A. J. T. Maas, F. Spieksma, J. J. van de Klundert. 2007. Exact algorithms for procurement problems under a total quantity discount structure. *European Journal of Operational Research* **178** 603–626.

Green, J., J. Laffont. 1979. *Incentives in Public Decision Making*. North Holland.

Grimm, V., F. Riedel, E. Wolfstetter. 2003. Low price equilibrium in multi-unit auctions: the gsm spectrum auction in Germany. *International Journal of Industrial Organization* **21**(10) 1557–1569.

Groves, T. 1973. Incentives in teams. *Econometrica* **41** 617–631.

Gul, F., E. Stacchetti. 1999. Walrasian equilibrium with gross substitutes. *Journal of Economic Theory* **87** 95–124.

Guler, K., M. Bichler, J. Petrakis. 2016. Ascending combinatorial auctions with risk aversion. *INFORMS Group Decision and Negotiation* **25**(3) 609–639.

Halldórsson, M. M., J. Kratochvil, J. A. Telle. 2000. Independent sets with domination constraints. *Discrete Applied Mathematics* **99**(1–3) 39–54.

Halldórsson, M. M., R. W. Irving, K. Iwama, D. F. Manlove, S. Miyazaki, Y. Morita *et al.* 2003. Approximability results for stable marriage problems with ties. *Theoretical Computer Science* **306**(1) 431–447.

Hamada, K., K. Iwama, S. Miyazaki. 2011. The hospitals/residents problem with quota lower bounds. In C. Demetrescu, M. Halldorsson, eds., *Proc. Annual European Symposium on Algorithms ESA 2011, Lecture Notes in Computer Science*, vol. 6942. Springer, 180–191.

Harsanyi, J. C. 1967. Games with incomplete information played by "Bayesian" players. Parts I–III. *Management Science* **14** 159–182, 320–324, 486–502.

Hartline, J., R. Kleinberg, A. Malekian. 2015. Bayesian incentive compatibility via matchings. *Games and Economic Behavior* **92** 401–429.

Hatfield, J. W. 2009. Strategy-proof, efficient, and nonbossy quota allocations. *Social Choice and Welfare* **33**(3) 505–515.

Hogan, W. W., B. J. Ring. 2003. On minimum-uplift pricing for electricity markets. Electricity Policy Group.

Holmstrom, B. 1979. Groves' scheme on restricted domains. *Econometrica* **47** 1137–1144.

Holzman, R., N. Kfir-Dahav, D. Monderer, M. Tennenholtz. 2004. Bundling equilibrium in combinatorial auctions. *Games and Economic Behavior* **47**(1) 104–123.

Hurwicz, L. 1972. On informationally decentralized systems. In C. B. McGuire, R. Radner, eds., *Decisions and Organizations*. North-Holland, 297–336.

Hylland, A., R. Zeckhauser. 1979. The efficient allocation of individuals to positions. *Journal of Political Economy* **87**(2) 293–314.

Innes, J., O. Thébaud, A. Norman-López, L. Little, J. Kung. 2014. Evidence of package trading in a mature multi-species {ITQ} market. *Marine Policy* **46** 68–71.

Irving, R. 1985. An efficient algorithm for the stable roommates problem. *Journal of Algorithms* **6**(4) 577–595.

Isaac, M., T. Salmon, A. Zillante. 2007. A theory of jump bidding in ascending auctions. *Journal of Economic Behaviour and Organization* **62** 144–164.

Jackson, M., A. Manelli. 1997. Approximately competitive equilibria in large finite economies. *Journal of Economic Theory* **77**(2) 354–376.

Janssen, M., V. Karamychev. 2016. Spiteful bidding and gaming in combinatorial clock auctions. *Games and Economic Behavior* **100**(1), 186–207.

Jaramillo, P., V. Manjunath. 2012. The difference indifference makes in strategy-proof allocation of objects. *Journal of Economic Theory* **147**(5) 1913–1946.

Jehiel, P., M. Meyer-ter Vehn, B. Moldovanu, W. Zame. 2006. The limits of ex post implementation. *Econometrica* **74**(3) 585–610.

Kagel, J., R. M. Marstad, D. Levin. 1987. Information impact and allocation rules in auctions with affiliated private values: a laboratory study. *Econometrica* **55** 1275–1304.

Kagel, J., Y. Lien, P. Milgrom. 2010. Ascending prices and package bids: an experimental analysis. *American Economic Journal: Microeconomics* **2**(3).

Kahneman, D. 2003. Maps of bounded rationality: psychology for behavioral economics. *The American Economic Review* **93**(5) 1449–1475.

Kahneman, D., A. Tversky. 1979. Prospect theory: an analysis of decision under risk. *Econometrica: Journal of the Econometric Society* 263–291.

Karloff, H., U. Zwick. 1997. A 7/8-approximation algorithm for max 3sat? In *Foundations of Computer Science, Proc. 38th Annual Symposium.* 406–415.

Karmarkar, N. 1984. A new polynomial-time algorithm for linear programming. In *Proc. Sixteenth Annual ACM Symposium on the Theory of Computing.* ACM, 302–311.

Kazumori, E. 2005. Auctions with package bidding: an experimental study. Technical report, The Center for Advanced Research in Finance, The University of Tokyo.

Kelly, F., R. Steinberg. 2000. A combinatorial auction with multiple winners for universal service. *Management Science* **46**(4) 586–596.

Kelso, A. S., V. P. Crawford. 1982. Job matching, coalition formation, and gross substitute. *Econometrica* **50** 1483–1504.

Kesten, O. 2010. School choice with consent. *The Quarterly Journal of Economics* **125**(3) 1297–1348.

Khachiyan, L. 1980. Polynomial algorithms in linear programming. *USSR Computational Mathematics and Mathematical Physics* **20**(1) 53–72.

Klemperer, P. 2002. What really matters in auction design. *Journal of Economic Perspectives* **16**(1) 169–189.

Koebberling, V. 2006. Strength of preference and cardinal utility. *Economic Theory* **27** 375–391.

Kokott, G., M. Bichler, P. Paulsen. 2017. The beauty of Dutch: equilibrium bidding strategies in ex-post split-award auctions. Technical University of Munich Working Paper.

Kraft, D., S. Fadaei, M. Bichler. 2014. Efficient convex decomposition for truthful social welfare approximation. In *Proc. Conference on Web and Internet Economics.* Springer, Cham 120–132.

Krishna, V., ed. 2009. *Auction Theory.* Elsevier Science.

Krishna, A., M. Ünver. 2008. Improving the efficiency of course bidding at business schools: field and laboratory studies. *Marketing Science* **27** 262–282.

Kroemer, C., M. Bichler, A. Goetzendorff. 2014. (Un) expected bidder behavior in spectrum auctions: about inconsistent bidding and its impact on efficiency in the combinatorial clock auction. *Group Decision and Negotiation* **25**(1) 31–63.

Krysta, P., T. Michalak, T. Sandholm, M. Wooldridge. 2010. Combinatorial auctions with externalities. In *Proc. 9th International Conference on Autonomous Agents and Multiagent Systems*, vol. 1. International Foundation for Autonomous Agents and Multiagent Systems, 1471–1472.

Kuhn, H. W. 1955. The Hungarian method for the assignment problem. *Naval Research Logistics Quarterly* **2**(1–2) 83–97.

Kwanashie, A., D. F. Manlove. 2013. An integer programming approach to the hospital/residents problem with ties. In D. Huisman, I. Louwers, A. Wagelmans, eds., *Proc. Conference on Operations Research 2013*. Springer, Cham.

Kwasnica, T., J. O. Ledyard, D. Porter, C. DeMartini. 2005. A new and improved design for multi-objective iterative auctions. *Management Science* **51**(3) 419–434.

Lavi, R., C. Swamy. 2011. Truthful and near-optimal mechanism design via linear programming. *Journal of the ACM (JACM)* **58**(6) 25.

Lavi, R., A. Alem, N. Nisan. 2003. Towards a characterization of truthful combinatorial auctions. In *Foundations of Computer Science, Proc. 44th Annual IEEE Symposium*. IEEE, 574–583.

Ledyard, J., D. Porter, A. Rangel. 1997. Experiments testing multiobject allocation mechanisms. *Journal of Economics and Management Strategy* **6** 639–675.

Lehmann, D., L. I. O'Callaghan, Y. Shoham. 2002. Truth revelation in approximately efficient combinatorial auctions. *Journal of the ACM (JACM)* **49**(5) 577–602.

Lehmann, D., R. Mueller, T. Sandholm. 2006. The winner determination problem. In P. Cramton, Y. Shoham, R. Steinberg, eds., *Combinatorial Auctions*. MIT Press, Cambridge, MA.

Leonard, H. B. 1983. Elicitation of honest preferences for the assignment of individuals to positions. *The Journal of Political Economy* 461–479.

Levin, J., A. Skrzypacz. 2017. Properties of the combinatorial clock auction. *American Economic Review* **106**(9) 2528–2551.

Leyton-Brown, K., E. Nudelman, Y. Shoham. 2009. Empirical hardness models: methodology and a case study on combinatorial auctions. *Journal of the ACM* **56** 1–52.

Li, S. 2015. Obviously strategy-proof mechanisms. Technical report, SSRN Working Paper. http://dx.doi.org/10.2139/ssrn.2560028.

Lucier, B., A. Borodin. 2010. Price of anarchy for greedy auctions. In *Proc. 21st Annual ACM-SIAM Symposium on Discrete Algorithms*. Society for Industrial and Applied Mathematics, 537–553.

Manlove, D. 2013. *Algorithmics of Matching Under Preferences*. Series on Theoretical Computer Science, World Scientific.

Manlove, D., G. O'Malley. 2012. Paired and altruistic kidney donation in the UK: algorithms and experimentation. In *Experimental Algorithms*, Springer, 271–282.

Manlove, D., C. T. S. Sng. 2006. Popular matchings in the capacitated house allocation problem. In Y. Azar, T. Erlebach, eds., *Proc. 14th Annual European Symposium on Algorithms*, Lecture Notes in Computer Science, vol. 4168. Springer, 492–503.

Manlove, D., R. Irving, K. Iwama, S. Miyazaki, Y. Morita. 2002. Hard variants of stable marriage. *Theoretical Computer Science* **276**(1) 261–279.

Martin, A., J. Müller, S. Pokutta. 2014. Strict linear prices in non-convex European day-ahead electricity markets. *Optimization Methods and Software* **29**(1) 189–221.

Maskin, E., J. Riley. 1984. Optimal auctions with risk averse buyers. *Econometrica* 1473–1518.

May, K. O. 1952. A set of independent necessary and sufficient conditions for simple majority decision. *Econometrica* 680–684.

McAfee, R. P. 1992. A dominant strategy double auction. *Journal of Economic Theory* **56**(2) 434–450.

McAfee, R. P. 2008. The gains from trade under fixed price mechanisms. *Applied Economics Research Bulletin* **1**(1) 1–10.

McAfee, R., P. J. McMillan. 1987. Auctions and bidding. *Journal of Economic Literature* **25** 699–738.

McKelvey, R. D., A. McLennan. 1997. The maximal number of regular totally mixed Nash equilibria. *Journal of Economic Theory* **72**(2) 411–425.

Milgrom, P. 2000. Putting auction theory to work: the simultaneous ascending auction. *Journal of Political Economy* **108**(21) 245–272.

Milgrom, P. 2017. *Discovering Prices: Auction Design in Markets with Complex Constraints.* Columbia University Press.

Milgrom, P., I. Segal. 2014. Deferred-acceptance auctions and radio spectrum reallocation. In *Proc. 15th ACM Conference on Economics and Computation.*

Milgrom, P. R., R. J. Weber. 1982. A theory of auctions and competitive bidding. *Econometrica* **50**(5) 1089–1122.

Mishra, D., D. Parkes. 2007. Ascending price Vickrey auctions for general valuations. *Journal of Economic Theory* **132** 335–366.

Moreton, P. S., P. T. Spiller. 1998. What's in the air: interlicense synergies in the Federal Communications Commission's broadband personal communication service spectrum auctions. *Journal of Law and Economics* **41**(2) 677–716.

Morgan, J., K. Steiglitz, G. Reis. 2003. The spite motive and equilibrium behavior in auctions. *Contributions to Economic Analysis and Policy* **2**, article 5.

Moulin, H. 1991. *Axioms of Cooperative Decision Making.* Cambridge University Press.

Mueller, R. 2006. Tractable cases of the winner determination problem. In P. Cramton, Y. Shoham, R. Steinberg, eds., *Combinatorial Auctions.* MIT Press.

Muller, E., M. A. Satterthwaite. 1977. The equivalence of strong positive association and strategy-proofness. *Journal of Economic Theory* **14**(2) 412–418.

Myerson, R. B. 1981. Optimal auction design. *Mathematics of Operations Research* **6** 58–73.

Myerson, R., M. Satterthwaite. 1983. Efficient mechanisms for bilateral trading. *Journal of Economic Theory* **29**(2) 265–281.

Nemes, V., C. R. Plott, G. Stoneham. 2008. Electronic bushbroker exchange: designing a combinatorial double auction for native vegetation offsets. Available at SSRN 1212202.

Nemhauser, G. L., L. A. Wolsey. 1988. *Integer and Combinatorial Optimization.* Wiley-Interscience Series in Discrete Mathematics and Optimization.

Nguyen, T., R. Vohra. 2014. Near feasible stable matchings with complementarities. Technical report, PIER Working Paper.

Nguyen, T., A. Peivandi, R. Vohra. 2016. Assignment problems with complementarities. *Journal of Economic Theory* **165** 209–241.

Nisan, N. 2006. Bidding languages. In P. Cramton, Y. Shoham, R. Steinberg, eds., *Combinatorial Auctions.* MIT Press.

Nisan, N. 2007. Introduction to mechanism design (for computer scientists). In N. Nisan, T. Roughgarden, E. Tardos, V. Vazirani, eds., *Algorithmic Game Theory.* Cambridge University Press.

Nisan, N., A. Ronen. 2001. Algorithmic mechanism design. *Games and Economic Behavior* **35** 166–196.

Nisan, N., A. Ronen. 2007. Computationally feasible vcg mechanisms. *J. Artif. Intell. Res. (JAIR)* **29** 19–47.

Nisan, N., I. Segal. 2006. The communcation requirements of efficient allocations and supporting prices. *Journal of Economic Theory* **129** 192–224.

Nobel Prize. 2012. The Sveriges Riksbank Prize in Economic Sciences in Memory of Alfred Nobel 2012. www.nobelprize.org/nobel_prizes/economic-sciences/laureates/2012/. [Online; accessed 19 August 2014].

O'Neill, R., P. Sotkiewicz, B. Hobbs, M. Rothkopf, W. Stewart. 2005. Efficient market-clearing prices in markets with nonconvexities. *European Journal of Operational Research* **1**(164) 269–285.

Osborne, M. J. 2004. *An Introduction to Game Theory*, vol. 3. Oxford University Press.

Ostrovsky, M., M. Schwarz. 2011. Reserve prices in internet advertising auctions: a field experiment. In *Proc. 12th ACM Conference on Electronic Commerce*. ACM, 59–60.

Oxley, J. G. 1992. *Matroid Theory*. Oxford University Press.

Pai, M., R. V. Vohra. 2008. Optimal auctions with financially constrained bidders. pdf.

Papadimitriou, C., ed. 1993. *Computational Complexity*. Addison Wesley.

Papadimitriou, P., H. Garcia-Molina. 2011. Data leakage detection. *IEEE Transactions on Knowledge and Data Engineering*, **23**(1) 51–63.

Papadimitriou, C., M. Schapira, Y. Singer. 2008. On the hardness of being truthful. In *Proc. Foundations of Computer Science, 2008, IEEE 49th Annual IEEE Symposium*. IEEE, 250–259.

Pápai, S. 2001. Strategyproof and nonbossy multiple assignments. *Journal of Public Economic Theory* **3**(3) 257–271.

Parkes, D. 2001. Iterative combinatorial auctions: achieving economic and computational efficiency. Ph.D. thesis, University of Pennsylvania.

Parkes, D., L. H. Ungar. 2000. Iterative combinatorial auctions: theory and practice. In *Proc. 17th National Conference on Artificial Intelligence*. 74–81.

Petrakis, I., G. Ziegler, M. Bichler. 2012. Ascending combinatorial auctions with allocation constraints: on game theoretical and computational properties of generic pricing rules. *Information Systems Research* **24**(3) 768–786.

Porter, D., V. Smith. 2006. FCC license auction design: a 12-year experiment. *Journal of Law Economics and Policy* **3** 63–88.

Porter, D., S. Rassenti, A. Roopnarine, V. Smith. 2003. Combinatorial auction design. *Proceedings of the National Academy of Sciences of the USA (PNAS)* **100** 11153–11157.

Pycia, M., U. Ünver. 2015. Incentive compatible allocation and exchange of discrete resources. Technical report. Available at SSRN 1079505.

Rassenti, S., V. L. Smith, R. L. Bulfin. 1982. A combinatorial auction mechanism for airport time slot allocations. *Bell Journal of Economics* **13** 402–417.

Roberts, D., A. Postlewaite. 1976. The incentives for price-taking behavior in large exchange economies. *Econometrica* 115–127.

Roberts, K. 1979. The characterization of implementable choice rules. In J. Laffont, ed., *Aggregation and Revelation of Preferences*. North-Holland, 321–349.

Robinson, M. S. 1985. Collusion and the choice of auction. *Rand Journal of Economics* **16** 141–145.

Roth, A. E. 1982a. The economics of matching: stability and incentives. *Mathematics of Operations Research* **7**(4) 617–628.

Roth, A. E. 1982b. Incentive compatibility in a market with indivisible goods. *Economics Letters* **9**(2) 127–132.

Roth, A. E. 1984. The evolution of the labor market for medical interns and residents: a case study in game theory. *Journal of Political Economy* **92** 991–1016.

Roth, A. E. 2002. The economist as engineer: game theory, experimental economics and computation as tools of design economics. *Econometrica* **70** 1341–1378.

Roth, A. E, T. Sönmez, M. U. Ünver. 2005. Pairwise kidney exchange. *Journal of Economic Theory* **125**(2) 151–188.

Rothkopf, M. H. 2007. Thirteen reasons why the Vickrey–Clarke–Groves process is not practical. *Operations Research* **55** 191–197.

Rothkopf, M. H., A. Pekec, R. M. Harstad. 1998. Computationally manageable combinatorial auctions. *Management Science* **44** 1131–1147.

Saban, D., J. Sethuraman. 2013. House allocation with indifferences: a generalization and a unified view. In *Proc. 14th ACM Conference on Electronic Commerce*. ACM, 803–820.

Salant, D. J. 1997. Up in the air: GTE's experience in the MTA auction for personal communication services licenses. *Journal of Economics & Management Strategy* **6**(3) 549–572.

Samuelson, P. A. 1938. A note on the pure theory of consumer's behaviour. *Economica* **5**(17) 61–71.

Samuelson, P. A. 1948. Foundations of economic analysis. *Science and Society* **13**(1) 93–95.

Sandholm, T. 2006. Optimal winner determination algorithms. In P. Cramton, Y. Shoham, R. Steinberg, eds., *Combinatorial Auctions*. MIT Press.

Sandholm, T. 2007. Expressive commerce and its application to sourcing: how we conducted $35 billion of generalized combinatorial auctions. *AI Magazine* **28**(3) 45.

Sandholm, T. 2012. Very-large-scale generalized combinatorial multi-attribute auctions: lessons from conducting $60 billion of sourcing. *The Handbook of Market Design*. Oxford University Press.

Sandholm, T., S. Suri. 2006. Side constraints and non-price attributes in markets. *Games and Economic Behaviour* **55** 321–330.

Sano, R. 2011. Incentives in core-selecting auctions with single-minded bidders. *Games and Economic Behavior* **72**(2) 602–606.

Satterthwaite, M. A. 1975. Strategy-proofness and arrow's conditions. Existence and correspondence theorems for voting procedures and social welfare functions. *Journal of Economic Theory* **10**(2) 187–217.

Scheffel, T., A. Pikovsky, M. Bichler, K. Guler. 2011. An experimental comparison of linear and non-linear price combinatorial auctions. *Information Systems Research* **22** 346–368.

Scheffel, T., A. Ziegler, M. Bichler. 2012. On the impact of package selection in combinatorial auctions: an experimental study in the context of spectrum auction design. *Experimental Economics* **15** 667–692.

Schneider, S., P. Shabalin, M. Bichler. 2010. On the robustness of non-linear personalized price combinatorial auctions. *European Journal on Operational Research* **206** 248–259.

Shapley, L. S., H. Scarf. 1974. On cores and indivisibility. *Journal of Mathematical Economics* **1**(1) 23–37.

Shapley, L. S., M. Shubik. 1971. The assignment game i: the core. *International Journal of Game Theory* **1**(1) 111–130.

Shoham, Y., K. Leyton-Brown. 2009. *Multiagent Systems: Algorithmic, Game-Theoretic, and Logical Foundations*. Cambridge University Press.

Shoham, Y., K. Leyton-Brown. 2011. *Multi Agent Systems – Applications, Game-Theoretic, and Logical Foundations*. Cambridge University Press.

Shubik, M. 1974. The dollar auction game: a paradox in noncooperative behavior and escalation. *Journal of Conflict Resolution* **47** 209–221.

Simon, H. A. 1996. *The Sciences of the Artificial*. MIT Press.

Sng, C. T. S. 2008. Efficient algorithms for bipartite matching problems with preferences. Ph.D. thesis, University of Glasgow.

Sönmez, T., M. U. Ünver. 2010. Course bidding at business schools. *International Economic Review* **51**(1) 99–123.

Syrgkanis, V., E. Tardos. 2013. Composable and efficient mechanisms. In *Proc. 45th Annual ACM Symposium on Theory of Computing*. ACM, 211–220.

Teo, C., J. Sethuraman. 2000. On a cutting plane heuristic for the stable roommates problem and its applications. *European Journal of Operational Research* **123**(1) 195–205.

Ueda, S., D. Fragiadakis, A. Iwasaki, P. Troyan, M. Yokoo. 2012. Strategy-proof mechanisms for two-sided matching with minimum and maximum quotas. In *Proc. 11th International Conference on Autonomous Agents and Multiagent Systems*, vol. 3. International Foundation for Autonomous Agents and Multiagent Systems, 1327–1328.

Van Vyve, M. *et al.* 2011. Linear prices for non-convex electricity markets: models and algorithms. Technical report, Catholic University of Louvain, *Center for Operations Research and Econometrics*.

Varian, H. 2006. Revealed preference. In M. Szenberg, L. Ramrattan, A. A. Gottesman, eds., *Samuelsonian Economics and the Twenty-First Century*, chapter 6. Oxford University Press, 99–115.

Varian, H., C. Harris. 2014. The vcg auction in theory and practice. *American Economic Review* **104**(5) 442–445.

Vazirani, V. 2003. *Approximation Algorithms*. Springer Science & Business Media.

Vickrey, W. 1961. Counterspeculation, auctions, and competitive sealed tenders. *The Journal of Finance* **16**(1) 8–37.

Vohra, R. 2004. *Advanced Mathematical Economics*. Routledge.

Vohra, R. 2011. *Mechanism Design: A Linear Programming Approach*, vol. 47. Cambridge University Press.

Von Neumann, J. 1953. A certain zero-sum two-person game equivalent to the optimal assignment problem. *Contributions to the Theory of Games* **2** 5–12.

Von Neumann, J., O. Morgenstern. 1947. Theory of games and economic behavior. Princeton University Press.

Walsh, W., M. Wellman, F. Ygge. 2000. Combinatorial auctions for supply chain formation. In *Proc. 2nd ACM Conference on Electronic Commerce*. ACM, 260–269. doi:10.1145/352871. 352900.

Wang, X., H. Kopfer. 2014. Collaborative transportation planning of less-than-truckload freight. *OR Spectrum* **36**(2) 357–380. doi:10.1007/s00291-013-0331-x.

Westkamp, A. 2013. An analysis of the German university admissions system. *Economic Theory* **53**(3) 561–589.

Wilson, R. 1987. Game-theoretic analyses of trading processes. *Advances in Economic Theory: Fifth World Congress*. Cambridge University Press, 33–70.

Zhang, W., S. Yuan, J. Wang. 2014. Optimal real-time bidding for display advertising. In *Proc. 20th ACM SIGKDD*. ACM, 1077–1086.

Zhou, L. 1990. On a conjecture by Gale about one-sided matching problems. *Journal of Economic Theory* **52**(1) 123–135.

Index

Printed in the United States
by Baker & Taylor Publisher Services